FISH AND FISHERIES

FISH AND FISHERIES

B.N. Yadav

(Totally Revised and Enlarged Second Editon)

2023

Daya Publishing House®

A Division of

Astral International Pvt. Ltd.

New Delhi - 110 002

Reprinted, 2023

ISBN: 978-81-7035-278-5 (PB)

Published by : **Daya Publishing House**®
A Division of
Astral International Pvt. Ltd.
– ISO 9001:2015 Certified Company –
4736/23, Ansari Road, Darya Ganj
New Delhi-110 002
Ph. 011-43549197
E-mail: info@astralint.com
Website: www.astralint.com

Digitally Printed at : **Replika Press Pvt. Ltd.**

Preface to Second Edition

I am thankful to teachers and students for warm reception accorded to the book "FISH AND FISHERIES". The book has been thoroughly revised and enlarged. Some new chapters like "Food, Feeding Habits and Alimentary Canal", "Skeleton", "Common Biota of Fish Ponds of India", "Fish and Pesticides", and "Fisheries Institutes in India" have been incorporated in the second edition of the book. Moreover, some chapters like "Respiration in Fishes" and "Reservoir Fishery Management" have been reorganised and written in detail. Latest data on world fish catch, and fish catches from the reservoirs of U.P. and Bihar have also been incorporated in this edition of the book. Some old sketches have been replaced and also some new fish plates have been added. I hope, this edition of the book will be more useful for the readers. Suggestions are always invited for further improvement of the book. I am also thankful to the publisher for taking interest and extending all co-operation in publishing this book.

B. N. Yadav

CONTENTS

CHAPTER 1

FISHES AND THEIR EVOLUTIONARY HISTORY

Fishes are among the earliest vertebrates going back to the Devonian period, 400 million years ago. Once the *ostracoderms* were abundant throughout the world but they became extinct, and only two types of cyclostomes survive as relics of these agnathan vertebrates. The jawed vertebrates, included among *acanthodes* and *placoderms*, also became extinct. Early sharks and bony fishes took a lead over all the above groups of vertebrates i.e. ostracoderms, acanthodians and placoderms. Today, the evolutionary history of the fishes has reached its climax. They are the masters of the water. A complicated adaptive radiation has taken place in the different groups of fishes.

The following are the important characters of fishes:

1. Fishes are cold-blooded animals and with a very few exceptions, they have stream-lined body.
2. With a combination of median and paired fins, they are well adapted for active life in the water.
3. There is a tail or caudal fin and one or two dorsal fins (on the back of the fish).
4. There is a median ventral fin and the anal fin.
5. There is one pair of Pectoral fins (anteriorly) and there is also one pair of pelvic fins located posteriorly.
6. In the bony fishes, the spiracle is much suppressed or it disappears completely.
7. In the most primitive Jawed fishes, there was *autostylic* jaw suspension, in the primitive sharks it was *amphistylic* and in the later sharks and bony fishes the jaw suspension is of hyostylic type.
8. The integument is either naked or beset with scales, dermal denticles or bony plates.
9. Endoskeleton is either cartilaginous or bony.
10. Gills are the chief respiratory organs but some times accessory respiratory organs may be present.

11. The heart consists of only impure blood and hence it is known as the venous heart. It has one auricle and one ventricle. The venous blood is pumped to the gills for aeration.
12. Gill slits may be covered by an operculum as in teleosts. The maximum number of gill slits is seven pairs.
13. There are 10 pairs of cranial nerves in fishes.
14. The lateral line system and receptors are well developed.
15. Paired nostrils are present which normally do not open into the pharynx except in lung fishes and lobe fin fishes.
16. The kidney in fish is commonly that of *mesonephros* type.

Origin and Evolution of Fishes

The study of fishes particularly the evolutionary history is a fascinating story. It is estimated that there are about 50000 species of fishes living today. They are among the earliest vertebrates going back to the Devonian period, the age of the fishes, about 400 million years ago. Some of the fishes live exclusively in fresh water, others are marine. There are few fishes which like to live partly in fresh water and partly in marine waters, but some of them prefer brackish water.

The first vertebrates known in the fossil record are represented by dermal fragments of an *agnathan* (jawless fish) found in the upper cambrian segments in Wyoming. They represent a *heterostracan* and the genus *Anatolepis* has been referred to this concern. This ancient form is also known from ordovician rocks in North America, Greenland and Spitzbergen.

Another evidence of vertebrate life comes from England particularly in the rocks of middle silurian age. Complete skeletons of two genera, namely *Jamoytius* and *Thelodus* have been discovered. These primitive jawless vertebrates probably occupied a position close to the ancestry of the lamprey and its close relatives. Jamoytius is supposed to be a possible relic of the unarmoured ancestors.

In *chondrichthyes* (Elasmobranchii), the chief tissue of skeleton is cartilage. The fertilization in these fishes is mostly internal and several species are viviparous. The gills are fixed to the sides of the gill-slits and the gill slits open to the outside. The sharks, the rays and the skates are common examples belonging to this class.

In the class *osteichthyes*, the chief tissue of skeleton is bone. The bonyfishes are supposed to constitute a higher group embracing three sub-divisions: the lobe fins (Crossopterygii), the lung fishes (Dipnoi) and the modern teleosts (Teleostei).

The Crossopterygians were thought to be an extinct group. The discovery of a strange fish, a *Coelacanth,* e.g. *Latimeria chalumnae* in 1938 in the Mozambique Bay of East Africa has provided an opportunity for the study of this group. The discovery of this fish was a *sensational* one. The crossopterygian fishes appeared in the middle Devonian time. They were on the direct line of descendent between fishes and amphibians. They genus *Osteolepis* of the Devonian time is a well known example of the early Crossopterygian. It possessed the following important characters:

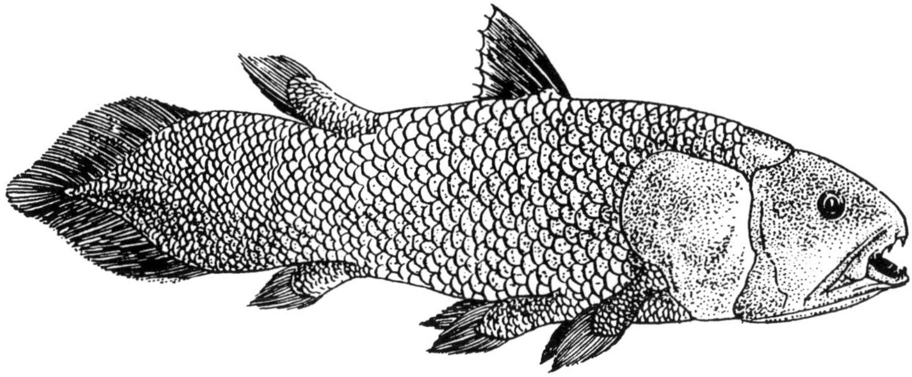

Fig. 1 : Latimeria chalumnae

1. The body was fusiform and the tail was strongly heterocercal.
2. There was lobate, archipterygial paired fins.
3. There were two dorsal fins present.
4. Rhombic scales of the cosmoid type were present.
5. There was a strong notochord.
6. The skull and jaws were completely bony in nature.
7. There were two large bones between the eyes and they were homologous to the parietal bones of other vertebrates.
8. A pineal opening was present.
9. Frontal bones were present in front of the parietals, also, in the rostral portion of the head, there was a series of small bones.
10. Circumorbital bones were present around the eyes, like higher bony fishes and amphibians.
11. Temporal bones were present on the sides of the head.
12. Post parietal region of the skull was separated by a prominent joint.
13. There was better ossification of the braincase, and joints of the skull and braincase provided enough flexibility.

In the early Crossopterygians, sharp and pointed teeth were present on the palate and they were adapted for grasping prey. Thus, they were definitely carnivorous fishes. Teeth had highly infolded enamel to form complex labyrinthine pattern. The scheme of bone arrangement in the fin was an indication of the evolution of limb-bones in the land living forms.

From the early crossopterygian stock, two general lines evolved—one was represented by the sub-order *Rhipidistia* and other by the suborder *Coelacanthini*. The osteolepids were *rhipidistians* which lived in freshwaters. In the middle Devonian time evolution took place in two lines from the rhipidistians. One line was that of the *holoptichians* (*genus-holoptichius*) of the late Devonian time. The body of *holoptichius* was robust and it was covered with large and rounded scales. The caudal fins were in close proximity to the tail of the fish. The Devonian genus *Eusthenopteron* also belonged to the group of rhipidistians. They were on the direct line toward the early amphibians. They showed some advancement over the osteolepid ancestors. Some important characters of *Eusthenopteron* are:

1. Its body was elongated.
2. It was probably a carnivorous fish.
3. The notochord was provided with a series of rings at regular interval and between the rings were small nubbins of bones in the dorsal side.
4. The each notochordal ring has a spine projecting up and back.
5. The tail was symmetrical and vertebral column extended upto the tip of the tail.

The other group of Crossopterygians, the *Coelacanths* were abundant in the marine deposits of Mesozoic era. They were far removed from the mainline of evolution toward the early land dwelling vertebrates. The cretaceous genus, *Macropoma* was a typical member of this group. The important characters of this group are:

1. They were marine forms.
2. They were deep-bodied and had lobate paired fins.
3. Though there was reduction of the internal elements of the lobe, however, there was increase in the relative size of the fins.
4. The tail was symmetrical and diphycercal.
5. There was an additional lobe between the upper and lower lobes of the fin in the tail region.
6. There was considerable reduction of bones in the skull and the skull was comparatively short.
7. The swim bladder was calcified and preserved in the fossil materials.

Latimeria is about five to six feet in length resembling *Macropoma* of the cretaceous period. It is characterized by rounded and large brilliant blue scales and lobed paired fins which are quite strong. In December, 1952, another specimen of *Latimeria* was caught off the coast of Madagascar. Since then, more coelacanths have been found in the vicinity of the Comoro Island, between Madagascar and Africa.

The more advanced orders of the teleosts which embrace most of the familiar fishes are:

1. *Isospondyli* (Clupeiformes): They are both fresh water and marine forms. They include *Hilsa, Sardins, Chanos, Herring, Salmons* etc. These fishes are characterized by the presence of cycloid scales, homocercal tail, sigle dorsal fin, absence of spines in the fin and absence of Weberian apparatus etc.
2. *Ostariophysi* (cypriniformes): It includes sub-orders (i) *Cyprinoids* (e.g. carps) (ii) *Siluroids* (e.g. cat fishes). In *cyprinoids,* Weberian apparatus is present, air bladder has ducts, Scales are present and ventral fin is abdominal. But, in *Siluroids,* there is no scale, Maxillary bone is reduced and 3rd, 4th, and 5th vertebrate are fused.

3. *Acanthopterygii* (Perciformes): It includes mostly marine fishes. They are spiny-finned, air bladder is a closed sac (Physoclistic), and Scales are cycloid. The important examples are Mackerels, Mullets, Perches etc.
4. *Heterosomata* (Pleuronectiformes): It includes flat fishes (*e.g. cynoglossus*) adapted to live at the bottom. Both eyes are present on the upper side, skull is asymmetrical, fin spines and air bladder are absent.

The lungfishes (Dipnoi) have been described later on and also in a separate chapter.

Fossil fishes: The oldest fish fossils have been unearthed from the rocks of the ordovician period about 500 million years ago. These archaic stocks are the *ostracoderms* or unarmoured prehistoric fishes. The important orders of these agnathous vertebrates are:

1.	Cephalaspida	e.g.	*Cephalaspis*
2.	Anaspida	e.g.	*Birkenia*
3.	Cyclostomata	e.g.	Modern Lampreys and Hagfishes
4.	Pteraspida	e.g.	*Pterapis*
5.	Coelolepida	e.g.	*Thelodus*

The important characters of ostracoderms have been mentioned below:

1. There was absence of jaws.
2. They lacked paired fins or at best had a single pair of fins behind the head.
3. There was no axial skeletons or vertebral column.
4. There was well developed armour or bony plates or scales.

It is probable that they represent independent lines of evolutionary development.

Cephalaspis was a bottom-dwelling Devonian genus which possessed the following important characters:

1. They were small animals about not more than a foot in length.
2. They were heavily armoured and the head was protected by strong solid shield.
3. The body was covered by vertical elongated bony plates.
4. The body was elongated. The body form was general fish like, terminating in a tail fin and bearing upon the dorsal surface a small median fin.
5. The head shield was flat and at its back margin it increased in depth, where it joined the body.
6. There was a pair of lateral fins at the corners of the head shield.
7. The head shield comprised a solid piece of bone, covering the top and the sides of the head and folded under around the margins of the shields.
8. Some of the cephalaspids, possessed very long lateral horns but in others they were completely lacking.
9. On the dorsal side, the head shield was pierced by the opening for the eyes.

10. There was a single nasal opening between the eyes and slightly in front of them, showing a relationship with modern lampreys.
11. Between the eyes and behind the nostril, there was a pineal opening, a light receptor.
12. There were three areas on the head shield that were depressed and covered by small, polygonal plates—supposed to be electric or sensory fields of some sort.
13. The under surface of the head was protected by a pattern of fine plates enclosing the lower surface of the head completely, except for a ventrally placed mouth.
14. On each side there were 10(ten) gill openings corresponding to ten gill pouches that occupied each side of the head shield.
15. In Cephalaspids, there were two semicircular canals in the ear, a character resembling lamprey.
16. In the brain there were large nerve trunks radiating out on either side to supply the sensory fields.
17. The head shield joined the bony armour posteriorly.
18. Soft rays were present in the heterocercal tail.
19. Paired fins joined the body on either side behind the horns of the head shield.

Now, Ostracoderms of the order *Anaspida* has the following important characters:

1. They were covered by bony plates or scales.
2. Eyes were lateral in position.
3. There was a single opening for the nostrils between the eyes. Behind the nostril there is a small pineal opening.
4. In anaspids, there was a slanting row of about eight gill openings on each side which run down from the head.

Birkenia which can be described as typical silurian anaspid, possessed the following characters:

1. It was a tiny fish like form which was narrow and deep bodied, adapted for active swimming.
2. There was a complex pattern of small scales, many of them being somewhat like grains of rice, particularly those, covering the throat.
3. The mouth was terminal in position and it was like a transverse slit.
4. True jaws were absent.
5. Behind the head, the body was covered with a series of scales or plates. These were vertically elongated and arranged in several longitudinal rows.
6. Birkenia lacked paired fins.

7. On the ventral surface of the body there were some additional spines in Birkenia.
8. There were several median spines, running in a row along the back.
9. There was a well developed anal fin.
10. The tail was no doubt, fish like in form but the lower lobe of the tail was larger than the upper lobe and it is known as the *reversed heterocercal* tail.
11. Heterocercal tail of Birkenia helped much in active swimming.

The earliest known ostracoderms belong to the order *pteraspida*. They possessed the following important characters:

1. Some of them were small, fusiform and free-swimming, but some were also large, flattened and bottom dwelling forms.
2. *Pteraspis* was small but heavily armoured, the head shield being rounded in cross section.
3. A long sharp beak (rostrum) extended beyond the mouth located ventrally.
4. Mouth in *Pteraspis* was present in the form of a transverse slit placed near the front on the lower surface of the head shield. There was a series of slender plates stretched across the slit which might have acted like jaws in absence of true jaws.
5. On each side there was a single exit for the gills on the dorsal middle-line of the head shield, a long spine projected up and back.
6. Small scales were present on the body of pteraspis and the tail was reversed *heterocercal.*
7. There was absence of well developed median fins and paired fins.

The bottom-feeding pteraspida (Heterostraci) are typified by *Drepanaspis,* a lower Devonian genus. It possessed the following characters:

1. It was very flat and broad.
2. The eyes were set apart on the sides of the head shield.
3. The wide mouth was located on the front of the shield.
4. The head shield was covered by several plates of varying size.
5. The tail region was comparatively small.

Order-*Coelolepida* comprises the genera *Thelodus* and *Lanarkia* found in the upper Silurian and lower Devonian periods. Some of the important characters are:

1. They were flattened animals with laterally placed eyes.
2. The tail was of heterocercal type.
3. The body covering consisted of minute denticles. There was no flat plates as in some other ostracoderms.
4. These denticles are considered as much reduced plates unlike denticles of sharks.

Acanthodians: The *acanthodians* were earliest known gnathostomes (vertebrates with true jaws), also known as "spiny sharks". They were found in the rocks of late Silurian age. By early Devonian years the acanthodians reached the peak of their evolutionary development but by the close of the palaeozoic era there was sharp decline. The actual relationship of this group is controversial. Some important characters of acanthodians are as follows:

1. They were freshwater animals living in rivers, lakes, and swamps of middle and late palaeozoic era.
2. There was enlarged upper jaw (Palatoquadrate) and well developed lower jaw or mandible.
3. Teeth were quite sharp and were present in the mandible.
4. Behind the scissor like primary jaws there was the gill arch the hyoid arch. The hyomandibular bone of the hyoid arch articulated with the palatoquadrate to form a connection between the braincase and the jaws.

The genus *climatius* is a good example of the early acandthodian. The genus was present during the late, Silurian and early Devonian period. The following are the important characters of *climatius:*

1. They were small gnathostome vertebrates, only a few inches in length with fish like bodies tapering towards the tail.
2. In the posterior region, the body was slightly turned up.
3. The tail was heterocercal.
4. Median and paired fins were present besides tail fin.
5. Two large triangular dorsal fins were present on the back which consisted of a web of skin, provided with a spine.
6. The large anal fin was also supported along its front edge by a spine.
7. There was a pair of pelvic fins in front of the anal fin.
8. Between the pelvic fins and anal fin, there were five pairs of small fins, running along the ventral portion of the body. These fins has spines just like the median fins.
9. The number of 'extra' paired fins varies from one genus to another. There is general agreement that such paired fins represent the remnants of continuous lateral fin folds (of the ancestors).
10. The entire body of climatius was protected by a dermal armour of small rhombic or diamond-shaped scales. Over the head, they took the form of regularly arranged small plates, never expanded into large units.
11. The eyes were quite large in *climatius* and each of them was surrounded by a ring of bony plates. The eyes were placed far forward and the scene of sight was dominant in these fishes.
12. The palatoquadrate was ossified in three separate pieces and was devoid of teeth.

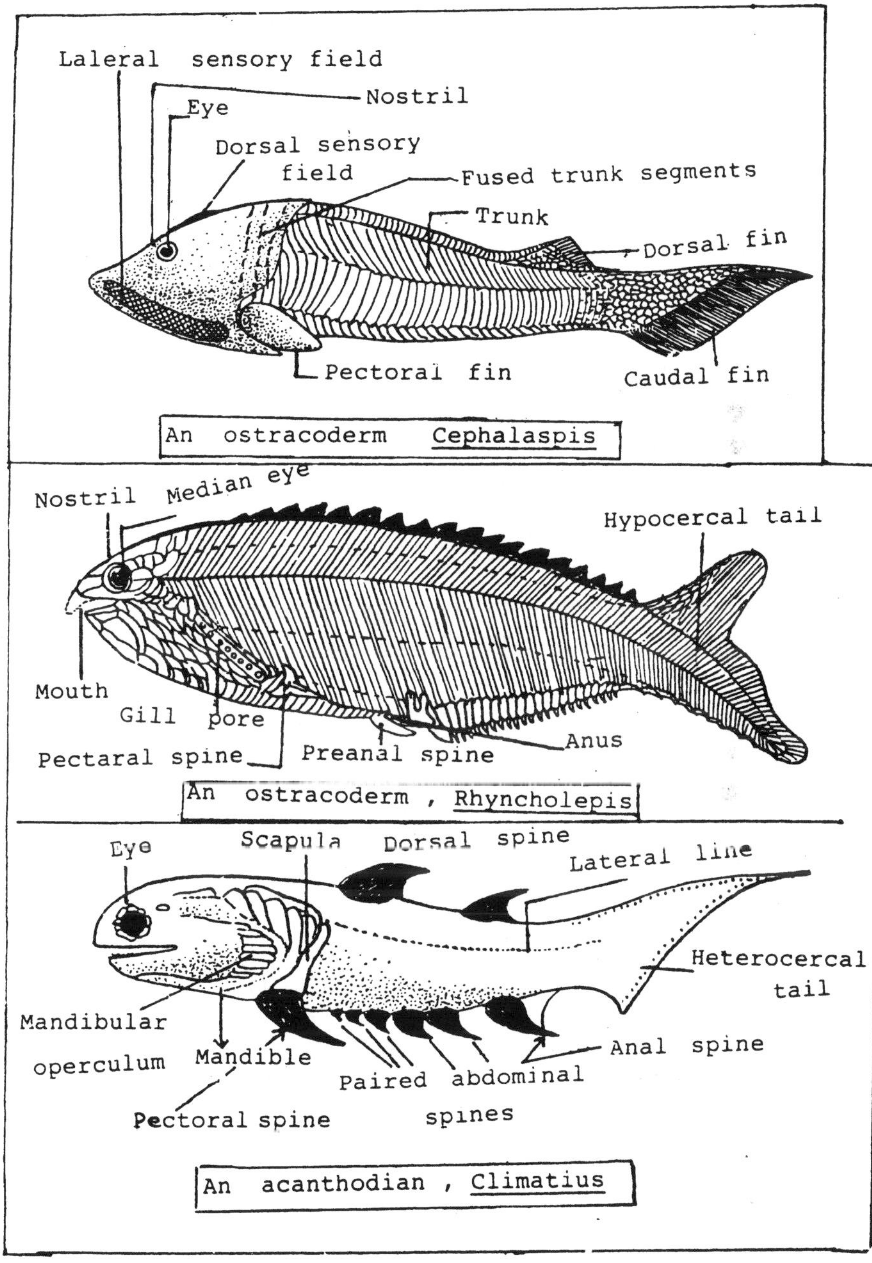

Fig. 2 : Ostracoderms and Acanthodian

13. The operculum was quite different in structure and origin in comparison to higher fishes. The operculum covering was made of stiff bony rods which enclosed the gill arches.

Appearance of Placoderms

Placoderms which were the ancient gnathostomes evolved during the middle palaeozoic time, but, by the end of the palaeozoic era all of them vanished from the earth. They were of course a heterogeneous lot. They were the evolutionary experiment which failed. The placoderms have been arranged in the following orders:

1. *Arthrodira* : During the Devonian period, they were dominant vertebrates.
2. *Petalichthyida* : Specialized placoderms with strong bony head shield
3. *Antiarchi* : Bottom living heavily armoured placoderms of upper Devonian time, they were generally small sized.
4. *Rhenanida* : They were "Shark-like" placoderms.
5. *Phyllolepida* : Flat, degenerate, placoderms of medium size
6. *Ptyctodontida* : Small mollusc-eating placoderms with reduced head
7. *Palaeospondyloidea* : Single genus with uncertain affinities, peculiarly shaped skull, scarcity of sufficient fossils

Besides lower jaws, the placoderms had strong upperjaws, firmly fused to the skull. There was a joint between the skull and the shoulder girdle. The head and the shoulder girdle were covered with dermal bones. The gills were situated far forward. In placoderms, paired fins were always present. According to some workers the Holocephali might be related to placoderms.

Early Placoderms

There are two important orders which include the early placoderms. These two orders are:

1. Rhenanida (Stegoselachians), and
2. Petalichthyida.

The Rhenanids : These Devonian vertebrates are supposed to be the early relatives of sharks. The genus *Gemuendina* from Devonian segments of central Europe is the best known example. The important characters are:

1. This flattened fish had a broad head and a tapering body covered with all tuberacles which resembles the denticles of sharks.
2. The mouth was terminal and was equipped with pointed teeth.
3. The eyes and the nostrils were present on the dorsal side of the head.
4. There as an enlarged pair of pectoral fins, giving this animal an appearance of modern rays.
5. The jaw structure was of primitive type.

The Petalichthyds : The genus *Macropetalichthys* belonged to this order. The important characters were:

1. There was a strong bony head shield and the braincase was ossified.

2. Behind the head shield, thoracic plates were present and also a pair of pectoral spine were present.
3. The macropetalichthyds were related to arthrodires. Both these groups diversed at an early stage in their histories and followed separate evolutionary paths.

The Arthrodires

They are commonly known as the armoured fishes or the joint-necked fishes of the Devonian time. For sometime, they were the most successful vertebrate but unfortunately they became extinct with the close of the Devonian period. The earliest known arthrodires were small and flattened vertebrates.

Coccosteus was a typical arthrodire in the old red sanstone beds of northern England and Scotland. The characteristic features of this genus were:

1. It was not more than one to two feet in length and had a fish like form of the body.
2. A series of large bony plates were present in the skull which firmly joined to one another.
3. In several arthrodires the skull was very deep and strongly arched.
4. The eyes were large and were protected by a ring of four sclerotic plates.
5. Small nostrils were present at the front of the skull.
6. There was as strong lower jaw which consisted of a single bone on each side. This bone was called the inferognathal bone. Opposing the lower jaw, two plates of bones were present on each side. These bones were known as anterior and posterior supragnathals and were attached to the front margin of the skull. They were tooth like in shape like the upper edge of interognathal bone. So, bony plates were functioning as teeth.
7. In *Dinichthys*, a more advanced arthrodire the plate had scissor like cutting edges, in the external basal plate of the skull there was a socket. Behind the skull there was a ring of thoracic plate on which there was a strong ball or condyle on either side. The ball was fitted in to the socket. The skull could be moved up and down conveniently.
8. *Coccosteus* and several other arthrodires could open the mouth by raising the skull with relation to the body. It allowed for a very wide gape, advantageous for the carnivorous creatures.
9. In *coccosteus,* the gills were located in the cheek region and there was no operculum.
10. The head and the thoracic region of coccosteus were heavily armoured but the dermal covering was from the posterior body portion or the tail.
11. The supporting column had a cartilaginous notochord bordered above and below by spines, but, there was no vertebral discs or centra.
12. The tail was heterocercal and besides tail fin, their was a median dorsal fin. One pair of large pectoral fins and one pair of small pelvic fins were present in *coccosteus.*

The early arthrodires (as Devonian *Arctolepis*) possessed somewhat different characters in comparison to more advanced forms such as coccosteus. Some of the characters of *Arctolepis* are:

1. They had well developed strong pectoral spines attached firmly to the body armour.
2. The jaws in Arctolepis were very weak.
3. They were bottom living forms.
4. The greatly enlarged pectoral spines probably served as anchors in the swift flowing currents in which they lived.

Thus, by middle and late Devonian times the arthrodires became fast-swimming, aggressive predators. The two giant genera *Denichthys* and *Titanichthys* were found in the upper Devonian cleveland shales of Ohio. They were very large fishes

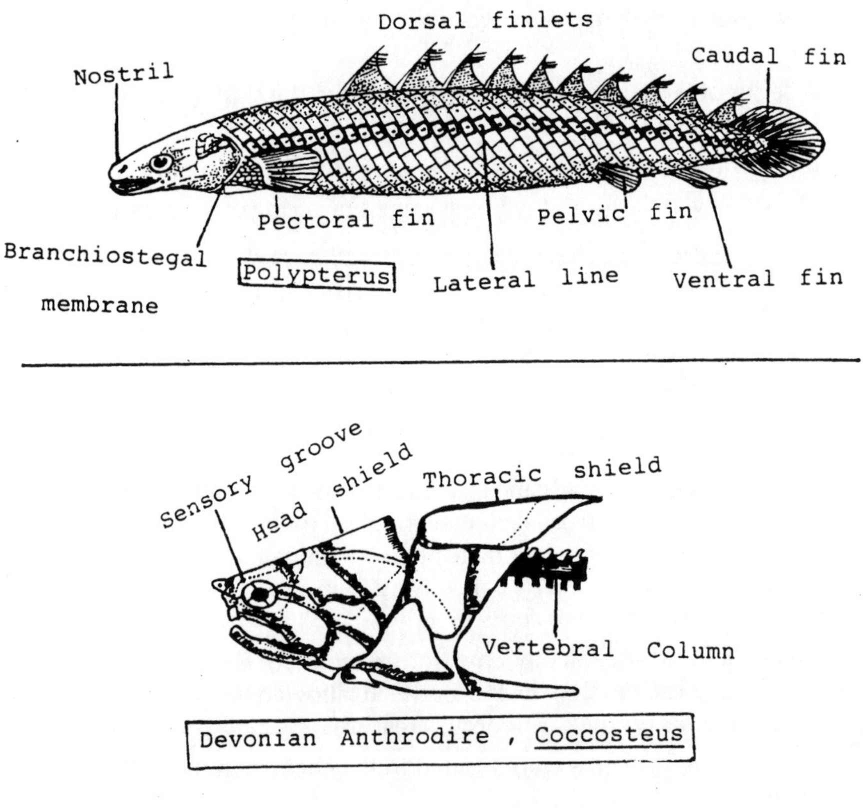

Fig. 3 : Polypterus and Coccosteus

reaching a length of even 30 feet. They were characterized by the presence of enormous skull and strong jaws equipped with large cutting plates. *Denichthys* was supposed to be the ruler of the environment it inhabited.

Ptyctodonts and Phyllolepids

Evolution of several aberrant lines took place during the transition period between Devonian to Mississipian times. The genus *Rhamphodopsis* belonged to *Ptyctodontida*. This genus possessed three important characters:

1. They were mollusc-seating small placoderms with heavy dental plates.
2. The head and thoracic armour were reduced.
3. There was a large dorsal spine besides the pectoral spines.

The genus *phyllolepis* belonged to the order *Phyllolepida*. They were probably bottom living forms of medium size. They were flat and had ornamented plates.

The Antiarchs:- Bothriolepis was a typical example of the order-Antiarchi and was found in the upper Devonian rocks. They possessed the following important characters:

1. It was heavily armoured, having the head shield composed of large plates and the box like long body shield.
2. Eyes were present on the top of the head shield.
3. There was a pineal opening in between the eyes.
4. The mouth was ventral and very small, and the lower jaw was weak.
5. There was a well developed functional lung.
6. There was long and pointed armoured pectoral appendage which could move freely.
7. Behind the body shield, the body of *Bothriolepis* was naked in contrast to that of *Pterichthys* where the posterior part of the body and tail were covered with scales.
8. The tail was heterocercal
9. There was a median dorsal fin also.

Palaeospondylus : For the time being this genus has been accommodated in the order *Palaeospondyloidea* though it has been supposed to be of uncertain affinities. Some important characters are as follows:

1. It possessed peculiarly shaped skull and well-ossified vertebral column.
2. It was a small placoderm in which the dermal armour was lost.

Sometimes, *Palaeospondylus* is regarded as a larval vertebrate but this interpretation is doubtful for this bony vertebrate. Several skull elements are difficult to be homologized and as such, this genus will remain a palaeontological question mark for ever.

Fossil Sharks : The genus *Cladoselache* was one of the first sharks known from the available fossil evidences. It was found in the upper Devonian cleaveland shales, along the South shore of Lake Erie. It possessed the following important characters:

1. The body was typical shark like or torpedo-shaped.

2. The tail was that of heterocercal type, there being two lobes of unequal size.
3. There were two dorsal fins, pectoral and pelvic fins and a pair of small horizontal fins, one on either side of the tail near its base.
4. The paired fins has very broad bases.
5. The fins of cladoselache consisted of an axial basalia and a fringe of radialia on the preaxial side. The fins are of Pleurorhachic being free from the body wall.
6. There was amphistylic method of jaw suspension.
7. Each tooth had a central cusp, with a low lateral cusp on each side. Such tooth structure was found in ancient fossil forms.
8. Behind the jaws there were six branchial arches (gill bars).

The cladoselache seems to form the central stem from which the later sharks evolved in various directions.

Pleuracanth sharks included the genus *Pleuracanthus* which evolved during carboniferous and permian times. Pleurocanthus had some important characters as given below:

1. They had elongated body with a very long dorsal fin extending up to a considerable length of the back.
2. They had a primitive amphistylic jaw suspension.
3. The tail was diphycercal which was secondarily derived from a primary heterocercal tail.
4. The paired fins were composed of a central axis from which fin rays radiated on each side.
5. There was a long spine projecting backward from the back of the skull.
6. There were many teeth and each one was composed of two long divergent cusps or blades. In between the two cusps, a small cusp was also present.

The earliest representative of the modern sharks were the *hybodonts* which appeared in the late Devonian period and continued till the beginning of the cenozoic era. *Hybodus* of upper permian and Mesozoic age was a typical genus. The important characters of this genus were:

1. They were an intermediate stage in the evolution of sharks, however, they retained the amphistylic skull.
2. The paired fins had narrow bases which were flexible.
3. Claspers appeared on the pelvic fins in the hybodont for the first time.
4. Teeth were broad and low crowned for crushing the hard food materials.

Two groups of sharks i.e. *heterodontid* and *hexanchid* sharks seem to be persistent connecting links between the hybodonts and the hosts of varied sharks living today. *Heterodontus* of Australia is an example of the heterodontid sharks and *Chlamydoselache* of Atlantic and Pacific waters represents the *hexachid* sharks. *Heterodontus* is supposed to be a modified descendant of the *hybodonts. Chlamydoselache* and the related genus *Hexanthus* were elongated predaceous sharks with amphistylic jaw suspension.

The hybodont sharks reached the pinnacle of their evolutionary development during the late paleozoic times but were replaced by the *heterodontid* and *hexachid* sharks during the Mesozoic. Gradually several advanced sharks evolved later on, in which the amphistylic method of jaw suspension was replaced by *hyostylic suspension.*

Right from the Mesozoic up to the present, the evolution of the higher sharks exhibits two general lines. One line of evolution is that of the typical sharks with pointed head, elongated and streamlined body. They are fast, aggressive and highly predaceous creatures. They have ventrally placed widely grasping mouth provided with sharp teeth. There are five pairs of gill slits, and there is a round spiracle in front of the first gill in each side. The body tapers posteriorly. The tail is very strong and heterocercal in nature. One or two dorsal fins may be present. Claspers are present on the pelvic fins in males. The paired fins have narrow bases.

The skates and rays constitute the other lines of evolution. They are basically bottom lining sharks. They are characterized by large pectoral fins, ventrally placed gills and reduced tail. The teeth are highly modified for crushing. Water is taken in through a large spircle which is dorsally located.

The sub-class *Holocephali* (now considered as an independent class) includes the chimaeroids or silver shark represented today by *Chimaera, Callorhynchus* and *Harriotta* of the deep sea oceanic, waters. They are active fishes with an elongated, pointed rostrum. The jaw suspension is that of autostylic type, upper jaw firmly fused to the brain case. The pectoral fins are large and fanlike and the tail is elongated into a long whiplash. They are the distinct offshoot of the earliest cartilaginous fishes during the triassic. They flourished in the cretaceous. The best known fossil example is *Helodus* of the lower carboniferous.

The Lung Fishes (Dipnoans)

The earliest record of Lung fishes is *Dipterus* of the middle Devonian age. It had two dorsal fins and an unequal tail fin. The head was covered with numerous small enamel coated bones. The braincase was poorly ossified. A process of chondrification was beginning in the partially ossified jaws. Paired fins were of archipterygial type. The scales of the body were thick and *rhomboid* made of *cosmine.* They continuosly progressed through ages as seen in the fossil remains of the fishes such as *Phaneropleuron, Scaumenacea* and *Ceratodus.*

Neoceratodus of Australia, *Protopterus* of Africa and *Lepidosiren* of South America are the three living genera of lung fishes. From *Dipterus,* the lungfishes evolved during the Devonian period. The central line of dipnoan evolution led to *Ceratodus* (Triassic and Mesozoic). *Neoceratodus* is considered as a direct descendant of Ceratodus. Other lungfishes have evolved as side branches from the central stem of dipnoan evolution. Secondarily simplified symmetrical tail of modern dipnoans are known as *gephyrocercal* fin.

Bony Fishes

Bony fishes (actinopterygians) are very successful creatures of water. They are highly advanced in the ossification of skeleton as a whole. In the primitive bony fishes the scales were heavy and generally of rhombic shape. The *cosmoid* scales were possessed by the lungfishes and *ganoid* scales were present in the early crossopterygians. In the *ganoid* scales the enamel layer was very thick, formed of *guanine*. The entire gill area is covered by a bony operculum. The spiracle is suppressed in the bony fishes. Hyostylic jaw suspension is found in most of the bony fishes In most of the fishes the air bladdèr is present.

Bony fishes first appeared in the deposits of middle Devonian period. The first bony fishes belonged to an order—Palaeoniscoidea (e.g *Cheirolepis*). The important characters of the ancient bony fishes were:

1. Osteichthyan cranial pattern
2. Presence of circumorbitals
3. Paired fish, the pectoral fins in front and the pelvic fins further back
4. The tail was heterocercal with large upper lobe.
5. Strongly developed notochord, and incomplete ossification of skull

Studies on *Cheirolepis* revealed that the bony fishes evolved through three different stages of actinopterygian evolution as indicated by the three infra classes given below:

1. *Chondrostei* (Primitive): Devonian through permian, some forms of which are surviving into the Recent also.
2. *Holostei* (Intermediate): Triassic through cretaceous, with a few forms which are surviving into the Recent also.
3. *Teleostei* (advanced): Cretaceous to Recent, rising to the highest point of evolution.

The important distinguishing characters of these three infra classes can be enumerated as follows:

In Chondrostei : The rhombic scales were present and the internal skeleton was partly cartilagenous. The spiracular slit was also present. Maxilla was fastened to cheek. The tail was strongly heterocercal. The lungs were not transformed into air bladder.

In Holostei :The rhombic scales were present and internal skeleton was partly cartilaginous. The spiracle was lost.Maxilla was freed from the cheek. Abbreviated heterocercal tail was present and lungs were transformed into air bladder.

In Teleostei : The scales were thin and rounded. The internal skeleton is completely ossified, Spiracle free and transformed into a pushing bone. The tail was homocercal. Pelvic fins became more forward, air bladder usually completely hydrostatic.

The genus *Amphicentrum* was a Pennsylvanian and Permian Palaeoniscoid fish. It was a specialized fish with elongated dorsal and anal fins. The structure of the tail was heterocercal though superficially it looked homocercal. The palaeoniscoids gave rise to two orders of chondrostean fishes i.e. *Polypterini* (Example—Polypterus) and *Acipenseroidei* (Example—Sturgeons, Paddle fishes). Several advanced palaeoniscoid fishes (Example— Redfieldia) were found during the Triassic period. They were characterized by:

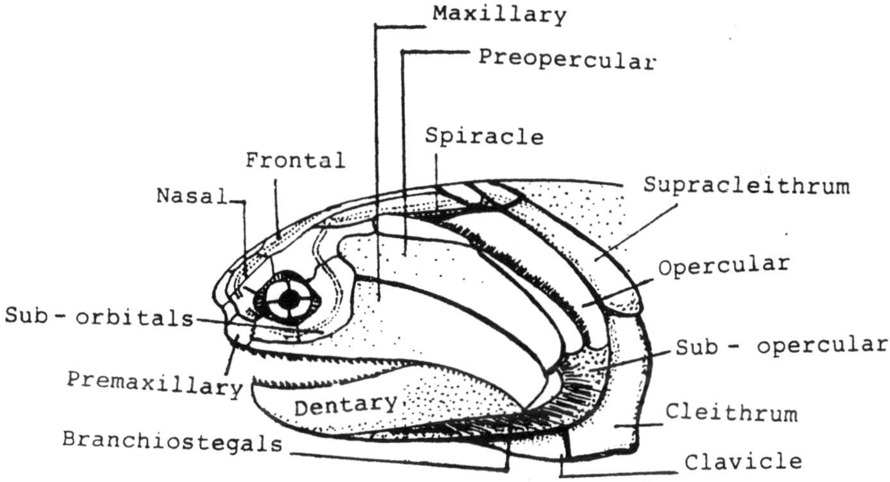

Skull of Palaeoniscid, Cheirolepis

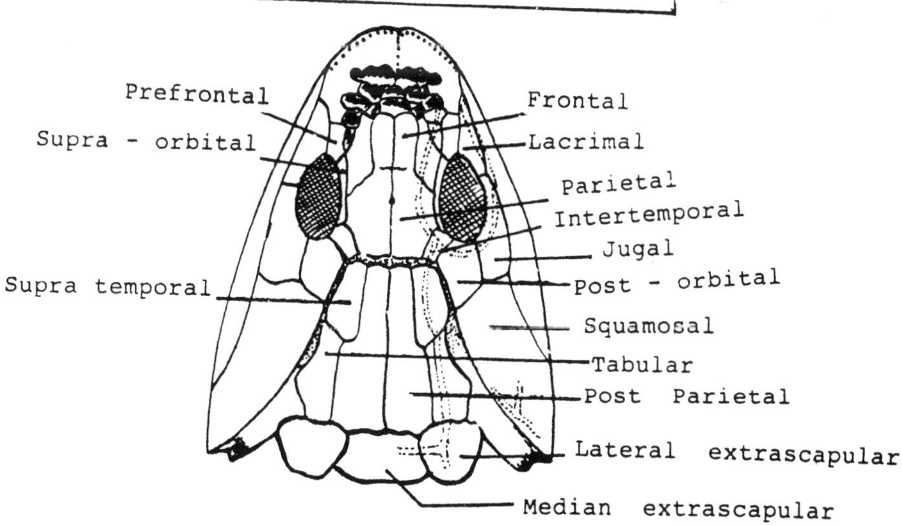

Dermatocrarium of osteolepis

Fig. 4 : Skulls of Cheirolepis and osteolepis

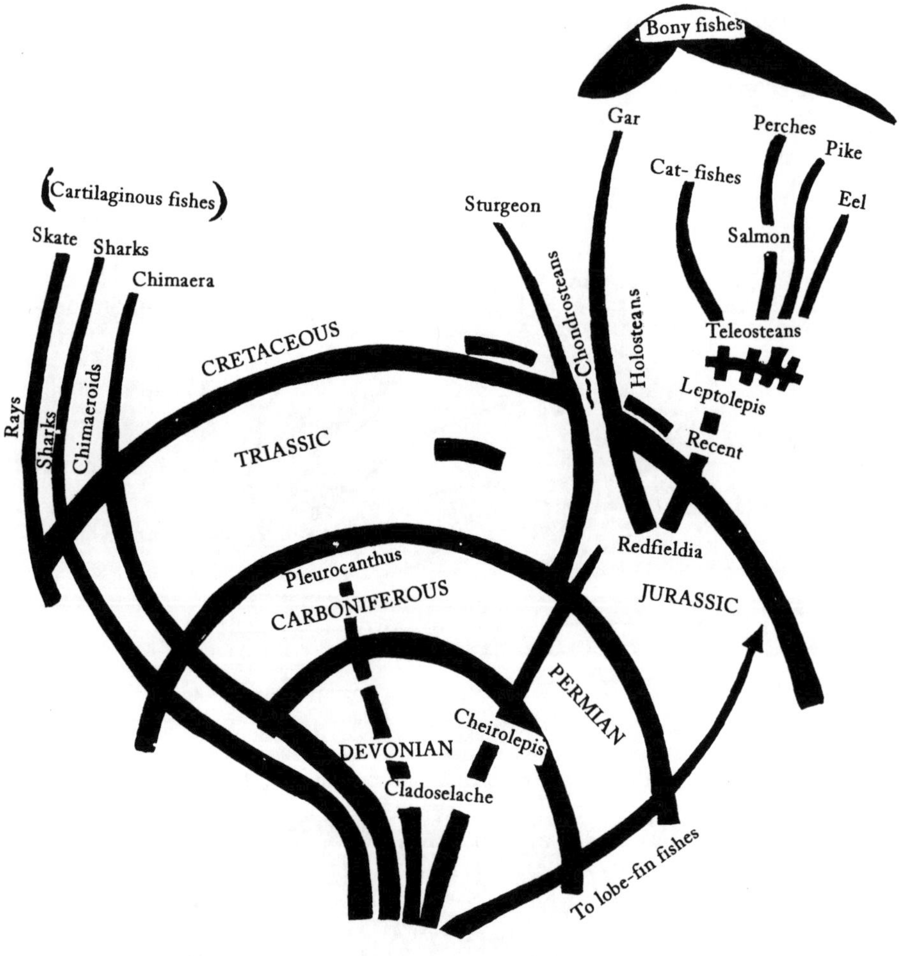

Fig. 5 : Evolution of Cartilaginous and Bony Fishes (based on Lois M. Darling).

1. Abbreviated upper lobe in the heterocercal tail
2. Reduction in the middle layer of each scale
3. Shortening of jaws, etc.

These fishes were considered as intermediate between Chondrosteans and the next higher group, the holosteans. The Mesozoic genus *Semionotus* was a typical example of the holosteans. Some specializations in this fish were like the early chondrostean fishes. *Dapedius* or *Microdon* on the Jurassic period also showed some evolutionary trends as shown in the deep-bodied chondrosteans of the late palaeozoic times. The genus *Aspidorhynchus* was also a holostean fish of the jurassic time.

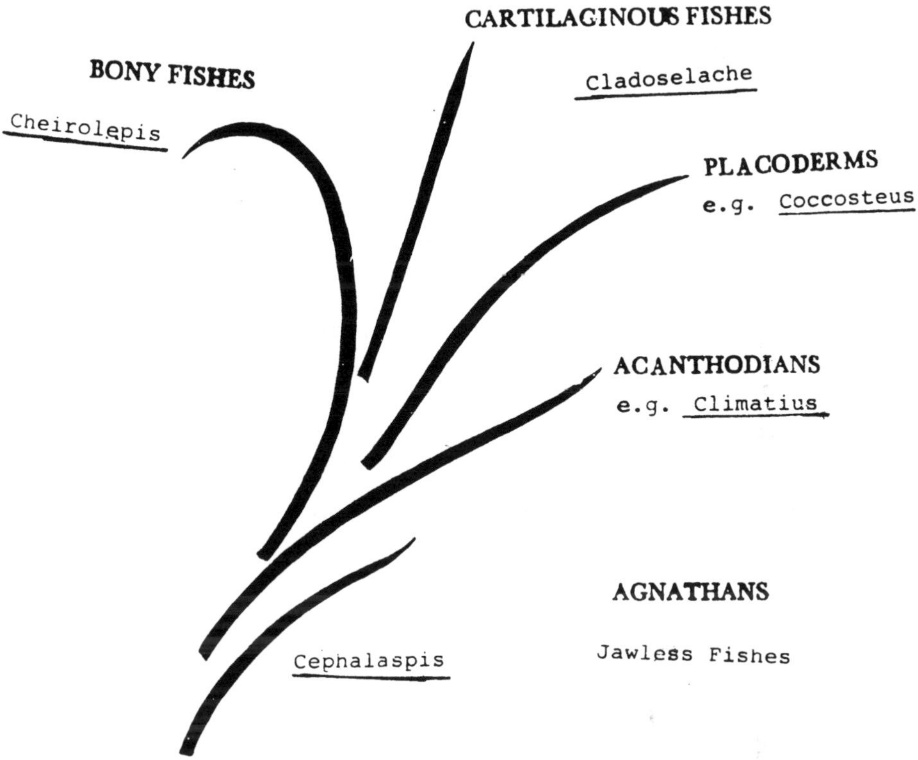

Fig. 6 : Evolution of Primitive fishes as prepared by Lois M. Darling.

The highest point of holostean evolution was reached during the jurassic and early cretaceous times and after that there was a decline. Two genera i.e. *Lepisosteus* and *Amia* persist into recent times also. Finally, the teleost fishes replaced holosteans during the cretaceous time.

The genus *Leptolepis* was the first teleost which appeared in the jurassic period. It was a nice intermediate form between the holostean and the teleosts. Numerous array of teleost genera and species have been outlined at the level of super orders in the following manner:

Leptolepidomorpha

The important characters are :

1. They were small-sized most primitive fishes having sardine like body form.
2. There was a single dorsal fin.
3. Pelvic fins are posterior in position.
4. Caudal fin was homocercal.
5. There were traces of ganoine on the surface of the scale.
6. They appeared during the upper triassic time and continued until the end of the mesozoic era.

Elopomorpha: Important characters of this super order are:

1. The elopomorphs, which were abundant during the cretaceous period were more advanced than their Leptolepidomorph ancestors.
2. There was development of hypural bones and the loss of ganoine on the scale.
3. Some elopomorphs evolved as the tarpons and their relatives.
4. Some of the elopomorphs branches off as highly and morphologically distinct *eels*.

Clupeomorpha : Important points of informations are as follows:

1. They were successful group appearing in the jurassic times.
2. Herring (Clupea), shad and sardines are more advanced than elopomorphs.
3. *Diplomystus* was a well known fish found in the deposits of the Eocene time.

Osteoglossomorpha : The important points of acquaintance are:

1. Osteoglossomorphs were found during the cretaceous period.
2. Some present day fishes have definitely descended from early osteoglossomorphs.
3. *Portheus* of the Niobrara beds of Kansas was of gigantic size.
4. *Osteoglossum* found today in Brazil, and snouted mormyrids of Africa have descended from the osteoglossomorphs.

Protacanthopterygii : The important characters are:

1. They appeared in cretaceous times and they were the ancestors of the most successful groups of the modern teleosts.
2. The primitive members of this suborder are the trouts and salmon.
3. Soft, fatty dorsal fin present, which was derived from the spiny dorsal fin.

Ostariophysi : The important characters are :

1. Most of the freshwater fishes living today have been included in this group.
2. Weberian ossicle is present and it connects the ear with the air-bladder.
3. The skull has a small chain of bones.
4. Carps, minnows, suckers and catfishes are common examples of this group.

Anterinomorpha : The following are the important characters:

1. The pelvic fins were posterior in position which is considered as a primitive character.
2. The maxillary bone has been excluded from the border of the mouth, and it is supposed to be an advanced character.
3. Flying fishes and killifishes are included in this group.
4. The palaeontological history of this group is not fully known.

Paracanthopterygii : Important characters are:

1. In paracanthopterygians, there is forward migration of the Pelvic fins like the acanthopterygians. Also, there are certain speciiizations in the mouth. The examples are cod, hadlock, the toad fishes and deep-sea angler etc.
2. They are said to represent a series of parallel adaptations from salmon like ancestors.

Acanthopterygii : The important characters of this sub-order are the following:

1. They are most numerous and advanced of the bony fishes popularly known as the spiny-finned teleosts.
2. Spines are prevalent in the anterior portion of the dorsal fin and in the anal fin.
3. Thin and rounded scales with tiny spines are present—they are *ctenoid* scales.
4. The endoskeleton is completely ossified.
5. The pelvic fins in these fishes migrate to an anterior position.
6. The maxilla is excluded from the mouth and it acts as a lever only in pushing the premaxilla forward.
7. There is an enormous range of adaptive radiation in these fishes. They include the perches, bass, sunfishes, snappers, pipe fishes, sea-horses, parrot fishes, trigger fishes, sword fishes, butterfly fish etc.

Concluding Remarks

The *Placoderms* lived in the Devonian period side by side with the *Ostracoderms*. Because of the presence of jaws, well developed fins and reduced exoskeletal armours in the former, they (placoderms) were supposed to be a superior case. The ostracoderms disappeared by the end of the devonian period. The oldest fish fossil have been unearthed from the rocks of the ordovician period (500 million years ago). These archaic stocks are the ostracoderms or unarmoured prehistoric fishes. *Jamoytius* is a possible relic of the unarmoured ancestors.

The *Chondrosteans* were the first fishes to evolve and that they were dominant during late palaeozoic times. Then it was shown that during early and middle mesozoic era the chondrosteans were replaced by holosteans. During the last phases of the mesozoic time and in the cenozoic era the holostean fishes were replaced by the teleosts. The final stage in the evolution of the teleosts seem to have been marked by a clear dichotomy into the specialized *paracanthopterygians* on the one hand and the parallel *acanthopterygian* or spiny-finned teleost fishes on the other.

The first Devonian crossopterygians as typified particularly by the genus *Osteolepis* formed the basal stock from which crossopterygians evolved. The evolution took place in two general lines, one being represented by the suborder—*Rhipidistia*, the other by the order *Coelacanthini*. The osteolepids were rhipidistans. The placoderms (e.g. *Gemuendina*) the Devonian vertebrates are also supposed to be early relatives of sharks.

CHAPTER 2

FOOD, FEEDING HABITS, AND ALIMENTARY CANAL

Fishes have become adapted to wide range of feeding habits. Some fishes are *herbivorous* (e.g. *Labeo rohita, L. fimbriatus*), some are *carnivorous* (e.g. *Wallago attu, Channa striatus*) and a large number of fishes are *omnivorous* also (e.g. *Clarias batrachus, Heteropneustes fossilis*). Most of the culturable fishes are *omnivorous* in their feeding habit. Some fishes depend for their nutrition, mainly on zooplankton and phytoplankton and as such, they are known as plankton feeders (e.g. *Cirrhinus reba, Hilsa ilisha*) and form a separate group as conceived by Hora and Pillay (1962). Schaperclaus (1933) divided the fishes into three groups on the basis of their feeding preference:

(a) 'Main food' or the Natural food, which the fish prefers under favourable condition and on which it grows well.

(b) 'Occasional food' or the natural food, that is well liked and are consumed, when available.

(c) 'Emergency food' which is ingested when the preferred food items are not available but the fish can just survive.

On the basis of relationship between the fishes and their food, Nikol 'skii (1963) divided food of fishes into the following categories:

(i) *Basic food*—Consumed by the fish, comprising main part of the gut content.

(ii) *Secondary food*—Present in small amounts in the gut of the fish.

(iii) *Obligatory food*—Which is consumed in the absence of basic food.

According to this author, the *herbivorous* and *detrito-phagic* species feed on vegetable matter and detrius, *carnivorous* feed on invertebrates, and *Predators* prey on other fishes. Nikol'skii (1963) also categorized that the species feeding on a variety of foods are *euryphagic,* those feeding on a few selected types of food are *stenophagic,* and those species which feed on a single type food are *monophagic.*

The plant materials consumed by herbivorous fish includes unicellular algae, filamentous algae and portions of several aquatic plants of larger size. Certain fish species also take small quantity of sand and mud alongwith the food materials. Zooplankton include protozoans, rotifers, micro-crustaceans, small invertebrates, larvae and eggs of several animals and they constitute the food of the carnivorous fishes. The annelid worms, snails, crustaceans, mussels, insects, small fishes and also frogs and tadpoles are consumed by certain fishes.

There may be variation in the food preference of the fry, fingerlings and adult of the same species of fish. The fingerlings of *Catla* (a surface feeder) feeds on planktonic algae, vegetable debris and water flees but the food materials of adult comprise algae, plant materials, crustaceans, rotifers, insects and vegetable debris. Similarly the fingerlings of *Heteropneustes fossilis* (a bottom feeder) feed on some insects and worms and the adults feed on insects, debris and algae and ostracods etc. In case of *Anabas testudineus* (an entomophage), the fry feeds on Protozoans, animalcules and water fleas. The fingerlings feed on mosquito, insect larvae, water fleas etc. The important food materials of the adult of this fish species include water fleas, vegetable debris, small fishes and some selected insects etc.

According to Das and Moitra (1955), the food spectrum of fishes varies in different seasons. It depends on the availability of food at different periods. Herbivorous and carnivorous fishes show some definite peak periods in feeding, in contrast to omnivorous fishes as the latter show little variation throughout the year. Das and Moitra (1955) also divided the fishes into three groups according to trophic niche, they occupy in the water. These groups are :

(i) *Plankton eating surface feeders*—e.g. *Catla catla, Puntius ticto, Glossogobius giuris, Gadusia chaptra, Hypophthalmisthys molitrix* etc. They may be either carnivorous or omnivorous.

(ii) *Column or mid feeders*—e.g. *Labeo rohita, Puntius sophore, Tor tor, Mystus cavasius, Wallago attu* etc. They depend on the organisms of the mid-water. They may be herbivorous, carnivorous or omnivorous.

(iii) *Bottom feeders*—e.g. *Cirrhina mrigala, Labeo calbasu, Puntius sarana, Cirrhina reba, Clarias batrachus, Heteropneustes fossilis* etc. Like the Column feeders they are herbivorous, omnivorous or carnivorous.

Feeding Intensity: The feeding intensity or the degree of feeding is related with season, maturity, spawning and availability of food materials. It is determined by calculating the *Gastrosomatic index* by the formula :

$$\text{Gastro somatic Index (GaSI)} = \frac{\text{Weight of the stomach content}}{\text{Weight of the fish}} \times 100$$

There may be seasonal variation in the gastrosomatic index of several species of fishes. It is maximum during the post spawning period and minimum during the breeding period.

Table : Food and Feeding Habits of Some Important Freshwater Fishes

Fish species	*Food*	*Feeding habit*
Anabas testudineus	Fry–Protozoans, animalcules and water fleas Fingerlings–Insect larvae, Mosquitoes and Water fleas etc. Adult–Insects, fish, vegetable debris and water fleas	Entomophagous
Catla catla	Fingerlings–Waterfleas, Algae and certain vegetable debris.	Surface feeder
	Adult–Algae, Crustaceans, Some plants, rotifers, insects etc.	Mainly Plankton feeder
Hypophthalmichthys molitrix	Fingerlings–Unicellular algae. Adult–Dinoflagellates, Protozoans, Species of Bacillariophyceae, Rotifers, macrovegetation and detrius etc.	Plankton feeder
Labeo rohita	Fingerlings–Plants, microscopic in size and vegetable debris. Adult–Plants, microscopic in size Decaying higher plants, Detris and mud.	Herbivorous
Labeo calbasu	Fingerlings–Microscopic plants and Vegetable debris Adult–As in *Labeo rohita.*	Herbivorous
Labeo fimbriatus	Several species of algae (families Bacillariophy ceae, Chlorophy ceae and Myxophyceae), Macrovegetation, animal matter and decaying organic matter.	Herbivorous Bottom feeder
Labeo bata	Both fingerlings and adults feed on algae, vegetable debris, detrius and mud etc.	Herbivorous Bottom feeder
Labeo kontius	Fingerlings–Filamentous algae, decaying leaves of aquatic plants, unicellular algae, insects, detrius and mud. Adult–Decaying leaves of aquatic plants, detrius, remains of insects, algae etc.	Marginal and Bottom feeder
Labeo gonius	Fingerlings–Vegetable debris, algae, detrius and mud etc. Adult–Vegetable matter, Plants of microscopic size, detrius and mud etc.	Bottom-Column feeder, herbivorous
Cirrhina mrigala	Fingerlings–Algae. Vegetable debris, detrius, mud etc. Adults–Algae, detrius, sand and mud decayed leaves of aquatic plants, algae.	Bottom feeder, herbivorous
Cirrhinus reba	Fingerlings–Algae, decaying plants, animal matter, detrius and mud etc. Adults–Phytoplankton, Decaying leaves, detrius and mud.	Bottom feeder, Planktophage
Glyptothorax pectinopterus	Adult–Protozoans, crustaceae worms, memotodes, diatoms etc.	Carnivorous
Noemacheilus montanus	Fingerlings–Unicellular algae, insect larvae. Adult–Insects, Molluscs, Filamentous algae, Macrovegetation, Sand and mud.	Omnivorous

Contd...

Fish species	*Food*	*Feeding habit*
Barbus carnaticus	Fingerlings–Filamentous algae and insects. Adult–Leaves of aquatic plants, filamentous algae, insects, detritus etc.	Omnivorous
Cyprinus carpio	Fry and Fingerlings–Mostly Nauplius larvae. Adult–Cyclops, rotifers, Nauplius, Euglena, Diatoms; Volvox, chironomus larvae, insects.	Voraciously Omnivorous
Ctenopharyngodon idella	Fry and Fingerlings–Unicellular algae, rotifers, crustaceans, chironomus larva. Adult–Aquatic vegetation, weeds.	Herbivorous
Carassius auratus	Adult–Copepods, Cladocerans crustaceans.	Carnivorous
Eutroplus suratensis	Fingerlings–Algae-both Unicellular and filamentous; water fleas and animalcula. Adults–Filamentous algae, Insects and minute crustaceans, Diatoms, Leaves of aquatic plants.	Omnivorous
Osphronemus goramy	Fry–Insect larvae, Zooplankton, crustaceans, soft parts of aquatic vegetation. Adult–Mainly aquatic vegetation, when emergency, it can feed on insects, small fish and frogs.	Herbivorous / Omnivorous
Wallago attu	Fry–Insects, fish-fry, fingerlings water fleas. Fingerlings–Fish fry, insects and smaller fingerlings. Adults–Insects, tadpoles and fish.	Carnivorous and Predaceous
Mystus seenghala	Same as *Wallago attu.*	
Channa striatus	Fry–Water fleas, insects, fish fry and Fingerlings. Fingerlings–Larvae of Diptera, zooplankton, fish fry. Adults–Small fish, tadpoles etc.	Carnivorous mainly
Tilapia mossambica	Fry–Unicellular algae Diatoms etc. Adult–Algal food, insects, Crustaceans, fish larvae detrius etc.	Mainly herbivorous but also Omnivorous
Heteropneustes fossilis	Fingerlings–Insect and several worms. Adult–Algae, copepods, insects and Ostracods etc.	Omnivorous
Clarias batrachus	Fingerlings–Insects, Crustaceans, debris. Adults–Smaller and Larger Crustaceans, Worms, insects, Small fish, decaying organic matter etc.	Omnivorous

Critical Reviews

The morphohistological characters of the alimentary canal of several teleosts are on record. The important contributions are those of Sarbahi (1940), Al-Hussaini (1947), Islam (1975), Kapoor (1953, 1957), Khanna (1961), Kamal (1964), Puspa Kamal (1964 a, b), Chitray (1966), Sehgal (1966), Moitra and Bhowmik (1967), Lal (1968), Mehrotra and Khanna (1969), Sehgal and Salaria (1970), Moitra and Sinha (1971), Sinha and Moitra (1972, 1975), Sinha (1983), Geeta *et. al.* (1991) and others.

Moitra and Sinha (1971) described some aspects of the morphohistology of the alimentary canal of *Chagunius chagunio*. Well developed and distinct villi have been observed in the buccopharyugeal region. A large number of taste buds and mucous cells were also seen in this area. Undifferentiated columnar cells become differentiated into mucous cells. Presence of taste buds in the oesophagus region appeared to be related to its peculiar mode of feeding. The compact villi were seen in the intestinal bulb for more efficient obsorption. An abundance of mucous cells and the strong musculature were considered as the characteristic features of the rectal region.

Sinha and Moitra (1975) described in detail the morphohistology of the intestine of *Cirrhinus mrigala* (Hamilton) during different life history stages. They revealed that the intestine was shortest in the fry (carnivorous) and longest in the adults (herbivorous) with intermediate values in the fingerlings (omnivorous). There was adaptation in the mucous folds according to the nature of diet. The food appeared to have a marked influence on the morpho-histology of the villi and the number of mucous cells per unit area in different stages. The sub-mucosa, muscularis and tunica propria were present in all the three stages. They also studied the functional morpho-histology of the alimentary canal of an Indian freshwater carp, *Labeo rohita* (Hamilton) during its different life history stages. They revealed that with advancing age, there is change from carnivorous type and consequently many histological changes take place in the alimentary canal.

Sarma (1973) has described the alimentary canal and gut content of *Hilsa kanagurta* (Blkr.). Because it is a plankton feeder, the adaptations are correlated with its feeding habits. Absence of teeth, numerous gillrakers, pharyngeal bristles, long alimentary canal and coiled intestine are some of the important features of adaptation.

Agrawal and Sharma (1966) have studied the morpho-histology of the digestive organs of *Mystus vittatus* (Bloch), an omnivorous siluroid fish. They found that the alimentary canal of this fish is of moderate size with inferior mouth. The bucco-pharynx has well developed teeth. The maxillary and mandibular valves are present. The stomach has cardiac and pyloric parts and the latter is thick and muscular, almost like gizzard. The lips and buccal epithelium were provided with mucous cells and taste buds. The oesophageal mucosa is lined with columnar cells. The tubular gastric glands are present only in the cardiac stomach and they are absent in the pyloric stomach. The intestinal wall is provided with top plates.

Pandey and Pandey (1974) have described the histomorphology of alimentary canal of *Nandus nandus*. There is adaptation in the alimentary canal in accordance with the nature of diet. The mouth has wide gape. The upper jaw is protrusible. Taste buds are present in the buccal cavity. Pharyngeal and horny pad teeth are present. The gill rakers are short and provided with teeth. A true stomach is present like other carnivorous fishes. The intestine is short like *Heteropneustes fossilis*, *Clarias batrachus* (Chitray and Saxena, 1962), and *Tilapia mossambica* (Pasha, 1964), is not demarcated into a rectum. A large number of the mucosa folds increase the surface of the gut (Chitray and Saxena, 1962) and Sehgal (1966). Kiran Kumari and co-workers (1989) have studied certain aspects of the alimentary canal of *Bagarius bagarius*.

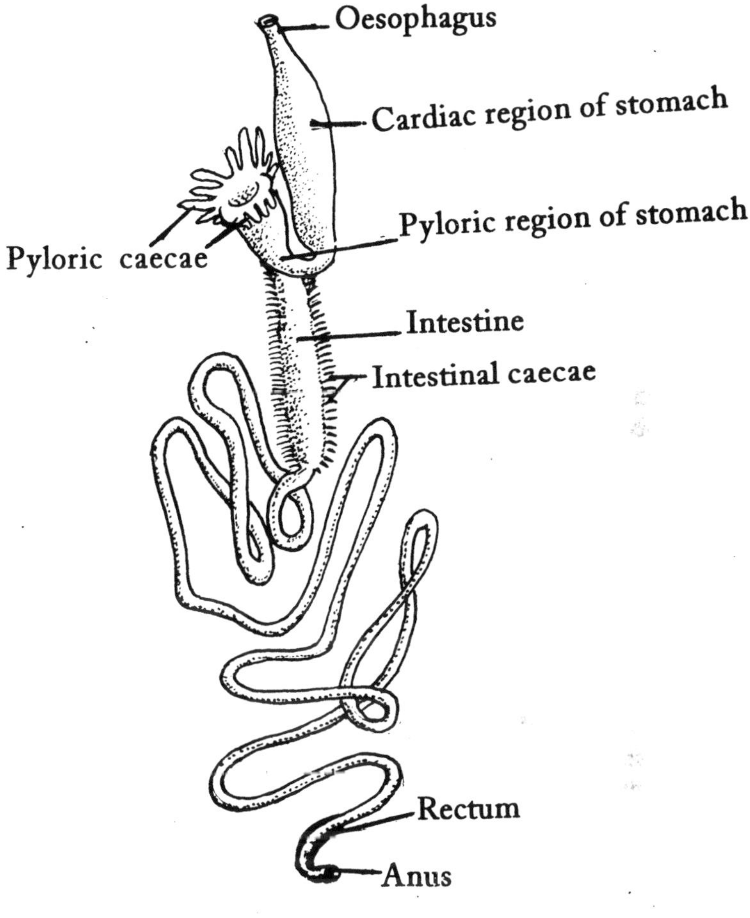

Fig. 7 : Alimentary canal of *Gadusia Chapra*

The anatomy and histology of the alimentary canal in relation to its feeding habits of a siluroid fish, *Wallago attu* (Bl. & Schn.) have been studied by Kapoor (1953). He has made comparative studies of the differences between the anatomy and histology of the alimentary canal of carnivores, herbivores and plankton feeders among Indian fishes. *Wallago attu* is a carnivorous and predator fish feeding on fry, prawns and other animal materials. Its feeding habits lead to certain morphological and anatomical adaptations. Anatomy and histology of the alimentary canal is in accordance with the carnivorous habit of this fish.

Al-Hussaini (1949) has described the functional morphology of the alimentary canal of some fish in relation to differences in their feeding habits, anatomy and histology. Chacko (1945) studied the food and alimentary canal of the Milk-fish, *Chanos chanos.* Mookerjee and Das (1945) have described the gut of carnivorous and herbivorous fishes in relation to their food at different stages of their life cycle. Kuthalingam (1956) has described in detail the food and feeding habits of the Indian

Mackerel *Rastrelliger kanagurta* (Russel). The author has studied the diet of the Indian Mackerel in the post larval, juvenile and adult stages in a large number of species. He has revealed that the post larval forms are strictly herbivorous and feed on diatoms and algae. In the juvenile form they become omnivorous and feed on all surface forms available in this area such as copepods, lucifers, ostracoderms, polychaetes, molluscs, diatoms and algae. This fish is definitely a carnivorous fish. Bapat and Bal (1952) have described the food of some fishes from Bombay. Bhimachar and George (1952) have studied the food and feeding habits of the Indian Mackerel *Rastrelliger kanagurta* (Russel). Bullen (1912) has also given some notes on the feeding habits of Mackerels and certain clupeids in the English Channel. Food and feeding habits of oil sardine and Mackerel has been studied by John and Menon (1942).

Moitra and Ray (1981) have studied the digestive enzymes and their relationships with the food and feeding habits in Indian freshwater fishes. Existing knowledge of the digestive enzymes of Indian freshwater perches are mainly due to the efforts of Agrawal and Singh (1963), and Agrawal and Sharma (1966). Moitra and Ray (1981) have made the qualitative estimation of the digestive enzymes in the Indian climbing perch, *Anabas testudineus* (Bloch) and their relationships with the food and feeding habits have also been discussed. They have revealed that *protease* activity is pronounced in the hepatopancreas, intestine and pyloric stomach which indicates that the fish is more suited to digest protein food. *Lipase* activity was more pronounced in hepatopancreas and intestine. *Amylase* was found to be more or less active in all the regions of the digestive system inspite of the carnivorous feeding habits of this fish. Agrawal and Sharma (1966) have studied the physiology of digestion in *Nandus nandus* (Ham.) and have revealed several important features. Agrawal and Singh (1963) have described the physiology of digestion in *Colisa fasciata* (Bloch and Schneider) in detail. The comparative activity of some digestive

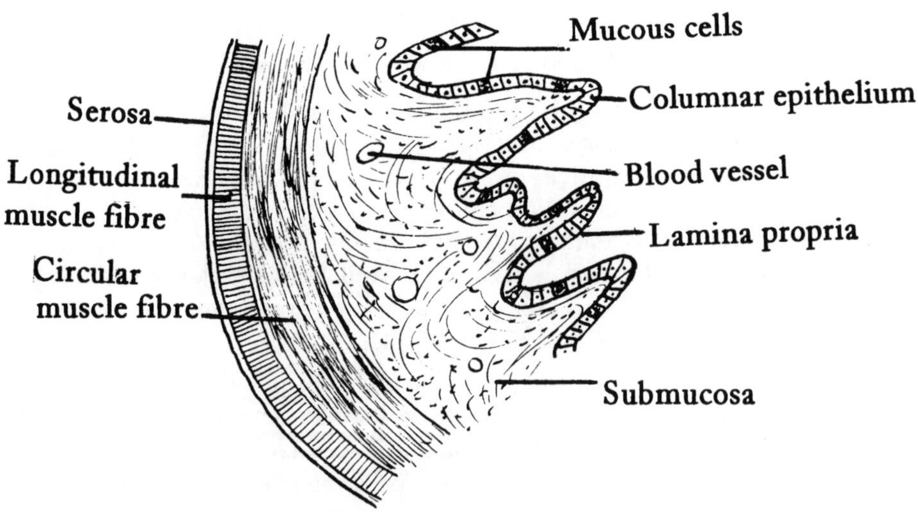

Fig. 8 : T.S. of instestine of *Clarias batrachus*

enzymes in the alimentary canal of *Tilapia* and perch has been made by Fish (1960). Ghosh (1976) has described the digestive enzymes and their correlation with the food habits in the catfish *Clarias batrachus*.

Geeta *et. al.* (1991) have described in detail the food and feeding habits of *Therapon jarbua* (Forsk.). They have studied in detail the food and feeding habit of this fish. It is a voracious predator. They procured the specimens from Veli lake (an estuary) of Kerala. This fish has a piscivorous feeding nature, closely followed by crustaceans. *T. jarbua* is a specific feeder of piscine diet and selectively feeds on them depending on the abundance of these forms in surrounding waters.

Moitra and Sinha (1972) have described in detail the structure, distribution and probable function of *Taste buds* and *Mucous cells* in the alimentary canal during the life history of *Cirrhinus mrigala* (Hamilton). Various types of food by this fish at different stages of its life-history in relation to variation in structure, distribution and function of taste buds and mucous cells have been critically analysed. The fry are definitely carnivorous. It could be confirmed by the fact that the relative length of the gut is low. The taste buds play a very significant role at this stage. The adult exhibits a herbivorous feeding habit and the role of taste buds is quite significant and as such, they are sufficient in number and are well organised. The authors have inferred that it is the actual diet (Plant or animal food) of the fish which is responsible for the development of taste buds and mucous cells.

In the fingerlings and adults, the taste buds are present in the oesophagus but in the fry they are absent in the oesophageal region, where there is no need of gustatory sense because of sight feeding habit. Gustatory sense is there in the oesophageal region of the fingerlings and adults and the final selection of food is affected. Numerical abundance of mucous cells in the oesophagus of fry, fingerlings and adults is an adaptation for lubrication of food. As the intestinal bulb and the intestine are concerned with storage, digestion and absorption of food, the mucous cells are very few in number. In the rectum the mucous cells secrete mucous which facilitate the expulsion of faeces. Mucous cells are rarely present in the fry and fingerlings because of simple nature of food materials.

Among the hill stream fishes also, some are carnivorous, some are herbivorous and some are omnivorous. The alimentary canal is adapted in accordance to a particular feeding habit of the fish. *Glyptothorax pectinopterus* is a carnivorous fish. The alimentary canal is a short and straight tube. *Garra gotyla* is basically a herbivorous fish. The alimentary canal is typically of herbivorous type having longer and coiled intestine. Adaptations in both the cases are in accordance with the nature of diet. A longer intestine is found in a fish whose food is poor in nutritional substance. The poor development of folds in mucosa is compensated by a long intestine which sufficiently increases the absorbing surface. Longer intestine in *Garra gotyla* ensures the extraction of the maximum nutritional matters. So, a long intestine compensates for the poor development of folds in the mucosa and high folds increase the surface of the mucosa (e.g. *Glyptothorax pectinopterus*) to compensate for a relatively short intestine. Modifications are in accordance with the availability of food materials also.

The fish *Glyptothorax pectinopterus* is better equipped for protein digestion because the Proteolytic activities are stronger in the pyloric stomach, intestine and hepatopancreas. Also, there is strong activity of lipase in the intestine of this fish which is an evidence for the fact that this fish is well adapted also for the digestion of the fatty substances injected alongwith the normal diet. The fat digesting enzyme is probably secreted mainly by the hepatopancreas in this case.

Glyptothorax pectinopterus is a carnivorous fish. In its stomach contents can be seen the crustacean larvae (e.g. daphnia), Chironomus larvae, Dragon fly nymph, May fly nymph, adult mosquitoes and certain nematodes. The stomach contents of the fish *Garra gotyla* were also analysed. This fish is basically a herbivorous fish. The food recorded are mostly Periphyton which include *Volvox globator, Ulothrix zonata, Oedogonium refescens, Spirogyra nitida, Oscillatoria* Sp., *Navicula* sp. etc. The feeding rate in *G.pectinopterus* is high during the months of September, December, April and May and it is low during the months of October, November, February and June. In *Garra gotyla*, the feeding intensity is higher in April and May and then from August to October, i.e. before the advent of breeding season and after the spawning period as evident from several studies.

The Alimentary Canal and Digestive Glands of *Wallago attu*

Wallago attu is a well known carnivorous and predaceous siluroid fish popularly known as freshwater shark. The morpho-histology of its alimentary canal is strictly in accordance with its nature of diet. The alimentary canal consists of Mouth, Buccal cavity, with a number of patches of teeth, a developed stomach and a short Intestine. Liver and pancreas are the main digestive glands.

The different regions of the alimentary canal are characterised by the presence of mucous folds which project into the lumen of the canal. Though mucosal epithelium of the buccal cavity is smooth on the whole, a few longitudinal and wavy folds are there on its posterior part. These folds are continuous with the oesophageal mucosal folds. These oesophageal folds increase in height. The height of the mucosal folds decrease in the stomach and they are thick and longitudinally arranged in a zigzag way. The height and complexity of these folds increase in the fundic part. The mucosal folds of the proximal intestine are web-like in appearance but, distally they are comparatively simple. Now, the various parts have been described in detail below:

The Mouth and Buccal Cavity : The mouth cleft is deep and is bounded by the upper and lower jaws which are provided with teeth. The mouth leads into the buccal cavity. The buccal cavity is spacious and it can be divided into anterior and posterior regions. The anterior region bears the maxillary, mandibular and vomerine teeth and horny pad teeth. The posterior region consists the pharyngeal teeth. Maxillary teeth, Vomerine teeth and Pharyngeal teeth are present on the roof of the buccal cavity but the mandibular teeth and horny pad teeth are present on the floor of the buccal cavity. Maxillary teeth are actually borne on the premaxillaries. Vomerine teeth are present on a pair of oval patches which are present on the vomerine bones. Pharyngeal teeth are also located on a pair of oval patches. Mandibular teeth are borne on dentaries. A pair of horny pads bear the so called horny pad teeth. These are quite superficially embedded. Teeth present on the jaws are of very large size but those on the horny pad are smaller in size. Teeth are *homodont* and *polyphyodont*. They are backwardly curved so as to prevent the escape of prey. The gill rackers provide additional grip for holding the prey. The base of the cranium forms the roof of the buccal cavity and the sides are supported by the branchial arches. The median *urohyal* supports the floor of the buccal cavity. At the anterior part, of the floor of the buccal cavity the mucosal thickening appears which forms a tongue like structure.

Histologically, the anterior region of the buccal cavity consists of *mucosa* , *submucosa* and *muscularis* but the posterior portion (Pharynx) is made up of *mucosa submucosa, muscularis* and *adventitia*. The mucosa of the buccal cavity comprises epithelium and its derivatives— the mucous cells, giant cells and the taste buds. The stratified epithelial cells are polygonal in shape with an oval or spherical nucleus which is centrally placed. Some of the cells are modified into mucous and giant cells. They are in abundance in the buccal cavity. The mucous cells are flask-shaped cells. Giant cells are circular or oval in shape and they are bigger than the mucous cells. Islam (1951) termed the 'giant cells' as club-shaped cells. These cells have been described earlier by Vanajakshi (1938) also. In addition to these cells, there are some taste buds also. Granular cells and muscle bundles are also present. Granules can be observed even in routine haemotoxy lin-eosin preparation. The basal layer of cells are columnar in appearance and they are supported on a well defined basement membrane.

The mucosa layer is followed by submucosa which comprises the upper and lower layers. The upper layer is composed of circular connective tissue fibres. At certain places, radial or longitudinal connective tissue fibres may be present. The lower layer is composed of loose connective tissue fibres. The muscularis consists of an inner longitudinal and an outer layer of muscles. The adventitia layer comprises fibrous connective tissue and is supplied with fine blood capillaries. Subserous connective tissue layer is also present. In the pharyngeal region the granular cells are mostly absent. The pharyngeal mucosa has also the layers of rete mucosum of malpighii (upper) and stratum malpighii (lower) just above the basement membrane. The buccal cavity leads into the oesophagus.

Oesophagus : It is a tubular structure. It passes through the septum transversum and enters the visceral cavity. It lies óver the lobes of the liver and pancreas. The fish (*Wallago attu*) is a physostomous one and as such, the air bladder has a pneumatic duct attached with the posterior end of the oesophagus. The oesophagus and other parts of the alimentary canal posterior to the buccal cavity are composed of *tunica mucosae, tunica submucosae, tunica muscularis* and *adventitia (serosa).* Histologically the oesophagus is similar to that of the posterior part of the pherynx. But the granular cells are absent. There is increase in the number of giant cells in the oesophagus. The retemucosum of malpighian layer is absent. The thickness of the tunica submucosae decreases and the serosa is thin in this region. The oesophagus leads into the stomach.

Stomach : *Wallago attu* has a true stomach lying in the left side of the visceral cavity. It is a sac-like pyriform organ divisible into cardiac, fundic and Pyloric parts. Histologically, the stomach consists of *tunica mucosae, tunica submucosae, tunica muscularis* and *Serosa.* The lining of the stomach is folded. The stratified epithelial layer of the *tunica mucosae* of the oesophagus is transformed into the columnar or gastric epithelium of the *tunica mucosa* of stomach. In the layer of tunica muscularis, the outer circular and the inner longitudinal layers of muscles reverse their position in the wall of the stomach. So, this is a difference with the oesophagus.

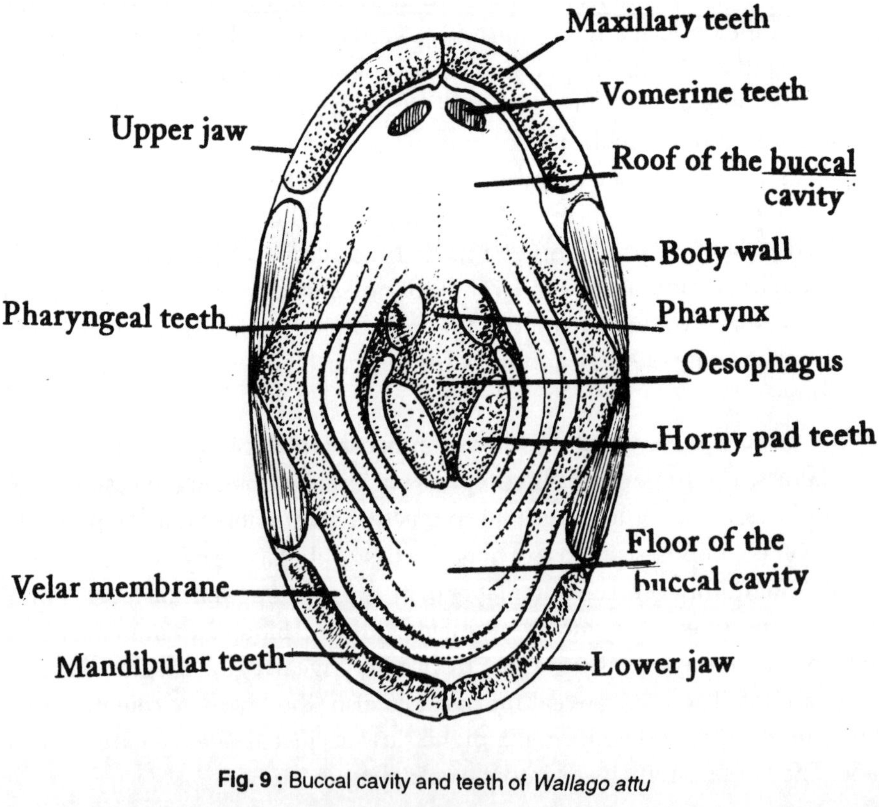

Fig. 9 : Buccal cavity and teeth of *Wallago attu*

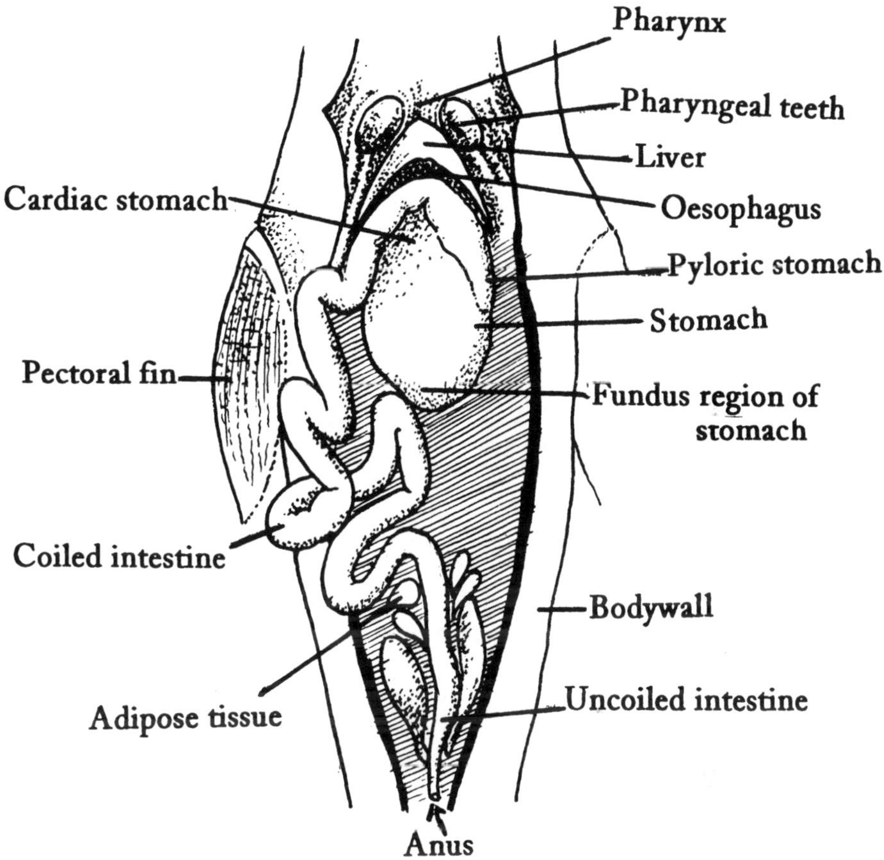

Fig. 10 : Alimentary canal of Wallago attu

The tunica mucosae comprises the columnar epithelium, gastric glands and lamina propria. The columnar epithelial layer is mainly made up of simple tall prismatic cells with granular cytoplasm and oval nucleus. Certain columnar epithelial cells are modified to form the gastric gland which are invaginated within lamina propria. These glands open at places into the gastric pits of tunica mucosae. Lamina propria is an extension of submucosa and is quite vascular. It projects into the glandular region forming the main supporting tissue of the gastric glands. The gastric glands are tubular and branched. At the pyloric region of the stomach the sphincter is formed by the thick circular muscle layer. Tunica submucosae which is present next to the tunica mucosae consists of fibrous connective tissue. The tunica muscularis comprises an inner circular and outer longitudinal layers of muscles. Serosa is made up of fibrous connective tissue and also bundles of subserous connective tissue. This layer becomes thin at the pyloric end of the stomach. The stomach leads into the intestine.

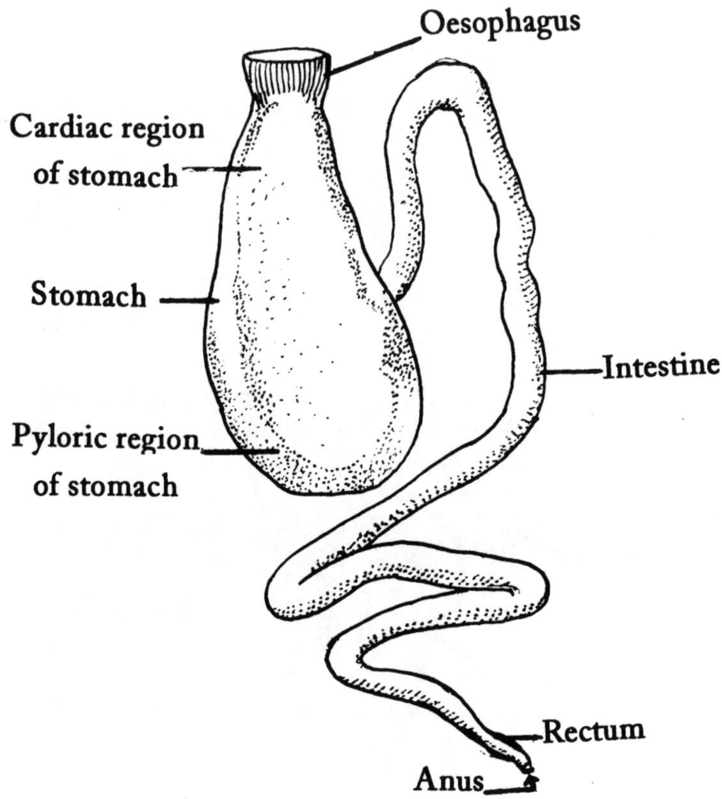

Fig. 11 : Alimentary canal of *Wallago attu* (taken out)

Intestine : The intestine is a coiled tube with moderate length. It can not be externally demarcated into different parts. However, there is variation in diameters of this tube at different places and there is difference in the disposition of the mucous folds also. The bile duct enters the proximal part of the intestine projecting into its lumen. The intestine, after making a few coils opens into the exterior through the anal opening as usual. Some parts of the intestine is surrounded by the adipose tissue and the position of the intestine is maintained by the mesentery.

Histologically the intestine comprises the usual four layers: *tunica mucosae, tunica submucosae, tunica muscularis* and *serosa.* The tunica mucosae consists of columnar epithelium and lamina propria. The free border of the columnar epithelium is also known as *brush border* or *top plate.* The epithelial layer consists of columnar or absorptive cells. The columnar cells contain nucleus towards the basal portion and the nucleus is oval in shape. In the columnar epithelium are present certain wandering cells and mucous cells. A number of unstriated muscle fibres are present in lamina propria and the latter supports the columnar epithelium. Tunica submucosae is made up of fibrous connective tissue which comprises unstriated muscle fibres. Tunica muscularis has an inner circular and an outer longitudinal layers of muscles. Serosa is a very thin layer made of the fibrous connective tissue. The anal operture is lined by striated epithelium which contains several mucous and giant cells. The circular layer of muscularis thickens but the serosa layer is very thin at the anal end.

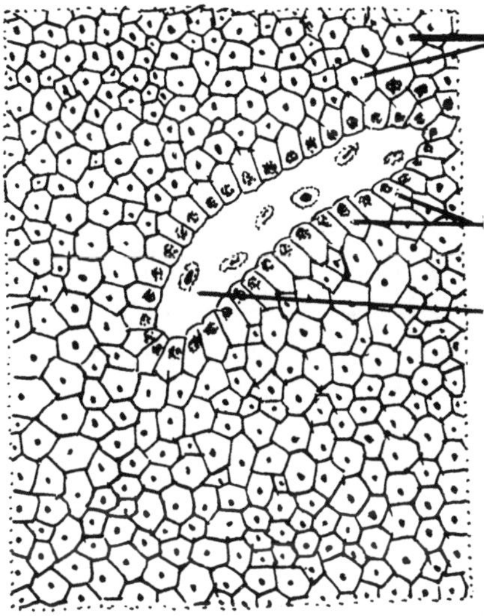

Fig. 12 : Hepatopancreas (histological picture)

The Liver and the Pancreas : The liver is bilobed and compact structure. The left lobe is slightly larger than the right lobe. It is dark brown in colour. Between the lobes of the liver is present a thin walled gall bladder of greenish colour. The neck portion of the gall bladder is continuous with the cystic duct. Hepatic ducts coming from the lobes of the liver merge into the cystic duct and the main bile duct is formed. The main bile duct runs through the left pancreatic lobe and opens into the duodenum. Histologically, the gall bladder has columnar epithelium, fibromuscular tissue and serosa. The columnar cells have oval nuclei. The columnar epithelial layer is the inner most layer which is followed by the fibromuscular connective tissue layer. The outer layer is that of serosa which comprises the connective tissue fibres. The blood capillaries pass into the bladder through the tissue of Serosa. The liver has a fibrous connective tissue covering which is sometimes spoken as capsule. The liver is made up of characteristic hepatic polygonal cells and ductules. Each hepatic cell has a granular cytoplasm and a prominent round nucleus. The groups of hepatic cells are supported by the reticular tissues. The bile duct is made up of columnar epithelial layer, fibro muscular tissue and serosa coat. The serous coat is the outer most layer, the fibromuscular tissue is located in the middle and the columnar layer of cells is the inner most layer.

The Pancreas is also a bilobed gland, the right lobe being larger than the left one. The pancreas mainly consists of the acini and the islands. Lobules or acini are the exocrine tissue of the pancreas which are composed of Polyhedral cells. The cells have rounded nuclei and the cytoplasm is granular. The acini are purely serous. In the centre of the acinus there may be present few spindle-shaped cells the controacinar cells. The pancreatic duct system is very prominent. The pancreatic islands (Islets of Langerhans) are the real endocrine tissues. They are formed by the aggregation of certain cells which are surrounded by connective tissues and are richly supplied with blood capillaries.

Digestive Organs of *Labeo rohita*

Freshwater teleosts exhibit variations in their food and feeding habits. *Labeo rohita* is a freshwater mid-feeder fish. It derives protein, carbohydrate, fat, vitamins and most minerals from algae and plants for its nutrition and growth. The alimentary canal in this fish is extremely long and it is associated with digestive glands. The alimentary canal can be conveniently divided into mouth, buccal cavity, pharynx, Oesophagus, intestinal bulb, intestine and rectum. The rectum finally opens into the anus.

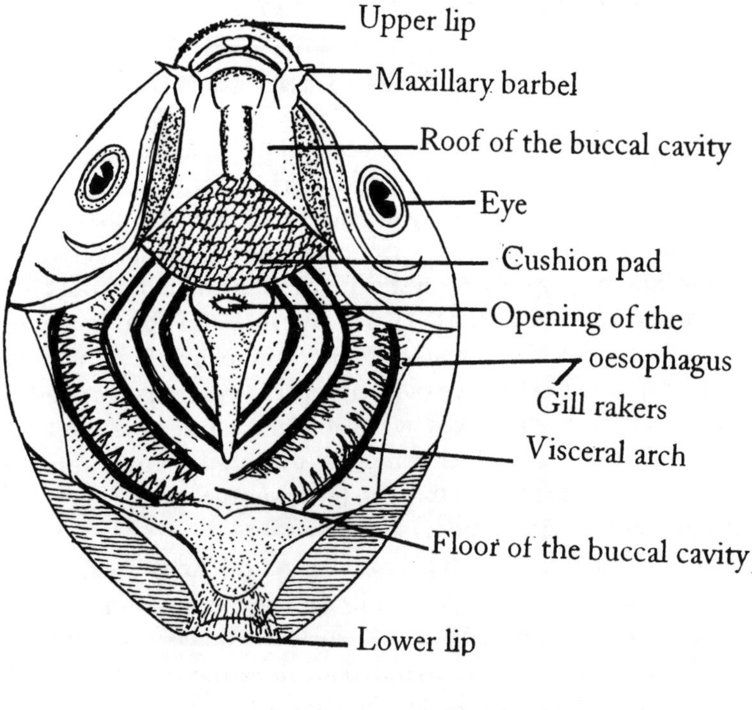

Fig. 13 : Buccal cavity of *Labeo rohita*

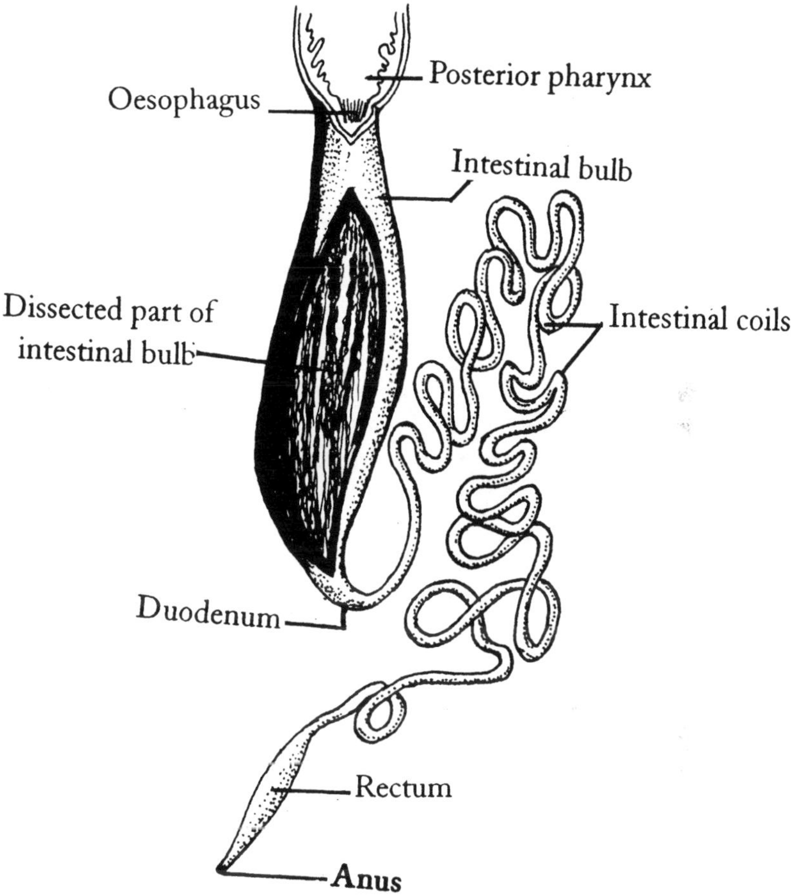

Fig. 14 : *Labeo rotita*—Alimentary canal

The mouth is depressed and bounded by upper and lower jaws. It is protrusible. The free edges of the lips are broad and are beset with four to five rows of conical papillae. The buccal cavity is dorsoventrally compressed cavity whose floor is flat with thick muscles and the roof is arched. Minute papillae are present in the mucous membrane of the buccal cavity. A distinct tongue is not present in this case. A triangular cushioned pad is present on the palate which is made up of over 100 honey comb-like structures. This pad is narrow anteriorly and broad posteriorly. The buccal cavity leads into the pharynx.

The pharynx is also dorso-ventrally flat and it is bound by gill arches. The whole pharynx is divisible into an anterior respiratory part and a posterior narrow masticatory part. The anterior part is perforated laterally by gill-slits. The posterior part of the pharynx has transversely folded ventral wall. The pharyngeal teeth are present on the ventrolateral walls. There are homodont teeth arranged in three rows. As usual, a tooth has a basal root embedded in the mucous membrane, and a cylindrical projecting crown.

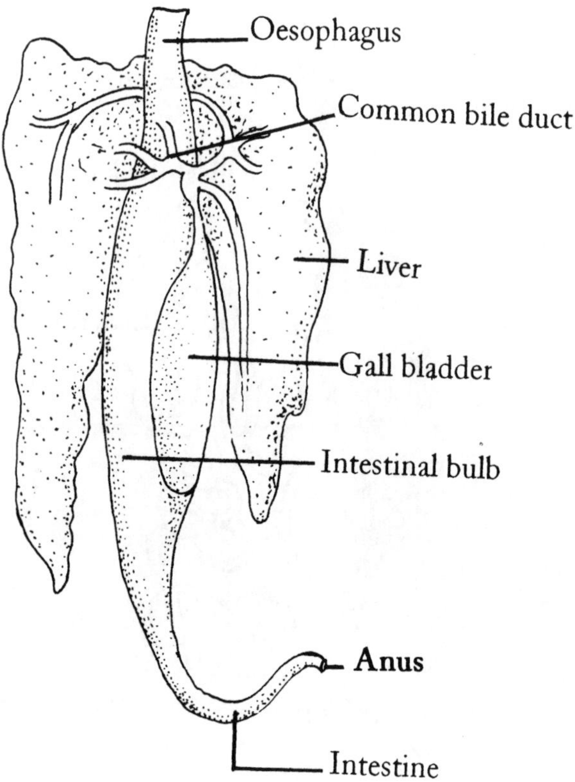

Fig. 15 : A part of the alimentary canal of *Labeo rohita* showing relationship of liver and gall bladder

The pharynx posteriorly leads into the Oesophagus which is a short thick tube. The mucous membrane forms several longitudinal folds. There is no true stomach in the case of *Labeo rohita.* Behind the oesophagus, the intestine widens to form the intestinal bulb which can be distinguished by its lumen only. It serves as storage for food materials. Histologically, the intestinal bulb resembles the intestine. The mucous lining contains *absorptive cells* with free striated margin, and *mucous cells.* The intestine is a thin walled tube which is very much elongated and enormously coiled structure. It has uniform diameter. It is well established that a longer intestine is found in a fish whose food is poor in nutritional substances. Larger intestine ensures the extraction of the maximum nutritional matters. In the anterior part of the intestine the transverse folds are oblique but in the posterior part the folds are longitudinal. The middle intestine is more active in ionic obsorption than the anterior and posterior parts. Intense ATPase activity has been reported by Sinha and Chakrabarti (1986) in the different types of mucous cells and basement membrane in the various parts of the intestine and other parts of the digestive system. The last part of the intestine widens to form the thin walled rectum which opens to the exterior through the anus. The pyloric caecae are absent in the alimentary canal of *Labeo rohita.* The relative length of the gut as described by Das and Moitra (1955) is 12.

Sinha (1983), on the basis of scanning Electron Microscope study has revealed many facts about the intestinal mucosae of *Labeo rohita.* According to him the modifications of surface mucosa of the anterior and the middle of the intestine, besides increasing the luminal surface, serves as storage for the undigested food. He has suggested that communication between the columnar cells and the submucosal layer through the basement membrane are affected by circular orifices. His observations revealed that a peer-shaped apical portion provided with prominent microridges of the goblet cell probably allowed the mechanical stress to develop for the accumulation of secretory mucins.

The liver and the pancreas are the major digestive glands. The liver is a very large gland of dark-brown colour. It has two lobes, the right and the left lobes.The left lobe is larger than the right lobe. The gall bladder is an elongated sac situated between the right and the left lobes. The cystic duct receives three hepatic ducts. The pancreas is a diffused gland extending into the liver and associated with the coils of the intestine. Histologically, the pancreatic acini are very prominent. The cells of the acini are columnar cells with zymogen granules in the apical part.

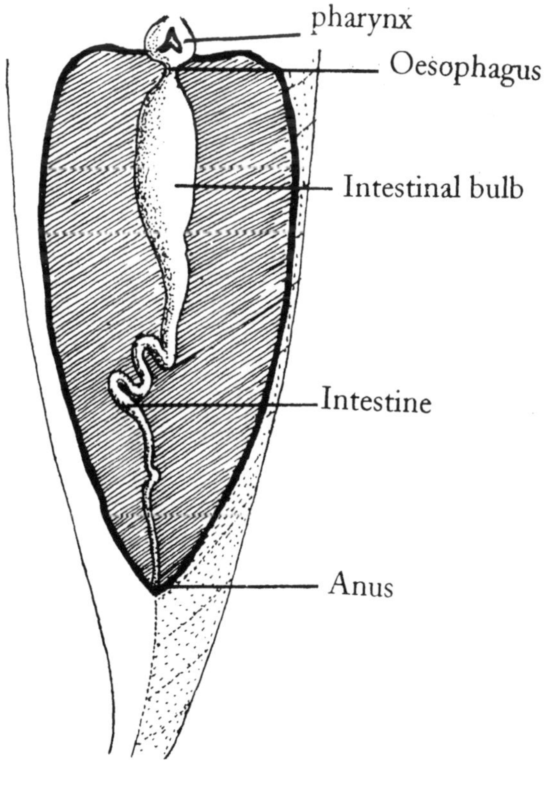

Fig. 16 : Alimentary canal of fry of *Cirrhinus mrigala*

Alimentary Canals of Fry and Fingerlings

Feeding habits have a marked influence on the morpho-histology of the alimentary canal in the fry, fingerlings and adult. In case of *Cirrhinus mrigala* Sinha and Moitra (1975) have described the morphohistology of the intestine during the different life history stages in relation to food and feeding habits. The intestine in the fry which is *Carnivorous* in feeding habit is the shortest and it is longest in the adults because of being *herbivorous*. The intestine is of intermediate values in the fingerlings which are *omnivorous*. The fries feed on zooplankton but when grow to fingerlings and adult the feeding habits change. In fry the villi are simple and unbranched but in the adults the villi become longer. Also, they are branched and complex. Sinha (1975) has revealed that in fries the functional taste buds are not present in the bucco pharyngeal epithelia. Only formative stages of taste bud have been observed. The fry have low relative length of the gut (RLG) because of carnivorous habit. For adjusting changed food and feeding habit in the fingerling stage further development of taste bud takes place from the formative stage. The RLG increases. In the adult the taste buds are fully developed and functional. RLG becomes the highest. Other histological changes also occur in the alimentary canal at different stages of development.

CHAPTER 3

SKELETON

The Skeleton not only determines the form of the body but it also provides protection, gives coverage and is concerned with haematopoiesis. In certain fishes skeletal modifications of fins facilitate the placement of sperms into the reproductive tract of the females.

Bilateral symmetry is the structural ground plan of skeletal organization in fishes. Body form and locomotion are the result of interaction of both the skeleton and musculature. The present chapter mainly deals with the endoskeleton of teleosts. The endoskeleton of teleosts is more or less completely ossified and it is composed of both replacing and investing bones. It consists of an axial skeleton and an appendicular skeleton. The axial skeleton of fish comprises the skull, the vertebral column, the ribs and the intermuscular bones. The appendicular skeleton is composed of Girdles (Pelvic + Pectoral) and fin supports. The description of endoskeleton described below is mainly of cyprinid fish *Labeo rohita*. These bones are present in several teleosts, sometimes with some modifications.

Axial Skeleton

The Skull : It is a complex structure comprising large number of replacing and investing bones. The skull is composed of (a) Cranium (which encloses the brain) (b) Sense capsules (with auditory, olfactory and orbital regions) and (c) the Visceral Skeleton (with suspensorium and the gill arches).

The brain case and the auditory olfactory, optic and otic capsules are the parts of *Neurocranium* but the jaws, hyoid arch, opercular series and the gill arches constitute what is known as *branchiocranium.*

The bones of neurocranium are grouped by their location into the following regions:

(a) Olfactory — region of the nasal portion
(b) Orbital — region surrounding the eye
(c) Otic — region of the ear (temporal), and
(d) Basicranial.

In the above mentioned regions are present both the *cartilage bones* and the *dermal bones*. The former is also known as replacement bones and they are deeper in

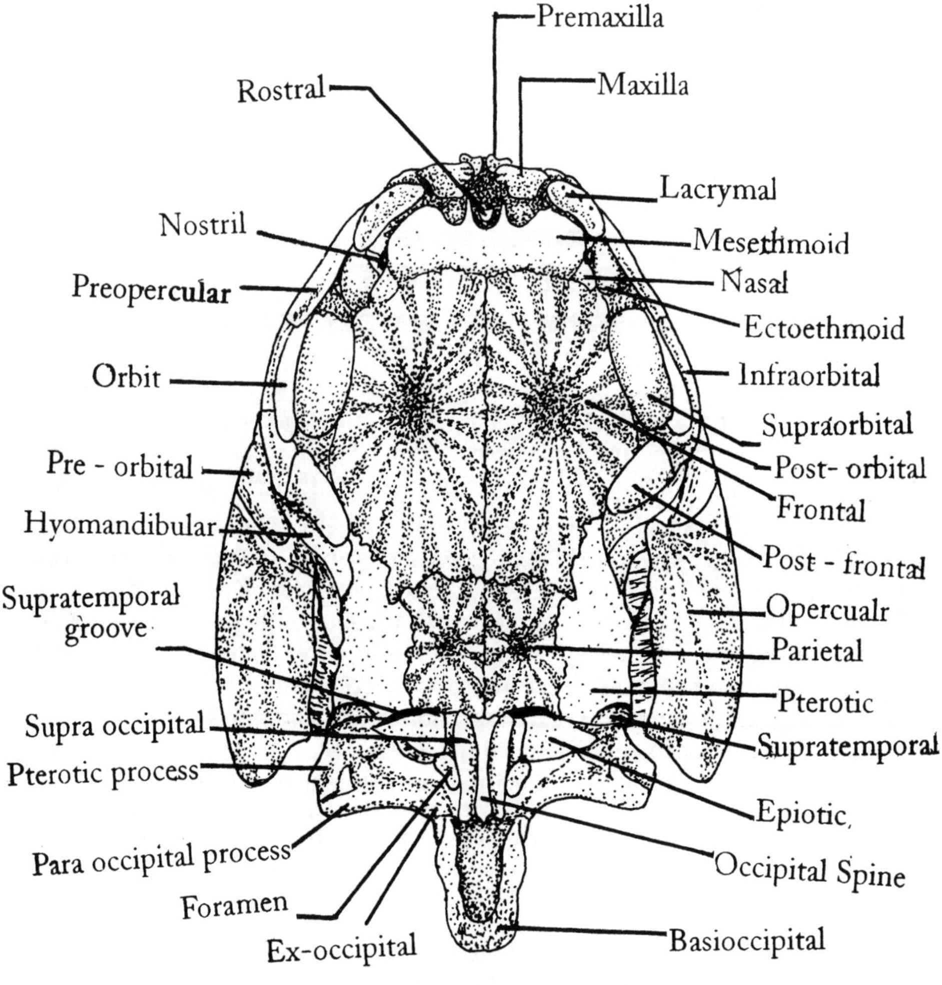

Fig. 17 : *Labepo rohita* skull (Dorsal view)

location in comparison to the dermal bones. They are first laid down as cartilage but later on replaced by bones. Dermal bone is superficial and originates in inner layers of the skin.

Olfactory region: The cartilaginous bones in this region are paired lateral ethmoids, paired preethmoids, and the median ethmoid. The lateral ethmoids are dorsolaterally covered by the prefrontals. The ethmoid and preethmoids are ventrally covered by the vomer and dorsolaterally by the nasals. Paired prefrontals, nasals and vomer (unpaired) are the dermal bones of this region.

Orbital region: The paired alisphenoids and the median orbitosphenoid are the cartilage-bones in this region. The frontals cover them dorsally. The sclerotic bones or circumorbitals surround the orbital region. These are paired dermal bones. Supraorbitals and infraorbitals are also present. Preorbitals are also known as

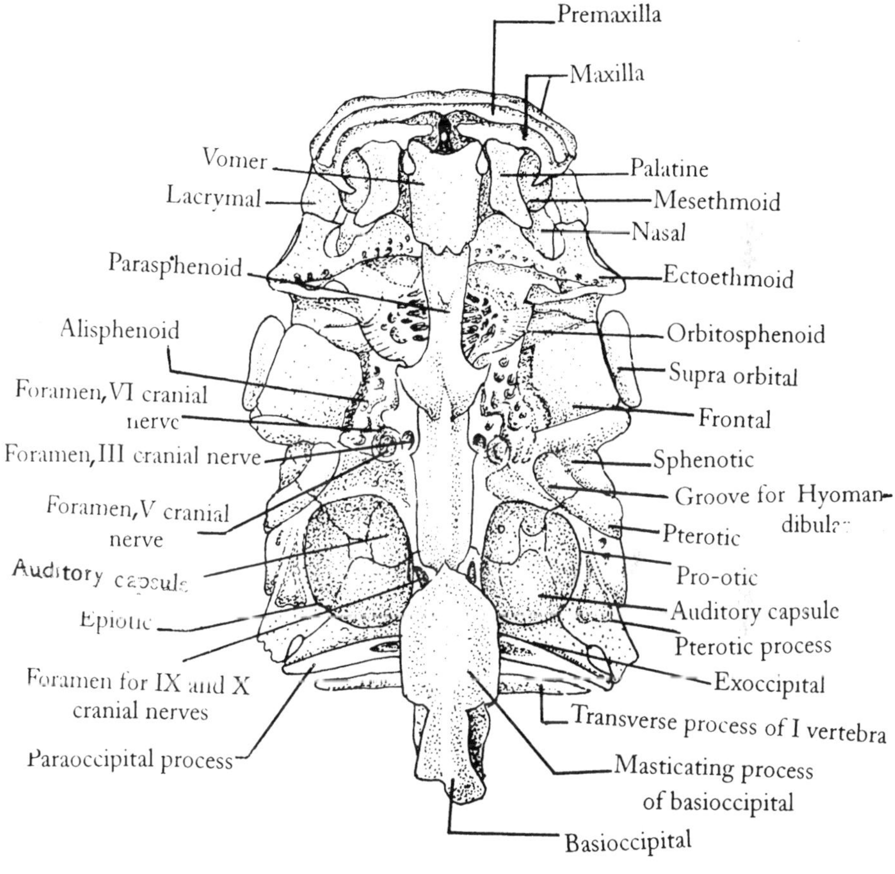

Fig. 18 : *Labeo rohita* skull (Ventral view)

lachrymal. In addition to this, jugal and true infraorbitals are also prominent. These are considered as infraorbitals.

Otic region: The cartilage bones in this region include paired sphenotics, pterotics, prootics, epiotics, opisthotics, exoccipitals and unpairled Supra Occipital. The dermal bones in this area are parietals, posttemporals and Supracleithra. These are paired bones.

Basicranial Cranial region: The only cartilage bone in this region is the unpaired basioccipital, which articulates with the first vertebra. The Parasphenoid is an elongated dermal bone extending from the olfactory region to the basioccipital.

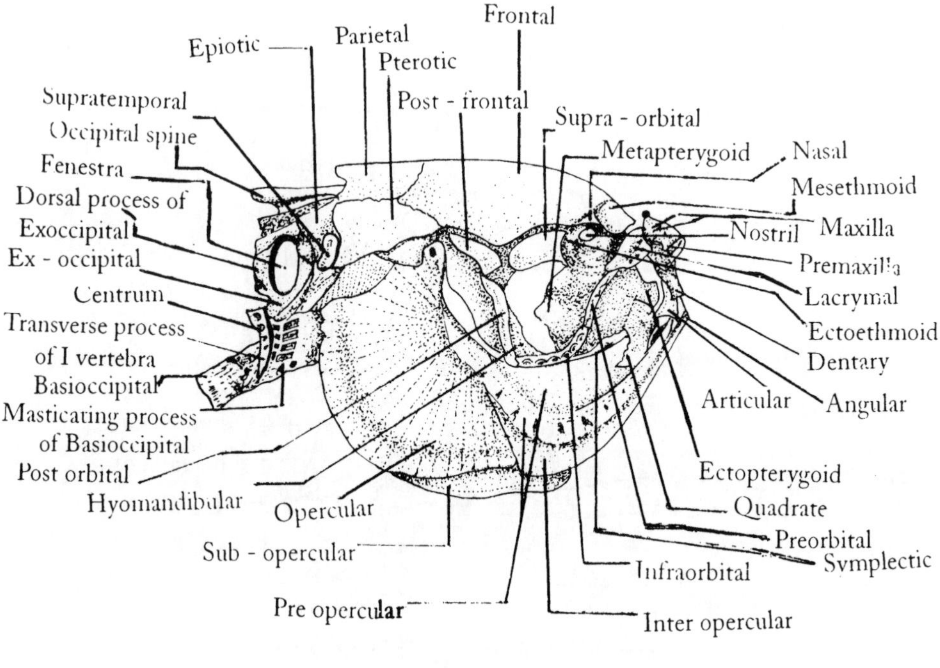

Fig. 19 : *Labeo rohita* skull (Lateral view)

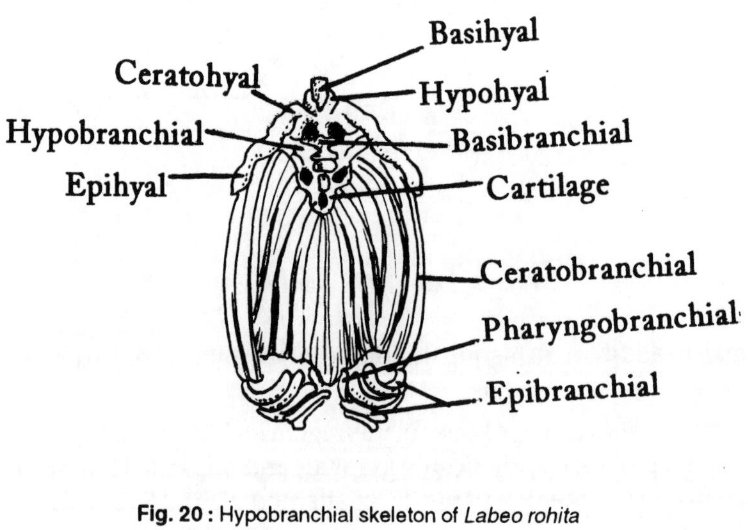

Fig. 20 : Hypobranchial skeleton of *Labeo rohita*

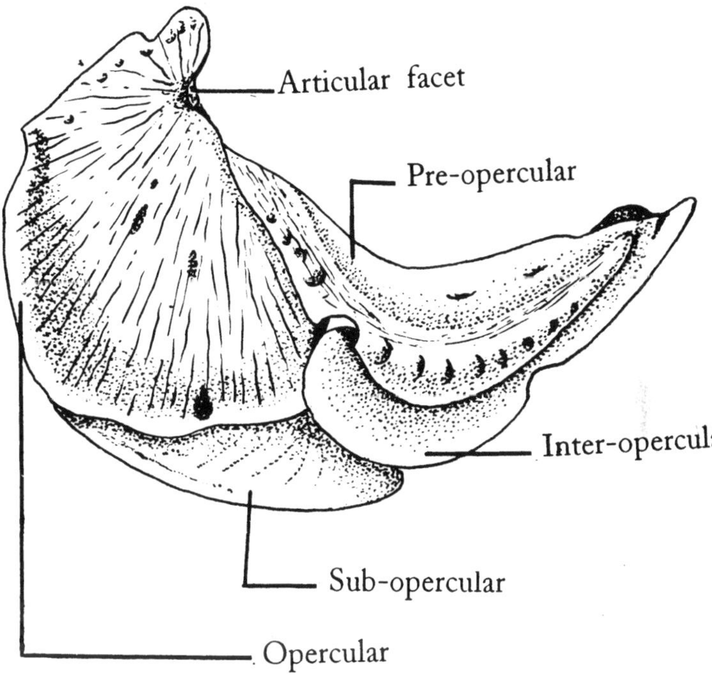

Fig. 21 : Operculum of *Lebeo rohita*

The *branchiocranium* is composed of different regions. The mandibular region are present in the upper and lower jaws and some associated paired bones. In the upper jaw the main cartilage bones are the quadrates, palatines and metapterygoids. The quadrates are the main constituent of the junction of the pterygoid, upper hyoid bones and the lower jaw. The palatines are toothed bones. Constituents of the dermal bones of the upper jaw are the premaxillae, maxillae, pteygoids and mesopterygoids. The premaxillae are also toothed but the maxillae are devoid of teeth. In certain fishes a small dermal bone, supramaxilla may be present which is attached to the maxilla in the posterodorsal side. In the lower jaw the articulars are the only cartilage bones associated with the quadrates. Angulars are the dermal bones of the low jaw, attached to the posteroventral part of the articular. The dentaries of the lower jaw may bear teeth in certain fishes.

The hyoid region is composed of cartilage and dermal bones. The hyomandibulars, symplectics, interhyals, epihyals, ceratohyals and hypohyals and basihyal are the cartilage bones. Except basihyal, all the cartilage bones are paired. The dermal and paired bones of the hyoid region are pre-opercles, opercles, subopercles, interopercles and branchiostegals. Only the uohyal (which is also cartilage-bone), is unpaired.

The hyomandibular dorsally articulates with the Sphenotic, Prootic and Pterotic bones. These three bones form facets for articulating the auditory region. The hyomandibular articulates with the metapterygoid antero-dorsally. It (hyomandibu-

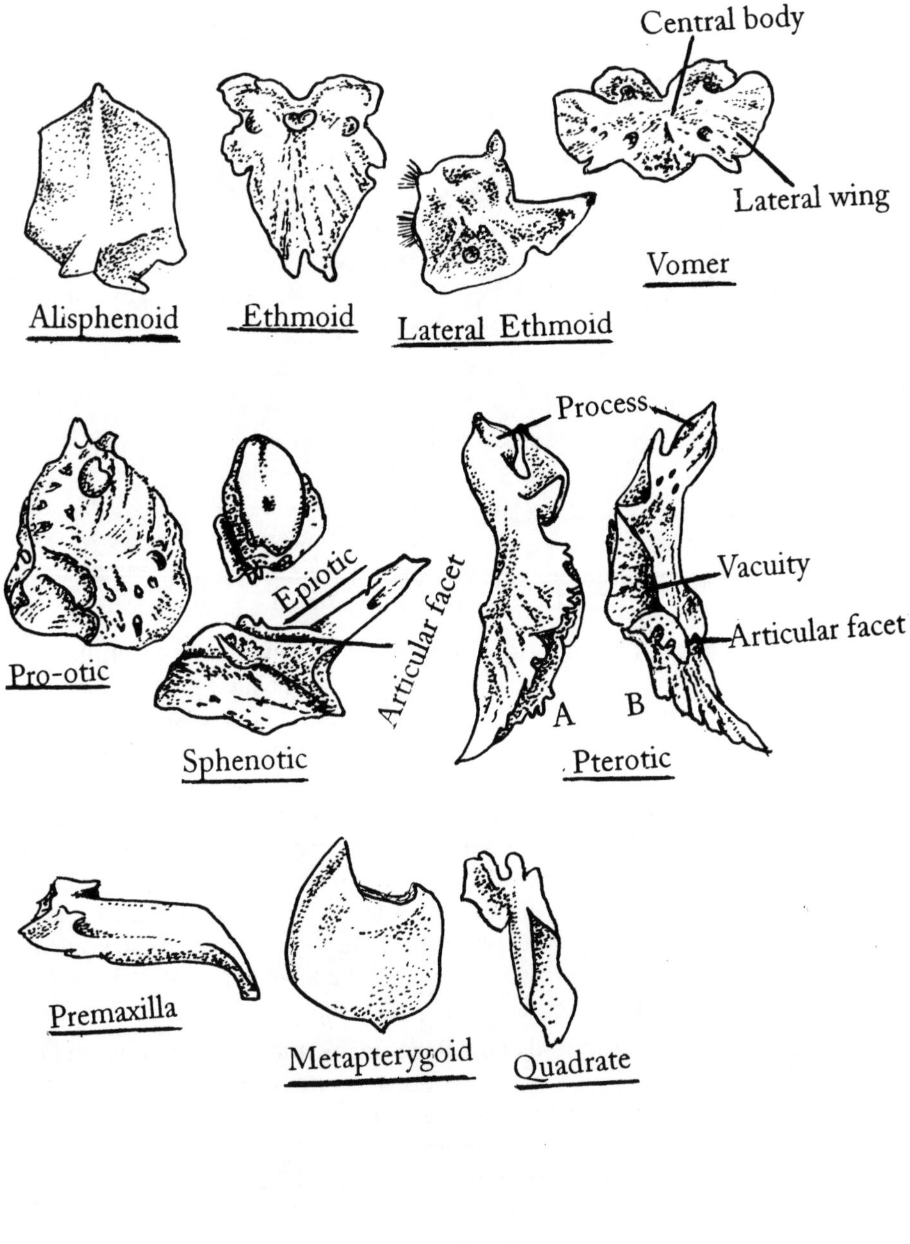

Fig. 22 : Some skull bones of *Labeo rohita* (Disarticulated)

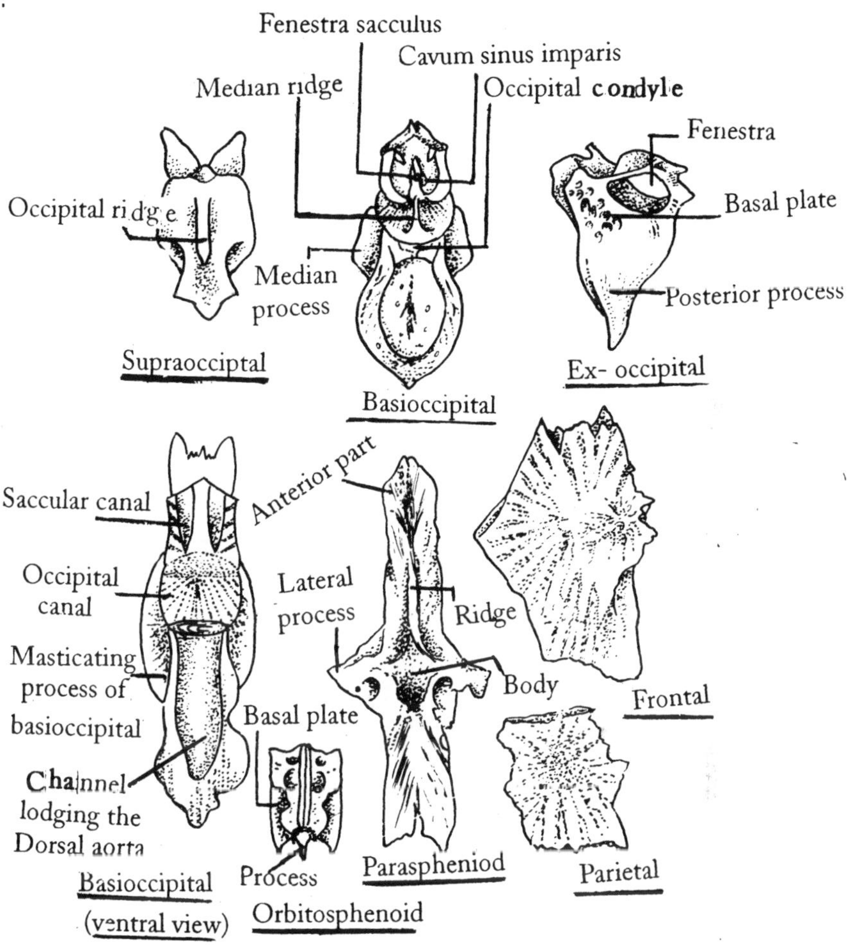

Fig. 23 : Some skull bones of *Labeo rohita* (Disarticulated)

lar) joins the interhyal and the Symplectic bone and the articulation is made effective by connective tissue and cartilage. The hyomandibular also articulates with the opercle. A facet for articulation with the hyomandibular is present on the inner side of the opercle. The symplectic is of small size and is attached to the quandate's groove. The epihyal is a triangular bone with bony processes. The interhyal connects the epihyal to the hyomandibular and the symplectic. The epihyal is present between the interhyal and the ceratohyal. The ceratohyal and epihyal interdigitate to make a stronger connection. The hypohyal articulates with the ceratohyal. The hyomandibular and the symplectic form the suspensorium.

Opurcular bones make up the gill cover on each side of the skull. It is composed of the pre-opercle, opercle, interopercle, and sub-opercle. The opercle is comparatively of large size in the series. The branchiostegal membrane is supported by branchio-stegal rays. The latter are attached to the hyoid bones (ceratohyals)

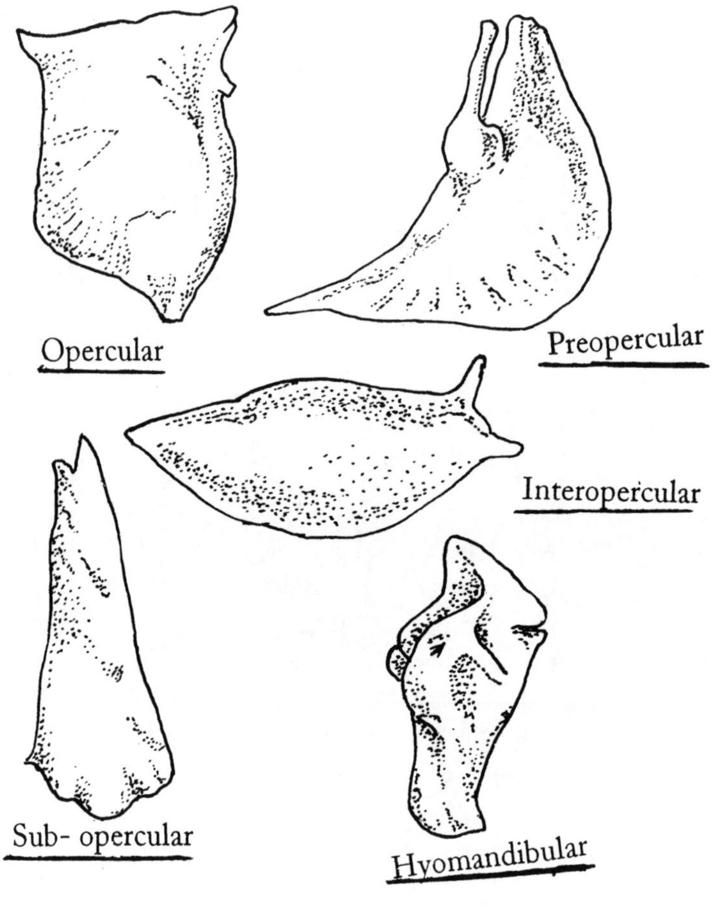

Fig. 24 : Opercular series of investing bones and Hyomandibular of *Labeo rohita*

anteriorly. Their number and attachment differ in different series of teleosts. The urohyal lies between the rami of the lower jaw. It has flat horizontal and vertical components.

The branchial region is made up of cartilage bones. These components of the gill arch are known as pharyngobranchials, epibranchials, ceratobranchials, hypobranchials and basibranchial. Only the basibranchials is unpaired but the rest are paired.

There are typically three basibranchials, three pairs of hypobranchials, and four pairs of ceratobranchials, epibranchials and pharyngobranchials each. Ceratobranchials and epibranchials are elongated rod-like grooved bones. Certain branchial bones have teeth on the pharyngeal surface in some teleosts. The dorsal pharyngeal teeth are suprapharyngeals, and the ventral are infrapharyngeals. In minnows the teeth are present on the fifth pair of ceratobranchials.

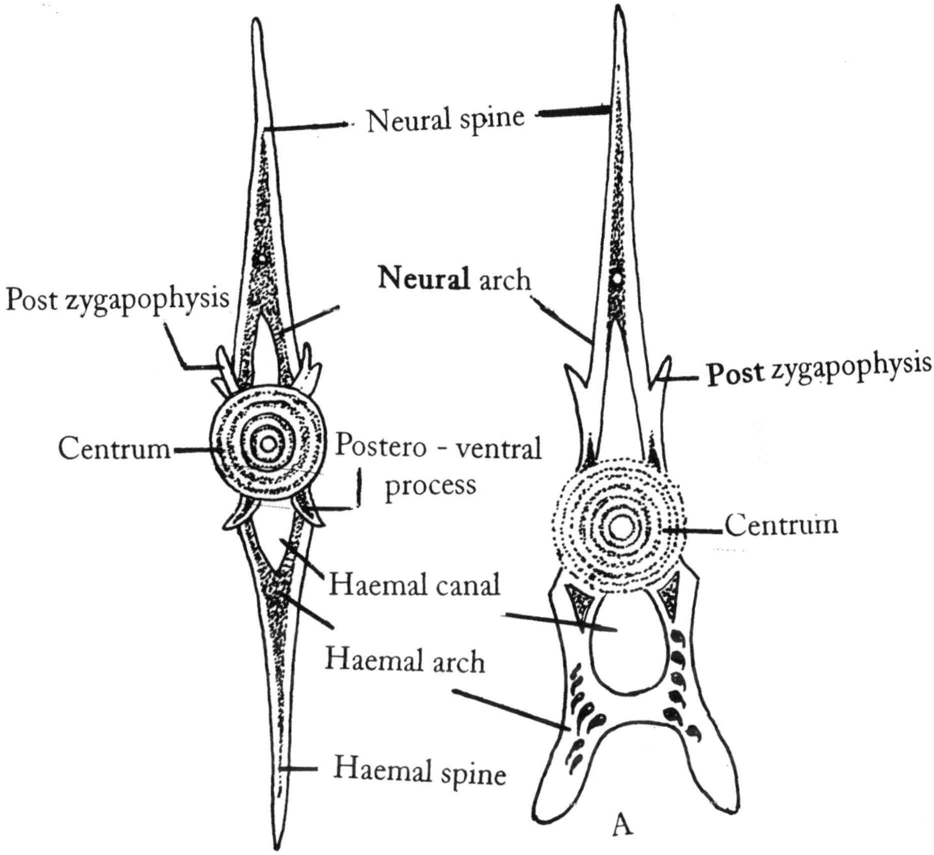

Fig. 25 : Precaudal (A) and caudal (B) vertebrae of *Labeo rohita*

Vertebral Column and Ribs: Labeo is a typical bony fish and the vertebral column is completely ossified in this case. There are 37-38 vertebrae. The vertebrae are amphicoelous. The whole vertebral column can be conveniently divided into (1) anterior trunk region consisting of 21 trunk vertebrae which bear movable ribs. (2) a posterior caudal region which is devoid of ribs. The caudal vertebrae have haemal arches.

The first four trunk vertebrae exhibit some structural changes because they connect the swim-bladder with the internal ear. The last trunk vertebrae (3-4) bear posteroventral processes. The last three caudal vertebrae also exhibit some structural modification as they support the caudal fin. The posterior most caudal vertebra is transformed into a solid rod like structure called the urostyle. It has a ventral groove in which the proximal ends of the hypourals are fitted. A typical trunk vertebra is amphicoelous. A pair of backwardly directed processes arise from the anterolateral borders of centrum. These processes enclose the spinal cord and unite above to form the neural arch. The neural arch gives a neural spine. It is dorsal in position, is quite long and backwardly directed. A pair of small processes are present anteriorly at the base of the neural arch. These are known as prezygapophyses. Another pair of such structure arise from the posterolateral edges of the vertebra and are known as postzygapophyses. These are pointed upwards and backwards. Also, a pair of short paraphyses originate from the ventrolateral surfaces of the centrum and they are directed backwards. The ribs are attached with the paraphyses with the help of ligaments and hence they are movable.

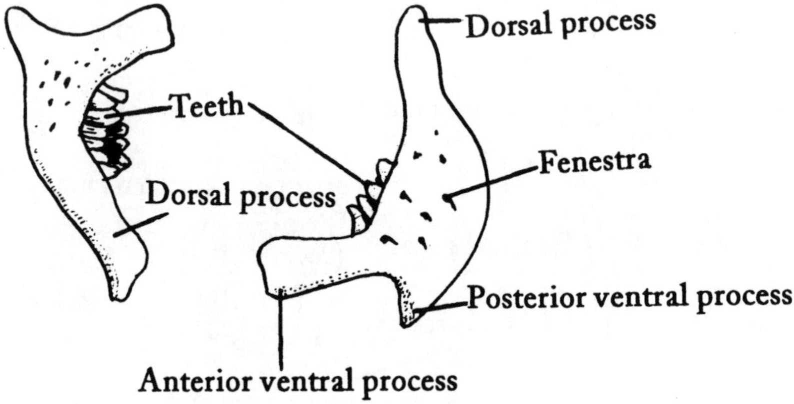

Fig. 26 : Inferior pharyngeal bones of *Labeo rohita*

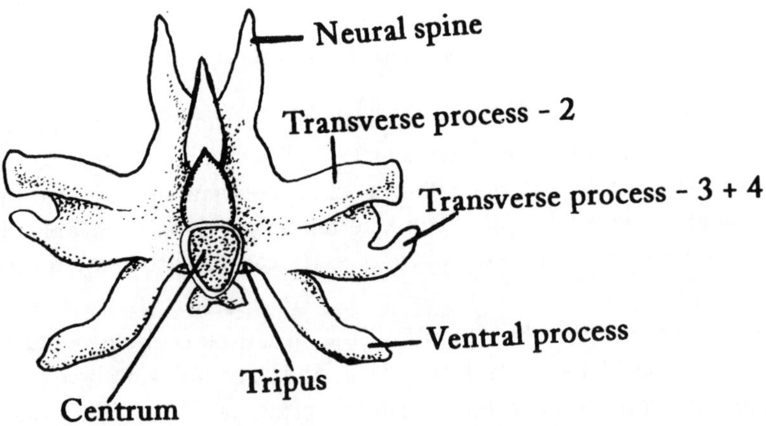

Fig. 27 : Complex vertebrae of cat fish (anterior view)

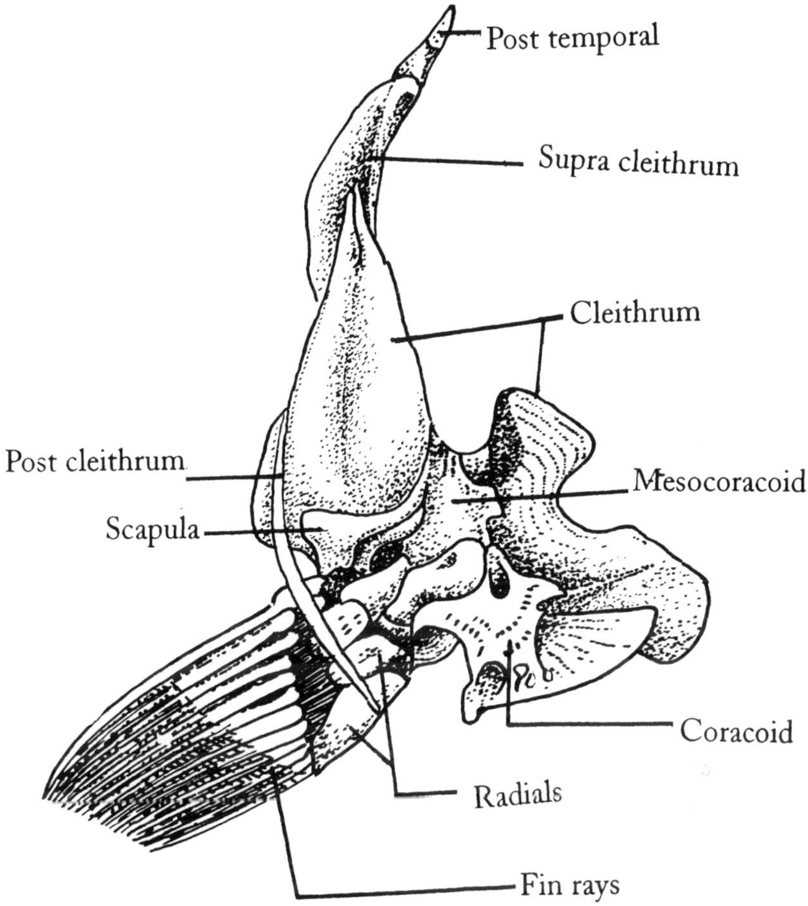

Fig. 28 : Half of the pectoral girdle of *Labeo rohita* with fin

The number of caudal vertebrae may be 16 or 17. Like the trunk vertebrae they have also the amphicoelous centrum.

Associated with the vertebra are a median dorsal, a median ventral and two lateral depressions. A neural arch with a backwardly directed long neural spine is also present. Prezygapophyses and Postzygapophyses are also present like the trunk vertebra. From the anterolateral margines of the centrum a pair of backwardly directed processes arise and they meet in the ventral line to form a canal which provides space for the caudal blood vessels. This process is called the haemal arch which produces the haemal spine. This spine is backwardly directed. At the bases of each haemal arch a pair of anteroventral processes are present. These are very small structures. Similar structures are present on the posterolateral side of the centrum. These posteroventral processes are directed downwards and backwards.

Actinopterous fishes in general have sometimes dorsal ribs and ventral or pleural ribs. In Labeo the pleural ribs are segmentally arranged. There are seventeen pair of ribs. They are slender bony rods attached with the distal ends of the paraphyses. The first pair of ribs are attached with the paraphyses of the fifth trunk vertebra. The ribs are present between the muscles and the peritoneum and they encircle the abdominal cavity protecting the internal organs indirectly. Also there are series of riblike intermuscular bones which are Y-shaped (forked) and support the connective tissue septa. The intermuscular bones originate from the neural arch of all the vertebrae. Lungfishes have bony pleural ribs which articulate with the basiventral cartilages. In crossopterygians, the ribs are short and of the dorsal type like tetrapods.

Appendicular firm skeleton: The Pelvic and Pectoral fins in teleosts are supported by girdles, but the median fins have no such supports. So there is a fundamental difference between the skeletal support of these two types (median and paired) of fins.

Median fin Skeleton : The skeletal support of median fin comprises (a) The endoskeletal radials (Somactidia) and (b) The dermal fin rays (dermotrichia).

The endoskeletal radials are bony rods and they lie within the body muscles. Each somactid is divisible into *Proximal, mesial* and *distal* segments. The dorsal fin rays (dermotrichia) support the fin fold and they are branched and jointed in *Labeo*. It is also called *Lepidotrichia*. Also, delicate horny-rays (actinotrichia) are present at the free edges of the median fins.

In the dorsal fin there are 15-16 *lepidotrichia* located on 14 radials. The proximal segment of each radial is enlarged and daggershaped. These are called *axonost*. The median segment is short and the distal part is very much reduced. The anal fin has eight fin rays supported by seven radials. The first six are well developed. Several flattened bony rods support the caudal fin. On the dorsal side of the urostyle are present two *epiurals* and a *radial* and on the ventral side there are nine hypourals. The fin-rays are connected with the *hypourals* and *epiurals.*

Pectoral girdle and fins : In osteichthyes, the pectoral girdle is composed of both cartilage and dermal-bones. This girdle is connected to the rays of the pectoral fin by some intermediate skeletal elements which are considerably reduced in the higher bony fishes. The pectoral girdle in *Labeo* consists of 'primary' endoskeletal and well-developed secondary dermal girdle. The primary girdle is made up of two lateral halves each one being transformed into three replacing bones e.g. *scapula, coracoid* and *mesocoracoid*. It is remarkable that the two halves of the girdle do not meet in the mid-ventral lines. Each side of this girdle consists of a *cleithrum* (clavicle), a *supracleithrum,* a *post-temporal* and a *post-cleithrum*.

Scapula is a ring-like bone with a large opening or foramen in it. This foramen is meant for the impass of the branchial artery and also the nerve. The coracoid is roughly a triangular bone attached to the scapula and mesocoracoid. The mesocoracoid is an inverted Y-shaped bone. The glenoid articulation is formed by coracoid and scapula. Three radials are attached to this and these radials are movable. The supra cleithrum leads to the cleithrum which is quite large. The post cleithrum attaches to the cleithrum ventrally and extends into the lateral trunk musculature. The cleithrum is the part of the secondary pectoral girdle and it covers the primary pectoral girdle. At the dorsal end the supracleithrum is attached the posttemporal bone which is a very minute bone.

The radials are directly articulated with the scapula. The pectoral fin is supported by 19 lepidotrichia. All of them are attached to radials, four in number.

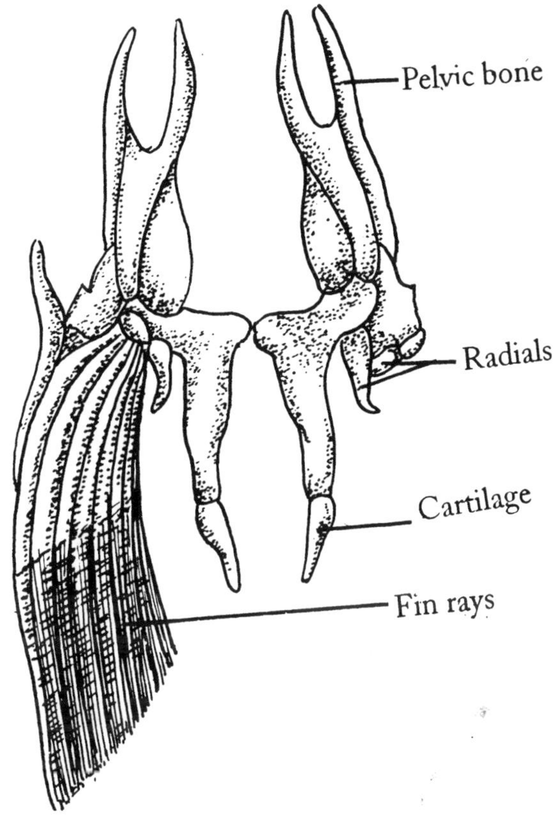

Fig. 29 : Pelvic girdle of *Labeo rohita*

Pelvic girdle and fins: The pelvic girdle is free from the vertebral column in all the fishes. The pelvic girdle is a pair of cartilage bones, the *basipterygia*. There may be quite separate or fuse sometimes. Radials are attached to *basipterygium* in lower bony fishes to support the pelvic fin rays but in the higher teleosts the radials disappear and as such the fin rays directly articulate with the *basipterygia*. The pelvic girdle is free from the vertebral column in all the fishes. In Labeo, the pelvic bone can be distinguished into an anterior and a posterior part. The anterior portion is elongated but the posterior part is stout and rod like in appearance. At the anterior part, there is a deep groove located ventrally and the frontal end is forked. The frontal forked end is attached with the ribs of the trunk vertebra (12th) by means of ligaments. The posterior stout rod-like parts of the two halves are united with the middle line.

In all, nine fin-rays and three radials support the pelvic fin. The fin-rays are attached to the radials and the radials are articulated with the pelvic bone, also called the basipterygium. The first two radials bear two fin rays but the rest fin rays are borne by the third radial.

Caudal fin supports: There is great variation in the major types of skeletal support of caudal fins. This has been discussed in the chapter—*"Shapes of tails, median and paired fins."*

CHAPTER 4

MIGRATION OF FISHES

Migration is a movement from one habitat to another as conceived by many, including Southwood (1962). According to Baker (1978) it is "the act of moving from one spatial unit to another." The animal thus changes the conditions of life by undertaking migration. The resources of habitats which are not permanently suitable for their mode of life are exploited by the migrants. According to Cohen (1970) about 120 species of fish move between fresh water and marine environments. According to Nikolsky (1963)—migration is an adaptation towards increasing the abundance of a species. Migratory behaviour is of course one of the phenomena in the life histories of the fish directed towards reproductive success.

The energy costs differ with the type of locomotion. An estimation from the data given by Schmidt–Nielson (1972) has revealed that a 100g fish might consume 240J in swimming 1 Km. Thus 1g of fat used as the fuel (and supplying 37kJ) would take the fish 154 Km.

Terms Used to Describe Fish Migration

Meek (1915) for the first time introduced two terms *Denatant* and *Contranatant* to describe the movements of fish in relation to the water current. *Denatant* is swimming, drifting or migrating with the water current, but, *Contranatant* means swimming or migrating against the water current. In the classic contranatant theory of fish migration as proposed by Russell (1937), prespawning migrations are active contranatant movements against the water current, while post-spawning migrations of spent fish are passive denatant movements with the current. Myers (1949) proposed some revisions and additions to the terms used to describe fish migrations. Myers' terms and descriptions are as follows:

1. *Diadromous* : These are real migratory fishes. They migrate between the sea and freshwater. They basically belong to the following categories:

(a) *Anadromous* : These are diadromous fishes which spend a major part of their lives in the sea but migrate to freshwater during breeding period for spawning particularly. Several marine fishes like *Salmon, Hilsa* and *Sea* lamprey travel long distance in the sea and reach the rivers to spawn in the freshwater. After egg laying, they return to their feeding places in the sea. The 'King Salmon' of America is a reknowned traveller which travels a distance upto 2000 miles of the Yukon river in

Alaska. *Hilsa ilisha* resides in the Bay of Bengal. During the breeding period they ascend the estuaries of the Ganges and reach fresh water. They used to migrate from the Bay of Bengal and regularly reached as far as Allahabad through the river Ganges. But now, because of the construction of Farraka barrage on the Ganges in Bengal, the migration of *Hilsa* has been restricted. The milk fish *chanos* is abundant in the coastal waters of the Arabian sea and with regularity they migrate towards the river mouth for spawning. When their eggs hatch out, larvae grow into fingerlings and the latter leave for the sea.

(b) *Catadromous:* These are diadromous fishes which spend a major part of their lives in freshwater and migrate to the sea to breed. The freshwater eel *Anguilla anguilla* travels several thousand miles in reaching the sea, starting from the river. They lay their eggs in the sea. The young larvae sw in back towards the freshwater. They undergo metamorphosis and change from *Leptocephalus* stage to *elvers.* They ascend the rivers. They become adult in freshwater and after obtaining maturity they start seaward migration again. This feature is regularly repeated.

(c) *Amphidromous :* These are diadromous fishes which migrate from freshwater to the sea, or vice-versa, not for the purpose of breeding but it is a regularity at some definite stages of their life cycle. The migration of some gobies fall into this category as reported by Myers.

(2) *Potamodromous :* These are also migratory fishes but their migration remains confined to freshwater only. Carps and trouts travel long distances for the purpose of spawning. After egg laying, they return back to the feeding ground again. Thus migration occurs wholly within freshwater.

(3) *Oceanodromous :* These fishes live and migrate wholly in the sea. *Herrings* and *Mackerels* are the common examples. They travel long distances in the sea and after laying their eggs at suitable places return to their feeding ground. The terms, *Spawning bed, Spawning ground* and *Spawning area* have different meaning. In the case of a fish with demersal eggs, the spawning bed is the actual site of egg laying. Numerous beds are located within the specific spawning ground. Within a spawning area there may be more than one spawning ground. The spawning area of the winter spawning herring of the Southern North Sea is the Southern Bight. Here, there are several clearly defined grounds for example near the Gabbard, North Hinder or Sandettie' Banks. On these grounds beds are located where the demersal eggs may be laid. Pelagic eggs however, do not have spawning beds. The eggs are released at some position in the spawning ground within the spawning area. The Arcto-Norwegian cod is considered as an example. The spawning area of these fishes is along the Norwegian Coastline from the Murman coast to Romsdal. The spawning grounds lie at Motovski, Gulf, Lofoten, Romsdal and some other places.

Types of Migration and Migratory Movements

Fish can move in vertical direction or in a horizontal direction either up stream or down stream. When fish move from one place to another in search of food and suitable water, it is known as *alimental migration.* Migration for the purpose of reproduction is known as *gametic migration.* The migration for securing a suitable climatic condition or a better climatic condition is known as *climatic migration.* For maintaining the water-salt balance (homeostasis), there may be *osmoregulatory migration* also. Some important terms relating to migration have already been described.

To reach their destination, fish adopt various methods for making migratory movements. *Drifting* is a passive movement when fish are carried by water currents. When fish are released from a particular point and spread out in all directions leading to uniform distribution of the species (by dispersal),—this is known as *random locomotory movement*. Fishes have definitely a sense of direction. They move towards, or away from a source of stimulation, following a definite direction. This is known as *oriental swimming movement*. Migration pattern is related to the currents, already described.

Migration and Homing

The periodic and directed travel mainly for feeding, breeding and overcoming adverse climatic conditions is said to be migration. Modern biologists have explained the phenomenon of migration in terms of evolution by natural selection. According to them, the animals migrate because their migrating ancestors left more descendants than did their conspecifics which did not migrate. Thus, reproductive success of migrants have been pointed out. Several definitions of migration have been cited earlier.

Homing has been defined as "The return to a place formerly occupied by the migrants instead of going to another equally probable places." There are well documented instances of homing and migration by salmon, herring, cod, hilsa, plaice and some other fishes. Even first-time spawners return to the parent area, to the parent ground, or to the parent bed. There are several examples of repeated annual returns to the parental or adopted home. Return of Norwegian herring to Norway coast, Cultus lake Sockeye to the Fraser river, Acro-Norwegian cod to Norway coast and Plaice to German Southern Bights are some of the important examples of first-time spawners to the parent area. Return of Cultus lake Sockeye to Cultus lake is a good example of first-time spawner to the parent ground.

Several workers believe in the *Olfactory Hypothesis* as sensory basis for homing in Salmonids. Hasler and Scholz (1980) have revealed that juvenile Salmon becomes imprinted to the unique chemical odour of the natal stream particularly during the smolt stage. This cue is used by them later on to locate their stream during spawning migration. It is interesting to note that imprinting can take place relatively late in the life history during the smolt stage in the second year, third year, or even fourth year of the life cycle.

Specific substances possibly pheromones which form odour, trail and guide the mature Salmon back to the native river. But, the pheromones are not considered as the sole olfactory guide. Non-pheromone attractants play the major role in the return of migration of salmon from the sea. Imprinting with artificial odours (e.g. *morpholine* or *phenyl alcohol*) results in higher return rates in comparison to non-imprinted fish.

The *Groundwater Seepage Hypothesis* developed by Harden Jones (1980) illustrates that the spawning area and spawning grounds of marine fishes which spawn in coastal waters could be identified with reference to certain chemicals which enter the sea by groundwater seepage. This idea links the anadromous species of some orders. Dr. Arnold reported that the plaice of the southern Bight of the North Sea use tidal transport during the period of migration. Fish can save energy when they use tidal transport during migration.

Life Histories

Salmon and *eels* migrate between the sea and freshwater. Most of the species of Salmon are *anadromous*. They spend much of their life in the sea and reach freshwater to spawn. The eggs are laid normally in the gravel beds or redds. In most species the young fish migrate to sea as *smolt* after 2-3 years in nursery streams or lakes. In certain species of Pacific Salmon the young one migrate to sea as *fry* immediately after hatching.

Eels are *catadromous* spending most of their adult lives in freshwater and migrate to sea for spawning. *Anguilla anguilla* spawns in the sargasso sea and are subjected to extensive drift migration across the North Atlantic during their larval stages. Two and half years after spawning, the newly metamorphosed *elvers* reach the European coastal waters.

Factors Influencing Migration

There are several physical and chemical factors which influence migration. The physical factors are depth of water, bottom materials, pressure, temperature intensity of light, photoperiod, nature of water current and turbidity etc. The characters like salinity, pH of water concerned, smell and taste of water are some of the important chemical factors.

In addition to the above mentioned factors, there are some biological factors also which include food memory, sexual maturity, physiological clock and the endocrine glands. Presence or absence of Predators and competitors may also be considered as biological factors. Baggerman (1962) has suggested that gonadal hormones play an important role in the migration of anadromous fishes.

Availability of food is such a factor which is responsible for large scale migration of several species of fishes. Fishes go out in search of feeding areas. Rising temperature of the sea during the summer season provides a stimulus to Salmon for seaward migration. When the temperature of river-water rises, fishes move up stream for spawning.

Several fishes can not tolerate salinity change and such fishes are called *Stenohaline*. For this reason, they do not undertake large migrations, and as such, they are confined to freshwater only. On the contrary, some fishes like *Anguilla, Salmon, Hilsa, Gasterosteus* and *Fundulus* etc. are capable of adapting themselves to large salinity changes and they are called *euryhaline*. They can easily undertake large scale migrations.

The intensity of light and also duration of light play important role in the migration of fish. Some of them are attracted towards light and hence easily trapped by providing light at suitable points. Migration of herrings can be seen during full moon. Baggerman suggested that the change in salinity preference in yearling coho-salmon at the onset of seaward migration is also because of long spring days.

Robertson *et. al.* (1961) have reported high levels of corticosteroids in the plasma of migrating and spawning Salmon and Rainbow trout. Probably it facilitated gluconeogenesis. According to Leloup and Fontaine (1960), an increase in the activity of the thyroid gland occurs in migrating Atlantic Salmon, *Salmo salar*, where fasting metabolism is facilitated. The thyroid gland has been implicated in migratory processes by many authors. Hyperplasia of the thyroid gland during the smolt stage of Salmon has been demonstrated by Hoar. Thyroid activities increase motor activity for seaward migration. For osmoregulation in sea-water gill Sodium Potassium activated adenosine triphosphatase (Na^+, K^+— AT Pase) is an important enzyme. The activities of this enzyme increase in migrating smolts prior to their entry into sea-water. A number of hormones including thyroxine have been implicated in this mechanism. There is a marked change in the thyroxine levels during the up stream reproductive migration.

Sticklebacks show freshwater treatment following thyroxine or TSH treatment but the Pacific Salmon shows a strong saltwater preference after TSH administration.

The interrenal gland has also been implicated in fish migration. Cortisol increases Na^+ excretion, water permeability and Na^+, K^+—AT Pase activity of the gill simultaneously with water and ion movement in the intestine and urinary bladder. Corticosteroids are said to be responsible for induction of oocyte maturation, for gluconeogenesis and also for coping the stress of environmental changes in aquatic life. There is variation in the corticosteroid levels in the plasma of eels during their life cycle and the hydromineral metabolism is greatly influenced.

There are evidences that thyroid changes and changes in plasma corticoid levels during migratory phases are modulated by thyroid-stimulating hormone and Adrenocorticotropic hormone.

Prolactin also plays an important role in the control of water and sodium movement in freshwater teleosts. It is a major pituitary factor for osmoregulation in these fishes. Prolactine synthesis or release is controlled by environmental salinity. Prolactin is thus involved in the migration of *Salmon, Gasterosteus aculeatus, Mugil cephalus* and some other fishes.

Corpuscles of Stannius also play some role in the migratory fishes. Morphohistological changes in corpuscles of Stannius in response to salinity changes (e.g. in Stickleback) have been pointed out. Evidences suggest that Corpuscles of Stannius definitely have osmoregulatory effects and also increase motor activity.

CHAPTER 5

AIR BLADDER AND WEBERIAN OSSICLES IN FISHES

The air bladder or gas bladder or Swim bladder is a white glistering saccular organ developing as a diverticulum from the wall of the pharynx in the gut. It is often present among the teleosts. It attains its full development among the spiny-rayed teleosts (Acanthopterygii). Sometimes it is difficult to make distinction between the swim baldder and the lung, particularly in the primitive fishes. A swim bladder may be single or double and it may open into the digestive tract. When it is connected with the digestive tract by open pneumatic duct it is known as *Physostomous*, whereas those which are completely closed are known as *Physoclistous*. Various studies on the air bladder have been made by several workers and notable among them are. Gunther (1848), Hasse (1873), de Beaufort (1909), Hora (1922), Das (1927), Jones and Marshall (1953), George (1956), Padmakar and Dehadrai (1967), Marshall (1960), Wittenberg and Wittenberg (1961), Randall (1970), Steen (1970) and others. The gas bladder is connected with the internal ear by weberian ossicles (Weberian apparatus).

General Description, and Structural Details of Air Bladder

In certain cases the air bladder extends the whole length of the body cavity as in *Clupeids* and it may send diverticulum into the head. In the minnows the air-bladder is two chambered anteroposteriorly. A constriction between the two chambers is formed by smooth muscle, working as sphincter. In the bottom dwelling loaches (Homalopteridae and Cobitidae) the anterior portion of the air-bladder lies in a bony capsule, and in the latter is present a jelly like fluid. The posterior portion of the air bladder almost disappears.

In *Acipenser*, the air-bladder is oval in shape with a smooth non-sacculated inner surface. It communicates with the oesophagus by a funnel-like orifice. In the Lepidosteidae there is a single air-bladder extending the whole length of the abdominal cavity. It communicates with the exterior through a larynx like vestibule provided with glottis. In cod (*Gadus morrhua*), the air bladder divides into a pair of caecal prolongations extending forwards to the head. These are often coiled. The air-bladder in *Notopterus chitala* (clupeiformes) is of *Physostomous* type. Its wall is white and tough and it extends beyond the body cavity limits. The abdominal or coelomic portion of the air-bladder is a sub-spherical sac divided internally into two lateral compartments by a vertical septum. The cranial or the precoelomic portion of the bladder is a narrow tubular prolongation of the sub-spherical sac. It divides further into two lateral auditory caecae and reach the outer surface of the auditory capsule of the respective sides. A constriction can be marked externally between the sub-spherical sac and the cranial or precoelomic portion. The caudal or post-coelomic caecae are two in number and they extend backwards along either side of the caudal skeleton. Each of the two caudal caecae communicates with a row of fourteen diverticulae, each of which forms a pair with those of the opposite side. Some of the diverticulae terminate by sub-dividing into an anterior and a posterior slender filiform caeca.

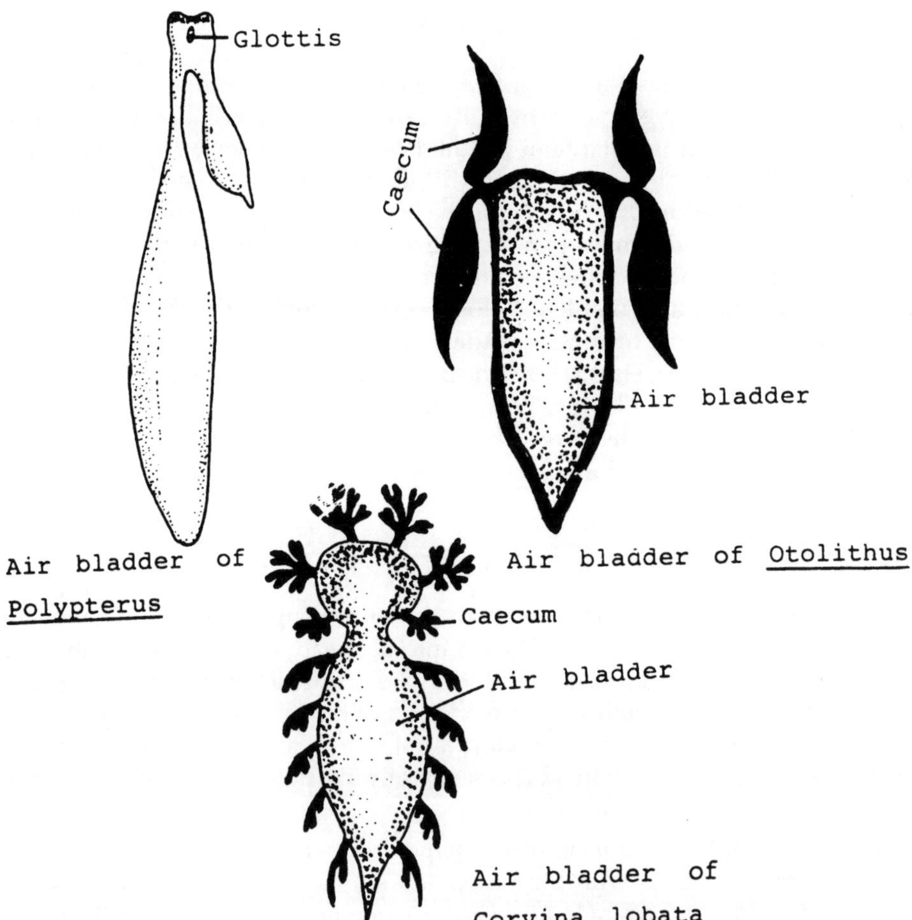

Fig.30 : Air bladders of some fishes

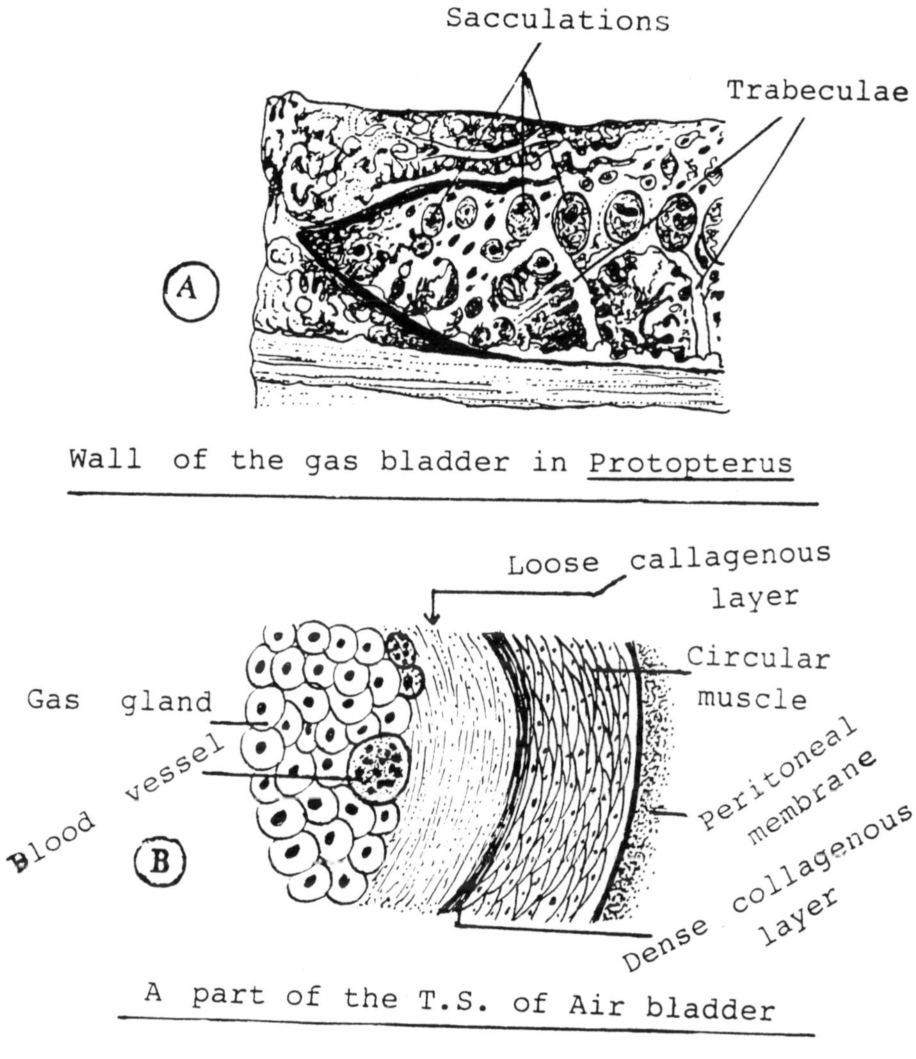

Fig.31 : Histological structure of air bladder

In several fishes, the walls of the air-bladder may be internally simple and smooth but it may also be divided by septa. It may be alveolar also as in *Lepidosteus* and *Amina.* In some catfishes (Sissoridae), only anterior chamber of the air bladder remains.

In *Polypterus* a primitive, rayfinned fish (living at present) the air bladder is referred to as lung. The air bladder is smooth walled and it is bilobed. The pneumatic duct is present in the ventral side of the digestive tract and it opens at the anterior and ventral part of the oesophagus by a small muscular glottis. Two lobes are present in the air-bladder, right one extending beyond the left and curving around the right side of the digestive tract. This lobe is dorsal to the intestine at its posterior end. The lungs are vascular having alveoli and sacculi. At present the lungfishes

(Dipnoi) include three surviving genera: *Protopterus, Lepidosiren* and *Neoceratodus*. In all the cases, the swim bladder is sacculated. The blood to this organ is derived from Pulmonary arteries. These arteries directly arise from the dorsal aorta. Partly oxygenated blood is carried to the air-bladder. Pulmonary veins directly carry blood to the left atrium. Two atria in the Dipnoi appear for the first time in the vertebrate series. In *Neoceratodus* the air bladder consists of only one lobe and it is connected ventrally with the oesophagus by pneumatic duct. During embryonic development the left lobe is present as diverticulum but in the adult it disappears. The pulmonary artery supplies the air-bladder. Two pulmonary veins unite and the single vessel thus formed, opens into the left atrium of the heart. In *Neoceratodus*, the atrium is not completely divided into two chambers (atria). The blood going to the air-bladder is oxygenated in the gills. In all the dipnoans the air-bladder is highly vascular and it becomes a true lung. In *Protopterus* and *Lepidosiren* these lungs are the principal breathing organs.

The air-bladder of *Channa punctatus* is of *Physoclistous* type. It is elongated, cylindrical, and tapers at both ends. This tubular structure pierces through the stream-lined body of this fish. It has two chambers—anterior and posterior chambers. The posterior chamber has comparatively thin wall. In between the two chambers, the muscular diaphragm is present. There is an aperture on the diaphragm for the passage of gases between the two chambers. There are 15-20 muscle bands radiating from this aperture of the diaphragm. Before joining the wall of the air-bladder, each muscle band divides into two or three smaller bands. The rim surrounding the aperture is fairly thick. The whole structure acts like the sphincter.

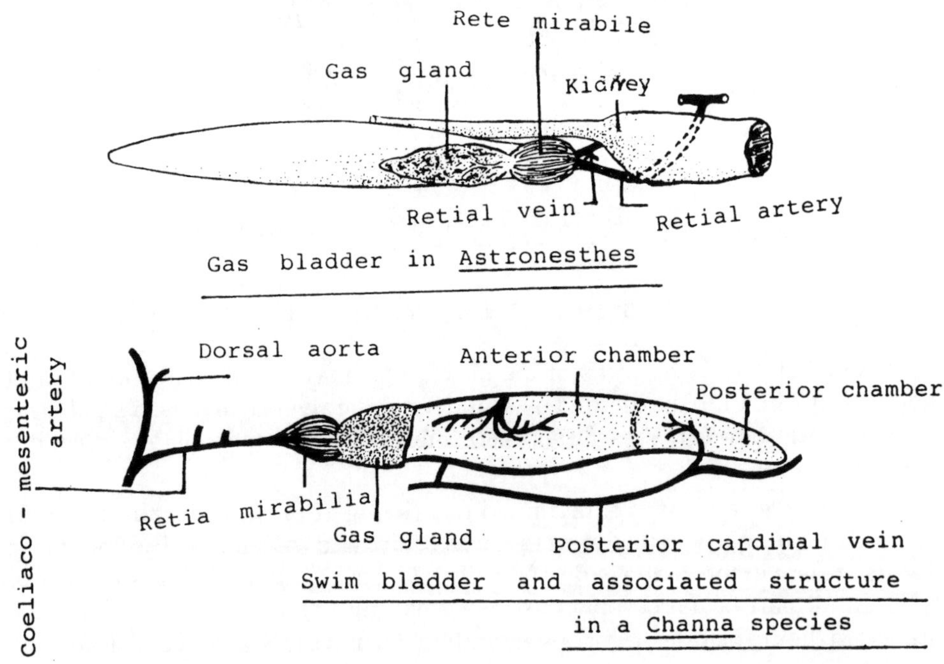

Fig.32 : Swim bladder and associated structure

The arterial blood supply to the air-bladder may be directly from the dorsal aorta or from coeliaco-mesenteric artery. The nerve supply to the air-bladder is derived from the vagus nerve.

The wall of the anterior chamber of the air bladder is composed of an outer layer, *tunica externa* and an inner layer, *tunica interna*. In the tunica externa, the outer most layer is that of *vascular peritoneal membrane*. This layer is followed by *circular layer* of muscle. Next to the circular layer, there is the *dense collagenous connective tissue layer*. The inner most layer is the *loose collagenous* connective tissue layer.

The tunica interna is formed of outer *loose elastic fibres* and the inner *epithelium*. The tunica interna is comparatively more vascular in comparison to tunica externa.

In the posterior chamber also *tunica externa* and *tunica interna* layers are present. The *vascular Peritoneal layer* in tunica externa is the outer most layer. It is followed by circular layer of muscles. The inner most layer is that of loose collagenous layer. The tunica interna of the posterior chamber is mainly composed of multi-layered transitional epithelium. Rounded Cells are present towards the lumen of the air-bladder however, towards the interior the cells are squamous.

The Gas Secreting Complex

The gas secreting complex in several teleosts has two basic parts: (1) the *gas gland* and (2) *Rete mirabile* (*Retia Mirabilia*).

The squamous epithelium is modified into glandular structure. So, the gas gland is a region of the bladder epithelium. It may be one layered or several cell layered in thickness. The blood vessel entering the anterior part of the air-bladder breaks up into smaller branches. They divide and redivide into multitude of capillaries. This area is highly vascular and constitutes *rete mirabile*. The blood is actually supplied from the dorsal aorta through a branch of *coeliaco-mesenteric* artery

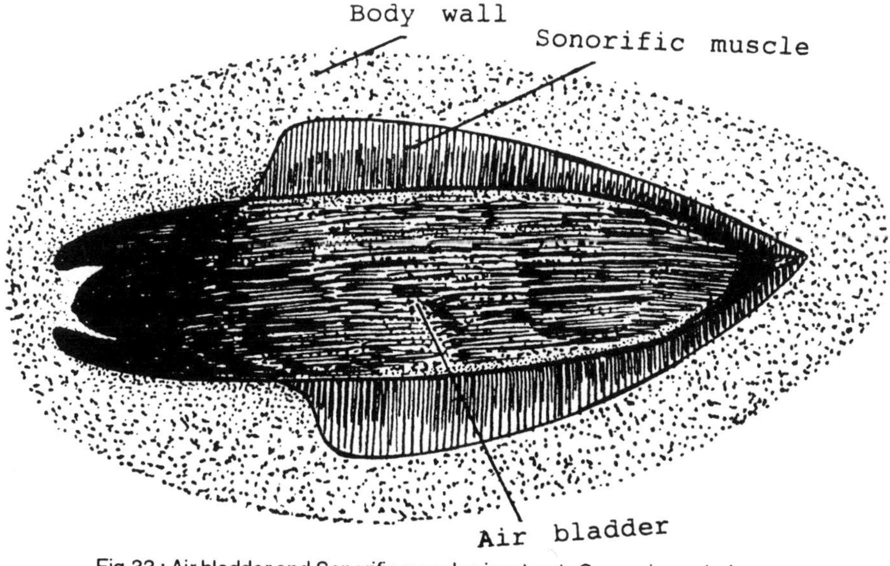

Fig.33 : Air bladder and Sonorific muscles in a trout, *Cynoscion nebulosum*

and it is carried off by a branch of the renal portal vein. In the eel (*Anguilla*) over 100,000 arterioles and slightly smaller number of venules have been observed in *retia mirabilia* which provide the latter a total surface area of 2 square meters. They are linked by efficient capillary connections in the epithelium of the air bladder. Oxygen is mainly built up along the capillaries at the wall of the air bladder. The gases in the air bladder consists of oxygen, nitrogen and CO_2. Because of the rapid dissociation of haemoglobin of the blood on account of reduction of pressure in water, the amount of oxygen increases much. The dissolved gases are transferred from the capillaries into the gas bladder by the epithelial cells.

Functions of the Air-Bladder

The following are the important functions of the air-bladder:

1. *Hydrostatic function* : The division of the fishes into *Physostomous* (bladder with opening) and *Physoclistous* (bladder closed) has not only the morphological basis but the functional basis also. In some physostomous species the air bladder loses the pneumatic duct, though this connection persists in the juvenile or young stage. Such a condition is known as *Paraphysoclistous* as in the mid-depth lantern fishes (Myctophidae). Soft rayed fishes (Malacopterygii) are Physostomous and those spiny-rayed fishes (Acanthopterygii) are Physoclistous. The perch-like fishes (Perciformes) which are considered as truly physoclistous teleosts, adjust the pressure in their air bladder through secretion or reabsorption of gases from or to the blood. The air-bladder balances the fish at different depths. When the fish moves up, the pressure on its body decreases. The air-bladder expands taking more air inside it. The body becomes lighter and the fish remain at that upper level of water without any muscular activity. Opposite things happen when they move to a lower level.

2. *As accessory respiratory organ* : The air bladder has become modified for breathing purpose in several fishes. The inner wall of the baldder becomes vascular. Also, it is partitioned by septa and cross septa as in lung fishes. In *Amia* and *Lepisosteus* the air bladder is sacculated and vascular, well adapted for respiration. The giant redfish (*Arapaima gigas*) of the Amazon which lives in swamps has well developed air bladder adapted for aerial respiration. The mudminnows (Umbra) have alveoli and also gas absorbing and secreting organs in the air bladder.

3. *Sound Production* : The air-bladder normally produces sound of low frequencies. The sounds are significant in breeding behaviour and in territorial defence. Excited minnows (cyprinidae), loaches (cobitidae) and eels (Anguillidae) produce higher pitches sounds by release of air from the bladder through the pneumatic duct. Herrings (Clupeidae) expel gas from the air-bladders through a duct which ends at the anus. During expulsion of gas from the air-bladder through pneumatic duct, simplest type of sound is produced.The grunting and gurgling noises are very common in many fishes particularly when they are taken out of water. Several organs are concerned with the production of sound but air bladder is very common among teleosts for sound production.

4. *Sound reception*: Reception of sound is also an important function of the air bladder. Bone and air bladder may act as sound conductors or resonators. Volume changes of the air-bladder cause the weberian ossicles to move. In this process,

pressure changes due to sound waves transmitted to the perilymph. From here it goes to the sensory cells of the labyrinth, the seat of sound reception as in *ostariophysi.* The *tripus* bone of the Weberian ossicle touches the anterior wall of the air-bladder. In the herrings (clupeidae) extensions of the air bladder grown into cartilaginous bodies (Pro-otic and pterotic bullae) in close apposition to the perilymph spaces of the internal ear. In the cods (Gadidae) an anterior extension of the air-bladder touches the head bones near the sacculus of the internal ear.

5. *Sensory function:* Air-bladder helps the fishes in maintaining a steady depth inside water. When fishes move to different depths of water, compression of enclosed air takes place. The air bladder in this condition functions as pressure receptor like a manometer, barometer or a hydrophone.

The Filling and Emptying of Air Bladder

The air bladder in most of the Physostomous fishes is filled by gulping air particularly in the early stage of development. These fishes are however, capable of gas secretion and absorption by means of blood supply in the adult stage (e.g trouts and salmon). Some of the fishes (*Gasterosteus, Hippocampus* and *Lebistes*) gulp atmospheric air in the larval stage, though they are physoclists. Gas secretion and absorption are physiological processes working of which depend on the needs of the fishes with changing depths in the water. The gas is prepared by the gas secreting complex i.e. gas gland and rete mirabile, the structures of which has already been described. It is present on the wall of the air-bladder. In the rete, mainly oxygen is built up, along the capillaries. The rete is capable of concentrating oxygen in the epithelium of the gas gland at higher tensions than the surrounding water. The epithelial cells of the gas gland subsequently transfer the dissolved gases from the capillaries into the air bladder. Besides oxygen, pure nitrogen is also concentrated in the air bladder. Fishes from deeper water (e.g. *Trigla*) fill the air-bladder mostly with oxygen, percentage of which varies from 16 to 50 at a depth of 1 metre. In the conger eel the percentage of oxygen reaches as much as 85 in the bladder at a depth of 175 metres. Reabsorption of gas from the air bladder is accomplished mainly by diffusion into blood vessels on the air-bladder wall, outside the gas secreting complex. Gas secretion and reabsorption is under the control of sympathetic and parasympathetic components.

Weberian Ossicles (Weberian Apparatus)

Structure and Working

In carps and siluroids (Cypriniformes) a chain of bones connects the swim bladder with the internal ear. This chain of bones forms the weberian apparatus which is very useful in sound reception. It connects the gas bladder with the ear. This apparatus was first described by Weber (1820). Weberian ossicles are derived from various parts of the anterior vertebrae and neighbouring elements. *Tripus* is the hindmost of them and is connected with the anterior wall of the air bladder. It is the largest bone of the Weberian apparatus and is connected to the next bone, the *inter-calarium* with the help of ligament. In certain cases when this bone is missing, tripus is connected with *scaphium,* and the latter in turn is attached to *claustrum* which is a very minute anteriormost bone. Between the scaphium and the intercalarium, the interossicular ligament is present.

The *claustrum* of each side touches the membranous window of the *sinus impar* lying in the basioccipital bone of the head and is an extension of the perilymph system of the inner ear. In the absence of claustrum (e.g. gymnotids), the scaphium touches the window of the sinus impar.

The *claustrum* normally articulates with the first vertebra. In certain cases it may simply form part of the neural arch of this vertebra. *Scaphium* is a large and broad structure as compared to *claustrum.* A ventrally situated peg-like process of the scaphium articulates with a depression present on the centrum of the first vertebra. *Intercalarium,* is either a nodule like structure without any connection with the vertebral column as in *Wallago attu* or it may have a rod-like appearance reaching the centrum of the second vertebra, as in *Labeo* and *Cirrhinus.* The *intercalarium* is attached with the *scaphium* anteriorly and posterioly with the *tripus* as already pointed out. Both attachments are affected by interossicular ligaments. The *tripus,* the largest piece of bone in the Weberian apparatus, may be fenestrated in some fishes (e.g. *Tor putitora*). The *tripus* has three important processes. Anterior process is connected with the interossicular ligament in posterior side of the *intercalarium.* The medial process articulates between the second and third vertebrae. The posterior process which is connected with the air-bladder is also known as transformator.

The connection between the air-bladder and internal ear can be shown in the following way: Air bladder—Weberian ossicles—Sinus impar—Sinus endolymphaticus—transverse canal—sacculus.

Weberian ossicles move when there is volume change of the gas bladder. They move in such a manner that pressure changes are conveniently transmitted to the perilymph and from there to the sensory cells of the inferior portion of the labyrinth, the seat of sound reception. By the movements of the ossicles, the pressure of the perilymph in the *sinus impar* increases and conveyed to sacculus. When the air

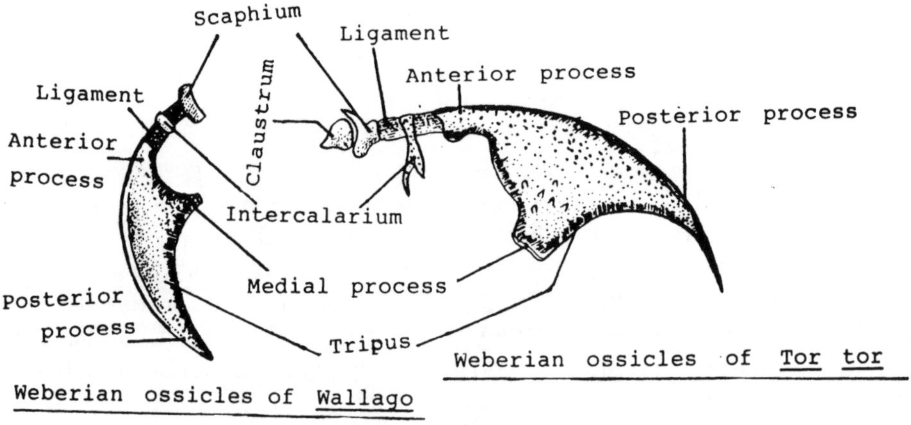

Fig. 34 : Weberian ossicles of two fishes

bladder is enclosed in the bony capsule or connective tissue (direct system of Wright), the rhythmic compression of the air bladder lessens. The weberian ossicles are not homologous with mammalian auditory ossicles (Jones and Marshall, 1953) and they help in registering hydrostatic changes.

Origin of the Weberian Ossicles

It has already been described that there is a remarkable chain of four bony structures and antero-posteriorly they have been named as *claustrum, scaphium, intercalarium* and *tripus*. There are various views regarding their origin which have been proposed by different workers.

Claustrum: It has been considered that its probable origin is from the neural arch of the first vertebra a suggested by Goodrich (1909), but Watson (1939) held the opinion that it originated from intercalated cartilage. Sorensen (1894) considers it as interspinous ossicle and according to Wright (1884) it is the modified spine of the first vertebra. Some authors (Hora, 1922; Mukherji, 1952) considered its origin from a part of the neural arch of the first vertebra. Charnilov (1927) revealed that the neural process of the first vertebra contributes in its formation.

Scaphium: Several workers (Wright, 1884; Sorensen, 1894; Hora, 1992; Charnilov, 1927; Mukherji, 1952 and others) considered that the scaphium was formed from the neural arch of the first vertebra. Segemehl (1885) revealed that it is formed from the neural arch of the second vertebra. According to Goodrich (1909) it is formed from the rib portion of the first vertebra, however, Watson (1939) believed that Scaphium is formed by the combination of the neural arch of the first vertebra and the mesenchyme.

Intercalarium: According to Wright (1884), Goodrich (1909), Hora (1922) and Charnilov (1927), intercalarium is formed from the neural arch of second vertebra. Bridge and Haddon (1893) considered it as a compound bone formed by neural arch and transverse process of the second vertebra. Sorensen (1894) held the view that intercalarium is derived from neural arch of second vertebra plus ossified ligament or from the ossified ligament alone. According to Watson (1939) it is formed from a part of basidorsal of second vertebra plus the ossified ligament.

Tripus: Sorensen (1894) claimed that tripus is formed from the rib of the third vertebra plus ossified ligament. To this combination the ossified wall of the air bladder also joins. According to Wright (1884) the transverse process of the third vertebra and ossified outer-wall of the air-bladder contribute in the formation of tripus. According to some authors (Watson, 1939; Charnilov, 1927), it is formed from the paraphysis and pleural rib of the third vertebra. Hora (1922) has described the formation of tripus from the transverse process of the third vertebra and the ribs of the third and fourth vertebrae. Thus it is a compound bone.

Summary of Functions of the Weberian Ossicles

1. As suggested by a Bridge and Haldon (1893), the Weberian ossicles are sensitive to changes in the volume of the air bladder because of variations in the hydrostatic pressure. When the fish becomes highly sensitive to changes in the volume of the air

bladder, it is able to control the escape of gases through the pneumatic duct. Dijkgraaf (1950) has also confirmed that the Weberian ossicles are concerned with the perception of even slow pressure changes and control the release of gases through the pneumatic duct. Thus the ossicles have a hydrostatic function leading to adjustment of the air bladder volume as conceived by Jones and Marshall (1956).

2. It is probable that the fish can detect variations in the atmospheric pressure with the help of Weberian ossicles just to take necessary precautions during adverse weather conditions. But, there is no experimental evidence to confirm this hypothesis.

3. According to Von Frisch (1932, 1938), the Weberian ossicles have an auditory function also. They transmit the variations of the bladder wall in the following sequence: Bladder wall—Perilymph of sinus impar—endolymph—Saccular otoliths, Fishes having Weberian ossicles are more sensitive to sounds of all frequencies and intensities as compared to fishes without this apparatus.

4. As suggested by Evans (1925), the Weberian apparatus helps the fish in the localization of sound. The vibrations received on the side of the bladder nearest the source is stronger that on the other side. But, the saccular otoliths of both the sides are connected to the sinus impar by a single transverse canal. Both the chains of the Weberian ossicles are attached to the sinus impar. Vibrations should be received by both the otoliths equally without any distinction between right and left. This hypothesis, however, has no support.

CHAPTER 6

RESPIRATION IN FISHES

Fishes are aquatic vertebrate. They utilise Oxygen for respiration dissolved in water, but some fishes can breathe atmospheric oxygen also. Gills are the primary respiratory organs in fishes and they are borne in a series of gill pouches. The gills are well designed for gas exchange between blood and water. There are some accessory respiratory organs also which serve the function of respiration. Studies related to gas exchange have been concentrated on the movement of oxygen and carbondioxide mainly. The gills form a sieve like structure in the path of the respiratory water flow and they are richly supplied with blood capillaries. Oxygen comes in contact with the gills by the bulk flow of water and diffuses into the blood down a gradient of between 40 and 100mm $HgPo_2$ as per available records. Oxygen is transported in the blood from the gills to the capillaries differing across the capillary walls into the tissue. The secondary lamellae forming the side walls of the gills represent the major respiratory portion as conceived by Hughes (1966) and Muir and Hughes (1969). The total surface area of the Secondary lamellae has been reported to be about 5 cm^2/g body weight (Gray, 1954: Hughes, 1966).

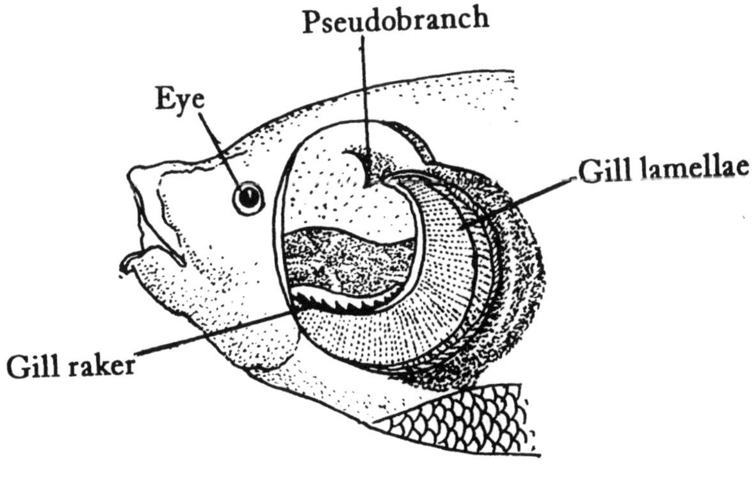

Fig. 35 : Position of gills in a teleost

The red blood cells contain haemoglobin, a respiratory pigment. Haemoglobin is the colouring protein of the blood, normally confined to the erythrocytes. Haemoglobin has ability to combine with oxygen reversibly. It is a conjugated protein possessing *heme* ($C_{34}H_{33}N_4$ Fe OH) which is an iron protoporphyrin portion of respiratory pigments. In the *globin* part of haemoglobin are normally present the peptide chains with variations in amino acid composition and their sequence. These chains are càlled alpha (α), beta (β), gama (γ) and delta (δ) chains.

Haemoglobin can loosely combine with oxygen forming oxyhaemoglobin.

Haemoglobin + $O_2 \rightleftharpoons$ Oxyhaemoglobin

Formation of oxyhaemoglobin depends upon the partial pressure of O_2. The attachment with oxygen takes place at iron in the *heme* portion. Iron is present in the ferrous form. Oxygen remains attached with the unpaired electrons of iron. The haemoglobin can also combine with carbon monoxide forming *Carbonyl haemoglobin*. Haemoglobin loses its capacity to combine with Oxygen in presence of carbon-monoxide. Haemotoxylin can combine with Carbondioxide forming Carbamino-haemoglobin compound. This combination takes place through amino group present in the globin portion.

$$\text{Hb. NH}_2 + \text{Co}_2 \rightleftharpoons \text{Hb. NH. CooH} \qquad \text{HbNH Coo}^- + \text{H}^+$$

(Carbaminohaemoglobin)

Bohr effect (Bohr *et. al.*, 1904) has been frequently discussed in connection with the physiology of respiration. It is a change in haemoglobin-oxygen affinity due to a change in pH.Oxygen-haemoglobin equilibrium is very sensitive to the metabolic needs of the animal.

Grigg (1967) has reported that a decrease in temperature increases the oxygen affinity of the blood (except in *tuna*). Several studies have revealed that fish blood has a high affinity for oxygen and is 95 per cent saturated even at low partial pressure. Even intraspecific variation can be seen in Oxygen affinity among fishes. For example in *Protopterus aethiopicus* the oxygen affinity is higher in comparison to that of *P. annectens*. This might be attributed to difference in structure of haemoglobins of these two airbreathing fishes. The equilibrium of oxygen with haemoglobin described with the help of oxygen dissociation curve. Haemoglobin components have been studied in several fishes and the electrophoretic data have been presented by Yamanaka *et. al.* (1965). The equilibrium of oxygen with haemoglobin is described with the help of oxygen dissociation curve. The oxygen equilibrium of single erythrocyte can be determined now (Huckauf *et al.* 1969).

The relationship between oxygen consumption and body weight is an exponential function.

$$R = kw^x$$

Here R is the volume of oxygen consumed per unit time, k is a constant, W is the body weight and x is an exponent ranging in value from 0.6 to 1.0. Factors like age, nutrition, disease, reproductive stage and some intrinsic regulatory mechanisms influence oxygen consumption in fishes also.

Respiration in Different Fishes

In scoliodon (an elasmobranch) there are five pairs of *gill pouches* situated in the lateral walls of the pharynx on each side. The gill pouch opens into the pharynx through a large aperture known as *internal branchial aperture* and it opens outside through the *external branchial aperture* also known as *gill slits*. The mucous membrane is produced into leaf like vascular structures called *branchial lamellae*. Each gill pouch has two sets of *branchial lamellae,* each set on the anterior and posterior walls. The lamellae of one side of each gill pouch constitute a *demibranch* (hemibranch). Thus each gill pouch has two demibranches. Two hemibranchs along with interbranchial septum and visceral arch constitute a holobranch (complete gill).

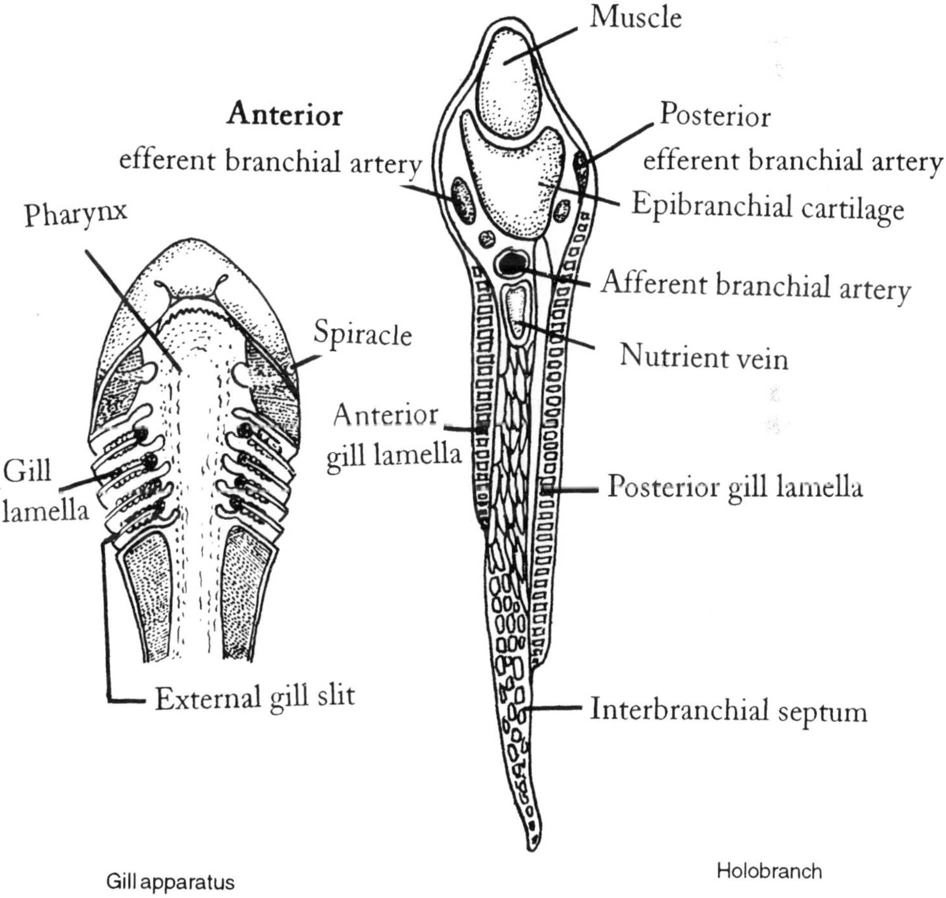

Fig. 36 : Respiratory structures of scoliodon

The interbranchial septa separate the gill pouches from each other. The *gill lamellae* are attached to the entire length of the interbranchial septum and as such, they are known as *lamelliform*. The inter branchial septum is supported by a cartilaginous rod called visceral arch and the latter gives out a series of *branchial rays* arising in a single row to support the septum. The visceral arches also bear comblike *gill rakers* at their inner end. The gill rakers protect the inter branchial aperture.

The hyoid arch lies in front of the first gill pouch. The rest posterior arches are called I, II, III, IV and V branchial arches.

The hyoid arch is a *demibranch* because it has only one gill on its posterior surface. The last branchial arch is devoid of gills. The remaining four branchial arches bear four *holobranchs*.

In between the mandibular and hyoid arches there is a pit in the inner wall of the pharynx which is known as the *spiracle*. In scolidon, it is a vestigial gill without lamellae. But, in certain elasmobranchs the spiracle may bear branchial lamellae and external branchial aperture. Thus the gill filaments in elasmobranchs are ridge like folds on the interbranchial septa.

In osteichthyes, the septum between the two apposed filaments become shortened, the filaments are free from one another even throughout their length depending on the extent of septal reduction. Normally, the gills are holobranchs in most of the cases but psendobranch gills may be present in certain forms. There are vestigial mandibular gills.

Gills are composed of primary gill-filaments which produce numerous secondary filaments. The secondary filament has a central core of vascular tissue. It is outlined by a thin layer of connective tissue and mucous epithelium. The central core consists of capillary net-work and supporting *Pilaster Cells.* The gill arch has afferent and afferent vessels. There is no existence of mandibular pseudobranch in *Latimeria* however, small hyoidean hemibranchs may be present. In Latimeria, as in other actinopterygians four pairs of holobranch are present. But the V gill arch is devoid of any gill. In *Amphipnous* there are no gills on the first and fourth branchial arches and only one demibranch on the second.

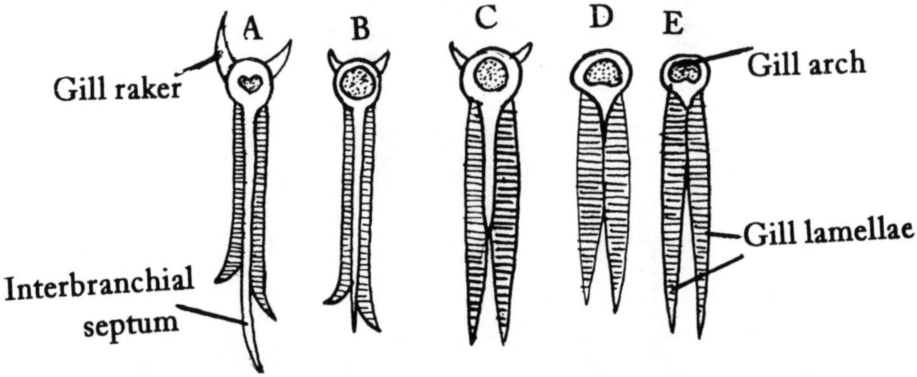

A - Elasmobranch, B - Holocephali, C - Holostei
D & E - Teleosts

Fig. 37 : Gill arches of different fish

Among the dipnoans, the *Neoceratodus* has a hyoidean demibranch, holobranch on the fourth and fifth arches. The sixth gill-arch bears an anterior hemibranch. Hemibranchs are absent in Lepidosiren and the second, third and fourth gill-arches have holobranchs. In certain fishes (e.g. Cod) the Pseudobranch is completely covered in the pharyngeal epithelium to form a gland like organ called *rete mirabile*. In *Catla catla* the pseudobranch is attached to the anterior gill. The hyoidean hemibranchs are absent in Lepidosiren. In latimeria the hyoidean hemibranchs are present but they are very small.

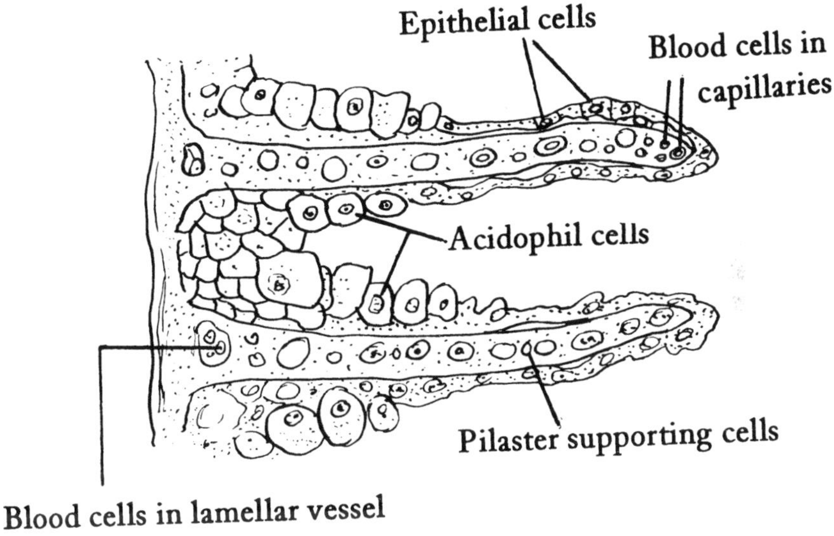

Fig. 38 : Section through two adjacent lamellae of a gill filament

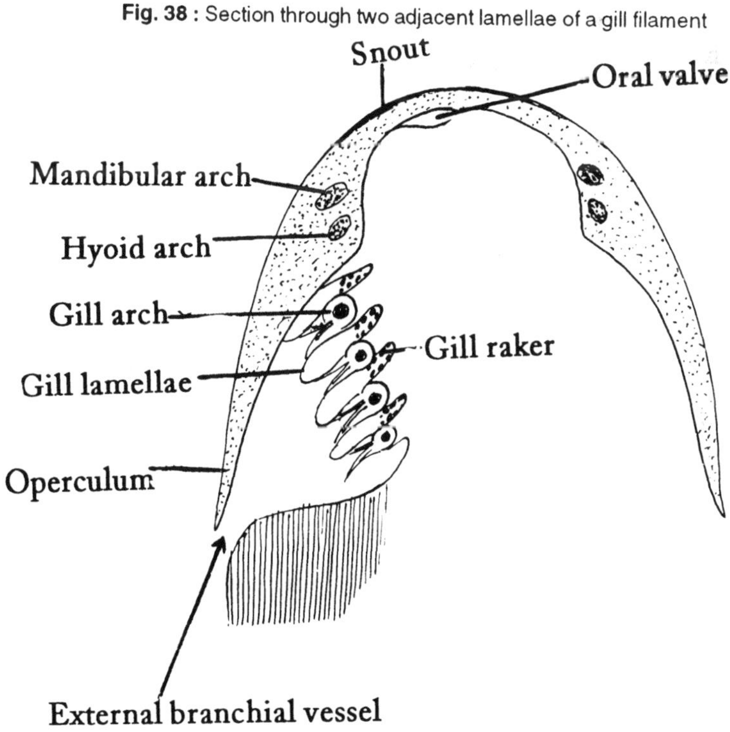

Fig. 39 : Respiratory region of a teleost (one side)

Dubale (1951) has revealed that the surface area of the gills is reduced in air-breathing fishes. According to this worker, the climbing pearch, *Anabas* the gills area is only about 1.44 cm^2/g. According to Hughes and Datta Munshi (1968) the respiratory epithelium in this fish is about 2 μ in thickness.

Capillaries in the Secondary lamellae are more involved in gas transfer than those in the gill filament. Studies have revealed that adrenaline increases lamellae blood flow (Steen and Kryusse, 1964).

Release of mucous in the gills increases diffusion distance for ions, water and gases. The production of mucous cell is said to be regulated by the hormone *prolactin* (Ball, 1969).

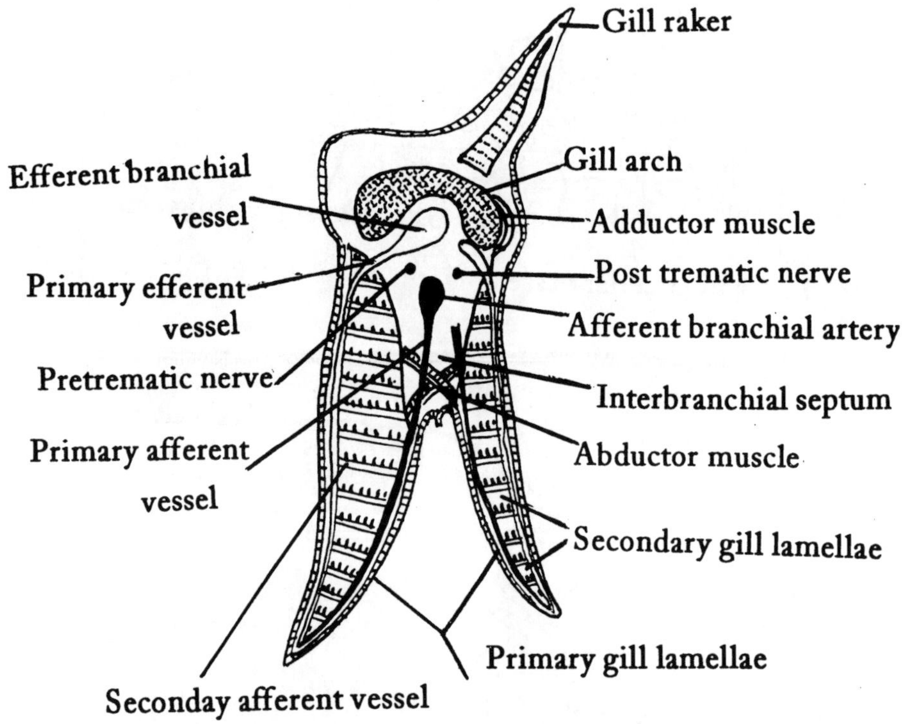

Fig. 40 : T.S. of gill of a teleost (based on Datta Munshi, 1960)

Lam (1968) observed that when the fish moves from sea water to freshwater, mucous from the gills is secreted. Recently several workers have observed excessive secretion of mucous by the gills of fishes following treatment of pollutants. The enzyne *carbonic anhydrase* is present in the fish erythrocytes and the gill epithelium. It is well established that carbonate is exchanged for chloride by an exchange diffusion mechanism across the gill epithelium as reported by Maetz and Garcia Romeu (1964).

Accessory Respiratory Organs in Fishes

Fishes are able to breathe oxygen dissolved in water by means of gills which are richly supplied with blood capillaries. Exchange of oxygen and carbondioxide takes place mainly through gills. But, sometimes their aquatic gills are insufficient in taking required amount of oxygen and getting rid of carbondioxide. So they have to take oxygen from air and as such, the fishes have evolved many respiratory adaptations for air-breathing. Thus, there are certain modified structures which assist the function of the gills. These organs are known as accessory respiratory organs. Thus, accessory respiratory organs are those organs that assist in the process of respiration. There are several fishes which have air-breathing tissues and are capable of spending several hours out of water. Air breathing function can be performed not only by the pre-existing structures like intestine, skin, gills, air bladder etc., but certain newly formed structures are also capable of utilizing atmospheric oxygen. These new structures are known as *neo-morphic* air breathing organs. They develop respiratory epithelium for this purpose.

Some notable contributions on the accessory respiratory organs of fishes are those of Das (1927, 1940), Sawaya (1946), George (1953), Munshi (1961, 1962, 1968), Johansen and Hanson (1968), Johansen and Lenfant (1968), Johansen (1968, 1970), Johansen *et. al.* (1970) , Prasad and Mishra (1982), Singh *et. al.* (1990), Munshi and Hughes (1992) and others. The following are the important accessory respiratory organs in fishes:

1. *Wet Skin Surface* : Any thin walled tissue, richly supplied with blood capillaries and having moist surface can easily serve as the organ for respiration, when it comes in contact with oxygen. In many fishes the skin is richly vascular and these fishes can respire through their skin which must be kept moist. *Anguilla anguilla* and *Amphipnous cuchia* are very common examples. When these fishes leave water, they can pass through damp vegetation and cover a short distance, thus making a land journey. Some larval fishes breath by skin until the gills are fully formed. Cutaneous respiration is performed also by Mudskipper (*Periophthalmus*).

2. *Parts of Alimentary Canal* : In certain fishes, various parts of the alimentary canal function as respiratory organ. The method has also been adopted by loaches (cobitidae) and some catfishes (Loricariidae). The pond-loaches (*Misgurnus fossilis*) swallows air and its intestinal wall extracts oxygen. They use the intestine at times for respiration. In the loaches, the middle and posterior parts of the intestine function both as digestive and respiratory organs. In some of the loaches the digestive phase of the intestine alternates with the respiratory phase. In certain cases the intestine serves as the respiratory organ during the summer months only. The weather fish of Europe swallows air and the latter is passed down into the intestine. The vascular reservoir of the intestine extracts oxygen from the air. The remaining gases are then emptied out through the vent. The rectum of the nesting catfish (*collichthys*) absorbs oxygen drawn in through the anus and hind gut i.e rectum absorbs oxygen from that.

3. *Arborescent Organs* : Gill cavity enlargement is found in *Clarias* (Clariidae) and related catfishes. Opening between the second and third gill arches leads to two sacs with bush like highly vascular structure known as arborescent organ. They are tufts of epithelial outgrowths and has cartilaginous supports which originate from II and IV gills. The entire structure inside the sac receives its blood supply from all the

afferent branchial arteries and oxygenated blood returns to the corresponding efferent vessels. The air-breathing organs of *Clarias batrachus* comprises (i) Suprabranchial chamber, (ii) Two beautiful rosettes of air trees, (iii) the fans, and (iv) respiratory membrane.

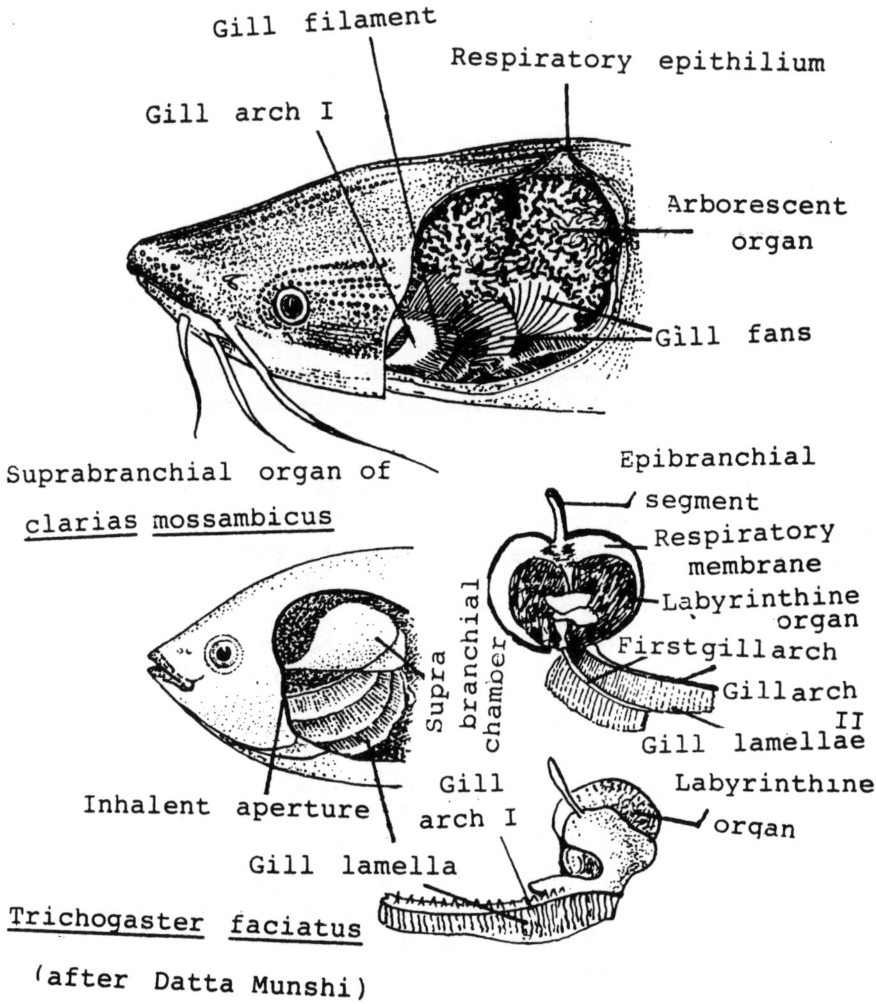

Fig. 41 : Accessory respiratory organs in two fishes

The suprabranchial chamber lying above the gills is divided into two cup like compartments lined by a vascular membrane. Two beautiful "rosettes" (dendritic organs) are present on each side. These are supported by the epibranchial cartilages of the II and IV branchial arches. The rosette consists of a core of cartilage and is covered by vascular epithelium showing eight folds. Fans are formed as a result of the fusion of some gill lamellae of each arch. The vascular area of the supra-branchial chamber shows several "islets." The gill-slit between the second and third gill arches serves as the inhalent aperture, through which air enters into the supra-branchial chamber. Air entering into the opercular cavity is directed into the suprabranchial chamber by two fans present on the 2nd and 3rd gill arches. The gill slit between the 3rd and the 4th gill arches functions as the exhalent aperture through which the air from the suprabranchial chamber goes into the opercular chamber and finally to the exterior. Partial vacuum in the supra-branchial chamber is created by its contraction and also by movement of the fans. When mouth opens, the bucco-pharyngeal cavity is enlarged and the air is inhaled.

4. *Saccular Organ :* In *Amphipnous cuchia* (synbranchiformes) the air-breathing organs consist of a pair of sacs which grow out from the pharynx just above the gills and air can be stored in the sacs for sometime; for gaseous exchange. The gills in this fish are rudimentary and the power of aquatic respiration has been lost. It comes to the surface of water to gulp air at frequent intervals. Each sac is provided with inhalent and exhalent apertures. The epithelium of the air sacs consists of vascular areas in the form of "Islets" having numerous "rosettes" or papillae. *Saccular organ* is also present in *Heteropneustes fossilis* (Bloch). Here the sac is very long and reaches the tail region. The gills are fused to form a valve over the orifice of the air sacs. The IV branchial artery supplies blood to this structure and the V efferent drains the blood. The "islets" are also covered by a thin epithelium which has numerous capillaries.

5. *Labyrinthiform Organ* : This organ is present in the climbing perch, *Anabas*, (Anabantidae) and has been thoroughly studied. This organ is derived from the epibranchial segment of first gill arch and is covered with folds of respiratory epithelium. The *Labyrinthiform organ* is located in the pocket of the pre-opercular dorsolateral area of the head region. This organ is also present in *Betta* and *Trichogaster*. The air-chamber in *Anabas testudineus* communicates with the bucco-pharyngeal cavity and the opercular cavity. There is lining of the vascular epithelium in the air chamber. The epithelium is sometimes folded. The labyrinthine organ is lodged in this air chamber.

In *Trichogaster* there is a supra-branchial chamber situated above the gills on either side communicating with the pharynx by inhalent aperture and with the opercular chamber by means of exhalent aperture. The labyrinthine organ is spiral in form with two leaf like expansions covered by vascular epithelium. The vascular area of the labyrinthine organ comprises large number of "islets" with parallel blood capillaries. The islets are derived from the secondary lamellae of a gill filament.

6. *Accessory Branchial Chamber :* The accessory branchial chamber is present in *Channa* sp. Because this chamber lies above the usual respiratory chamber, it is also known as supra-branchial chamber. There are two chambers which are incompletely separated. Diverticula of the mouth and pharyngeal cavities develop. The diverticula are provided with folded respiratory epithelium which has rich blood supply from the afferent vessels. In *Channa marulius* and *Channa striatus* the suprabranchial cavities are developed in the roof of the buccopharynx. These cavities are highly vascular. It is lined with respiratory epithelium which is raised into folds and tongues and shows respiratory "islets". The branchial cavities possess some alveoli also. The flat epibranchial of the first gill arch is also covered by

vascular membrane which assists respiration. It also has a highly branched respiratory labyrinthine organ.

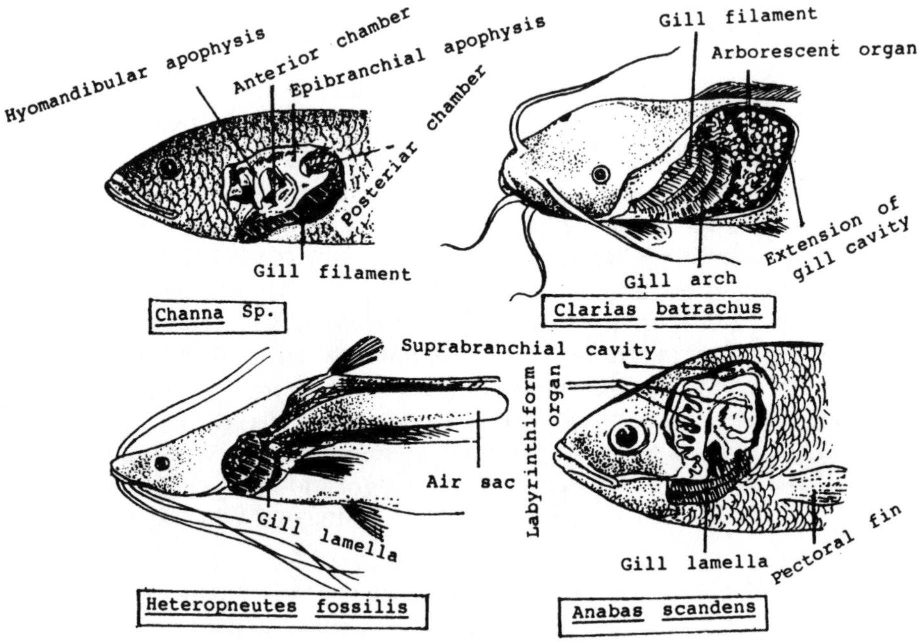

Fig. 42 : Accessory respiratory organs in some more fishes

7. *Air Bladder:* Many fishes use the air bladder as a temporary or supplementary organ of respiration. The gars (*Lepisosteus*) and the bow fin (*Amia*) are examples of facultative air-breathers with a highly sacculated or alveolar air-bladder. In lung fishes, the inner walls have become thin and richly vascular. It is partitioned by the development of Septa and cross septa to form a series of alveoli. Thus the surface area is greatly increased. *Neoceratodus* of Australia comes to the surface for breathing air. In *Protopterus* of Africa and *Lepidosiren* of South America, each lung sac cavity is further divided into a series of large and small irregular alveoli. The alveoli subdivide into tubules which finally terminate into small pockets. In *Notopterus chitala*, a physostomous fish, the gills are reduced and the air-bladder is very much developed and is almost like the lung of the higher vertebrates. The fish can leave out of water for few hours. When in water, it periodically gulps air. The main portion of the air bladder lies in the abdominal part inside the body cavity and bifurcates into two lateral bronchi like tubes. In the trunk region of the tube there are 14 or 15 blind pouches with finger like processes. The pouches and their processes have profuse supply of blood capillaries. Thus the air bladder in this case serves as true lung and makes the chital fish almost an air-breather.

Note on the Origin and Evolution

Recently some workers have based the origin and evolution of the neo-morphic air-breathing organs of teleosts on induction of ectodermal cells in the gill mass, either during the embryonic or post-embryonic developmental stage. The conversion of the gill lamellae into respiratory epithelium of the suprabranchial chamber (as in siluroidae) has also been taken into consideration by some workers. There is general agreement that the neo-morphic accessory respiratory organs evolved earlier in freshwater forms in comparison to fishes of other environments. *Heteropneusts fossilis* is said to represent the first stage in the evolution of these organs in freshwater habitat. In *Channa morulius* (Channidae) these organs are of the most archaic type but in *Channa gachua* it is quite advanced in the evolutionary history. *Monopterus cuchia* as revealed by Singh *et al.* (1990) is more evolved than *M. albus.* In the family Anabantidae, *Osphronemus nobilis* is the most primitive but *Anabas testudineus* is the most evolved when critically examined. Prasad *et. al.* (1982) have revealed that *Colisa fasciatus* occupies the intermediate position between the above two forms.

CHAPTER 7

EXCRETION AND OSMOREGULATION

There is a close relation between excretion and osmoregulation in fishes. The kidneys and gills are the main organs to serve these two functions. A functional *pronephros* is preset in the fishes which is replaced later on by *mesonephric tubules*. As a result of metabolic activities, serveral by-products are formed. Some of these compounds are useful to the body and others are removed. The term excretion means separation and elimination of the metabolic waste products from the body. During *osmoregulation*, not only water movement and water volumes are controlled but the ionic concentration of the body is also regulated. Fishes are described as *ammonoletic* animals and nitrogen is excreted predominantly in the form of ammonia. Because ammonia is highly soluble, it can readily diffuse out into the surrounding water medium. In freshwater fishes kidney functions as a water excretory device. Nitrogenous excreta diffuses out through the gill surface also.

In marine teleosts the kidney chiefly serves as an excretory device for magnesium and sulphate ions. Some marine teleosts excrete considerable amount of NH_3 and small quantity of urea. Marine teleosts excrete nitrogen in the form of trimethylamine oxide (TMAO). The process of reabsorption and secretion by the kidney tubule are more or less active and involve energy utilization in the form of ATP.

Kidney Structure

The kidneys of fishes are paired elongated structures above the gut and below the vertebral column. Each kidney opens to the exterior through a duct, which may fuse to form a single duct, commonly known as *urinogenital sinus* (e.g. shark) or so called urinary bladder (e.g.some bony fishes). The *mesonephric* kidney is made up of a large number of kidney tubules, each one enlarged at its extremity to form the *Renal Capsule*. A mass of capillaries, known as the *glomerulus* is present in the capsule. Blood is filtered under high pressure in the glomerulus.

The teleostean kidney is divisible into two parts—the head kidney and the trunk kidney, which are well marked in histological preparations. The head kidney in several cases encloses the adrenal gland. According to Ogawa (1961), marine teleostean kidney can be divided into five types:

Type I : In this case, two sides of the kidney have completely fused, and the head and the trunk regions can not be clearly distinguished (e.g.herrings—Clupeidae).

Type II : When only the middle and posterior portions are fused and there is clear distinction between the head kidney and the trunk kidney, e.g. marine fishes (Plotosidae) and eels (Anguillidae).

Type III : Only Posterior portion of the kidney is fused and the anterior portion is represented by two slender branches. There is clear distinction between head and trunk. Most of the marine fishes possess this type of kidney. The examples include the bill fishes (Belonidae), Mullets (Mugilidae), Lantern fishes (Scopelidae), mackerel (scombridae), sculpines and sea ravens (cottidae), pompanas and sacks (carangidae), and Pleuronectidae (flounders).

Type IV: Only extreme posterior portion is fused and the head kidney in particular, can not be recognized (e.g. Sea horses and pipe fish—syngnathidae).

Type V: In this type, the two kidneys are completely separated (e.g.anglers-Lophidae).

The head kidney (anterior kidney) consists of lymphoid, haematopoietic, interrenal (cortical) and chromaffin (medullary) tissues. Some haematopoietic tissues and pigment cells are distributed in the tubules and vascular spaces of the trunk kidney. The corpuscles of Stannius are also located on the postero-dorsal side of the kidney. Several nerves are present in the renal parenchyma. Dilations formed as a result of fusion of two archinephric ducts may form a bladder like enlargement for storage and modification of the urine. Renal arteries supply blood to the kidneys. In glomerular forms they give rise to afferent arterioles supplying the glomerular capillaries which in turn drain into efferent arterioles. There is no true renal system in freshwater teleosts as studies by Moore (1933). In many, caudal vein forms the left and right cardinal veins. In euryhaline teleosts, the peritubular capillaries receive blood from various combinations of caudal and segmental veins forming a renal portal system.

Nephron in freshwater fishes: A glomerular nephron is characterized by the following regions:

1. A corpuscle containing vascular glomerulus
2. A ciliated neck region
3. Proximal segment with prominent brush border and several lysosomes
4. A second proximal segment with less developed brush border and numerous mitochondria
5. A narrow, ciliated intermediate segment
6. A distal segment having clear cells and elongate mitochondria, and finally
7. A collecting duct system.

There is very little information regarding glomerular freshwater teleosts. Grafflin (1937) and Smith (1932) have reported that in *Microphis boaja* Bleeker, nephron consists of only two regions which is comparable to the aglomerular nephron of the marine teleosts.

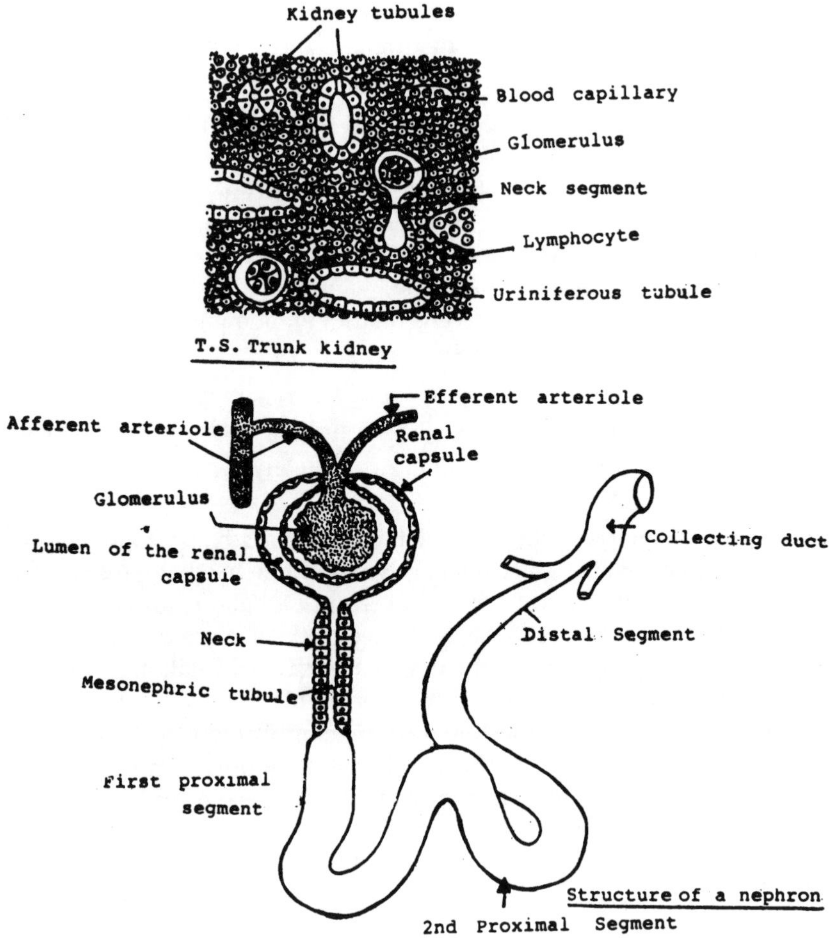

Fig. 43 : T.S. through teleostean Kidney and structure of a nephron

Nephron in Marine fishes (teleosts) : The glomerular nephron of the marine teleosts is composed of following regions: (1) Renal corpuscle with glomerulus, (2) A neck segment, (3) two or three proximal segments, (4) intermediate segment between the first and second proximal segments, (5) collecting tubule, and finally (6) collecting duct system.

Aglomerular nephron in syngnathidae (e.g. *Hippocampus* and *Syngnathus*) show similar morphology in the brush border segment with interdigitating basilar processes which contain mitochondria. Extensive arborization has been reported in the nephron of *Hippocampus.* In *Lophius piscatorius,* there is absence of basal process. The interdigitations are shallow and unlike *Hippocampus,* these are not related to mitochondria. *L.piscatorius* is supposed to be partly aglomerular.

Euryhaline glomerular nephron: In the marine pleuronectid, *Paralychthys lethostigma,* the nephron is composed of the following parts:

1. Poorly vascularized small glomerulus.
2. Ciliated neck segment.
3. First proximal segment.
4. Second proximal segment.
5. A ciliated tubule, and
6. A collecting duct system.

The remarkable variations exist in the intermediate segment and in the distal segments. Intermediate segments have been described in two species of *Anguilla* by Grafflin (1937), and two species of *Salmo* by Trump (1968). They consist of ciliated terminal portions of second part of the proximal segment. In other species the intermediate segments are mostly absent. Similarly most of the species possess distal segments but in *Fundulus heteroclitus* and *Gasterosteus aculeatus*, this segment is lacking.

Kidney Function in Freshwater Teleosts

Freshwater teleosts are hyperosmotic regulators. Here, extrarenal system is located in the gills where the regulation of the ionic composition of the blood is carried out. The problem before teleosts and cyclostomes inhabiting freshwater is to get rid of excess of water that enters the body because of osmosis. Loss of salts has to be compensated by diffusion. Freshwater fishes may drink little water or may not drink at all. They produce large quantities of dilute urine (hypotonic) and thereby maintain proper water balance. Some fishes can obtain sufficient quantities of salts in their diets in addition to renal retention and thus, salt loss is compensated. The function of kidney is to conserve filtered electrolytes. The urine is dilute almost free of sodium and chloride. A powerful monovalent ion reabsorptive mechanism operates however, there is a low tubular permeability to filter plasma water. Urine flow is greater in freshwater teleosts than the marine forms. Recent works have suggested that euryhaline fishes in freshwater drink their medium. The urine flow and glomerular filtration rate (GFR) of *Catostomus commersonii* increase with rising temperature (Backay and Beatty (1968). Sometimes GFR varies in response to salinity changes as in euryhaline flounder, *Platichthys flesus* (Lahlou, 1966).

Na^+ and Cl^- are completely reabsorbed from the ultrafiltrate in the tubule. Thus there is always a possibility of Potassium undergoing net secretion or net reabsorption against its concentration gradient. The urine concentration of K^+ and Na^+ vary inversely in *Catostomus commersonii* as reported by Hickman (1965) which suggests possible existence of a Na^+ for K^+ exchange pump. Mg^{++} and Ca^{++} concentrations are low as measured in urine and Cal^{++} in particular is strongly reabsorbed against its concentration gradients. The first segment of proximal tubule is concerned with the reabsorption of glucose, amino acids and macromolecules but the reabsorption of electrolytes and organic solutes takes place in both parts of the proximal tubule. The urine is mostly acidic with very few exceptions (rainbow trout). Some nitrogenous compounds like creatinine, uric acid, ammonia and urea are excreted through the gills. These substances have been found to be absent in the urine of *Cyprinus carpio*.

Kidney Functions in Marine Teleosts

The kidney performs a significant role in the regulation of ionic composition of the blood. In the kidney of marine teleosts the nephron is simple and it lacks the distal segment. The glomeruli either degenerate or they are completely absent. The kidney is a hyposmotic regulator. In myxinoid cyclostome only the body fluid is approximately isosmotic with the seawater. There is no question of osmotic regulation, however, ionic regulation is essential. There is much lower concentration of mg^{++} and So_4^{--} in the blood than seawater. Sodium concentration in the blood is high, the concentration of Calcium and Potassium is low. Ionic regulation is accomplished by general body surface and gills. In hag fish, selective intestinal absorption and renal retention accomplish this function.

The kidney in marine teleosts is concerned with excretion of magnesium and sulphate, the osmoregulatory by-products. A small fraction of divalent ions swallowed penetrates the intestinal mucosa and enters the blood stream. Hickman (1968) has revealed that all the absorbed magnesium and sulphate are excreted by the kidney. Sodium, Potassium, Chloride and Calcium ions are absorbed by the intestine and appear in the urine. All degrees of glomerular degeneration are seen in euryhaline marine teleosts. Urine flow of marine teleosts is determined by tubular activities than by the volume of glomerular filtrate. In aglomerular teleosts, it is determined by the amount of water that diffuses into the tubule. In marine teleosts, the blood supply is predominantly venous, the caudal vein entering the posterior end of the kidney. The segmental, subcardinal and epibranchial veins may also contribute in their blood supply. A large posterior cardinal vein drains the kidney. The concentration of magnesium sulphate and phosphate in the urine is always greater than their plasma concentration. The $^u/_p$ ratios for magnesium and sulphate may reach upto 100-300, thus, the ion species are actively secreted into the urine. The divalent ion transport system is directly governed by the quantity of Mg^{++} and So_4^{--} in the peritubular blood at the vascular surface of the tubular cells.

Kidney Function of Euryhaline Teleosts

Euryhaline teleosts can adjust both in hyperosmotic and hyposmotic environments. They include both anadromous and catadromous forms. The nephron of euryhaline fish resembles that of stenohaline fishes. Euryhaline fishes have kidneys with typical marine teleost glomerular nephrons and there is lack of distal segment. There is well developed glomeruli in euryhaline fishes but there are some exceptions (e.g. *Paralichthys lethostigma)*. Euryhaline species have higher filtration rate in freshwater than in seawater. Glomeruli have marked effects on them when the fishes are continuously exposed to one habitat. As reported by Ford (1958), the pink Salmon fry (*Onchorhynchus gorbuscha*) when kept in freshwater had more glomeruli than those raised in seawater. In *Lebistes reticulatus* (guppies) reared in sea-water for a period of $2^1/_2$ years, there was 40 per cent reduction in the number of glomeruli in comparison to their controls in freshwater, and also, the renal corpuscles seemed to be smaller in the sea-water- group—as reported by Daikoku (1965).

Lung Fishes

During aestivation, *Protopterus* accumulates urea in the body because of the fact that water is not available for its removal. About 2 to 4 per cent urea may be present in the body fluid after several months of aestivation. Nephrons of *Protopterus aethiopicus* and *Lepidosiren paradoxa* have been thoroughly studied by Edwards (1955), Grafflin (1937), and Guytron (1935). The nephron consists of the following parts:

1. A renal corpuscle containing a glomerulus with capillaries.
2. A ciliated neck region.
3. The first segment of the proximal tubule consists of lysosome like droplets. A second segment of this tubule is also present.
4. The intermediate segment is ciliated and it is lined by low cuboidal cells which are often ciliated.
5. A distal segment is also present. It has striated cytoplasm formed by the elongate perpendicular mitochondria.
6. A collecting duct system is present.

Lungfishes are freshwater forms and they are anuric during aestivation. Its urine is slightly different from the freshwater teleosts. The urine is very dilute containing Sodium and Ammonia.

Excretory Products

The excretory products are ammonia, urea, uric acid, creatine, creatinine, amino acids and trimethylamine oxide (particularly in marine fishes). Kidneys, liver, gills and some other tissues are concerned with the excretion of these substances. The principal source of Nitrogen is protein of food. Liberation of ammonia from the proteins takes place as follows:

$$\text{Proteins} \xrightarrow[\text{enzymes}]{\text{Proteolytic}} \text{Amino acids} \xrightarrow[\text{(in liver)}]{\text{Deamination}} \text{Ammonia}$$

Urine of both freshwater and marine fishes has very low nitrogen value. Urine nitrogen is lower in freshwater than in marine fish. Much nitrogen is excreted in ammonia by the gills. Highly diffusible substances such as urea and amine or amine oxide derivatives are eliminated through branchial excretion, but the less diffusible nitrogenous end products like creatine, creatinine and uric acid are excreted mainly by the kidneys. Ammonia, urea and trimethylamine oxide have been described in detail below:

Ammonia : Ammonia is the chief nitrogen and product of nitrogen metabolism, It is poisonous (toxic) substance formed as a result of deamination of amino acids. No expenditure of energy is required for the conversion of Protein nitrogen to ammonia. Deamination of glutamate, leads to the production and capture of free energy. In generating ATP, coupling of the glutamic acid dehydrogenase reaction with transamination system is very important. Glutamic acid dehydrogenase requires NAD^+ or $NADP^+$, which when reduced, can enter the chain of oxidative phosphorylation.

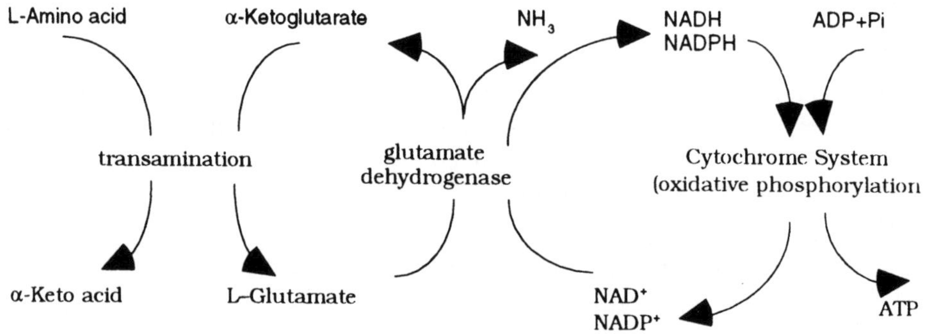

Deamination of amino acids and production of ATP via coupled transamination and glutamate dehydrogenase (Established Pathyways)

Excretion of nitrogen in the form of ammonia, which is lipid soluble takes place by diffusion without any loss of water. NH_4^+ is instantaneously converted into NH_3 and as such it is not a rate-limiting step in its elimination. Ability of NH_4^+ to exchange with Na^+ absorption by the gills of freshwater fish has been demonstrated. The exchange of NH_4^+ for Na^+ serves two functions; eliminates nitrogenous end product and also facilitates the accumulation of Na^+. Very small amount of ammonia is excreted by the kidneys.

Braunstein (1939) and Braunstein and Byechkov (1939) demonstrated the main route for ammonia formation by the deamination of amino acids, via transamination system. This pathway described in the figure earlier couples the transamination of various L-aminoacids with α-Ketoglutarate to form L-glutamate. The latter is then deaminated by L-glutamate dehydrogenase.

Braunstein (1957) suggested another possible pathway of amino acid deamination. Several workers (Zydowo, 1960; Makarewicz and Zydowo, 1962; Makarewicz, 1963) have also suggested the source of ammonia in the gills of carp and other freshwater teleosts. Branchial tissues have much higher activities of *adenosine monophoshphate aminohydrolase.* This partly involves the amination of *inosine monophosphate* by aspartate first. Subsequently, deamination of the product, *adenosine monophosphate* by *AMP-deaminase* takes place as shown below in the figure:

Inosine monophosphate + Aspartic acid ⟶ Adenosine monophosphate + Fumaric acid

$$\text{Adenosine monophosphate} \xrightarrow{\text{AMP-deaminase}} \text{Inosine monophosphate} + NH_3$$

Scheme showing the deamination of amino acids via adenosine monophosphate aminohydrolase.

Urea: Urea is a nitrogenous compound and is less toxic. It is more soluble in water than NH_3. It is formed from ammonia and carbondioxide by a complex cyclical process called *ornithine cycle.* It has been found that urea occurs in the blood of the marine Coelacanth, *Latimeria chalumnae* which is probably formed in the liver via the ornithine-urea cycle. However, there is controversy over the synthesis of urea in teleosts via the ornithine-citrulline-arginine cycle. Brown and Cohen (1960) failed to detect the hormones *carbamoyl phosphate synthetase* and *ornithine transcarbamylase* in the liver of teleosts. These two hormones are involved in the first two steps of the *ornithine cycle.* So, urea can not be synthesized in teleost livers by ornithine cycle. It has been suggested that Purines are a likely source of urea in fish. Studies on the degradation of uric acid by several workers (Przylecki, 1925; Stansky, 1933; Brunel, 1937; and others) have revealed the presence of *urate oxidase, allantoinase* and *allantoicase* in the livers of many teleosts. It has been proposed that urea was produced in a three-step process:

$$\text{Urate} \longrightarrow \text{allantoin} \longrightarrow \text{allantricate} \longrightarrow \text{Urea}$$

Urea synthesis via the Purine pathway can be illustrated in detail as follows:

$$\text{Uric acid} \xrightarrow[\substack{+\\ O_2}]{\text{Uricase}} \text{Allantoin} \xrightarrow[\text{Allantoinase}]{H_2O} \text{Allantoic acid} \xrightarrow{\text{Allantoicase}} \text{Urea}$$

Trimethylamine Oxide (TMAO): It is weakly basic non-toxic end product of nitrogen metabolism. It can be found in the blood and body fluids of fishes, particularly the marine species. It has an osmoregulatory role along with urea. There is very low concentration of TMAO in freshwater teleosts as compared to marine forms. Its concentration fluctuates in euryhaline fishes, such as *Salmon.* The amount of TMAO increases in tissues during marine phase of the euryhaline species.

Control of Kidney Function: Production of urine is the main function of the Kidney. It takes place by the co-ordinated activity of the different units of Kidney. Filtration takes place in the glomerulus of the Renal capsule because of difference of pressure in the blood vessels. Reabsorption and secretion take place by urinary tubular (Nephrons). A low blood pressure reduces the GFR and also decreases the rate of urine formation. Adrenaline and Nor-adrenaline injections increase the GFR and also increase the rate of urine formation. Some hormones like aldosterone (or mineralocorticoids) of the adrenal cortex, and antidiuretic hormone (ADH) of Pituitary gland control urine formation.

Osmoregulation

Osmoregulation is a type of homeostasis which controls both the volume of water and the concentration of electrolytes. The nature of osmoregulatory problem is quite different in various groups of fishes in different environments. Osmoregulation is very much essential for aquatic creatures. Krogh (1939) reported that Calcium is involved in the process of Osmoregulation in aquatic animals. Podoliak and Holden (1965, 1966) confirmed this work of Krogh with some fishes (e.g. rainbow trout).

Many species of fishes are *Stenohaline* i.e. they have a limited salinity tolerance. Sea-water is more concentrated in comparison to the body fluids of the fishes, naturally water tends to diffuse out and as such, the marine fishes have to drink water. Freshwater fishes lose salts and water enters into the body through the membranes of the gills and the oral cavity. These membranes are semipermeable. The concentration of salt in the body of fresh-water fishes is greater than that of the water in which they live. Kidneys play an important role in water -salt balance and they take active part in the excretion of the nitrogenous waste products.

Fresh Water Fishes

The osmotic pressure of body fluids depends on mineral and organic compound content. The osmotic pressure of the body fluids in freshwater fishes is always higher than that of the surrounding water and the latter diffuses into the body through oral membranes, gills and even intestinal surfaces. In certain species of fishes water may enter through the skin also. A large amount of *hypotonic* urine is produced by the freshwater fishes in general. The freshwater fishes possess more glomeruli (even more than 10000 in number in the kidney in comparison to the kidneys of marine fishes. The kidney is also larger in size and is well vascularised. It has been calculated that the freshwater teleosts produce urine which is normally 5-12 per cent of the body weight, per day. Water excretion is the main function of the kidneys in these fishes but small quantity of nitrogenous compounds, containing

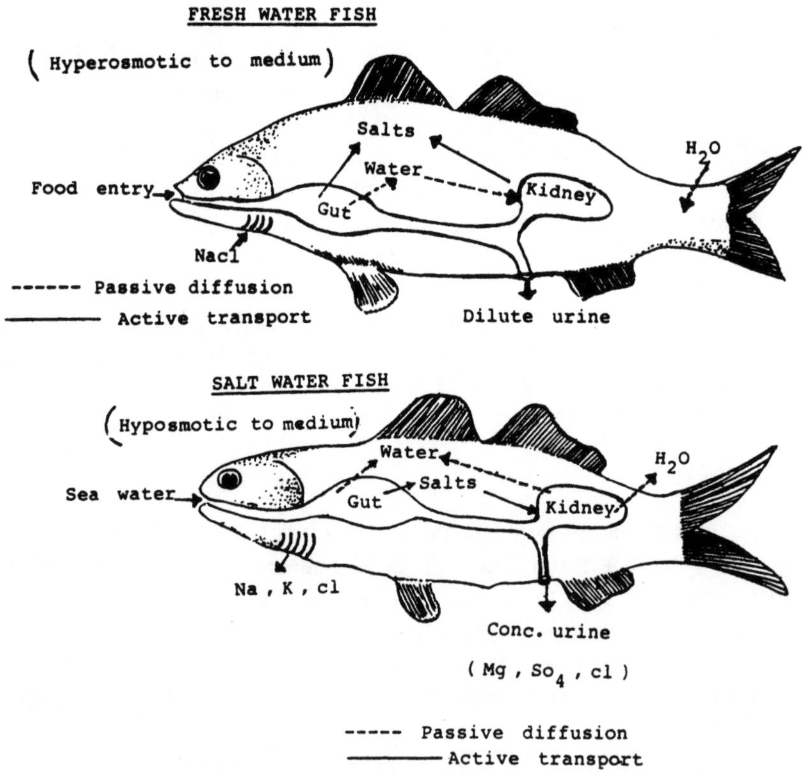

Fig. 44 : Water and salt balance in Fresh Water and Marine fishes

creatine, creatinine, aminoacids, ammonia and urea are also present in the urine. In freshwater bony fishes (osteichtyes) the freezing point depression (Δ) of urine is around -0.025°C. The renal system is selectively permeable to specific salts under the influence of regulatory principles from some endocrine glands.

Salt Balance

Hagfishes are isosmotic to their surroundings and so they do not drink water. The slime produced from their skin is high in Mg^{++}, Ca^{++} and K^{+} content. Their surplus salt is removed through the gills. Monovalent ions (e.g. Chloride surplus) reach the blood stream from the intestine and leave through the gills. But, the divalent ions (Mg^{++} and Ca^{++}) remain in the intestine when they combine with oxides and hydroxides. Thus the insoluble compounds formed in the alkaline medium pass out alongwith the faeces. Chloride cells eliminate excess of chlorine ions in the marine fishes and they absorb these ions in the freshwater fishes.

Because of the osmotic concentration of the body fluids in freshwater fishes is always higher than the surrounding water, some salts (e.g chlorides) are lost into the water by the process of diffusion which takes place mainly through surface tissues like buccal epithelium, gills and skin. Some salts may be lost in the faeces and urine also. Phillips (1944) showed that high levels of Nacl in diet resulted in a water edema in brook trout and it led to the death of the fish. The quantity of salts lost per day varies in different species of fishes. The gold fish *Carassius auratus,* loses 5 per cent of body chlorides per day but in *Salmon,* about 17 per cent of salts have been found to be lost. In the proximal part of the renal tubule active reabsorption takes place and as such the loss of salt is minimum in freshwater fishes. Krogh (1939) found that after holding in distilled water certain fishes (Perch, Catfish, Gold fish etc.) absorbed chloride from sodium chloride solution.

Salts are replaced by two ways: firstly through food and secondly by the absorption of salt ions from the surrounding water. Absorption of Salt ions from the water takes place mainly through gills and oral membrane. Absorption of ions of Sodium (Na^{+}), Calcium (Ca^{++}), Lithium (Li^{+}), Cobalt (Co^{++}), Strontium (Sr^{++}), Bromine (Br^{-}), Chlorine (Cl^{-}), Acid phosphate (HPO_4^{--}) and Sulphate (SO_4^{--}) can be demonstrated. These ions are absorbed by chloride cells located at the base of the gill lamellae. It has been suggested that the process of absorption is under the control of endocrine glands. Berg and Gorbman (1953) found that ^{125}I was utilized by the thyroid gland of Platyfish. Chavin and Bouwman (1965) traced ^{125}I from the materials in to the thyroid gland of goldfish and finally back into the blood stream as a component of thyroxine.

The *Euryhaline* species can withstand a wide range of salt concentrations in the aquatic medium e.g. *Anguilla, Salmon, Gasterosteus* etc. There are certain fishes however, which survive within a narrow range of salinities i.e. they have limited salinity tolerance and they are known as *Stenohaline* species. There are several factors associated with salinity tolerance, which include the area of gill surface, histological structure of the gills, oxygen consumption rate, salt tolerance of certain tissues and permeability control etc. Calcium decreases the permeability of the fish's membrane and prevents the loss of ions, when there is abrupt ionic changes in the environment.

Marine Fishes

In contrast to freshwater environment marine fishes live in the sea where salt concentration is higher than that of the body fluids of the fishes. Naturally, water is lost through the semipermeable membrane by the process of diffusion. Fishes have to drink sea-water in order to make up the loss and thus salt content of the body increases. There is no chance of dehydration after drinking sea-water. Increase of salt in the blood is then eliminated. There is marked reduction in the urine output, for conservation of water and the uriniferous tubules are modified for this purpose. The hagfishes (marine), as pointed out earlier, do not drink sea-water because there is no loss of salt through the semi-permeable membranes. The concentration of blood is same like that of the surrounding water. Required amount of water is obtained from the blood of the hosts.

In elasmobranchs there is no danger of dehydration because they maintain their blood at a higher concentration in comparison to surrounding water. Urine is formed as a result of filtration process in the glomerulus. The urea present in the urine is reabsorbed by special segments of the kidney tubule. Moreover, the gills in the case of elasmobranchs are impermeable to urea and as such, the urea is retained in the blood in large quantities. Thus osmotic concentration of the blood is raised and it becomes higher than that of the sea-water.

The high osmotic pressure of the blood is maintained also by the presence of trimethylamine oxide (TMAO). It makes up 7 to 12 per cent or more of that part of osmotic pressure in sharks, rays and skates by organic compounds. It is reabsorbed from the glomerular filtration like urea. It is important in elasmobranch osmo regulation.

Urea has an important role in the physiology of the elasmobranch. Urea cycle maintains the water balance when water is absorbed through the gills, the blood becomes diluted and this leads to increase urine flow. The levels of blood and tissue urea goes down and urine flow becomes slow. A new cycle of urea retention starts then. The fishes are supplied with sufficient quantity of water for meeting urine requirements. Excretion of salts takes place through faeces and urine. Some salts may be reabsorbed by Kidney tubules. Salts are never excreted through gills in the case of elasmobranches. There is high concentration of urea in the blood of elasmobranch living in freshwater.

In marine teleosts, there is considerable reduction in the size of the kidney tubules. The distal segment of the convoluted tubule is absent in most of the cases. The neck segment also is either absent or constricted in certain species. Nitrogenous waste products are excreted mainly through the gills in the form of ammonia. Traces of urea, ammonia and trimethylamine are present in the urine. Water is lost through the gills and other tissues because of lower concentraion of blood in comparison to the sea-water. The marine teleosts, therefore drink water. There is redution in the size and numebr of glomeruli also. Water is reabsorbed in the kidney tubules. There is physiological control over excess of urine formation and as such large amount of watrer does not pass out though the glomeruli. In many teleosts the glomeruli become degenerate. Even aglomerular kidney may be present in some marine teleosts. Salt secreting cells are present in the gills and oral membrane to help the process of excretion because large amount of salt accumulates in the body tissues because the fisehs frequently drink sea-water to avoid dehydration.

Diadromous Fishes

Diadromous fishes are adjusted both to the fresh water and the salt water phase of the life cycles. Studies on *Anguilla* suggested that the chloride cells can function as secreting and also absorbing units.

Andromous fishes like Salmon, Sea-lamprey and *Hilsa* travel long distance in the sea and reach the rivers to spawn in the freshwater. When their eggs hatch out, larvae grow into fingerlings and the latter leave for the sea. These fishes are able to adjust in water of different salinities, though, they may not be *euryhaline.* It is suggested that hormonal activities play some role in this connection. Salt secreting cells are fully developed in the young fishes and only then they enter the sea. During seaward migraion the enzyme Sodium Potassium activated *adenosine triphosphatase* (Na^+K^+ —ATPase) has been detected in the migratory fishes. It is supposed that this enzyme is necessarily concerned with osmoregulation.

Catadromous fishes (for example *Anguilla anguilla*) spend a major part of their lives in freshwater and migrate to sea for breeding purpose. They lay their eggs in the sea. The young larvae swim back towards freshwater. They undergo metamorphosis and change from *Leptocephalus* stage to *elvers*. It becomes *euryhaline* and enter the river. It has been suggested that during migraion, the hormonal activities facilitate them for adjustment in osmotic regulation.

Control of Osmoregulation

It is well established that endocrine glands are responsible for water-salt balance including urine flow in fishes. The filtering rate of renal corpuscles is affected by hormones. A change in the blood pressure is brought and about the amount of urine output is controlled. A number of hormones including *thyroxine* have been implicated in the process of osmoregulation. Diffusion and absorption of the gills have been found to be greatly influenced by hormones. Adrenocortical hormones are also concerned with osmoregulation. In *Anguilla,* medullary hormone, *adrenaline* has been shown to have strong vasodilatory effect on the gill vessels. It reduces or completely stops chloride secretion. There are evidences that *Prolactin* is a major Pituitary factor for osmoregulation in migratory fishes. The role of caudal neurosecretory system, *Urophysis* and other endocrine factors in osmoregulation in fishes have been reviewed by Bern (1967), in addition to the hormones secreted by interrenal gland. Hypothalamus and gonads have also been implicated in the process of mineral balance (e.g. in *Salmon*).

CHAPTER 8

FISH DISEASES

Like other animals, fishes can be subject to many diseases particularly when farming is intensive. Bad quality of water can cause more or less serious diseases. When the water is polluted, the death of all sizes of fishes is rapid. Large scale mortality is seen in the fish population due to parasitic infections. Health of the fishes depends a good deal on the sanitary conditions prevalent in the water body concerned. Normally, fish diseases can not be transmitted to man with the exception of a few parasitic tape worms (e.g. *Diphyllobothrium*). Disinfection of water bodies with *benzalkenium chloride, quicklime* or *Cyanamide, Potassium permanganate* and a bath in common salt solution are some of the means for controlling the spread of fish diseases in general. Important contribution related to fish disease are those of Davis (1956), Tripathi (1957), Gopalkrishnan (1961), Gupta (1961), Deufel (1963), Mc Fadden (1969), Kumar *et. al.* (1986), Kumar and Dey (1988), Rath (1989) and others. In addition to various piscine pathogenic microorganisms, viruses are the principal agents of fish diseases. The diseases of fishes may be classified as follows:

1. Bacterial diseases
2. Viral diseases
3. Fungal diseases
4. Diseases caused by Protozoans
5. Diseases caused by worms
6. Diseases caused by crustaceans
7. Environmental diseases, and
8. Nutritional diseases.

Now they are being described in detail along with their preventive and curative measures.

Bacterial Diseases

(a) *Abdominal Dropsy:* The most feared disease of carp is the *infectious abdominal dropsy.* The bacterium known as *Aeromonas (Pseudomonas) punctata* is the primary cause of this disease. During the spring season, the belly of the fish swells by the accumulation of yellow or pink coloured liquid in the body cavity. This is the intestinal infection, however, liver and kidney are also affected. The ulcerative form is recognised by profuse ulceration of skin evident by the presence of bloody areas on the body and the muscle is seriously affected. When the fishes are infected they feel pain and unrest which is evident by their frequent jumping. In some cases fins may be partially destroyed. It has been suggested that viruses are also responsible for causing this disease.

Control measure: Dead fishes should be immediately removed. Dropsy resistant carps should be selected for culture. When the carps are stocked and there is possibility of infection, antibiotics should be mixed with artificial food or they should be injected in a bath. *Chloramphenicol* is effective against *Aeromonas punctata*. *Oxytetracycline* and *Streptomycin* are also very much effective. For injection purpose 1 to 1.5mg of *chloramphenicol* has been advised for a fish of 100g body weight. For mixing the antibiotics with food, a fish with 100g body weight should be provided 1 mg of it per day. Some workers have also advised to dip the fish in copper sulphate solution (1:2000) and $KMno_4$ solution (5ppm) for two minutes.

(b) *Furunculosis of Salmonids:* It is a bacterial disease caused by *Aeromonas salmonicida*. Salmons and trouts are very easily attacked. About 2 year Salmonids are rapidly killed. This bacterial infection is transmitted through the digestive tract and the skin. The bacteria breed in the liver, spleen, kidneys and the blood. *Aeromonas salmonicida* is a rod-shaped bacterium 2-3 μm in length. Under the skin bloody boils of different sizes can be easily traced. The centre of infection is present along the muscular fibres. Inflammation of the intestines, spotted liver, haemorrhages at the bases of the fins, in the gill covers and in the muscles are also important signs of this disease. Mass mortality has been reported in trouts.

Control measures: The disease can be treated with sulphonamides, nitrofurans and antibiotics by mixing them in the food. Mc Graw (1955) and Deufel (1963) have advised a daily dose of 10g of Sulphamerazine and 3g of Sulphaguanide for a period of eight days in 100kg of trout. If necessary, the treatment should be repeated after 4 weeks. Ballet (1962) has prescribed 10g of chloramphenicol for 100g of fry over a period of 10 days, and 5g of it for 100kg of fingerlings or trout over a period of 6 to 10 days. Oxytetracycline may also be administered. For egg infection 1 percent providoneiodine has been recommended which is less toxic in comparison to other disinfectants in the case of trout eggs according the Mc Fadden (1969).

Dead fishes should be carefully removed and destroyed at a distant place. The pond should be disinfected with quicklime or calcium cyanide. Pond water should be pure, and its temperature moderate and oxygen concentration of water should be higher.

Viral Disease

(a) *Viral haemorrhagic septicaemia (VHS) of trout:* It is the most important example of viral infection discovered for the first time by Schäperclaus (1941) and later on confirmed by Zwillenberg (1965). This virus has RNA genome and measures 50nm in diameter. This disease becomes suddenly chronic causing very high mortality rate. The growth rate of the fish decreases earlier. The metabolic changes can be easily marked. The kidneys and liver are the most affected organs. This disease has been reported in all age groups of fishes. Haemorrhages in some muscles and perivisceral tissue, bleeding in air bladder, liver discolouration, kidney swelling, bleeding in gills and fins, enteritus etc. are the important symptoms. Fishes show abnormal movement and position in water. Swollen eyes (exophthalmos), general anaemic condition, reduced haemoglobin percentage, protruded anus, muscular oedema, swollen belly, haemorrhages in the air-bladder and in the muscles, presence of neutral or alkaline liquid in the stomach, red intestine, decaying and disintegrating liver, posteriorly swollen kidneys sores on the skin, pale gills etc. are some of the important signs of the disease. In addition to freshwater fish viruses, there are also marine viruses such as lymphocytosis virus (LCV).

Control measures: There is no effective treatment of VHS disease. Fishes should be brought from the uncontaminated farms. Infected or dead fishes should be immediately removed. High stocking densities should always be avoided. Fatty food should be avoided and vitaminous food should be preferred. Disinfected ponds with clean bottoms should be selected.

(b) *Infectious pancreatic necrosis* (IPN) of trout: It is also viral disease which causes heavy mortality of young trout. It is very common in fry and young fish. This virus contains RNA genome and measures 70nm in diameter. When the fishes are infected they revolve on their longitudinal axis. They swim without any sense of direction and finally becomes unable to move. They become dark in colour. The eyes protrude and the stomach and intestine are filled with a whitish liquid. The gall bladder shows signs of necrosis, both liver and spleen are pale. Acinar cells of pancreas show severe necrosis followed by rupture and release of zymogen granules. There is potential bleeding in liver, kidney, pylorus and other internal organs. Intestine is filled with mucous. Anaemic condition is there. Spiral swimming, inflammed anus and haemorrhage of gills and fins are also the characteristic features.

Treatment: There is no effective medicine for this disease, however, Economon (1963) has suggested the use of povidoneiodine which may be useful in controlling the disease.

(c) *Spring Viraemia of Carp (SVC)*: It is caused by *Rhabdovirus carpio*. The fishes become dark in colour. Distended abdomen, haemorrhage in gills and skin and loss of balance are important signs of this infection.

(d) *Channel Catfish Virus (CCV)*: It is caused by DNA gonome virus which measures 10nm. Fish hangs vertically in water showing loss of balance. Haemorrhage of visceral organs may be seen in this disease. Intestine, is filled with yellow mucous fluid, bleeding of internal organs, musculature and air-bladder, anaemic kidney and skin are important features.

(e) *Infectious Haematopoietic Necrosis (IHN)*: It is common in fry and young fishes. The colour of the fish becomes dark. Exophthalmus condition, bleeding in gills and fins, distended stomach and inflammed anus are important features in this case.

Fungal Diseases

(a) *Saprolegniasis: Saprolegnia* develops not only in the diseased or dead fishes but they develop in the weakened and injured fishes also. This parasitic fungus makes a way through the external lesions. Woolly grey-white or light brown blotches on the fins, eyes, skin, gills or mouth show signs of infection. Eggs are also completely covered by this fungus. Tufts of "cotton wool" on the skin (dermatomycosis) is a common fungal disease in several fishes.

Control measures: Potassium Permanganate both (1g per 100 litres of water) for 60-90 minutes has been recommended. Fishes may also be submitted to salt bath (10g/litre water) for 10 minutes or copper sulphate bath (5g in 10 litres of water) is also useful. Also, 1 to 2 ml of malachite green solution (1g of malachite green in 450 ml of water—as stock solution) may be used in one litre of water for a bath lasting for about one hour. 1g of Malachite green may be used for 5 to 10m^3 of water in a pond. Fungal development on trout eggs may be stopped by daily formaline bath for 15 minutes (1 to 2 ml of 30 per cent formal in 1 litre of water). Gottwald (1961) has suggested a concentration of 10 mg of malachite green per litre of water for 15 minutes bath every two days.

(b) *Gill rot or branchiomycosis*: Gill rot is caused by the fungal genus *Branchyomyces* in most of the cyprinids and pike. This disease is very common in densely stocked ponds when there is abundance of phytoplankton and organic matter. The disease manifests during the summer season. The gill becomes pale, and on the gills grey regions can be seen. Also, the gills show red coloured patches. Later on, they are partially destroyed and then they are attacked by *saprolegnia.*

Control measures: Dense stocking and rich supply of inorganic matter should be avoided. During the hot weather even the artificial feeding should be reduced. There is need for a good supply of freshwater.

200kg of quicklime should be spread per hectare but the pH of water is kept always less than 9 (nine). 12 kg of copper sulphate per hectare for pond with an average depth of 1m. has been recommended by Schäperclaus. This quantity of copper sulphate is used in four monthly distribution of 3kg between May to August. A copper sulphate bath (1g in 10 litres of water) for 10 to 30 minutes has also been found to be useful. A bath of Benzalkonium Chloride (1 to 4ppm) may also be used for 1 hour.

Diseases Caused by Protozoans

Numerous Protozoan parasites can live on the external or internal parts of the fish bodies and they can affect various tissues. Some of the diseases have been described below:

(a) *Costiasis:* This disease is caused by a flagellate known as *costia necatrix* when there is prolonged crowding on tanks. They live on the skins, fins and also the gills. Costiasis can be easily seen in salmonid fry and young carps. Slimy secretion appears on the skin, the fins and gills. Seriously affected part of the skin show red patches. Affected gills are brown and partially destroyed. They swim very slowly and become extremely weak and the fish and fry die very soon. This disease appears when living conditions are not favourable e.g. scarcity of food, too acidic water etc.

Control measures: A formaline bath (40ml of formaline in 100 litres of water) for

15 minutes has been advised. For trout fry and small carp a salt bath (10g of Sodium Chloride/litre of water) for 20 minutes has been found to be useful.

(b) *Whirling disease*: This disease is caused by *Myxosoma cerebralis*. Their spores present on the bottom of the pond are very resistant. The fishes are infected by these spores when they (fishes) are very young. The disease is very common among trouts in Europe and North America. In the intestine the young fish, the spore liberates sporozoites which, when carried by the blood, settle in the soft cartilages of the head region. The growth of the fish is much poor. *Myxosoma cerebralis* produces necrosis of the bone and cartilage. Deformation of canals in the ear takes place. This causes loss of balance. The young fishes whirl round and fall on the bottom. Some fishes develop black tail after infection in the sympathetic nerve. Deformation of spine, shortening of the jaws and the gill over, deformation of spinal column, and appearance of small cavities in the head are some of the important signs of this disease.

Control measures: The dead fish should be removed and buried with quicklime. The nursery pond and the flattening ponds should be separate. The nursing ponds must be emptied till September every year to stop infection of water. Storage tanks should be disinfected with quicklime or Calcium Chloride or benzalkonium chloride or formaline or sodium hypochlorite. Tack (1951) advised the use of 0.5 to 5 kg of Calcium cyanide per square metre on the bottom of the pond. Danish Salmonid farmers rear fry in concrete tanks to avoid infection. This is done for a period of two months or so until the fishes reach 5 or 6 cm.

(c) *Ichthyophthiriasis:* This disease is caused by a ciliated Protozoan *Ichthyophthirius multifiliis*. The young parasites attach between the dermis and the epidermis of the fishes. This parasite can cause great losses among carp, trout and other young fishes. Small greyish white spots ranging between 0.1-1 mm in diameter are visible on the skin of the fishes. The gills are also attacked by these parasites. The fish can be seen jumping in the water to get rid of the parasite by rubbing themselves against some object.

Control measures: As the parasites are under the epidermis, it is not possible to get rid of the disease.The diseased fish should be carefully removed. Transfer of fishes from one pond to another has been suggested. Rychlicki (1968) has advised to spread 1500 kg of quicklime per hectare and this should be again repeated after an interval of two days. Commercial formaline (1/4000) bath and Pyridyl mercuric acetate (1/500000) bath, each for 1 hr has been recommended. A common salt (30g/litre) has also been advised.

(d) *Boil disease (Myxobolosis):* The boil disease or ulceration is caused by a sporozoan, *Myxobolus*. Tiny knots are formed in the skin of the common carp *(cyprinus carpio)*. Gills and other parts may be affected in certain fishes (e.g.*Tinca*).

Diseases Caused by Worms

(a) *Piscicolosis:* Fishes are attacked by *Piscicola geometra*, the blood sucking leech. It is of course an external parasite. It is provided with a sucker at each end of its body, with the help of which it attaches to the body of the fish and sucks the blood. This is a cylindrical, ringed worm not more than 3 cm in length, 1mm in diameter. The parasite makes several incisions in the body of the fish through which fungal attack is feared.

Control measures: The fishes may be dipped into the solution of lysol (1 ml of lysol in 5 litres of water) for 5-10 seconds. Then, they are ringed in fresh water immediately. Lysol is a mixture of cresol (50 per cent) and soap (50 per cent). A salt bath (10g of Sodium chloride in one litre of water) for 20 minutes has also been recommended.

(b) *Ligulosis:* Ligulosis is caused by a yellowish-white tape worm known as *Ligula intestinalis.* This worm is about 15 to 40 cm long and 0.6 to 1.5 cm wide. This disease can be seen frequently among cyprinids found in open water. This parasite is capable of multiplication and constitute half the total weight of the host fish. As the food of the fish is consumed by the parasite, there is retardation of growth in the fish. The disease can be prevented by eliminating water foul.

(c) *Disease caused by Dactylogyrus: Dactylogyrus* is also known as the gill fluke. It is a small flat trematode which can be of great danger of young carps. *Dactylogyrus vaslator* is a common species that attacks the gills of carps. It is only 1mm in length. A large number of this parasite can attack the young fish at a time. The gills swell and become grey at the edges and then they are partially destroyed.

Control measures: Dense stocking should always be avoided. The first nursing pond should be rich in food when utilized. During the spawning period only, the spawning pond should be put under water. During the winter season, the first nursing pond should be left dry. A formaline bath (1 ml/litre of water) for 15 minutes for the large fishes, and 0.25 to 0.50 ml/litre of water for 30 minutes for the young fishes has been recommended. A salt bath (25g in a litre of water) for 10 minutes is also much effective.

(d) *Diplostomosis:* This disease is caused by the trematode, *Diplostomulum. "Parasitic Catract"* is formed in the eye of the fish by destruction of the lens and as a result, vision is lost.

(e) *Gut blocking:* A cestode, *Eubothrium* causes mechanical damage to the gut because of its large scale multiplication and subsequent blocking of the lumen of the gut.

Diseases Caused by Crustaceans

Argulosis: Argulus is a crustacean parasite of fish. There are several species of *Argulus* which attack the fishes. Its colour is green-yellow. *Argulus foliaceus* is only 8mm in length and *Argulus coregoni* reaches a length of 12mm. *Argulus* attaches the skin of the fish at the base of the fins by means of hooks and suckers situated under the eyes. There is a sharp pointed dart like a horn in between the antennae. The sting can cause wounds which become a source of another infections. Anaemia may result because of wounds, subsequently leading to death of the fish. *Argulus* discharges toxic substance from the poison gland, which is very harmful for the host fish. The parasite causes red blotches on the skin. The fish shows signs of nervousness.

Control measures: Lysol bath as described earlier is useful. A potassium permanganate bath (1g in 1 litre of water) for 40 seconds has also been recommended. In the pond 0.015g of lindane, per cubic metre of water has been found to be effective.

Environmental Diseases

The physico-chemical properties of water are of great importance in fish culture. Certain fishes are very much sensitive to Physical and Chemical deficiencies of water.

(a) *Too much acidic water:* When the pH of water goes below 5.5, the water becomes gradually toxic to fishes. The whitish film covers the body of the fish and mucous is secreted. Naturally mortality starts. In some waters, colloidal iron will settle on the gills and thus breathing will become increasingly difficult.

In such cases 500kg of calcium carbonate should be spread in one hectare of the pond so that the desired pH of water can be obtained.

(b) *Too much alkaline water:* The pH of water should always be kept below 9.0, otherwise, it will be again toxic for the fishes. This also affects the gills and fins of the fishes. Control over the distribution of quicklime and biogenic decalcification by controlling and reducing submerged vegetation can help in reducing the pH of water.

(c) *Temperature variations:* Higher temperature variation is also harmful for the fishes. A difference in temperature between 10 to 12°C is well tolerated by the fish. A suitable water temperature for Salmon is 10°C, for Perch it is 12°C, for *tilapia* the range is 10°-23°C and for major carps it is between 20°C-37°C.

(d) *Lack of oxygen:* Oxygen deficiency causes suffocation in water for the fishes and mortality can start. Fresh water should be allowed to enter into the pond and presence of aquatic plants should be maintained. The oxygen requirement varies in different fishes. At 20°C, salmonids require 9mg/litre strength of dissolved oxygen in water, carps need only 6-7 mg/litre but silurids and cichlids need even lower concentrations.

Nutritional Diseases

Overfeeding is not always beneficial for the fishes. It may cause several diseases and finally death of the fishes. *Lipoid hepatic degeneration* of Salmonids, *Enteritis* in some fishes (When intestine is inflammed and a yellow-red liquid passes through the anus), and *hepatoma* of rainbow trout (appearance of tumour behind the pectoral fins) are all nutritional diseases.

Following are the control measures for nutritional diseases. That, food must be distributed in good condition and excessive feeding should be avoided. Food should be rich in vitamins and it should not be much fatty and salty. When the weather is very cold or very hot, feeding should be deliberately reduced. The amount of daily ration should not exceed 2.5 per cent of the weight of the fish. One day fasting in every week has also been recommended by several workers.

CHAPTER 9

ELECTRIC ORGANS IN FISHES

Among several families of fishes, electric organs are well developed and they can produce electricity. These organs can produce electricity. These organs can generate electric field outside the body. Electric fishes have been divided into two types—strongly electric and weakly electric, depending on the strength of the current. The electric organs are used for capturing prey, as organs of defence and they are also used as direction finders. The electric eel (*Electrophorus electricus*) is the best known example of the fishes that can produce electricity. These fishes attain a length of eight feet and are eel like in appearance. They live in the shallow muddy waters of Amazon, Orinoco and other rivers of South America. This fish can discharge about 500 volts of electricity on land but in water there is considerable reduction in the strength on the current. However, the discharge voltage is enough to cause discomfort to man and other animals. *Torpedo, Malapterurus* and *Mormyrus* are known as the electric fishes from the ancient time.

Important contributions on the various aspects of electric organs in fishes are those of—

Sherrington (1906), Remmler (1930), Albe-Fessard (1950, 1951), Bigelow and Schroeder (1953), Szabo (1954, 1955,1958,1961), Bennett (1961, 1964, 1966, 1968, 1970), Bennett and Grundfest (1961, 1966, 1969), Mathewson *et al.* (1961), Bennett *et al.* (1964), Pappas and Bennet (1966), Cole (1968), Bullock (1970), Schwartz *et al.* (1971) and others.

Important Fishes with Electric Organs

Some important fishes which can generate electricity are the following:

1. Skates and ordinary rays (Rajidae)
2. Electric rays and Torpedos (Torpedinidae)
3. *Mormyrus* (Mormyridae)
4. *Gymnarchus* (Gymnarchidae)
5. Electric eel and Knife fish (Electrophoridae)

6. *Gymnotus* (Gymnotidae)
7. Electric Catfish (Malapteruridae)
8. Star gazer (Uranoscopidae)

In addition to the above mentioned fishes some other members belonging to the families Rhamphichthyidae, Sternarchidae and Sternopygidae have also been reported to possess the electric organs.

Description of Electric Organs

The electric organs differ in their shape and position in different species but their basic microscopic structure is almost the same. The organ is made up of disc-like cells known as *electroplaxes* or *electroplates* facing the same direction in the members of the particular species. The electroplates are embedded in a jelly-like substance and they are bound together by connective tissue into an elongated tube or compartment. The electroplates are quite large cells of low resistance and they can be studied by microelectrode techniques. One face of each electroplate is supplied by nerves and blood capillaries. Each electroplate is a multinucleate cell having transparent cytoplasm. It looks different from the muscles. The electric organ actually looks like a clear gelatinous mass.

The electroplate shows characteristic foldings and convolutions of one or both surfaces. On the non-nervous face of the electroplate, large papillae can be seen but the surface supplied with nerves is smooth. This improves the efficiency of the electric discharge because the internal resistance is lowered. In some fishes (Raja, Torpedo) there is repeated branching of the nerves and the whole surface of the electroplate is covered by the nervous net-work.

In *Electrophorus* the nerves end on a number of short papillae. In *Mormyrus,* the points of contact are much more reduced. The contact is at one point only in case of *Malapterurs.* The Electroplates are well innervated in all the electric fishes. The electric organs are located at different parts of the body. Shocks can be transmitted when the fish is molested. Shocks are also transmitted when the fish comes within the range of its preys which are knocked senseless and then swallowed whole.

In Mediterranean *Uranoscopus* and the American *Astroscopus* also the muscle tissues are modified into electric organs. These are innervated by the oculomotor nerves and, are confined to the region of the eyes. The African Mormyrids can produce weak shocks with the help of modified caudal muscles. The *Malapterurus electricus* is the only siluroid fish known to be electric.

The African *Gymnarchus niloticus* gives out weak electrical impulses at the rate of not more than 300 per second throughout life. Also, it can detect changes in the electric field caused by any obstacle in the murky river water. This has some evolutionary significance in the gradual development of powerful electric organs in fishes. In the Gymnotid (*Steatogenys elegans*) the electric organs are present in the groove below the dermis, right from the anterior margin of the lower jaw up to the base of the pectoral fin. In *Mormyrus kannume,* the discharge is continuous but the impulse is very weak at a variable frequency—is the lowest but when the animal is alarmed the rate increases to 80-100 impulses per minute. *Mormyroblasts,* the

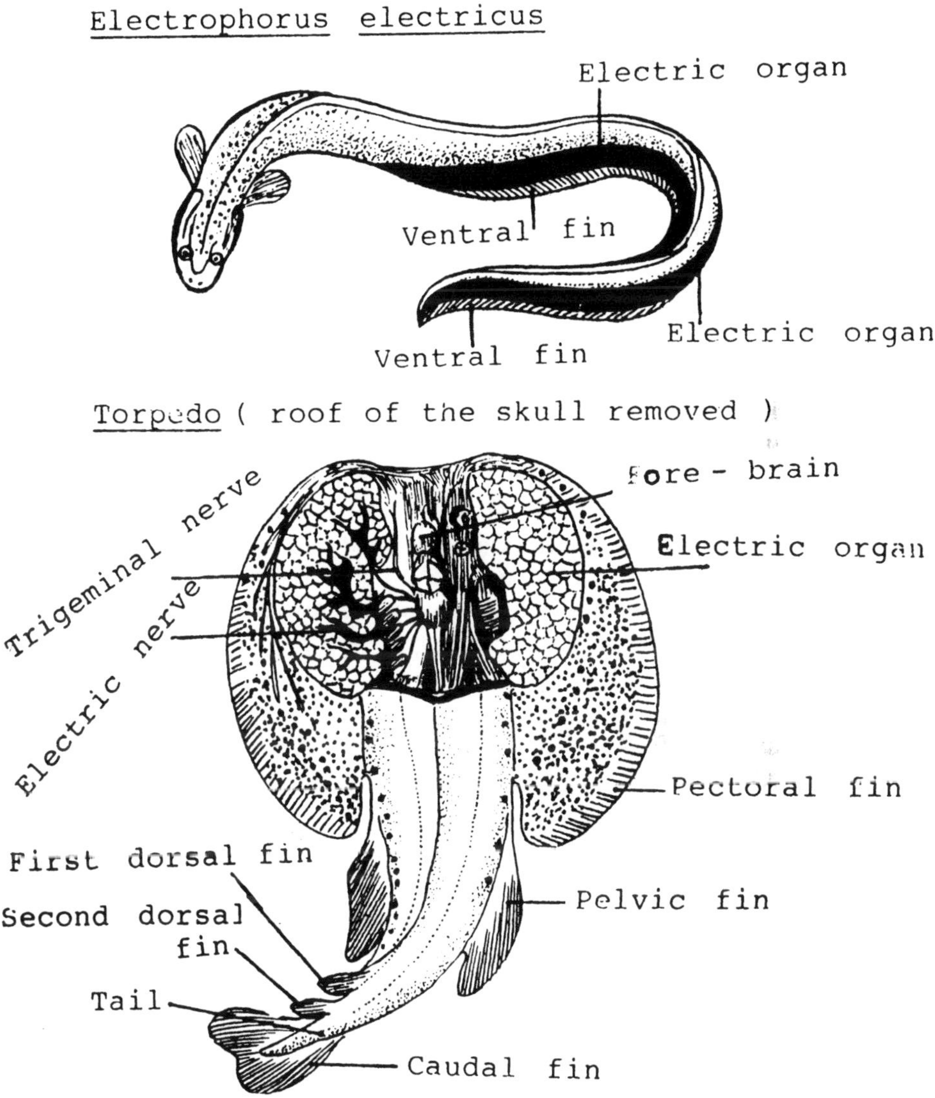

Fig. 45 : Fishes with electric organs

neuro-glandular epidermal cells are probably involved in perceiving electrical disturbances within the electromagnetic field. The enormously large size of the brain in *Mormyrus* is probably related to the co-ordination of impulses concerned with direction finding in this fish.

Thus, the electroplate-cells are well innervated. The neural system controls the electric organs. There are evidences that the functional requirements for rapid communication between cells are met through electrically mediated transmission.

This mode of transmission also facilitates the mediation of chemical transmission.

Details of Electric Organs of Some Important Fishes

Torpedo: There are two large and two small organs on each side of the head. The small organs are enclosed within the larger organs. The kidney-shaped mass on either side of the middle line is supplied by a prominent nerve originating from a special lobe of the brain. The organ comprises about 45 vertical hexagonal columns each possessing nearly 400 electroplates. The innervated side of the electroplate is electrically negative. The current in Torpedo passes from the dorsal side, which is positive, to the ventral side, which is electrically negative. The discharge is between 30 to 50 volts normally.

Electrophorus electricus: In *Electrophorus electricus* (electric eel), the electric organs are present on each side of the fish and one is larger than the other. The organ extends along the whole length of the body and consists of about 6000 electroplates. The nerve supply to this organ comes from the spinal cord. The *Electrophorus electricus* can discharge a current of about 250 volts (maximum 100 watt). It is sufficient to give a severe shock to man and some other creatures.

Malapterurus: A peculiar electric organ is located in the skin of this fish which forms a thick semitransparent covering on the body. The organ is divided into several compartments by the presence of large number of connective tissue septa. Each compartment consists of a large number of electroplates with their nervous ends towards the tail. All the electroplates in each half of the organ are connected to the processes of a single nerve cell in the grey matter of the spinal cord. The polarity in this fish lies from tail to head.

Origin of Electric Organs

It has been thoroughly studied that each electric plate is a transformed muscle fibres. In *torpedo* the electric organ has been derived from some of the branchial muscles which no longer move the gill arches. The electric organ of the electric eel, the skates and Mormyrids have developed from the lateral muscles of the tail. In *Malapterurus,* the electric organs develop from some body muscles. Electroplates of the three evolutionary lines of torpedinids, gymnotids and *Malapterurus* have fine but disorganized filaments without Z-line.

In *Gnathonemus* (mormyrid) there are thick and thin filaments and Z-lines also. In *Astroscopus* (star-gazer), the electric organ is formed from some of the eye-muscles and striations are easily seen. There are well organized Z-lines and thin filaments in both *Astroscopus* and rajids.

The Electric Discharge from Different Species

The members of four families i.e. *torpidinidae, electrophoridae, malapteruridae* and *uranoscopidae* are strongly electric but the members of the remaining families are mostly weakly electric forms. There is some variation in the polarity and the strength of the electric current generated by different fishes. The strength of the current has been estimated in certain electric fishes which have been mentioned below:

1.	Ray (*Torpedo sp.*)	—	40 volts
2.	Ray (*Narcine sp.*)	—	37 volts
3.	Skate (*Raja clavata*)	—	4 volts
4.	Star-gazer (*Astroscopus*)	—	50 volts
5.	Electric cat fish (*Malapterurus*)	—	350-450 volts
6.	Electric eel (*Electrophorus*)	—	370-550 volts

The source of energy for the current is the movement of Sodium ions firstly and then secondly potassium ions from strong to weak solutions. The Sodium ions enter into the cell first due to increase in the Sodium permeability of the membrane.

The discharge occurs from the electric organ in the form of a continuous series of pulses as a result of reflex responses. Strong or weak currents are produced according to the needs of the fishes. In *Electrophorus* it has been found with the help of micro-electrodes that the membrane potential across the posterior innervated surface reserves its polarity at the peak of the discharge. However, there is no change in the potential at the non-innervated surface.

Functions of the Electric Organ

The electric organs serve as the organ of offence and defence. It is used as the offensive organ during food hunting process. *Torpedo* and *Electroporus* paralyse their preys before eating them. Some fishes use the electric organs as the organs for defence against the enemy (e.g. electric catfish and *Narcine).* There are some fishes (mormyrids) which create an electric field around them in muddy water for their safety. The weak electric current helps the fish in finding direction (electro-echolocation) particularly in dark water. The lateral line system is of great use because it serves as current detector. In several mormyrids, the electric organ is of some use in the recognition of sex within the individual species.

CHAPTER 10

SOUND PRODUCTION IN FISHES

Sound production comes under the field of *aquatic bioacoustics*. Sound is the best channel for long range communication under water. By hydropone recording it has been proved that various species of bony fishes produce sound. Several structures like swim bladder, fin spines, vertebrae, teeth and even opercula are associated with sound production. The grunting or gurgling noise can be heard when some fishes are taken out of water. In the loach (cobitidae), the rapid expulsion of air bubbles through the anus results in the production of sound. The air bladder acts as a sound producing organ in several species of fishes e.g. *Hippocampus, Balistes, Diodon, Tetraodon, Ostracion, Channa, Gadus, Dactylopterus, Pangassius, Therapon Triacanthus, Sciana, Pristipoma* and other fishes.

Major reviews on the subject include those of Agassiz (1850), Dufosse'(1874), Smith (1927), Burkenroad (1930, 1931), Dijkgraaf (1932, 1934, 1947, 1949, 1952, 1963), Dobrin (1947, 1948), Fish *et al.* (1952), Kellogg (1953), Fish (1954, 1964), Fish and Mowbray (1959), Tavolga (1960, 1962, 1964, 1965), Marshall (1962, 1963), Moulton (1963), Protasov (1965), Salmon and Winn (1966), Caldwell and Caldwell (1967), Schneider (1967), Breder (1968) and others.

Different Ways of Sound Production

(A) *Stridulation*: In several fishes, sound is produced by stridulation in which one surface is rubbed against another. Some fishes possess opposing patches of denticles in the pharynx and produce sound while feeding. Stridulation of pharyangeal teeth takes palce in connection with activities like alarm and territoriality (as in *Haemulon*). In Sunfish (mola) and squirrel fish, sound is produced when pharyngeal teeth are ground against one another. The swim bladder usually acts as 'resonator' in many cases. Some fishes produce sound by means of modified molariform teeth, as in the case of puffers (Tetraodontiformes). In trigger fish, surgeon fish and a few catfishes, the spines of the dorsal, pectoral, anal and pelvic fins produce sound. The hyomandibular bone produces sound in *Dactylopterus*. A portion of the gill cover is used for stridulation in the bull head (*Cottus*). Stridulation of bones of the Pectoral girdle has been reported in *Balistes*. Salmon *et al.* (1968) studied the phenomenon of sound production in seven species of triggerfish and revealed that sound is produced by the rubbing of Pectoral fins against the body sides. Tavolga (1960) reported that certain serranids beat the opercula while producing sound.

Stridulation by the movement of special fin rays and spines has been reported in *Galeichthys felis* and *Bagre marinus*. When dorsal fin spines are moved in *Gasterosteus aculeatus*, low intensity sound is produced. In *Amphiprion, Hippocampus* and *Syngnathus louisiance*, the method of sound production is the stridulation of the posterior margin of the skull with vertebral elements.

(B) *By Air-Bladder* : Vibration of the walls of the air-bladder produces sound in several teleosts. This vibration is caused by the "elastic spring mechanism". In certain cases, expulsion of air or gas takes place from the air bladder through the pneumatic ducts and mouth. In this case sound is necessarily produced. Eels (Anguillidae) produce high pitched sounds by expelling air from the bladder through the pneumatic ducts. Breathing sounds are said to be produced by a few teleosts, some loaches and European siluroids. The loaches (e.g. *Misgurnus fossilis*) can produce sound by the expulsion of air bubbles through anus. Sounds can be detected in the fish at the time of emission of air bubbles, particularly when there is a pneumatic duct between the airbladder and oesophagus. This type of sound production has been elaborately described in some eels and catfishes by Dufossé (1874) and Fish (1954). Burkenroad (1930) reported that Pharyngeal denticle stridulation was affected by deflamation of the air bladder in the grunts. Fish (1954) observed that bone stridulation generates a sound in *Myxocephalus* particularly at a point near the anterior end of the bladder. A sound is also produced in *Balistes* with the help of pectoral fins when the latter beat against the body wall that covers the air-bladder.

Hazlett and Winn (1962) have described the sonic mechanism of *Epinephelus striatus* where a pair of sonic muscles are present. Generally one pair of large sonic muscles arising from the lateral wall musculature adjoin the lateral walls of the air bladder. Their vibrations occur in a series of drum like beats or knocking sounds. A pair of short muscles associated with sonic mechanism originate on the occipital region of the skull, insert on the ribs and connective tissue on the antero-dorsal surface of the airbladder. The mechanism has been fully described in *Epinephelus striatus, Holocentrus rufus, Therapon* and *Sebasticus*. In catfishes as described by Muller (1842, 1843) there is a fused shelf of bone over the antero-dorsal surface of the air bladder. In certain species, shelf of bone is very thin known as "elastic spring" (Sorensen, 1894). In *Galeichthys felis*, one pair of sonic muscles originate from the epiotic bone of the skull and are inserted on the upper surface of the elastic spring. Vibrations of these muscles cause the air bladder to vibrate. Tavolga (1962) has revealed that the functioning of bony shelf is antagonistic to the contraction of the sonic muscle. Tower (1908) studied the sonic function of the air bladder of toad fish. It was also confirmed by Tavolga (1964). It was considered that the fundamental frequency of the emitted sound is equivalent to the vibration frequency of the sonic muscles.

Sonic muscles are capable of rapid contractions and recovery cycles. The elastic spring maintains tension of the sonic muscles. By the contraction of sonic muscles volume and pressure changes take palce in the air bladder and as a result pulsation of the air bladder starts.

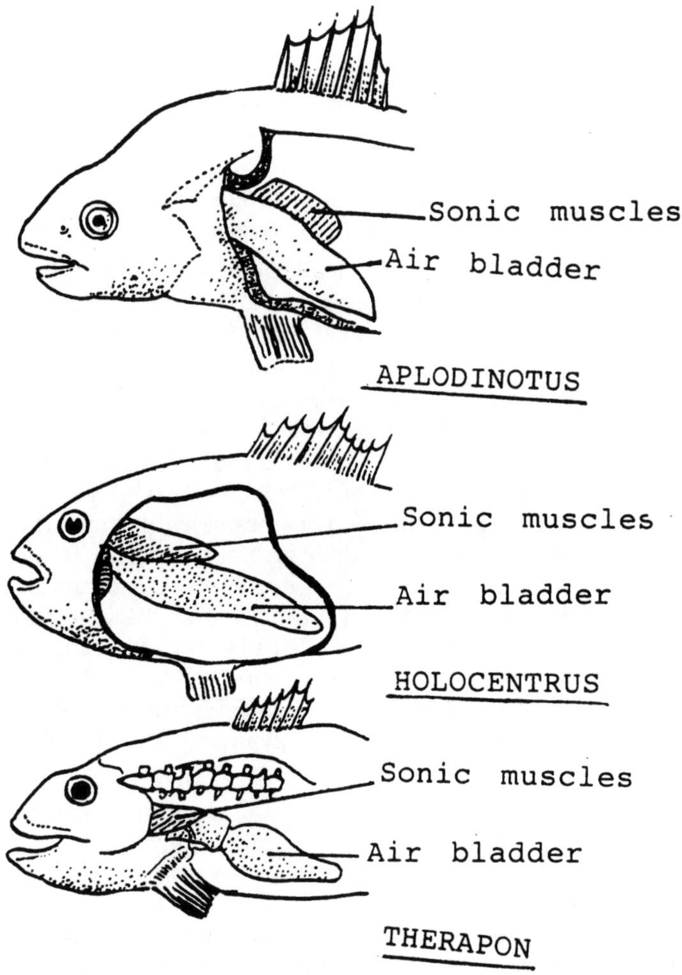

Fig. 46 : Swim bladder and sonic muscles in some fishes

(c) *By the Movement of Fish in Water:* Under this head, hydrodynamic and swimming sounds are included. Displacement of water is caused by the swimming fishes. Displacement and compression waves may be rhythmic subsonic vibrations when produced by the fins and body of these fishes. Moulton (1960) holds the view that the sounds may be internal in origin i.e. it is produced by muscular and skeletal movement inside the body of the fishes. When the fishes rapidly turns its body or there is a change in the velocity, the sounds are intensive. The turning of head also produces strong displacement of water leading to compression waves.

How Sound is Intensified: The sound is intensified by the vibratory movement of the free edges of the septa present in the chamber of the air bladder. The walls of the bladder vibrate by the contraction and expansion of the muscles associated with the bladder. The internal partitions make the air bladder slightly more complicated, acting as resonator intensifying the sound. For example, in *therapon* (Perciformes) and singing midshipman the air bladder is vibratory in nature.

Noises Produced by the Fishes: Water is really a good medium for the propagation of sound. So, all sorts of noises produced by different fishes travel a considerable distance. A deep *grawling sound* of the American catfish can be heard from a distance of 100 feet. Electric catfish (*Electrophorus electricus*) can produce a remarkable *hissing sound.* Globe fishes (Tetraodontidae) and trunk fishes (ostracionidae) produce sound almost *"grawling like dogs"*. *Hippocampus* also utters a monotonous sound. The Horse mackerel (*Caranx hippos)* produces a peculiar sound, like *grunting* of pig. *Drumming, humming, purring, whistling* and *creaking* sounds can be produced by the drums (Sciaenidae).

Biological Significance

In the breeding season the sound serves to attract the opposite sex. Sound may be used to frighten the aggressors invading the breeding area. The sounds function as an echo-locator in midwater. It also helps the individuals to congregate in large numbers producing shoals and thus it increases the chances of fertilization of the ova.

CHAPTER 11

BIOLUMINESCENCE

Luminescence occurs in fishes also but exclusively in the marine species (some elasmobranchii and Antinopterygii). Light may be generated within the tissues (intracellular luminescence) or it may be a result of discharge of luminous secretion (extracelluar luminescence), or light may be generated by symbiotic bacteria (bacterial luminescence) also. In the process of light production, various kinds of photogenic organs are involved. A photogenic tissue contains different kinds of cells. The most important purpose of bioluminescence is to illuminate sourrundings. The colour of the light is blue in *Stomias ferox* (Stomiatidae), green in *Coelorhynchus* hubbsi (macrouridae), blue-green in *Anomalops katoptron* (Anomalopidae), blue-white in *Paratrachichthys prosthemius* (Trachichthyidae), yellow in *Echiostoma barbatum* (Melanostomiatidae) and green-yellow in *Argyropelecus olfersi* (Sternoptychidae). Thus different colours are emitted by different fishes.

There is vast literature dealing with the light producing organs in fishes. Some pioneer contributions are those of Ohshima (1911), Hickling (1925, '28), Harvey (1931, '52, '55, '57), Waterman (1939), Kasto (1947), Haneda (1950, '51, '53,'57,'66), Nicol (1957, '58,'60,'62), Bassot (1959, '60, '63, '66), Iwai (1960) Iwai and Okamura (1960), Haneda and Johnson (1962), Boden and Kampa (1964), Cohen (1964), Hastings (1966), Johnson (1967), and Kier (1967).

Light Organs: There is great variation in the location of the light organs in different fishes. In *Acropoma* they are present in the ventral musculature. They are distributed in large number over the lower surface of the body in *Etmopterus*. In certain Isospondyli and light organs (Photophores) are arranged in rows. On the lower surface of the trunk and head area (as in *Cyclothone*). Light organs are present beneath the eyes of *Astronesthes.* Luminous bulbs are present on the dorsal fin ray of *Ceratias* and barbel of *Stomias* (stomiatidae). Luminous glands are also present in the ventral abdominal wall of *Malacocephalus* and on the lower jaw of *Monocentris.* In the case of *Gazza* the luminous glands surround the oesophagus and the glandular palisades contain bacteria.

The anatomy of the light producing organs has been described in detail under several heads as given below :

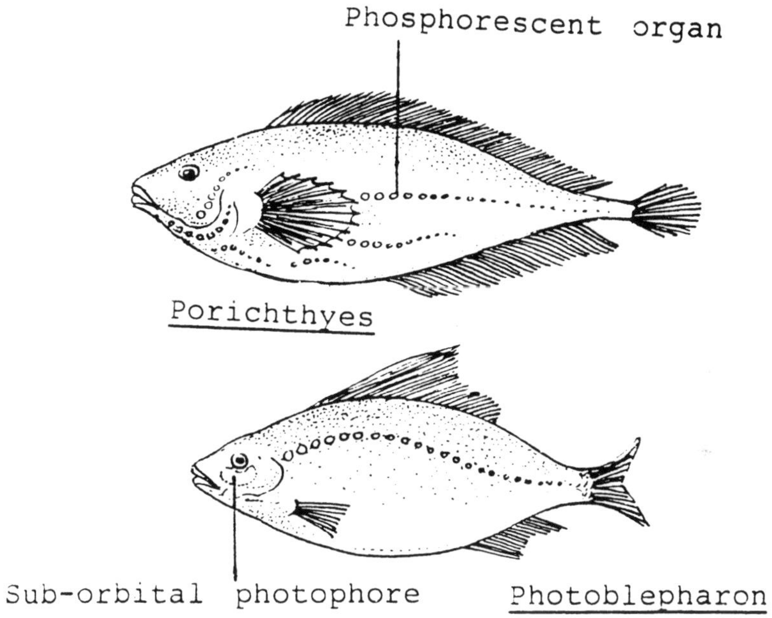

Fig. 47 : Light producing organs of two fishes

1. *Simple Organs:* Photophores of several sharks belong to this category. Here the photophores are very small, not more than 0.1 to 0.3 mm in width. Each of them comprises the light generating cells—the *photocytes.* Simple organs are with or without an interrupted mantle of pigment. Grouping of cells in the photophores are also called 'lenses' or lenticular cells'. In the distal area the photocytes contain acidophilic granular material. A layer of melanophore invests the photophore. The light organs of *stomias* lies in the gelatinous corium and consist of packet of photocytes. In *Chauliodus* there are thousands of simple light producing organs all over the body which constantly glow even at the depth of 500m. The light organs present on the chin barbels of *Stomias* are also simple in nature. The *Ceratias* owe their light to symbiotic bacteria and the light organ is a simple one.

2. *Compound Organs*: In addition to photogenic tissue and pigment mantle the compound organs comprise some putative dioptric accessories, lenses and also reflectors. For example, the subocular light organs of *Astronesthes* can be considered. It is a large organ laying in deep dermal tissue. A cell-free space separates it from the superficial epidermis and dermis. This organ contains a mass of photocytes arranged in cords and bands. In the inner surface there is a thick reflector and also a pigmented mantle.

Nerves and blood vessels penetrate the pigment and reflector layers and they invade the photogenic tissue also. Behind the photophore, there is a band of muscle. This muscle extends below the photophore and continues upward to become inserted on its external side. Besides, below the light organ, there is a black pigmented pocket in the dermis. When the muscle contracts, the outer face of the photophore is pulled downward causing the brighter surface to be concealed.

Simultaneously, some part of the pigmented upper wall of the photophore is moved in front of the patent window. Thus the mechanism for rotating and concealing the organ is somewhat peculiar.

The dermal photophores of *stomias* have a hemispherical reflector and a pigmented sheath. Two types of glandular cells (A & B) can be distinguished in the photogenic central tissue. A capping plate or lens is present on the outer surface.

In myctophids, shallow cup like light organs are present which lie in the corium. Black pigment and a reflector containing fine platelets are usually present. Elongated the spindleshaped photocytes are confined to a small area only. The photocytes belong to category A as seen in *stomias.*

3. *Alveolar Organs and Sacs in the Body Wall*: Glandular sacs embedded in the dermis are subdivided into chambers, alveoli and tubules in several fishes. They have one or more openings to the exterior. They may also be associated with some bacteria which are responsible for luminescence. *Photoblepharon* and *Anomalops* are good examples. The light organ has a mass of secretory tubules. There is a reflector and a layer of pigment internally. Various types of glandular cells and also bacteria are present in the tubules. The light organ shines through the window in the skin. The pigmented screen of *Photoblepharon* can be drawn up over its external surface but in *Anomalops* (Anamalopidae) the light organ is turned downwards by rotation and thus the light emitting surface becomes concealed. In *Monocentris* (Monocentridae) the light organ is situated beneath the mandible in the form of luminous discs. The organ comprises tubules and canals lined with glandular epithelium. The light organ is invested by connective tissue sheath containing chromatophores. Okada (1926) and Haneda (1966) have revealed that light is produced by luminescent bacteria of the tubules.

4. *Visceral Organs*: Light organs are associated with viscera of the fishes also. In *Gazza* (Leiognathidae) the luminous organ encircles the oesophagus. There are tubular gland invested by reflector and pigment. The light is dispersed by translucent ventral muscle and is spread over the whole lower surface of the body. The light escapes through a ventral aperture but a part of it passes dorsally and is reflected by the swim bladder and peritoneum.

In *Acropoma* (Acropomatidae) the light organ is U-shaped glandular tube present in the ventral body wall. A white opaque reflector separates the lateral from the ventral muscles of the body wall. The ventral muscles of the body wall are translucent. Haneda (1950) has described that reflected light from the gland is scattered within the muscle, appearing as a diffuse flow over the lower surface of the fish.

In *Parapriacanthus* (pempheridae) the luminous organs include the thoracic duct, opening into the caeca, and the anal duct, opening to the exterior by a pore near the anus. The thoracic organ lies above the pigmented screen, which is present between the luminous organ and the ventral surface of the fish. Reflectors are present above and on either side. Light is spread outward and downward through the translucent tissues of the lower trunk area. Fishes of the family *opisthoproctidae* have visceral light organs derived from the rectum which emit light directly or indirectly.

Fine Structure of Luminous Organs: Bassot (1960, '63, '66) has made detailed studies on the structure of glandular cells and has been able to describe several categories of *photocytes* in the *photophores* of stomiad fishes. The photocytes have been divided into A and B categories. In the A photocytes, there is abundance of basophilic endoplasmic reticulum and they are rich in secretory granules which are made up of glycoprotein. These photocytes usually occupy the inner and deeper region of the photophore. Photophores may be tall and radially arranged (as in *Chauliodus*), they may be densely packed smaller cells (as in *Maurolicus*), or they may be grouped in acini opening in to a common canal (as in *Gonostoma*).

Category B photocytes are usually present in the outer region of the photophore. They are secretory in nature. They contain fine granules, glycoprotein, glycogen and sufficient ribonucleic acid. There is abundance of rhibosomes. In *Chauliodus* these photocytes are enclosed by the A photocytes but in *Argypropelecus* they lie externally. They are pigmented in *Maurolicus*. The B photocytes are absent in *Gonostoma*.

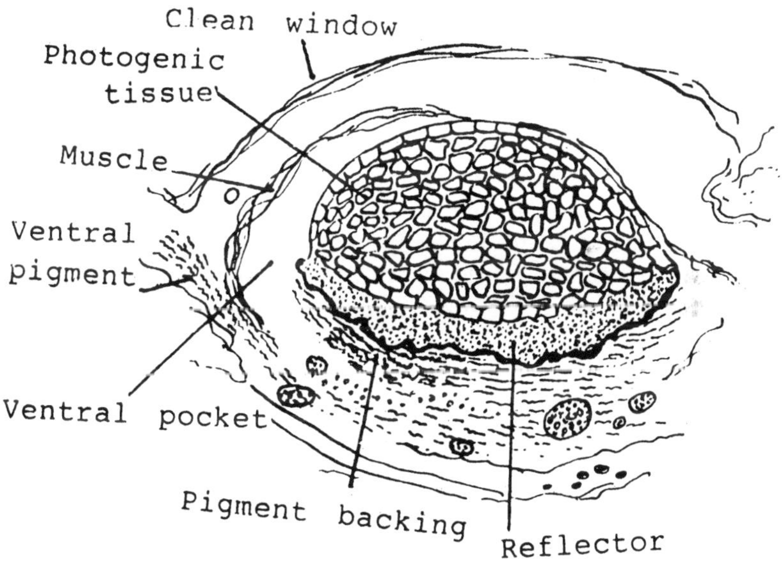

Fig. 48 : T.S. through a subocular light organ of *Astronesthes richardsoni*

The photophore of *Porichthys* contains the lens cells, the photocytes and supportive cells. The photocytes also contain numerous vesicles and lamellar membranous whorles. There are long microvilli extending from the photocytes into surrounding channels (extra cellular). Compound photophores contain a mass of clear epithelial tissue over the photogenic mass. The cells have a homogeneous cytoplasm there being no usual cytoplasmic inclusions. It looks like an ocular lens. The structure is known as lenses or accessory dioptric bodies. Such lenticular structures occur in the light organs of *porichthys* and *opisthoproctus* (Opisthoproctidae) and many other fishes. In *stomias* the lenslike body lying over the photogenic tissue is formed from B category cells, basically derived from A cells. The cells become transformed into the specialized cells of the lens.

Usually, the photophore contains a reflector together with a backing of dark pigment. In stomiatoids, the reflector contains elongated connective tissue cells. They are rectilinear and lie tangential to the curvature of the photophore. Platelets of guanine, arranged in regular piles above one another are present in the cells. These hexagonal platlets are almost parallel to the surface of the reflector. In *Porichthys* each of the small, thin hexagonal platelet lies inside a membrane-bound sac within the cell.

Chemical Basis of Luminescence: The mechanism by which light is produced, is a bio-chemical process and it is well established now. The gland cells of the photophores secrete a substance known as *luciferin.* Now, this substance (luciferin) in presence of the enzyme *luciferase* is converted into *oxy-luciferin*. This oxyluciferin emits light. The luminescent glands of many fishes (*Apogon, Parapriacanthus*) yield the crude extracts of luciferin and luciferase. They produce light when they are combined together. The reaction is oxygen dependent as suggested by Johanson and Haneda (1958).

Regulation of Light Emission: It has been already described that light is emitted either by the symbiotic bacteria or by the glandular secretion of the photophores. But, in all the cases there is some sort of arrangement to regulate the emission of light. The light emission of photophores is under nervous and/or endocrine control.

Direct Control: Several elasmobranchs belonging to the order Squaloidea produce light spontaneously for a long period. In *Etmopterus niger,* light is emitted spontaneously but intermittently. Luminescence can be induced by electrical stimulation in this case as revealed by Hickling (1928). When *E.frontimaculatus* is handled, it produces light, of course, after several minutes. The control mechanism is not perfectly known.

In certain teleosts (*Cyclothone, Portichthys etc.*) the serial photophores are innervated. Nerves enter the photogenic cells. The photophores of *Porichthys notatus* and *Echiostoma barbatum* emit light following administration of adrenaline. Electrical stimulation causes the photophores of *Porichthys* to emit light. It has been advocated by several workers that the serial photophores of some teleosts are definitely under nervous control, probably of the peripheral sympathetic system. In certain cases the possibility of hormonal control can not be ruled out. Sources of innervation is unknown in many cases. Thus different components of the nervous system are also possibly involved.

Indirect Control: In certain fishes there are devices for screening or concealing light organs and also they can change the intensity of light emitted. It has already been discussed that there is a mechanism of rotation in the stomiatoid fishes. In *Chauliodus and Astronesthes* there is a small muscle which passes down and is inserted on the lower or outer surface of the luminescent organ. The light organ rotates downward following the contraction of the muscle. The bright surface is concealed in the ventral pigmented cleft. Its upper pigmented surface is brought against the aperture of the window. Because the photocytes are innervated the probability of their being under the direct nervous control can not be ruled out. Naturally, rotation is controlled by some other function. In *Chauliodus* and *Stomias* the light organs are efficient reflector being present on the cheek of the fish when exposed. The brightly reflecting surface is concealed during the process of rotation when the organ is not in use or when these dark fishes are endangered. In the light organ of *Photoblepharon palpebratus,* there is a fold of black tissue, a membranous curtain which lies along the ventral edge of the light organ. The fold can be drawn up over the organ and the light is concealed. The light organ of *Anamalops* emits light intermittently, appearing intervals of several seconds when the fishes are in inshore waters. The light is produced mostly in darkness. *Photoblepharon* is also a surface dweller but it produces light continuously as reported by Haneda (1953, 1955). In both the above fishes, the light organ is innervated by trigeminal nerve. In *Acropoma* as revealed by Haneda (1950), light can be dimmed by contraction and expansion of chromatophores and this action of chromatophores controls the amount of light. Haneda (1938, 1951) believed that in some members of the deep-sea fishes belonging to the family gadidae, light emission is greatly influenced by concentration or dispersion of pigment in melanophores present in the skin over the light organ.

Significance of Luminescence

Significance and employment of luminescence can be described under the following heads:

1. *Luminescence is an enticement:* That, light is an enticement and it attracts other animals which are captured and utilized as food. The luminous bulb on the fishing tentacle of deep-sea ceratioids, the luminous chin barbels of stomiatoids and the photophores in the mouth of *Chauliodus* are some of the good examples. But there are some arguments against the fact that light emitted attracts the prey. Production of light is supposed to be a hazardous business in the deep sea. However, there is some truth in this hypothesis and it is believed that the light is a lure and it attracts other animals for consumption.

2. *Luminescence confuses predators:* Sudden flashing of photophores or discharge of luminous secretion diverts attention of the predators. Thus, producton of light facilitates an escape of the fish by confusing the enemy. The role is ascribed to the caudal glands of lantern fishes. Luminous secretion is discharged in *Ceratias* from the cephalic luminous glands. In *searsia* the luminous secretion is produced by the sac in the 'shoulder' and the light emitted is very bright.

3. *Luminescence illuminates surroundings:* When the surrounding is dark, there is need for its illumination sometimes. The cheek organ of *Anamalops* is used as a torch. Some stomiatoid fishes also emit beam of light from the luminescent cheek organ to snap the copepods and other small creatures.

4. *Luminescence is a warning signal:* There is much information regarding warning colouration in noxious animals. Some fishes also illustrate this function. For example, the midshipman *Porichthys* possesses a toxic spine. The fish flashes when it is attacked by predatory fish and the latter has to reject.

5. *Luminescence is an intraspecific signal:* In certain fish communities, each species has a definite peculiar pattern of light organs which are capable of providing a recognizable character. The particular light is distinguished by the members

belonging to that species. It is the characteristic feature of the light that enables to keep the members in a separate school (*Anamalops*). Not only this, the light organs of the two sexes may be sometime different but they can easily recognize each other as in the case of lantern fishes. In this case the male has one or many light glands above, but the female below the caudal penduncle, as observed by Marshall (1954). The post-orbital light in several members of melanostomiatidae is larger in male and smaller (or absent) in females. It suggests that the female is guided by male during movement through seawater. In *Porichthys*, when the gravid female becomes luminous the male responds by flashing. Then the male drives the female to the sight of the nest beneath the stone where the female deposits the eggs. This reproductive behaviour has been well observed by Crane (1965).

6. *Ventral luminescence obliterates the object:* In many deep sea fishes the longitudinal rows of photophores face downward (Isospondyli and Iniomi). The ventral body surface seems as bright as the background. The ventral and lateral photophores are so organized that the light emitted is narrowly restricted to a ventral path. When the belly of fish is laterally compressed (hatchet fish) the region lying the shadow below is much reduced. In the deep-sea water the intensity of light is considerably low and light emitted by the lower surface of the fish matches environmental light. Ventral location of light organ is a precautionary measure against the predators. There is abundance of predators in the epipelagic waters. The light emitted in the ventral side is not clearly visible to fishes and other animals above them.

CHAPTER 12

BREEDING, DEVELOPMENT AND PARENTAL CARE IN FISHES

The sexes are separate in fishes but the sexual dimorphism is not a very common phenomenon. Many fishes have a very short breeding season. The secondary sexual characters and accessory structures are necessary for courtship, sexual display and pairing of male and female, simultaneously alongwith the development of primary sex organs. Hermaphrodite gonads have also been reported in some perches, darters, and black basses. Some basses even start their lives as male and eventually become females. Fishes in general are egg laying creatures (oviparous). But, a few groups are viviparous and bring forth their young ones alive. In more than a dozen families in sharks viviparity occurs. In the Amazon molly (*Mollienesia formosa*), only females are produced because the male characters do not pass to the zygote. The males are actually females that undergo a change of sex.

Breeding

Ovaries and testes are paired organs. They are elongated structure lying close to the kidneys. In the breeding season the gonads are much enlarged. The matured oocytes pass to the exterior through the oviduct where the fertilization is external. The oviducts open either by special aperture or by sharing with the kidney ducts. In several bony fishes the eggs are dropped into the body cavity. There is no permanent oviducts and as such the eggs pass out through temporary genital funnels to the exterior. A narrow duct leads from each testis to the genital opening near the anus for the exit of the sperms.

In the viviparous forms (sharks mostly) the fertilization is internal in the oviduct. There are two uteri and each may harbour 7 to 8 young ones during gestation period. There may be more young ones also. The embroys get suspended by the neck of the yolk sac (after the yolk is used up.)

Among the teleosts viviparity is rather rare, however, in some fishes viviparity has been reported as in the surf fishes (Embiotocidae) of the North Pacific and Blennies (Blennoidae), *Lebistes* and *Gambusia affinis* etc. Among the rays, skates and relatives (Rajiformes), ovo-viviparity is a very common feature. *Latimeria,* the living coelacanth is also ovoviviparous.

Fishes attain sexual maturity at different ages. Some fishes are ready to reproduce at the age of one year, others when two or three year old. In eels, the females are ready to spawn at the age of 10 or 11 which is considered as a special feature in a lowly creature like fishes. *Lebistes* and *Gambusia affinis* become sexually mature at the age less than a year.

The time and periodicity of spawning vary from region to region depending on the climatic conditions. In Europe, several food fishes breed in the first half of the year. The spawning season of the plaice (*Pleuronectes*) is January to April and that of Cod. (*Gadus*) in the north sea from February to May. The spawning season of sole (Soles) falls in the month of April and it continues up to July. In India, most of the carps and catfishes breed with the advent of rainy season with a little regional fluctuations. In the eastern part of India, carps and catfishes lay their eggs from June to August, but in the northern regions the spawning season starts from July and continues up to the mid of September. Breeding of *Hilsa* starts in Bengal during the South-West monsoon from June to August but in Orissa it takes place in June-July. *Notopterus* spawns in the month of June, July and August. Some other freshwater fishes like *Clarias, Heteropneustes, Anabas* and *Channa* breed during the monsoon period.

During the breeding season, the fishes (female) lay a large number of eggs. It has been estimated that the Cod, Salmon and Plaice may lay from 250000 to 500000 eggs in a single spawning season.

Development

As soon as the egg is fertilized by the entry of the sperm, the pronuclei of the egg and sperm fuse. Thus the chromosomes that carry the genes come together and a complicated development starts immediately. The division of the zygote starts and a large number of cells are formed. This process of division is known as *cleavage*. The *meroblastic cleavage* is very common among fishes but it may also be *holoblastic* in certain fishes (*e.g. Lepidosiren, Acipenser, Amia,* and *Lepisosteus*). As a matter of fact, the early development of these fishes is almost intermediate between holoblastic and meroblastic cleavage types. In the primitive hagfishes and in the sharks and their relatives (chondrichthyes) the egg is of telolecithal type and cleavage is confined to a small disc of cytoplasm towards the animal pole. It is similar in the bony fishes (osteichthyes). The first cleavage in most of the teleosts (e.g. *Cirrhinus mrigala)* is meridional. The second furrow appears at right angle to the first and thus, four *blastomers* are formed. Further cleavage planes divide the egg vertically and horizontally and as a result *morula* stage is reached after about four hours of fertilization. Cleavages result in the formation of two kinds of cells, blastoderm and periblast cells. The blastoderm cells are mainly responsible for producing the embryo. The periblast cells lie between the yolk, and cells of the blastoderm and cover the yolk mass. They become syncytial and are concerned with mobilization of yolk reserves. The blastulae of several fishes are disc like and hence called blastodiscs. The blastocoele appears between the outer blastoderm and the central periblast which covers the yolk beneath the blastoderm. *Gastrulation* takes place mainly by the methods of *Epiboly* and *Emboly*. The former results in an extension of

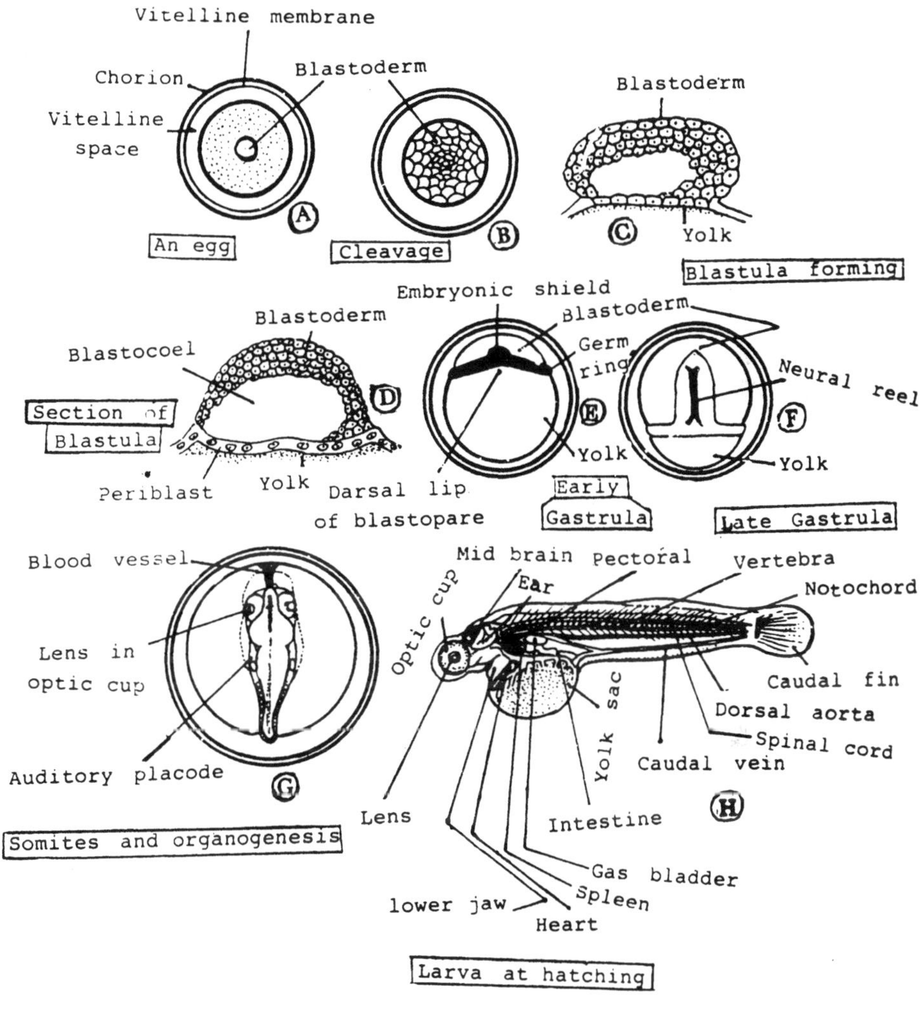

Fig. 49 : Some stages in the development of a teleost

the blastodisc over the yolk and is definitely associated with the growth of the periblast and the formation of *germ–ring*. In the process of emboly invagination of the rim of the blastoderm takes place. This process includes the invagination of material accompanied by marked convergence of invaginating and superficial material. These materials are brought to the dorsal mid-line of the future embryo. The germ ring passes down the equator of the yolk. It is the stage when the process of mesodermal segmentation begins.

As a result of gastrulation, the germinal layers are formed. These layers differentiate and form the developing young fish. When the young one is out of the shell it is known as a *larva* or *fry*. The larval period in some fishes lasts only for a short period, say for few hours. In sea lampreys it lasts for about five years. But, in most of the fishes the larval life is a matter of few weeks.

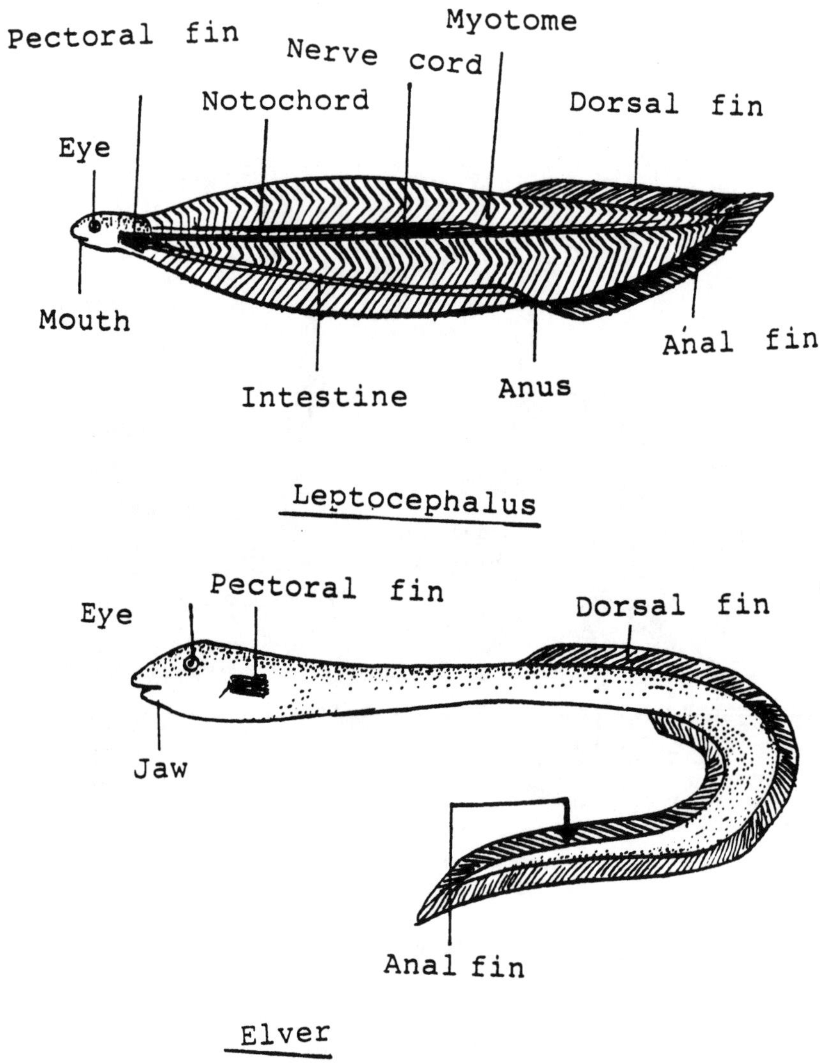

Fig. 50 : Two stages from the life-history of eel

In some fishes, the early larval stages feed on a yolk sac and at this stage larvae are known as *Pro-larvae*. When the yolk is completely used up, the young fish is called an advance fry or *alevin*. A fry loses the larval characters and becomes a miniature adult called "fingerlings". They enter an active feeding stage and further growth takes place. The larvae of the freshwater eels, called *Leptocephali* are flattened and glassy band like individuals. But, after metamorphosis it becomes rounded eel like form just before entering freshwater. The post-Leptocephalus stage which is opaque, pencil-like form is known as *elvers*. The larvae of *Cynoglossus* swim in a vertical upright position but later on, after metamorphosis they adopt the bottom living habit. The eye (lower) moves to the upper side.

Parental Care

Rearing or care of the offsprings is a very important achievement in the trend of evolution. This phenomenon of parental care is well developed in several groups of fishes.

There are various ways and means which facilitate the fishes in overcoming the hostile forces. It is actually very important in perpetuation of the race.

Fishes are lowly creatures and produce millions of eggs every year. There are large number of interesting cases where parents protect and take care of the fertilized eggs and the young ones. Various means for affording care to fertilized eggs and the young ones by one or both sexes among fishes are remarkable. Selection of spawning sites, laying of eggs at suitable places, nest building, protection of eggs and young ones are some of the important aspects of parental care.

Some *anadromous* fishes (*Acipenser, Salmo, Onchorhynchus*) ascend freshwater streams of spawning. The freshwater eels (Anguilla) have a *catadromous* habit, descending into the ocean for laying eggs.

Some fishes are efficient nest builders. The nest may be a simple trough or a hollow cleaned out in the sandy bottom of the stream where the eggs can be laid conveniently. In this case the male guards the eggs. The *Salmon* is a common example in this case.

The mud fish (*Protopterus*) hollows out in the mud of the swamp rich in aquatic weeds and grass which afford protection. This hollow becomes the nest in which the female lays eggs. The nest is built mainly by the male. It is the male who takes care of the eggs. He swims around the nest and chases the predators. Sometimes he aerates the water of the nest for the benefit of the eggs and young larvae.

The African Osteoglossid (*Clupisudis*) makes a nest by cleaning a space in the aquatic vegetation. The nest is built in about 2′ of water and it is about 4′ across. The walls of the nest is several inches in thickness, made up of stems of grasses. The floor of the nest is constituted by the smooth bare ground.

Gymnarchus (Mormyrid) forms a large floating nest projecting several inches above the surface of the water. The opposite end forms an entrance about 6″ below the water.

The nest of *Gasterosteus* is much more elaborate. The male labours hard for gluing fragments of plants together. The glue is a special product of the kidneys. When the nest is ready, the male goes in search of a female who comes and lays some eggs in the nest. Some of the eggs are fertilised by the male. The male again goes in search of another female, courts her also and invites her to the nest. The process is operated till the nest is completely filled up by eggs. The male now guards the eggs till they hatch out and the young ones leave the nest subsequently.

North American *Amia* also constructs a crude nest which is circular in appearance. The nest is placed at the swampy end of a lake rich in aquatic herbage. When the nest is completed one or more females attend. The fertilized eggs adhere to the bottom materials of the hollow. Eggs are guarded by the male. When the young fishes hatch, they leave the nest in a body under the care of the male who keeps them together by encircling around them.

Some catfishes (Amiuridae) of North America make a crude nest in the mud. In this process of excavation both parents share. Sometimes the nest is also placed in crevices in the river banks, beneath logs, under the stones or even in buckets or other receptacles in the water.

Tilapia mossambica (Below)

The young one taking shelter in the female buccal cavity when danger apprehended

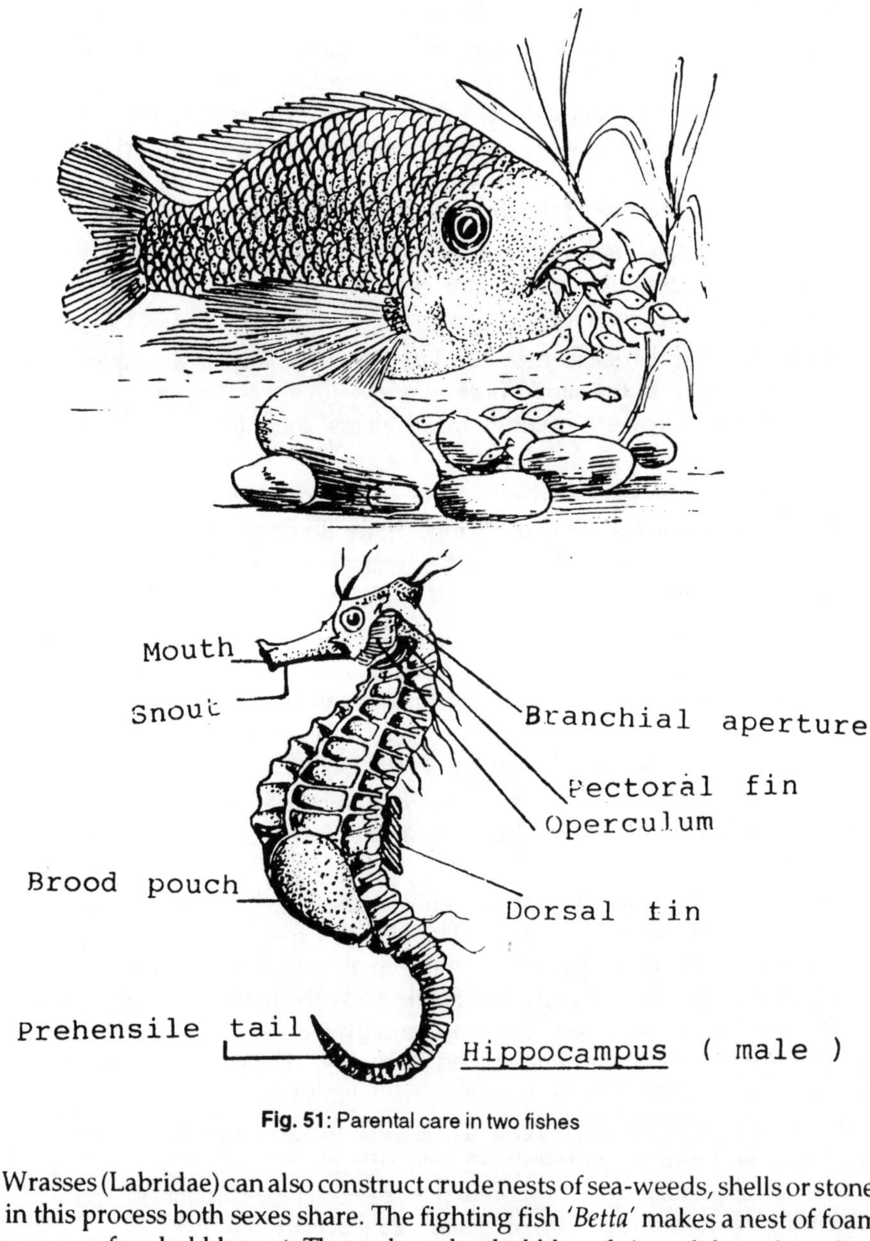

Fig. 51: Parental care in two fishes

Wrasses (Labridae) can also construct crude nests of sea-weeds, shells or stones and in this process both sexes share. The fighting fish *'Betta'* makes a nest of foam. It blows a surface bubble nest. The male makes bubbles of air and then glues them by mucous from his mouth. Thus a dome-shaped floating mass is formed. After elaborate courtship, the females lay eggs which are fertilized by the male. The male catches the eggs in his mouth and after providing a coating of mucous, sticks them to the undersirable of the nest. Finally, about 150 to 200 eggs are massed together in the nest. Both parents guard the nest till the larvae hatch and young ones leave the nest.

The Butter fish (*pholis*) lays its eggs in the valves of empty oyster shells. Sometimes the eggs are also laid in the holes of rocks made by the boring molluscs. The mass of spawn is just like a ball, about the size of a Brazil nut. Both male and female fish cooperate in this operation. Now, whether the male guards the eggs by coiling around them or the female does so, is not clearly known. It is probable that both parents take their turn in guarding the eggs.

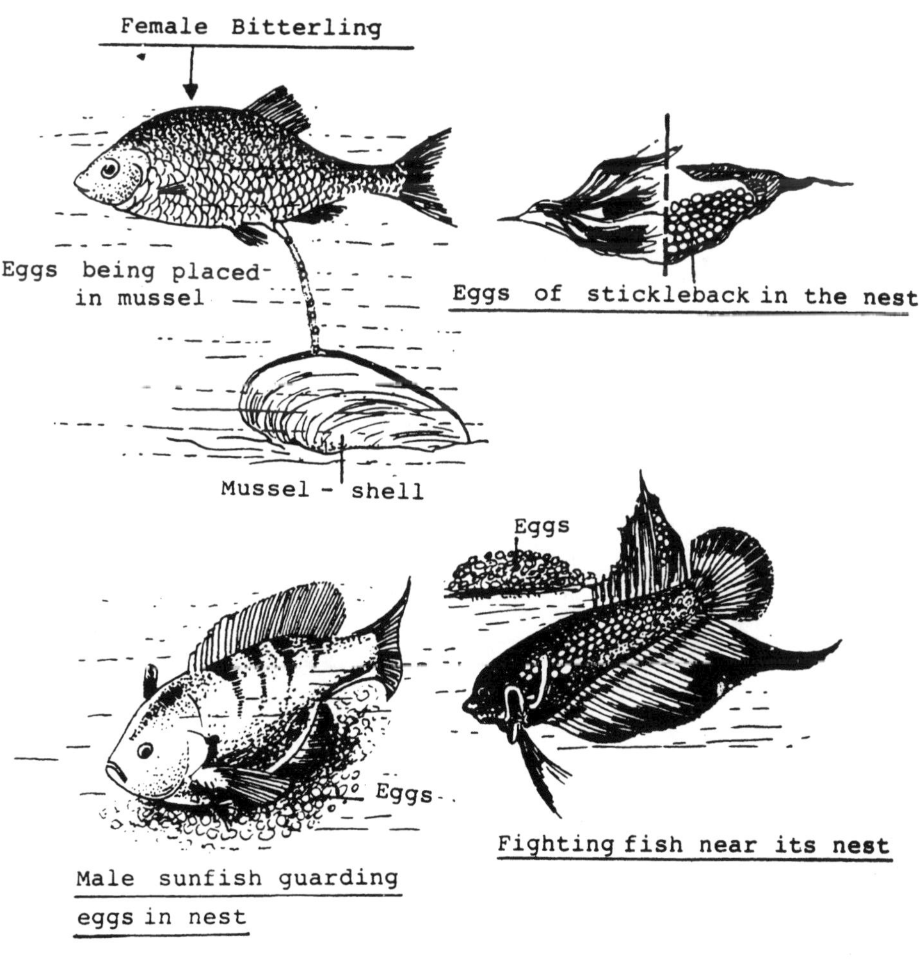

Fig. 52 : Parental care in some more fishes

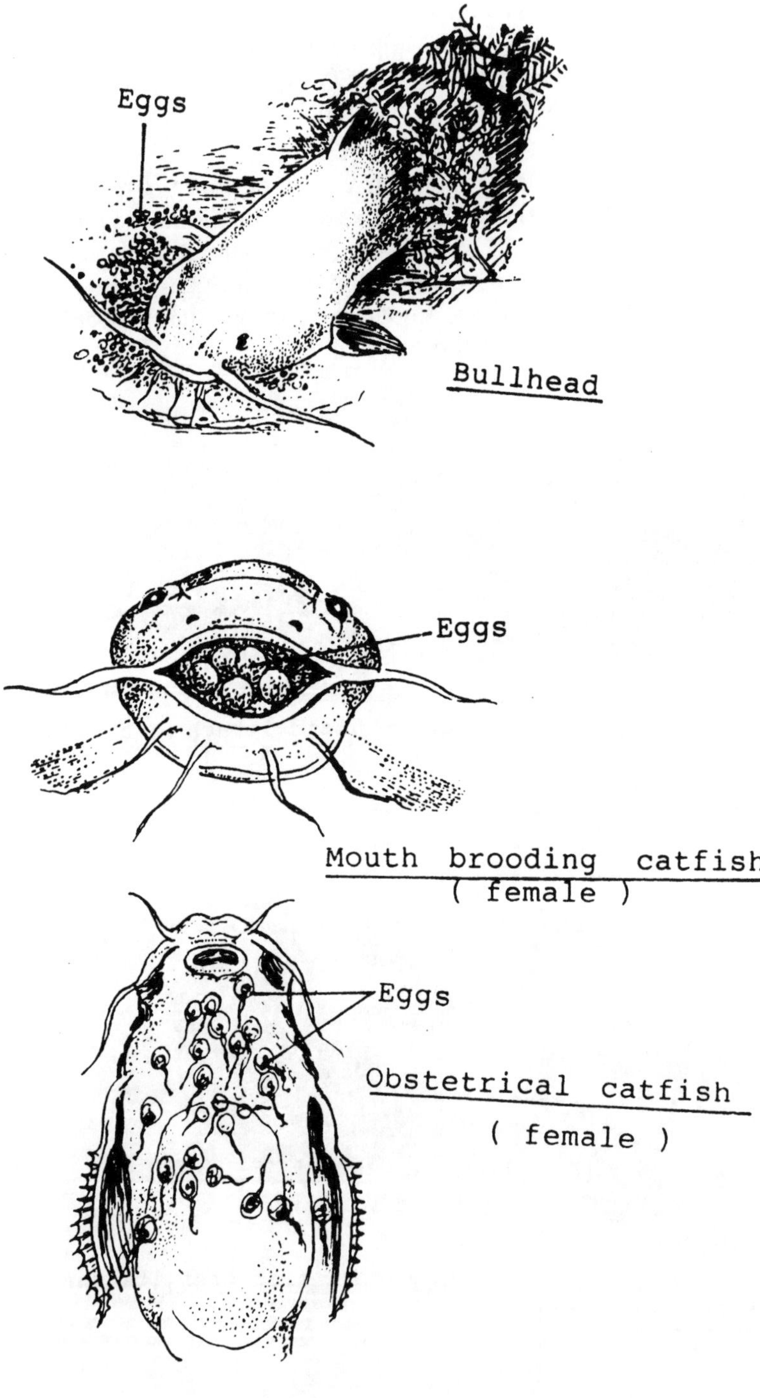

Fig. 53 : Some examples of Parental care

In the genus *Kurtus* (Perciformes), the male has a bony hook projecting from the fore-head. The egg mass becomes attached to this hook in such a way that one bunch of egg lies on either side of the male when he swims in water.

The eggs of the *Rhodeus* (European carp) are deposited in the mantle cavity of the freshwater mussel. The eggs undergo development inside the shell. The eggs are also aerated by the respiratory current of the mussel.

In the Brazilian catfish (*Platystacus*) the lower surface of the body of the female becomes soft and spongy when the skin swells during the breeding season. The female lies on the eggs when they are fertilized. The eggs become attached to the skin by small stalked cup-like structure. The cup is vascular and it nourishes the embryo. Thus the fertilized eggs are fixed until hatched.

In the *Hippocampus* and *Syngnathus*, the eggs are placed by the female in the brood pouch of the male. The brood pouch is present beneath the tail. During the breeding season the brood pouch becomes thick and vascular. The vascular wall of the brood pouch nourishes the developing embryos. The eggs are transferred into the male brood pouch with the help of genital papilla developed in the cloaca of the female. It acts as an intromittant organ. When the embryo is completely developed, certain apertures in the pouch become visible and through these apertures, miniature sea horses come out.

In the marine catfishes (Aridae) the male undertakes the care of eggs. The eggs are collected in his mouth. They are retained in the mouth during the entire period of development. During this period the male completely stops feeding.

The African cichlid fishes also carry the eggs in the mouth and this duty is performed by the female in this case. Even after hatching the young fishes do not leave the shelter of the maternal mouth so easily. Later on, they swim about in small shoal, accompanied by their parents.

In the Brazilian fish, *Loricaria typus,* the lower lip of the male enlarges to form a pouch and becomes suitable for labial incubation of the eggs. In two catfishes, *Bagre marinus* and *Galeichthys felis,* the mouth is employed as an oral incubator. Each male carries in his mouth 10 to 30 developing eggs. The African fishes, *Tilapia mossambica* are called "mouth brooders" because the newly hatched young ones escape at times of danger into the oral cavity of the female.

Recently, Coyer (1982) has reported that in giant kelp-fish, *Heterostichus rostratus,* the male guards the eggs after the spent female leaves. Male defence of the egg-laden nest is vigorous against all cospecifics and some algae searching fish predators.

CHAPTER 13

LARVIVOROUS (LARVICIDAL) FISHES

The relationship between fishes and mankind is very important. Some species of fishes are themselves of little food value but they are of immense utility to public health because of their larvivorous feeding habits. These fishes always prefer larvae of several insects as their favourite food. Thus such fishes are of great importance, because they control the spread of several dreadful diseases like malaria, filaria, yellow fever etc. which are caused through the agency of insects. These diseases can be eradicated with the help of these fishes by gradually decreasing insect population. This biological control of larvae destruction is the best way of controlling the adult insect population. Several larvicidal fishes feed upon mosquito larvae and as such, their introduction in different water bodies will definitely control the population of mosquitoes most effectively. Contributions on larvicidal fishes, including their feeding habits are those of Atkins (1901), Chaudhuri (1909), Bentley (1910), Sewell and Chaudhuri (1912), Prasad (1919), Covell (1927), Hora (1927), Chatterjee (1934), Hora and Nair (1938), John (1940), Chacko (1948), Chacko and Ganpati (1949), Hora and Mukherji (1953), Singh et al. (1977) and others.

Qualities of Larvicidal Fishes

(i) They should be smaller in size.

(ii) It should be capable of free breeding, irrespective of nature of water composition.

(iii) It should have little food value.

(iv) These fishes should not be so delicate, rather they should be hardy to withstand the adverse ecological conditions.

(v) It should be a carnivorous fish and its main diet should be insect larvae.

Important Larvivorous Fishes

A large number of species of fishes, both indigenous and exotic, are larvivorous in nature. Some of them have been listed below :

1. *Gambusia affinis* (a cichlid) — An exotic fish
2. *Lebistes reticulatus* (a cichlid) — An exotic fish

3.	*Carassius carassius* (a cyrinid fish, commonly known as 'gold fish'	—	An exotic fish
4.	*Aplocheilus lineatum* (a minnow)	—	An indigenous fish
5.	*Oryzias melanostigma* (minnow)	—	-do-
6.	*Aphanius dispar* (a minnow)	—	-do-
7.	*Amblypharyngodon* (a cyprinid)	—	-do-
8.	*Danio rerio* (a cyprinid)	—	-do-
9.	*Rasbora daniconius* (a cyprinid)	—	-do-
10.	*Esomus danricus* (a cyprinid)	—	-do-
11.	*Puntius sophore* (a cyprinid)	—	-do-
12.	*Colisa faciata* (anabantid)	—	-do-
13.	*Barilius vagra* (a cyprinid)	—	-do-
14.	*Notopterus notopterus* (an osteoglossid)	—	-do-
15.	*Oxygaster* (a cyprinid)	—	-do-

Gambusia affinis is only 2 1/2" - 3" in size. It has great liking for the larvae of mosquitoes and hence sometimes known as mosquitoes fish. Certain species of *Gambusia* (e.g. *G. affinis holbrooki*) can be kept in the aquarium also. It starts breeding only when it is 1 1/2" in length. Maturity in this fish is reached only after four months. It depends on water temperature and food supply. It is a successful destroyer of mosquito larvae and they are extensively used for this purpose not only in India but also in California, Hawai, Formosa, Philippines, Burma, Japan and some other countries. It has been reported that this fish is able to consume 165 larvae in 12 hours. It can survive even under ice sheets and mud. *Gambusia nicaraguensis* is about 2 1/2" in size and it starts breeding when it is 2" in length. Temperature requirement of this fish is between 50° and 90°F. Various species of *Aplocheilus* (*A. punchax, A. lineatus*) are highly efficient larvivorous fish. They feed on ants, larvae of mosquitoes and several insects. They are 3" in size and breeding takes place only in the adult fishes.

Oryzias melanostigma is also a very efficient larvivorous fish. It is only 1 1/2" in length. This fish matures earlier in brackish water, than in fresh water.

Hora and Mukherjee (1953) have classified the larvicidal fishes into following groups on the basis of efficiency in mosquito control. These groups are :

(1)	*Typical surface feeders*	—	e.g. *Gambusia* and *Aplocheilus* etc.
(2)	*Surface feeders*	—	e.g. *Oryzias, Lebistes* etc.
(3)	*Sub-surface feeders*	—	e.g. *Carassius, Rasbora, Danio, Esomus* etc.
(4)	*Column feeders*	—	e.g. *Puntius, Colisa, Anabas* etc.
(5)	*The fry of carps* also destroys the larvae	—	e.g. *Labeo, Catla, Mugil* etc.
(6)	*Predaceous fishes*	—	The young, adult and fry, all are destructive to larvivorous species and other fishes. They are not suitable for mosquito control.

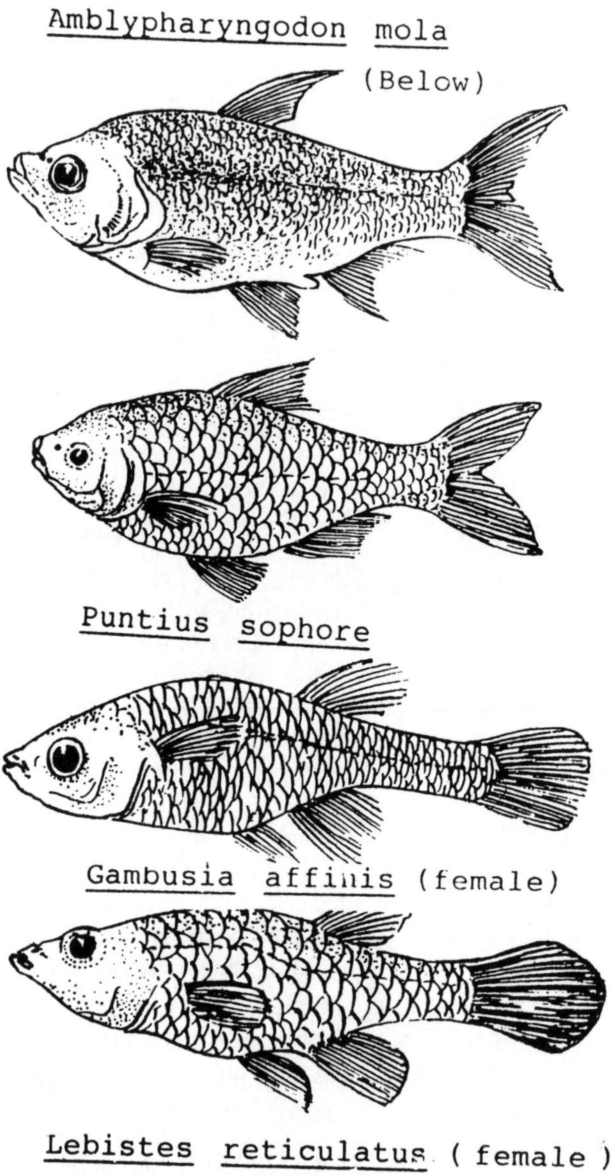

Fig. 54 : Some larvivorous fishes

For mosquito control, larvicidal fishes are introduced into various water bodies where mosquitoes breed. The predatory fishes should be completely removed. The vegetation in the water body should not be so dense. The most suitable stocking ratio recommended for *Aplocheilus* is two females and one male, however, for *Gambusia* it is one male and one famale for effective control of mosquitoes in a small body of water.

CHAPTER 14

HILL-STREAM FISHES

The fast flowing hill-streams, rivers and rivulets call for a special modification of the fish fauna. The individual modification is chiefly manifested in being small sized and development of certain structures mostly for adhesion. Of course, there are some internal adaptations also. Now the hill-stream fishes are being recorded from several new places and more and more species have been discovered. Some fishes temporarily inhabit the hill streams and migrate at certain periods of their lives for specific purposes. But, several others live permanently in the rivers and streams of the hills. Several structural modifications have been encountered in the fishes living in hill-streams. There is great range of variation of characters in the hill-stream fishes. Some important contributions on the various aspects of hill-stream fishes are those of Chaudhuri (1909), Jenkins (1910), Hora (1921, 1922, 1923), Menon (1954, 1964), Haws and Goodnight (1961), Menon and Datta (1964), Lal *et al.* (1966), Badola (1972, 1975), Ganguly *et al.* (1972), Ganguly and Datta (1973), Tilak and Hussian (1974), Joshi and Tondon (1977), Bhatt and Singh (1981), Jayaram (1981), Singh *et al.* (1981), Shah and Agrawal (1985), Sharma and Joshi (1986), Channa and Hajam (1989), Pandit and Yousuf (1989), Singh *et al.* (1989), Hussain (1989) and others.

Important Hill-Stream Fishes

The important hill-stream fishes include—*Garra, Balitora, Bhavania, Psilorhynchus, Parasilorhynchus, Schizothorax, Noemacheilus, Barilius, Barbus, Crossocheilus*—All belonging to order—Cypriniformes and family—Cyprinidae). Also, *Glyptosternum, Glyptothorax, Pseudoeheinis, Laguvia* and *Erethistes* (All belonging to the order Siluriformes and family—Sisoridae) are on the record. Mishra (1984) has reported several species of hill-stream fishes from Nepal-Bihar border. Some important among them are—*Labeo dyocheilus* (McClelland), *Labeo microphthalmus* (Day), *Puntius terio* (Ham.), *Garra gotyla sternohynchus* (Jerdon), *Botia geto* (Ham.), *Lepidocephalus annandalei* (Chaudhuri), *L.thermalis* (val.) and *Noemacheilus rupicola* (Mc Clelland).

Conditions in the Hill-Streams

The fishes living in the hill-streams are influenced by the following conditions:

(a) The fauna is considerably influenced by the current of water. The water current is stronger in comparison to rivers and streams on the plains. Fishes develop adhesive organs for attachment to rocks and other objects.

(b) Because of rapid flow of water some types of vegetation can not grow, however, there is abundance of algae on the stones and rocks. There is scarcity of insects and their larvae. Thus, some modifications are in accordance with the availability of food materials.

(c) Hill-stream fishes always require some shelter where they can hide themselves.

(d) As the hill-streams are shallow, fishes have to bear intense sunlight.

(e) Because of continuous rapid flow, the water is well aerated and the oxygen content is higher in comparison to other waters.

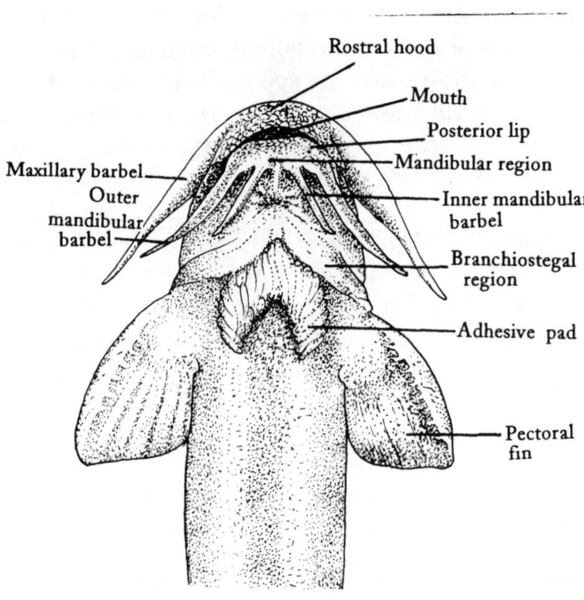

Fig. 55 : Ventral view of anterior region of *Glyptothorax*

Modifications in the Hill-Stream Fishes

There are several external and internal modifications in the various systems of these fishes which have been described below:

(1) *Changes in the external form*: Strength of the current has much to do with the shape and size of the fishes. The size of the fish is very small and it is convenient for them to move in the fast flowing stream. They can easily hide under the stones and rocks. Some of them are dorsoventrally flat (*Balitora, Garra* and *Glyptosternum* etc.)

and in some cases the body becomes leaf like (e.g. *Glyptothorax* and *Pseudoecheneis*). The ventral profile in several fishes is straight but the dorsal profile is slightly arched, as in *Garra* species. The head in several fishes is small with pointed snout. The shape of the body is such that it offers least resistance while passing through water.

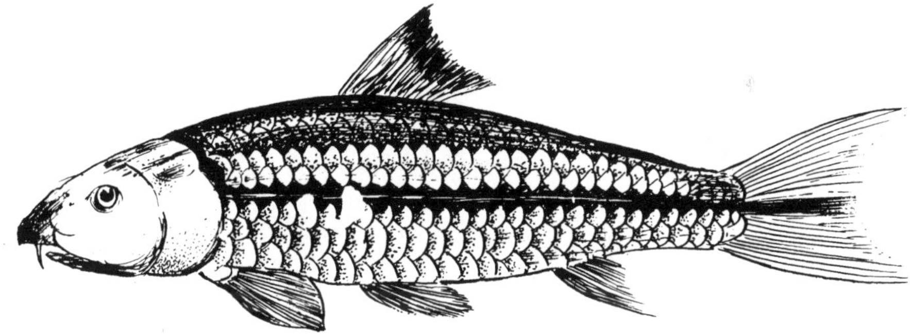

Garra sp.

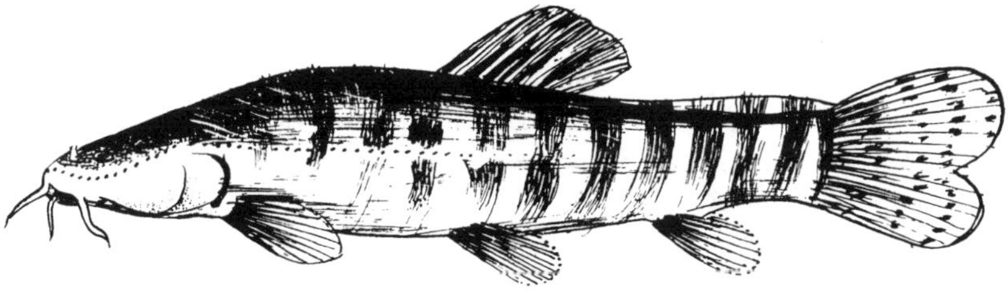

Noemacheilus montanus

Fig. 56 : Two Hill-stream fish

(2) *Scales*: In the cyprinid fishes living in hill-stream, the scales are small in size and partly embedded in the skin. Scales are reduced or absent on the ventral surface. In *Schizothorax* and *Noemacheilus* scales are very minute and they are embedded in the skin. In most other fishes, ventral scales disappear in the chest region which is

employed for adhesion. In some species, scales are absent except in the scapular and anal regions. Absence or reduction of scales probably lessens the resistance of the fish during its movement through water.

(3) *Paired fins*: In the hill-stream fishes, the paired fins are used for adhesion also. They require powerful muscles and also other structural modifications. There is increase in the number of outer fin rays. They become thick and flat. The paired fins are shifted onwards and come to lie horizontally just to facilitate adhesion to rocks and other objects. In *Pseudoecheneis* of the Himalayas there is plaited disc between the pectoral fins which help in adhesion.

(4) *The caudal fin and its peduncle*: Hill-stream fishes have long, narrow, band-shaped caudal peduncle which is supposed to be an adaptation for life in fast flowing water of the stream particularly at high altitude, as in the case of some species of *Noemacheilus, Glyptothorax striatus, G. saisii etc.* Also, the lower lobe of the caudal fin is larger than the upper one as in *Garra nausta* and *Glyptosternum labiatum*.

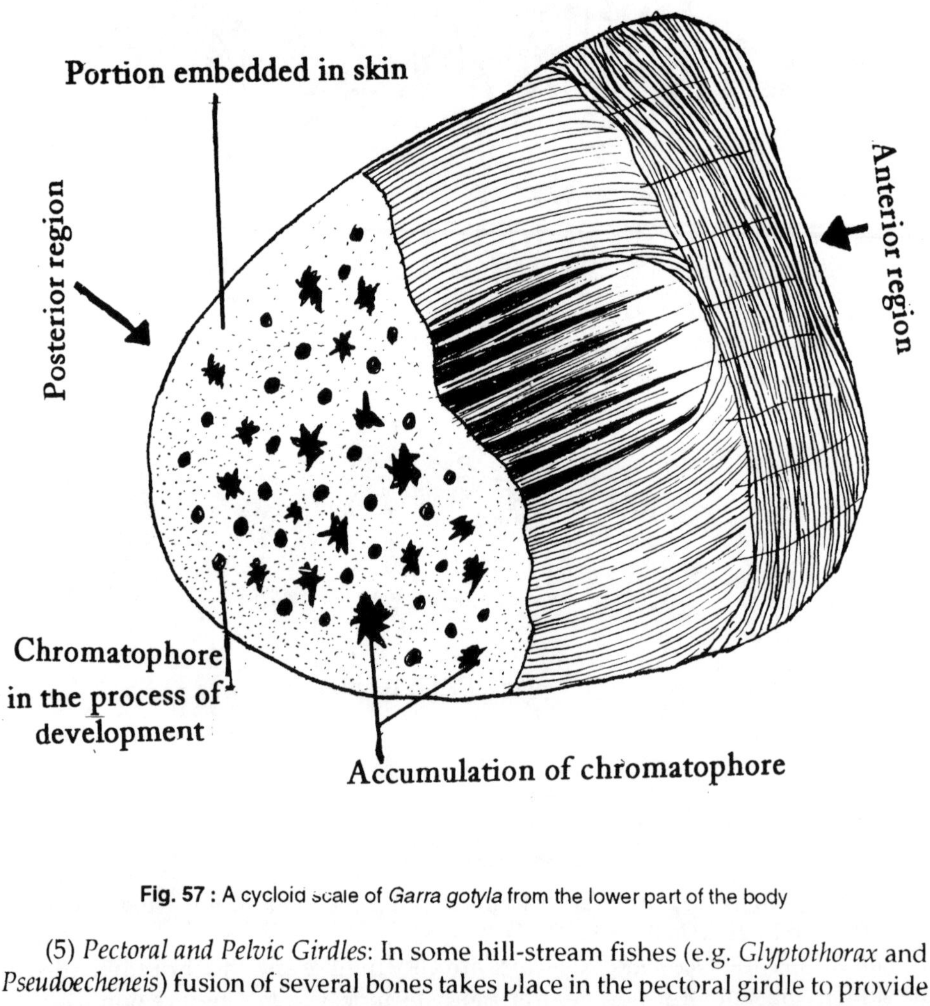

Fig. 57 : A cycloid scale of *Garra gotyla* from the lower part of the body

(5) *Pectoral and Pelvic Girdles*: In some hill-stream fishes (e.g. *Glyptothorax* and *Pseudoecheneis*) fusion of several bones takes place in the pectoral girdle to provide

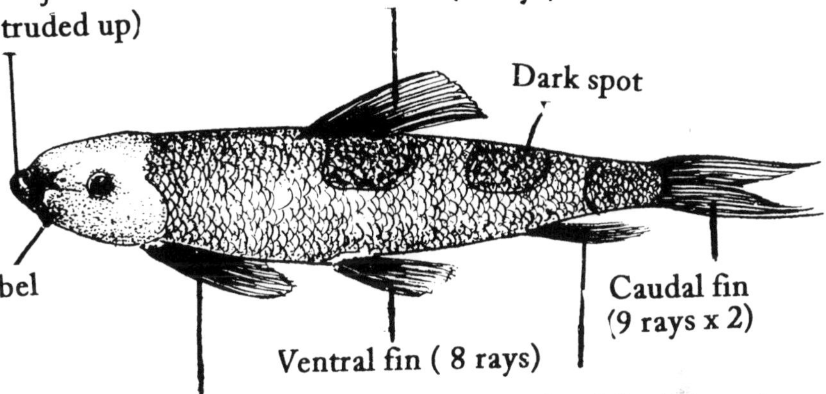

Fig. 58 : *Garra notata* (Lateral view)

strength. There is slight modification in the shape of the girdle, owing to horizontal position of the fins. Keel-like elevated ridges are present on the ventral surface of the inner clavicular bone which provides suitable attachment to their muscles. The ridges end posteriorly in spine like process. Adductor and abductor muscles attached to the girdles are well developed. Certain other muscles also develop to make the movement of the spine convenient. In Pelvic girdle also, there are some special muscles which help in keeping the fins closely pressed against the rocks and stones.

(6) *The Mouth, Lips and Barbels*: The mouth in several hill-stream fishes is crescentic or semicircular in shape and ventral in position, far behind from anterior end of snout. The jaws are strong and covered with horny covering to be employed to scrap off the algal food from the rocks and stones. The barbels are much reduced because the longer barbels would have been inconvenient during movement through water. Barbels are short, thick and fleshy at the base in *Pseudoecheneis* and *Glyptothorax.* In Noemacheilus the lips are modified to form sucker like arrangement. In *Balitora,* lips are cut to form tentaculate process and form an effective sucker capable of adhesion. In *Glyptothorax* and also *Glyptosternum,* the lips are spread around the mouth and forms a broad sucker for adhesion to rocks and stones. In *Glyptothorax pectinopterus,* the anterior lip is covered and masked by rostral skin. Rostral hood has a pad-like appearance near the mouth and has fleshy backward extensions on either side.

(7) *The Eyes*: The eyes of the hill-stream fishes are smaller in size, the larger eyes are not favourable in the fast flowing streams with intense light. The eyes are generally placed dorsally near each other. *Balitora brucei, Glyptothroax, Glyptosternum* and *Pseudoechenies etc.* bear typical small eyes.

(8) *Gill openings and Branchiostegal rays*: Gill openings are restricted to sides only. The openings are much reduced and as such, respiration suffers a bit. However, as the water is well aerated, it can be retained in the branchial chamber and the pectoral fins are kept in constant motion and thus the problem of respiratory difficulty is solved. In *Garra* the gill openings are wider.

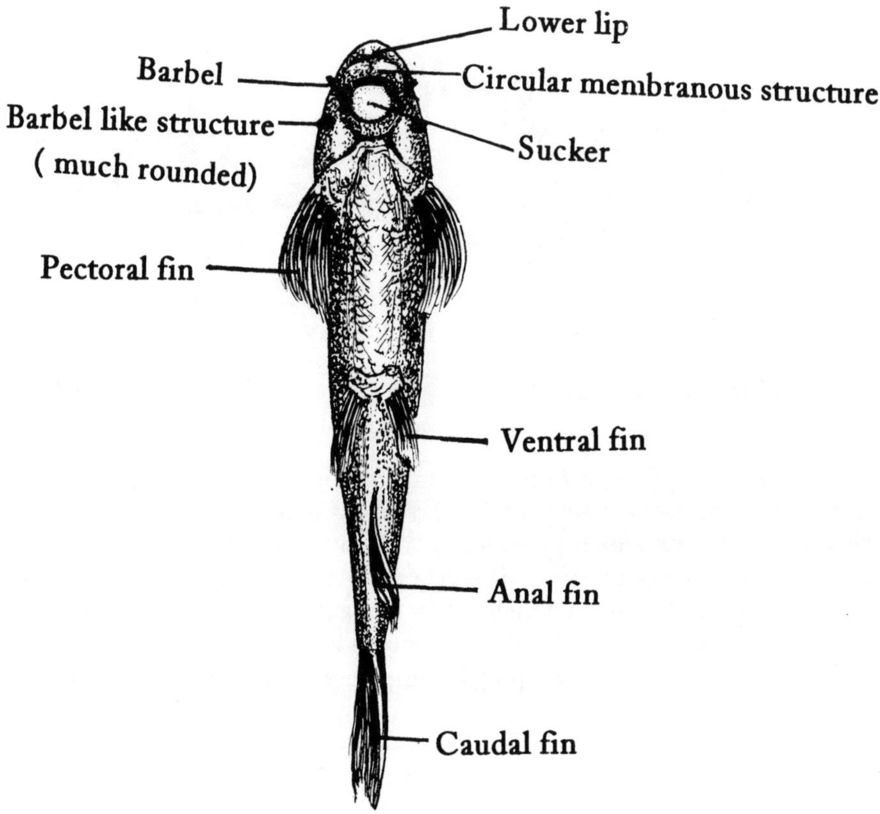

Fig. 59 : *Garra notata* (Ventral view)

The branchiostegal rays and membranes are very much reduced in the hill-stream fishes. The reason may be backward shifting of the mouth and reduction of gill slits. In *Glyptothorax pectinopterus,* the ridges and grooves of the region of branchiostegal rays arise from a pit-like depression situated midventrally on the posterior margin of the mandibular region.

The grooves and ridges run obliquely towards the antro-ventral side of the pectoral fin. The integument of ventral surface of the branchiostegal rays are obliquely fluted. The surface is on the whole, rough.

(9) *The Air Bladder*: There is considerable reduction in the size of the air-bladder because it is useless as a hydrostatic organ on the hill-stream fishes. The air bladder is normally encapsulated by a bony case. In *Noemacheilus botia,* the anterior chamber of air bladder consists of two laterally situated halves connected to each other by a median ventral transverse canal enclosed into a bony case. Each half of the capsule opens laterally by a wide aperture. The posterior chamber is wanting in the adult. In most of the cases (e.g. *Glyptothorax, Glyptosternum* and *Pseudoecheneis),* the

airbladder is divided into two lateral chambers, connected with each other by a short narrow transverse tube.

(10) *Skin and Other Modification*: The skin is modified in several ways to form organs of adhesion. It forms the suckers, cushion like pads and grooves and ridges in different parts of the body for the purpose of adhesion to rocks and stones. In *Glyptothorax pectinopterus* there is a thoracic adhesive pad. It consists of an inverted 'U'—shaped area lying just posterior to the region of the branchiostegal rays and in between the two pectoral fins. It has longitudinal ridges and grooves alternately arranged. In *Glyptosternum* and *Pseudoecheneis* also the skin on the ventral side of the body in between the bases of the pectoral fins is thrown into grooves and ridges. In *Erethistes elongata,* striations are well marked on the chest and belly. Striations are also present on the chest of *Laguvia.* In the case of *Pseudoecheneis sulcatus* also, the adhesive apparatus is present on the chest which consists of transverse ridges and folds. The under surface of the barbels and the skin at their bases are striated in *Glyptosternum,* of course, not in all the species. In *Garra,* the adhesive organ is present in the form of a suctorial disc of semicartilaginous pad present on the chin formed of the lower lip.

Histology of the Adhesive Apparatus

The epidermis is formed of several layers of cells which are of different shapes and size. The cells rest on the connective issue layer. The outer layer of epidermis is modified into stiff and strong spine like processes resting on the homogenous protoplasmic layer. The spines are slightly curved. The rectangular cells are arranged in layers just below the epidermis. A prominent nucleus is situated normally in the centre of each cell. Below the rectangular cells there is layer of the columnar cells (Pillar-like cells), followed by a loose connective tissue sheet.

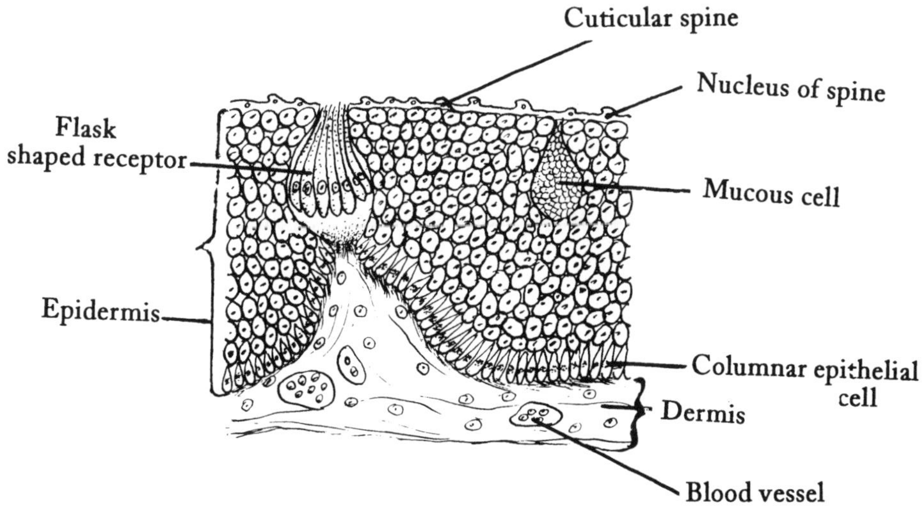

Fig. 60 : A part of the transverse section through the posterior lip of *G. pectinopterus*

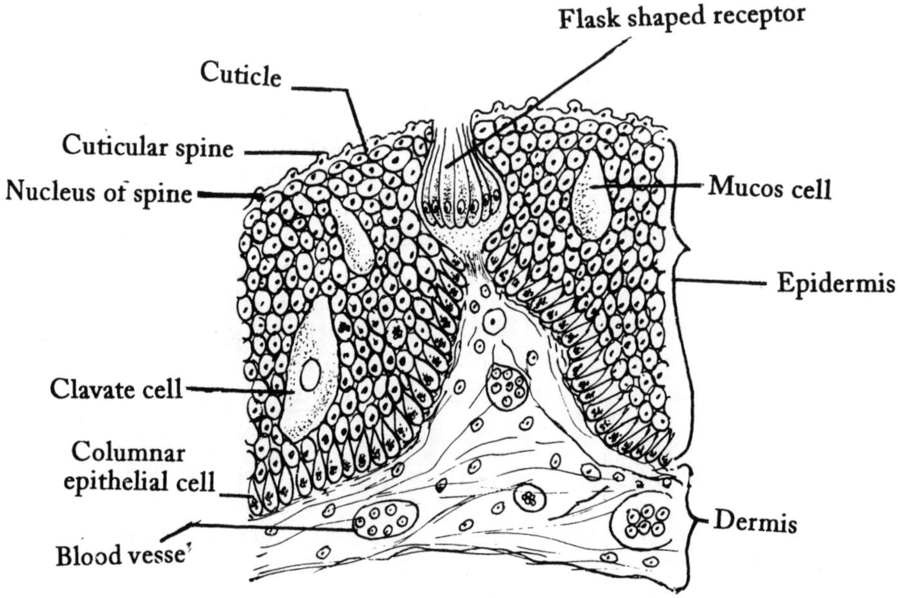

Fig. 61 : A part of the transverse section through rostral hood of *G. pectinopterus*

In *Glyptothorax pectinopterus,* the outermost layer of adhesive pad consists of non-cellular cuticle which is thin and transparent. The cuticle is produced into a large number of stiff elongated pointed spines. There is an oval granule at the base of each spine. Below the cuticle, there is a single row of rectangular beak-shaped cells. The cytoplasmic beaks are directed posteriorly. Each beak-shaped cell contains a larger rounded nucleus with a prominent nucleolus. The base of the beak-shaped cell is flat. Below the beak-shaped cells are present 4 to 5 tiers of rounded cells which are known as *formative cells.* The formative cells of the upper tiers are bigger in size in comparison to the lower cells. Towards the inner side of the formative cell, there is a layer of closely packed cloumnar cells with finely granular cytoplasm. All the cellular layers described, constitute the epidermis and the latter is followed by the dermis, made up of connective tissue, blood vessels and nerves.

The histological picture of the lip reveals that the cuticle is produced into short cuticular spines. The cells below the cuticle are lossely packed . These cells are oval or circular. The deepest layer of the epidermis is composed of a single row of columnar cells. In between the epidermal cells, there are flask-shaped and spherical receptors. Each receptor is made up of 8 to 12 cells. The free outer ends of the receptor cells have hair-like protoplasmic processes which project up to the surface of the cuticle. The receptors receive their nerve and blood supply at the base. Few *clavate* and mucous cells are also seen in the epidermal region.

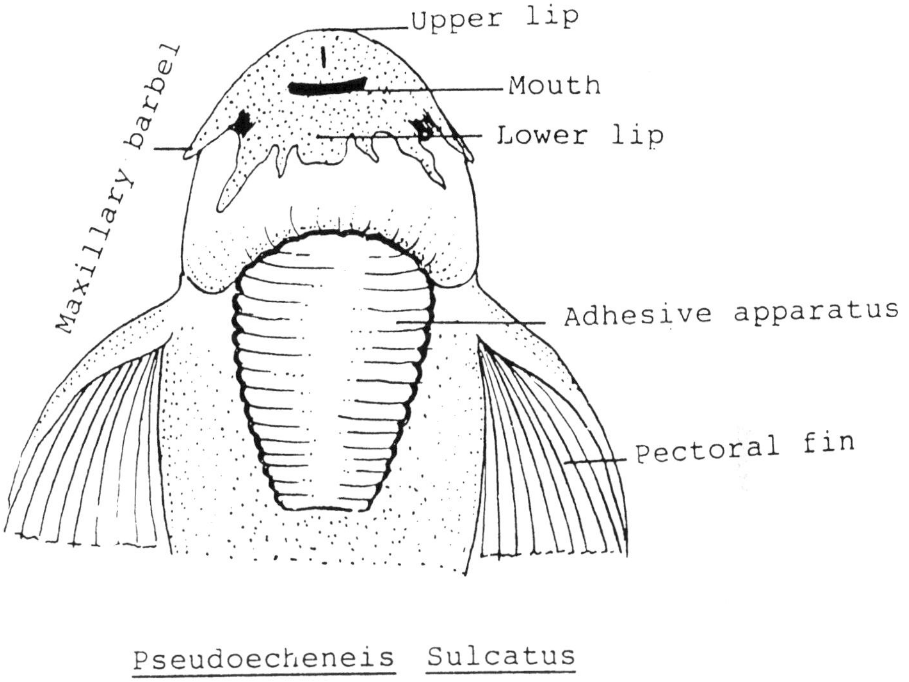

Fig. 62 : Adhesive apparatus of hill-stream fish

Comments on the alimentary canal: Some hill stream fishes are carnivorous and some are herbivorous. The alimentary canal is adapted in accordance with particular feeding habit of the fish. For example, *Glyptothorax pectinopterus* is a carnivorous fish and in this case the alimentary canal is a short and straight tube. *Garra gotyla* is basically a herbivorous fish and as such the alimentary canal is typically of herbivorous type having longer and coiled intestine. Thus adaptations in both the cases are strictly in accordance with the nature of diet. A longer intestine is found in a fish whose food is poor in nutritional substances. The poor development of folds in

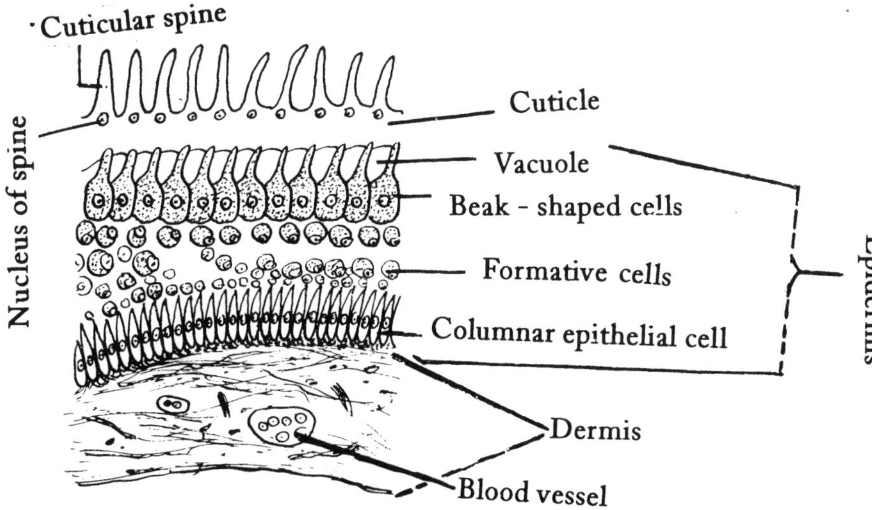

Fig. 63 : A part of transverse section through the thoracic adhesive pad of *Glyptothorax pectinopterus*

mucosa is compensated by a long intestine which sufficiently increases the absorbing surface. Longer intestine in *Garra gotyla* ensures the extraction of nutritional matters. So, a long intestine compensates for the poor development of folds in the mucosa and high folds increase the surface of the mucosa as in *G.pectinopterus,* to compensate for a relatively short intestine. Modifications are in accordance with the availability of food materials also.

Origin of the Hill-Stream Fishes

This issue has been critically examined by Hora (1922). Whether the fishes reached the hill-stream accidently or step by step colonisation took place was for sometime a controversial issue. But on the basis of some facts it has been accepted by all schools of thoughts that the fishes, originally living in the sluggish water of the plains slowly ascended the hill-streams in search of food and shelter. Subsequently, they acquired characters making them suitable for living in the hill-streams. There is no possibility of reaching these fishes in the hill-streams accidently.

Crossocheilus latius can be conveniently placed between specialised hill-stream forms and the fishes of the plains. The overalll structure of *Garra* suggests their gradual evolution from sluggish water forms. According to Hora (1920), the developmental stages of *Garra* recapitulate the history of the evolution of this genus. So, there are several examples to support this concept of origin.

CHAPTER 15

EXOTIC AND TRANSPLANTED FISHES

Fishes imported in a country for culture purpose are known as Exotic fishes. This culture is known as "exotic fish culture" as such. Exotic species are mostly superior quality fishes and they can tolerate climatic changes and quickly adapt to the new environment. Indigenous species of fish are definitely economical and easy to culture, still there is need to culture exotic fishes. Suitable indigenous species are not always available. Also some available indigenous species are not up to the mark as the cultivable fish.

The exotic fishes include the game fishes (*Salmo trutta, Onchorhynchus nerka* etc.) food fishes (*Tilapia mossambica, Ctenopharyngodon idella, Cyprinus carpio, Puntius javanicus* etc.) and larvivorous fishes (*Gambusia affinis, Lebistes reticulatus* etc.)

Regional transplantation of certain species of fish have also been practised in India and it has been found to be quite profitable. *Labeo* species have been successfully transplanted from Bengal to Madras. The milk fish *Chanos chanos* and bekti, *Lates calcarifer* have been found to survive in freshwaters of Madras. *Mugil cephalus* and *Polynemus tetradactylus* can also be acclimatised to freshwater. The fingerling stages are most suitable for transplantation purpose.

Cyprinus carpio is the most suitable species of fish which has met most of the requirements. It is cultivated in Asia for more than 2000 years and in Europe for about 600 years. For fish culture, economic and commercial considerations are very important.

Some notable works on various aspects of exotic and transplanted fishes including their feeding habits and breeding are those of —

Chen and Lin (1935, Lin (1935, 1964), Kulkarni (1939,1946), Bhimachar *et al.* (1944), Hofstede (1949), Panikkar and Tampi (1954), Saanin (1955), Chow (1958), Kuronuma (1958, 68), Alikunhi and Chaudhuri (1959), Hickling (1959, 1967), Menon *et al.* (1959), Aliev (1961, 1963), Chang Kong Tam (1962), Hora and Pillay (1962), Vinogradov *et al.* (1963), Alikunhi and Sukumaran (1964), Berg (1964), Wu and Chung (1964), Tang (1965), Alikunhi (1966), Saring (1966), Chaudhuri *et al.* (1967), Singh *et al.* (1967), Woynarovich (1968), Alikunhi *et al.* (1971) and others.

Description of Some Exotic Fishes

Some important exotic fishes have been described below :

(1) *Trout : Salmo trutta fario* (Brown trout), *Salmo gairdneri gairdneri* (Rainbow trout) and *Salmo gairdneri irideus* are the important species of game fishes which have been introduced into India. *S. trutta fario* was introduced in 1863 from England. They have been introduced in to Kashmir (1901) and Kerala (1909) also. Some members of this species have been imported from Japan also and they were introduced into Nilgiris (T.N.). *Salmo gairdneri gairdneri* have been imported from various places like England, Newzealand, Germany, Japan and Ceylon and their transplantation is successful in Nilgiris (T.N.) since 1968. *S. gairdneri irideus* species were also imported from England and were introduced into parts of India like Kashmir (1904, 1912), Kerala (1940), and Nilgiris (1967). *Salvelinus fontinalis* (brook trout) has been imported from Canada in 1968 and has been introduced into Kashmir and Himachal Pradesh. *Onchorhynchus nerka* has been introduced into Nilgiris from Japan (1968). *Salmo salar* has been introduced into Kashmir from North America in 1968.

(2) *Carassius carassius* : They are commonly known as crucian carp or the golden carp. They are food fishes but they are larvicidal in nature. They were brought from England in 1874 and introduced into Nilgiris waters. They have also been transplanted in Andhra Pradesh farms. It can breed in ponds throughout the year.

(3) *Tinca tinca* : They are known as tench. They are food fishes and are the native of central Europe. They were introduced into Ootacamund (T.N.) from England in 1874. They have now fully acclimatised into cold waters of Nilgiris. Attempts are being made to transplant them in plains also.

(4) *Cyprinus Species:* The common carp is the native of temperate regions of Asia but it is now conveniently cultivated in different parts of the world. There are three varieties of this fish.

(i) *Cyprinus carpio* Var. *specularis* (Mirror Carp)

(ii) *Cyprinus carpio* Var. *communis* (Scale Carp)

(iii) *Cyprinus carpio* Var. *nudus* (Leather (Carp)

The mirror carp was introduced for the first time in 1939 from Ceylon into Nilgiris. Later on they were carried to Bangalore and in 1947 they were introduced into Nainital lake. Some fishes were introduced into Kumaun Humalayas. The Scale carp was brought from Bangkok in 1957 and transplanted in Cuttack. All the above varieties are fast growing omnivorous species. The leather carp is also successfully cultured in Ootacamund lakes. The mirror carp is well established in Kashmir, Himachal Pradesh, Bihar, Manipur, Sikkim, Delhi and other places. It is supposed to be an ideal fish for hilly areas particularly. They are food fishes.

(5) *Hypothalmichthys molitrix* : This fish is also known as Silver carp. It is a food fish. In India, the silver carp was was brought from Japan in 1959 and transplanted in Cuttack. The Silver carp is the native of China but to-day it has been introduced into Burma, Philippines, Hongkong, Japan, U.S.A., Malaysia, Pakistan, Ceylon,

Nepal, India and other countries. This fish breeds in the rivers of China and Japan but in India they breed when pituitary injection is administered. The silver carp grows very fast and they can be cultured along with *Catla catla* in ponds.

(6) *Ctenopharyngodon idella* : This fish is commonly known as the grass carp. It is also a food fish. It was brought to India from Hong Kong in 1959 and was introduced into the ponds of Central Inland Fisheries Research Station at Cuttack. Now from India this fish has been sent to Nepal, Philippines and Burma. The male fish matures at the age of 2 years, but the females mature at the age of three years. They can be bred successfully by hypophysation. The grass carp and the silver carp can tolerate slightly brackish water. At the age of three years the individual fish can attain a weight of up to 7 kg.

(7) *Osphronemus goray* : It is commonly known as gourami. This fish was brought from Java and Mauritius in as early as 1865 and they were introduced into Nilgiri and also Calcutta. This fish can not survive below 15°C. It breeds in ponds and streams. Parental care is important for this fish. Male and female take part in nest building. Eggs laid are fertilized by the male. Both parents guard the nest. It is a good fish with an excellent flavour on the flesh. They have now been introduced into Bengal, Orissa and Bombay.

(8) *Tilapia mossambica* : These fishes are originally found along the east coast of Africa. They were however imported from Bangkok in 1952 and were introduced in Mandapam for the first time by Central Marine Fisheries Research station. Tilapia fries feed on zooplanktons and phytoplanktons but the adults are exclusively herbivore. They are commonly called mouth brooding cichlid (because of the reason that the female keeps the eggs in the mouth). They can be cultured in several environments including saline waters. It breeds at the age of two months. Breeding takes place throughout the year except in subtropical climate where reproduction is interrupted during cold season. Vass and Hofstede (1952) have recorded that the incubation period in this is 13 to 21 days but Panikkar and Tampi (1954) reported it to be 10 to 14 days.

Growth and survival rates are very high in this fish. These fishes are not suitable for culture along with carp because the biological balance is disturbed. *Tilapia* is a food fish.

(9) *Gambusia affinis* : It is commonly called the mosquito fish. It was imported from Italy in 1928 and it is now widely distributed in parts of India. They feed effectively at the surface of the water on the wriggling larvae of mosquitoes. In male, the pectoral fin is modified as claspers. Live bearing is highly developed in this fish. The fish becomes sexually mature at ages less than a year when it is an inch only or less.

(10) *Lebistes reticulatus* : It is commonly known as the guppy. It was brought from S. America in 1908. It belongs to the family poeciliidae to which *Gambusia affinis* also belongs. It is a larvivorous fish. It also becomes sexually mature at the ages less than a year and when it is not more than an inch. Live bearing is also highly developed. In males of this fish, members may be of variable sizes at the same age. It has movable

spatuliform teeth. This fish is well distributed in Rameshwaram, Thanjavur, Madras city, Malabar, Cuddapah and Kurnool etc. in Southern parts of India. This species has been recorded by Babu Rao *et al.* (1975) for the first time from Kulbhor river near Loni in Maharashtra.

(11) *Puntius javanicus* : They are commonly known as *tawes*. It is a food fish and was imported from Indonesia in 1972. It is a column feeder and was introduced for weed control. When chance permits, they can feed on the larvae of mosquitoes also. It was for the first time introduced into Kalyani (W.B.). It breeds in pond with riverine conditions. Hypophysation has been practised for breeding purpose in India. It has been reported that a single female lays 100000 eggs weighing about 600 g. The hatching period is 14 hrs.

Concluding Remarks

Now the exotic fishes are being successfully cultured in different parts of India without any harm to the existing indigenous forms. The indigenous fauna is not harmed by the introduction of exotic fishes, but sometimes the balance of natural fauna is up set. *Tilapia* is incompatible with the major carps with respect to food and space. The population of *tilapia* in pond goes on increasing, resulting in overcrowding if care is not taken towards their frequent removal. During the breeding season this fish makes pit at the bottom and this habit is considered as a menace to the growth of bottom living algae. As the bottom living algae form the vital food of *chanos*, the culture of *tilapia* and *chanos* in one pond is not suitable.

CHAPTER 16

CLASS-DIPNOI

The Dipnoi (double breathers) is an important group of bony fishes which evolved during the Devonian period. They are also known as "Lung-fishes" and actually represent a transitional group between fishes and amphibians. Several fossil forms like—*Dipterus* (Dipteridae), *Phaneropleuron, Dipnorhynchus, Uronemus (Uronemidae), and Ceratodus* (Ceratodontidae) are on record. But, the members of only three genera are surviving at present and they are *Neoceratodus, Protopterus* (Protopteridae) and *Lepidosiren* (Lepidosirenidae). There are four important species of *Protopterus.* They are *P. annectans, P. aethiopicus, P. dollei* and *P. amphibius*. Of the *Neoceratodus, N. forsteri* is a common species.

Class-Dipnoi comprises only two orders: *Monopneumona* (with sinlge lung) e.g.*Neoceratodus,* and *Dipneumona* (with double lungs) e.g. *Protopterus* and *Lepido-siren paradoxa.*

The earliest fossil fish represented by the genus *Dipterus* was a fish of the middle devonian age which possessed many of the generalized choanate characters like—long fusiform body, strong heterocercal tail, archipterygial type paired fins, two dorsal fins and large heavy cosmoid scale. Some specialized features of this fish were: poorly ossified brain case composed of numerous bony plates, particularly ossified jaws, and dentition highlly specialized with suppressed marginal teeth in both the jaws.

The central line of dipnoan evolution led to ceratodus which were distributed during the Triassic and subsequent period of the Mesozoic era.

Living Forms of Dipnoi

There are three living forms of the lung fishes included in the class Dipnoi. They have been described below:

(1) *Neoceratodus:* These are found in the Burnett and Mary rivers of Queensland (Australia). It has stout and cylindrical body and may attain a length of 6 feet. They are most primitive among the living forms and resemble the lung fishes of Triassic age. It has highlyvascular lung. It can not live without water. They frequently come to the surface and breathe air. This fish is able to walk along the bottom of the rivers

or ponds by using paired fins. It is a direct descendant of ceratodus. It has pointed head with large rounded scales all over the body. There is great reduction in the internal skeleton including the skull bones. Elongated and leaf shaped paired fins are present, the fleshy portion of which is covered with scales. Simplified tail is known as a *gephyrocercal* fin formed by the fusion of original dorsal, caudal and anal fins.

(2) *Protopterus:* It is found in rivers and marshes of West Africa. This fish is less bulky than Neoceratodus. It can live for months without water. With the advent of dry season, it burrows into the mud leaving one or more openings on contact with the outer air. It has one pair of lungs. The paired fins are reduced to long, slender whiplike appendages. They are characterized by *gephyrocercal* tail.

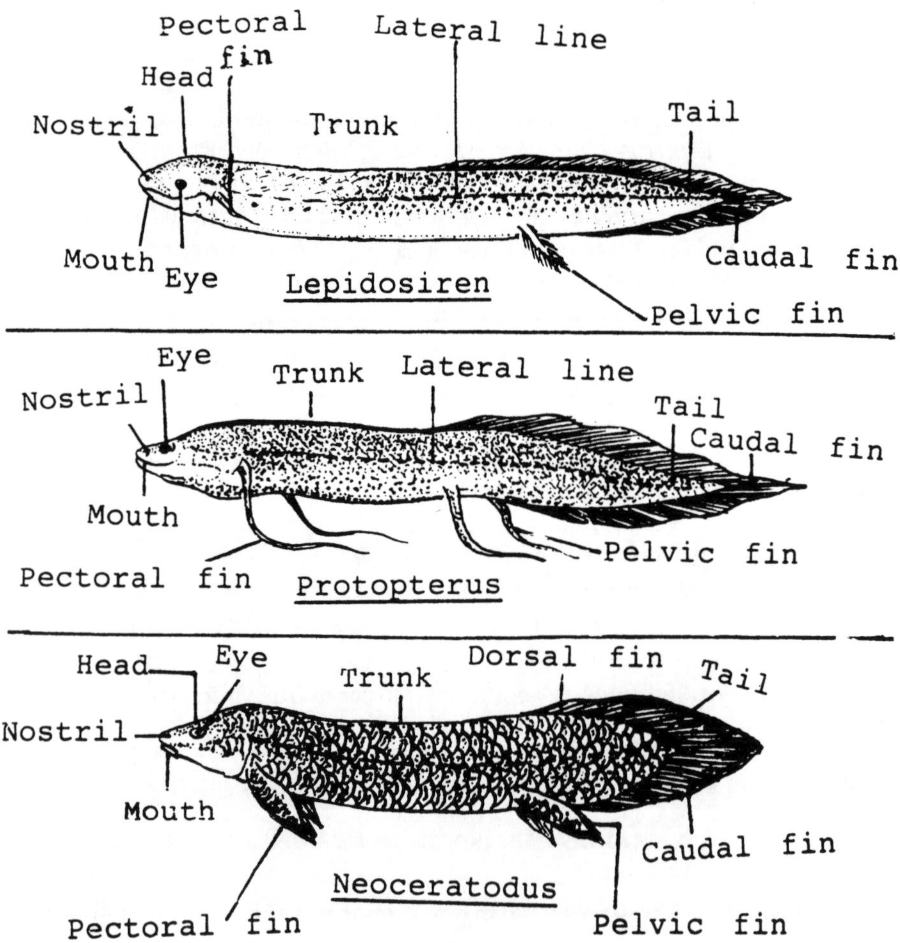

Fig. 64 : Lung Fishes (Living)

(3) *Lepidosiren:* They are found in the swamps of the Amazon basin (South America). They are eel-shaped creatures with small scales. It has two lungs. In dry

season it also burrows in mud like *Protopterus.* There is great reduction of paired fins in this fish and as such they look smaller. Like *Protopterus* it has gephyrocercal tail showing evolutionary trends similar to that of *Neoceratodus.*

General Character of Dipnoi

1. Paired fins are more or less acutely lobate and there are overlapping cycloid scales which are embedded in the dermis. In *Dipterus* the scales were covered with a layer of *cosmine.* In the living dipnoi paired fins are supported by jointed dermal fin rays which are bony in nature. The fins are of the archipterygial type. The tail is diphycercal with continuous dorsal and ventral median fins. Dipterus had a heterocercal tail, there were two separate dorsal and one anal fin.

(2) Two internal nostrils are present on the ventral surface of the skull and open into the roof of the mouth, facilitating aerial respiration as in frog.

(3) The skull is *autostylic* i.e hyoid arch does not take part in the formation of suspensorium. Large dental plates are firmly fused to the bones of the jaw. They are composed of thick dentine.

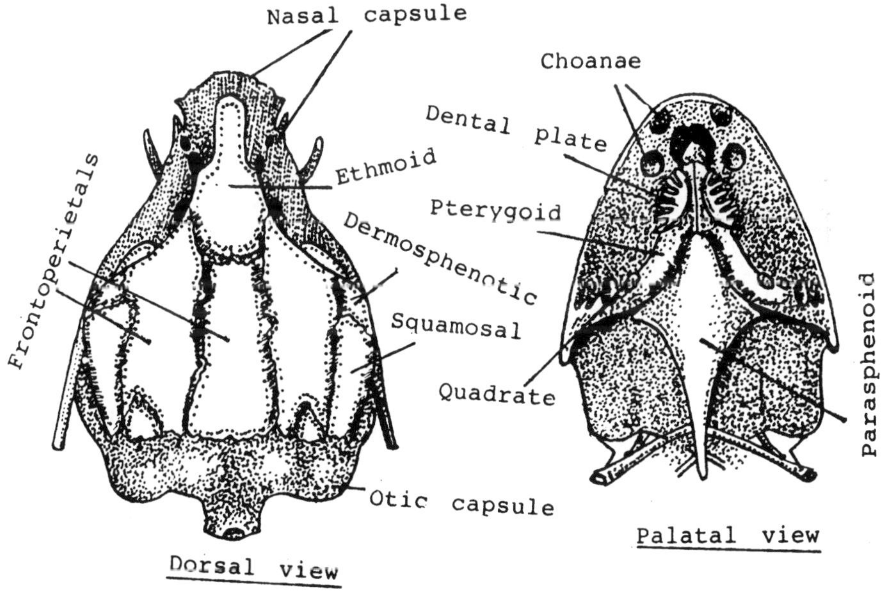

Fig.65 : Skull of *Neoceratodus*

(4) There is only one external branchial aperture and there is absence of spiracles. The air bladder is highly developed to form a breathing lung having cross-septa and alveoli. Lungs are well vascularized.

(5) There is a persistant and unconstricted notochord covered with a fibrous sheath. The skeleton is largely cartilaginous.

(6) In the skull, premaxillae, maxillae and the nasal are absent. The hyomandibulars are also absent. Dentaries are absent in the lower jaw and teeth are borne by the coronoids. There is great reduction in the ossification of the skull.

(7) Mouth is situated on the ventral surface of the head. The pharynx leads into the oesophagus. The oesophagus is connected with the stomach and the latter leads into the intestine. The rectum opens into the cloaca which opens by an aperture at the root of the tail. The liver is bilobed. The gall bladder lies between the two lobes of the liver. The pancreas is embedded in the intestinal wall. There is a well developed spiral valve in the intestine. Hepatic caecae are absent.

(8) In the brain single optic lobe is present. The cerebral hemispheres are quite large. The Pineal body is also present.

(9) In Neoceratodus there is only one lung but in *Protopterus* and *Lepidosiren* there are two lungs. Both aquatic and pulmonary respiration take place in the lung fishes. In Protopterus, only the 4th and 5th branchial arches bear gill filaments though there are six branchial arches. An anterior hemibranch is there on the hyoid arch and a posterior on the 6th arch.

Four pairs of gills are present in *Neoceratodus.* Each branchial arch bearing a double row of gill filaments. The fifth branchial arch is gill-less. In the larvae of Lepidosiren, four pairs of functional gills are present.

(10) In lung fishes the heart is almost three chambered like the Amphibians. The atrium is completely divided into two chambers by interauricular septum but the sinus venosus is imperfectly divided into two chambers. Blood (oxygenated) returning through the pulmonary vein enters the left side of the atrium, while the deoxygenated blood is poured into the right side of the sinus venous and enters the right auricle. Then by means of the spiral valve within the conus arteriosus, blood from the right auricle changes its direction towards the last (4th to 6th) aortic arches. From here, some of it can get into the lungs, while oxygenated blood from the left auricle is shifted towards the openings of the arteries leading to the head. Thus

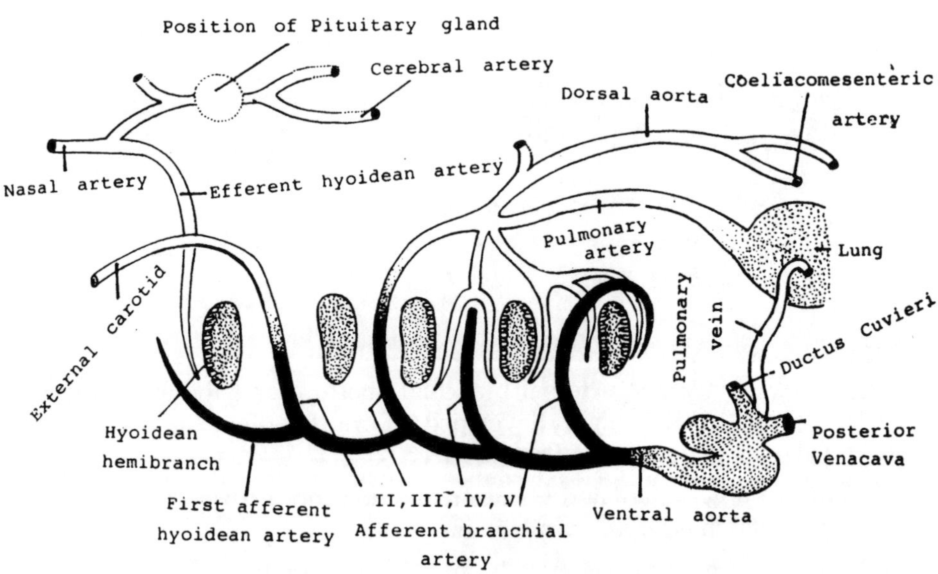

Fig. 66 : Blood vascular and respiratory systems in *Protopterus*
(Partly based on Parker and Haswell)

venous blood goes into the posterior branchial arches and carried to the lungs finally. So, both branchial and pulmonary circulations are met with.

There are generally four functional gills each a holobranch and supplied therefore by aortic arches 3rd to 6th. The afferents are always one per arch in Dipnoi and each holobranch carries two efferents. From near the dorsal end of each 6th arch, there arises a pulmonary artery to the lungs. In larval lung fishes, capillary loops supply the external gills from the branchial arches 4th to 6th.

(11) One pair of mesonephric kidneys are present. They discharge into the cloaca through the ureters. In the female one pair of ovaries are present. Oviducts open anteriorly into the coelom. They join posteriorly and open into the cloaca. In the male, one pair of testes are present which are close to the kidneys. The process of spermatogenesis is performed by the anterior part of the kidney but the posterior part acts as a vesicula seminalis. The two vasa deferentia join and open into the cloaca. Mullerian ducts are present in the vestigial form.

Affinities of Dipnoi

Characters of Dipnoi show that this group has not undergone much change during the long period of its existence. From time to time they have been linked with several groups of fishes, and amphibians but finally they have been given the status of a separate class because of the presence of several striking features.

A few important points of resemblance with the different groups have been mentioned below:

(A) *Affinity with Elasmobranch*— because of—
  (i) Cartilaginous endoskeleton present
  (ii) Persistent notochord
  (iii) Spiral valve in the intestine.

(B) *Affinity with Holocephali*—on the ground of—
  (i) Nature of dental plate
  (ii) Autostylic jaw suspension
  (iii) Position of Lateral line system.

(C) *Affinity with Ganoid fish*—because of—
  (i) Structure of paired fins
  (ii) Cosmoid scale (similar)
  (iii) Air bladder modified as lungs.

(D) *Affinity with teleost*— On the basis of—
  (i) Similar lobate fins
  (ii) Cycloid scale with consmine layer
  (iii) Operculum covering the gill opening
  (iv) Resemblance with actinopterygii in the structure of paired fins.

(But, for presence of lungs, autostylic jaw suspension, diphycercal caudal fin etc. they were supposed to be distinct).

(E) *Affinity with Amphibians :*

The points of resemblance between the modern dipnoans and amphibians are as follows:

(i) Lungs are present for breathing in addition to gills

(ii) Resemblance of Blood Vascular System as described already

(iii) Larvae of *Protopterus* and *Lepidosiren* possess external gills like tadpole larva of frog.

(iv) Autostytlic jaw suspension

(v) Presence of cloaca in both groups

(vi) Pulmonary artery and pulmonary vein present.

(vii) Large cerebral hemisphere and small cerebellum

(viii) Similar mode of development

(ix) Three-chambered heart in Dipnoi, like amphibians

(x) A pair of external nostrils opening in to the buccal cavity.

But, there are some specialised characters also, possessed by the members of this group (Dipnoi) and because of these characters the amphibian affinity has been ignored.

These characters are:

(i) Loss of premaxilla and maxilla

(ii) Lack of ossification in skull parts

(iii) Specialized tooth plates

(iv) Fusion of verterbrae in the back of the skull

(v) Ventral ribs

(vi) Structure of paired fins.

Conclusion

Thus the relationship of Dipnoi with fishes and amphibians seems to be deceptive. All the characters possessed by Dipnoi are not present either in fishes or in amphibians. Only a few resemblances are supposed to be due to convergent evolution. Some zoologists held the opinion that Dipnoi are the direct ancestors of amphibians. But this view has been ruled out. Lung fishes seem to be physiologically transitional between fishes and amphibians. According to Romer "the lung fishes are not the ancestors but the uncles of the land dwellers" because the ancestral Dipnoi and crossopterygii are supposed to have been derived from a common stock as conceived by Watson.

There is a general agreement that Dipnoi evolved as a well defined side branch of the bony fishes by the mid-devonian time and were certainly derived from the ancestral *Crossopterygian* stock from which the Osteolepids and *Coelacanths* arose. This concept seems to be more convincing. The South American and African lungfishes have diversed as side branches from the ancestral stem of dipnoan evolution. Thus Berg's view of giving the Dipnoi the status of an independent class is plausible.

There is absence of Dipnoi in the oriental region. As we know, the lungfishes do not occur in India at present, but there are evidences that they were present in the geological past. The fossil remains of Dipnoi (genus—*Ceratodus* Agassiz) have been found in the Maleri beds of the Godavari Valley during the Upper Triassic period, which spread to the Southern hemisphere reaching the area of Assam. Probably during the Upper Cretaceous time they dispersed to South Africa, South America and Australia. Such idea has been proposed by Hora and Menon (1952) and Menon and Prasad (1961).

CHAPTER 17

CLASS-HOLOCEPHALI

The Class Holocephali includes three living representatives today and they are *Chimaera, Callorhynchus* and *Harriotta*. All are found in the deep sea oceanic waters. They are the distinct offshoot of the earliest cartilaginous fishes of the Mesozoic era and flourished in the cretaceous. The best known fossil example of the lower carboniferous time is the *Helodus*. Some important extinct representatives of the class Holocephali are : *Squaloraja* and *Myriacanthus.*

Chimaera monstrosa (Chimaeridae) is a very active fish and is commonly known as rat fish or king of herrings. They eat small invertebrates and fishes. They are poor swimmers and move by undulations of the back half of the body. It has an elongated pointed rostrum. They are abundant on the coasts of Japan, Europe, Australia, New Zealand, North America and Africa. The Pectoral fins are large and fan like, and the tail is elongated into a long whiplash. In the male, there is a club-shaped frontal clasper on the head (Cephalic clasper). In front of the each pelvic fin there is an anterior clasper armed with denticles in addition to ordinary clasper behind the fin. Thus there are five claspers in all. In the mouth there are crushing plates instead of the teeth. A skin flap (operculum) covers the gills on each side. The tail appears to be diphycercal in this fish.

Callorhynchus antarticus is commonly found in the South Pacific. It has a pointed rostrum produced forward and ending in ventrally directed position serving as a tactile organ. In the male, a frontal clasper is also persent. Its tail is clearly heterocercal.

Harriotta is found in the North Altantic. It has a prominent elongated, tapering and depressed rostrum. The pectoral fins are very large. In this the frontal clasper is absent and other claspers are smaller in size. The tail is not turned in the upward direction.

External Features

The body is shark like in appearance. *Chimaera* is about 2 feet long but some fishes reach a length of 6 feet. The mouth is small and it is present in the ventral side. There is a single nasal aperture and four pairs of gills covered by cartilaginous operculum on each side. They open outside by a single branchial aperture. Eyes are very large. There is absence of spiracle and there is no cloaca. The urinogenital aperture and anus are quite separate and distinct. There are two dorsal fins and a ventral fin. The 2nd dorsal fin in *Chimaera* is much elongated. Pectoral fins are very large but pelvic fin is small. The first has cartilaginous spine. The lateral line is grooved in *Chimaera* but a closed tube in *Callorhynchus*. Skin is generally smooth and silvery. In *Chimaera* the placoid scales are restricted to certain parts of the body. *Callorhynchus callorhynchus* has a peculiar extended snout, part of which is turned back, below and infront of the mouth. This is a pad supplied with nerves and is sensory in nature.

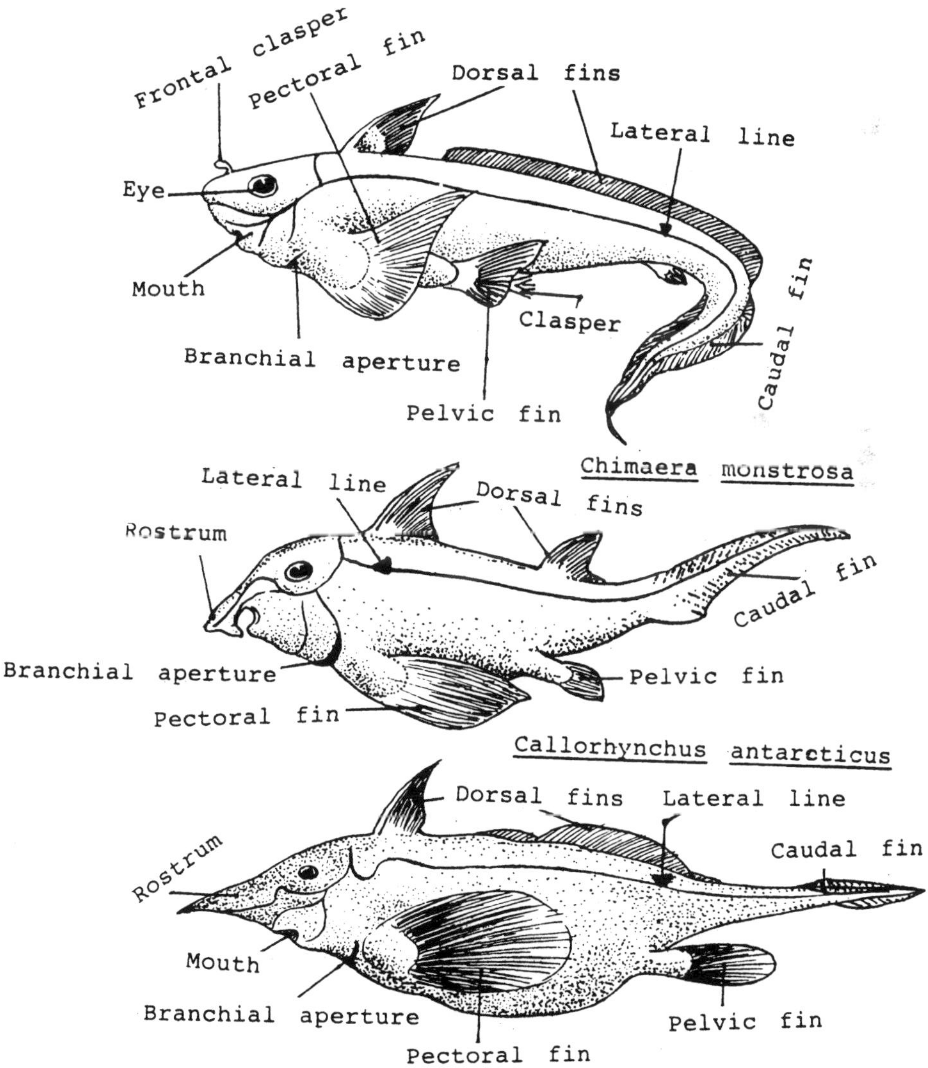

Fig. 67 : Members of Holocephali

Endoskeleton : The endoskeleton is cartilaginous. The vertebrae are reduced to separate nodules and the notochord is persistent and uncostricted. The palato-quadrate is fused with the neurocranium, providing support for the lower jaw. Mouth has crushing plates, two pairs in the upper jaw and one pair in the lower jaw. They have not enamel but vitrodentine and reduced pulp cavities. An inter-orbital septum is present dorsal to the brain case. Two halves of the pelvic girdle are not fused. In the notochordal sheath of *Chimaera* calcified rings are embedded. The neutral arches of the first few vertebrae are fused providing attachment to the first dorsal fin in the form of a plate. In *Callorhynchus,* the snout is supported by three cartilaginous rods which grow from the cranium. These rods are very much reduced in chimaera. The skull is *holostylic*. The Pitutary fossa is comparatively deep and inclined backward. The *condyle* is saddle-shaped articulating with the vertebral column. The hyoid resembles the branchial arches. Above the *epihyal* there is a small cartilage, the *pharyngohyal.* In the first dorsal fin the *pterygiophores* are fused in a single plate.

Digestive Tract : Teeth are present in the form of strong plates with irregular surface and sharp edges.

In the upper jaw there is one pair of *vomerine teeth.* Behind the vomerine teeth there is a pair of large *palatine teeth.* In the lower jaw, there is a single pair of large *mandibular teeth.*

The alimentary canal is straight. There is no true stomach, and there is a special valve in the intestine. Mouth is adapted to crush the small invertebrates and fishes with the help of plates.

Nervous System : The cerebral hemispheres are small in size and they are spindle-shaped. The medulla oblongata is laterally produced into large frill-like body which is known as the *restiform bodies.* The diencephalon is long, thin and trough-shaped. The olfactory peduncle bears at its extremity, a compressed olfactory bulb. The Pineal body is small and rounded and has a hollow stalk. The Pituitary body has intra and extra-cranial portions.

Respiratory System : There are three pairs of *holobranchs* (complete gills), two *hemibranchs* (half gills). The fifth branchial arch is gill-less. The holobranchs are present on the first three branchial arches, one hemibranch is present on the first three branchial arches, one hemibranch is present on the anterior face and another on the posterior face of hyoid.

Blood-Vascular System : The blood-vascular system of Holocephali resembles that of Scoliodon in all essential respects. The heart consists of *sinus venosus, atrium, ventricle* and *conus arteriosus* like dogfish. *Conus arteiosus* has three rows of valves.

Urino-Genital Organs : The main excretory organ is in the form of a pair of lobed deep-red kidneys which are short and stout in comparison to scoliodon. They are slighthy longer in males. The anterior part of the kidney consists of true uriniferous tubules. The kidney is segmented both anteriorly and posteriorly. The posterior part is narrow.

A large number of mesonephric ducts arise from the kidneys and they mostly open into the vas deferens, however, the last six open into the uninogenial sinus. In the female the ducts open into the urinary bladder (urinary sinus).

The female reproductive organs comprise a pair of ovaries, large shell glands and uteri. Reproductive organs are formed on the elasmobranch pattern. In the male there are two ovoid testes containing immature sperms. These sperms pass through the vasa efferentia and reach into the vas deferens which coils to form the epididymis. The epididymis is closely applied to the anterior part of the kidney. The sperms aggregate into *spermatophores* surrounded by membranous structure and they are full of gelatinous substance. The bundles of sperms are embeded in the gelatinous material. The lower part of the vas deferens dilates to form the *vesicula seminalis.* This dilated portion is imperfectly divided into compartment by transverse partitions. The spermatophores are passed into these compartments and then pass into the urinogenital sinus. The fertilization is internal and the egg becomes surrounded by a horny egg-shell secreted by the shell-glands.

Affinities

The Holocephali show some resemblances with the elasmobranchs and some with the teleosts. Besides these characters, this group possesses a number of specialized characters which are not present either in Elasmobranch or in teleosts and as such, this group has been given the status of independent class. The characters have been analysed below:

Resemblances with the Elasmobranchs

(1) In Holocephali the skeleton is cartilaginous, replacing and membrance bones are absent.
(2) The vertebral column has a persistent notochord with cartilaginous arches.
(3) Limbs and girdles are formed on the elasmobranch plan.
(4) The skin is silvery and smooth but some placoid scales are present on the claspers.
(5) A pair of claspers are present posterior to the pelvic fins in the male (like elasmobranch) however, anterior and frontal claspers are also present.
(6) The basic plan of the brain resembles with the elasmobranch but the development of restiform bodies and elongation of diencephalon are remarkable differences.
(7) A spiral valve is present in the intestine.
(8) The air bladder is absent like elasmobranchs.
(9) The tail is heterocercal in many holocephalians.
(10) The Urinogenital organs are of the selachian type.
(11) The conus arteriosus is present in the heart and contains three rows of valves as in the case of elasmobranchs.

Resemblances with Teleosts

(1) Gills do not open outside, rather they are covered by means of operculum like teleosts.

(2) There is a single external branchial aperture.

(3) The gill filaments project beyond the inter branchial septum, the latter being much reduced.

(4) The spiracle is absent.

(5) There is no cloaca and the urinogenital aperture lies behind the anus.

Special Features of Holocephali

In addition to the above mentioned characters, the Holocephali have some specialized characters also with are as follows :

(1) The skull is of holostylic type and the palatoquadrate is fused with the cranium.

(2) Extra claspers (Anterior and Cephalic claspers) are also present unlike other groups.

(3) The dention is peculiar in having large plates. Teeth are not covered by enamel but a layer of vasodentine is present. Sharp edges are there in the plates. The pulp cavity is much reduced.

(4) There is loss of scales and spiracle.

Conclusion

Thus in Holocephali we find some characters like elasmobranchs and others like teleosts. Besides, there are some special features also, already mentioned. The Holocephali arose from some shark ancestor during the Mesozoic era, possibly in Triassic period. Originally the Holocephali were considered as an order under the subclass-*Bradiodonti* of the Class—Elasmobranchii but now it has been given the status of independent class and it seems to be justified.

CHAPTER 18

SKIN AND SCALES

The skin is the outer covering of the body and is a complex sheet of tissues having several cells in thickness. The skin performs many functions e.g.protection against injuries, shocks, and external germs. In certain cases it is also respiratory, excretory and osmoregulatory in function. Sense of touch also predominantly develops in the skin. It also prevents loss of body heat and loss of water. Change of colour of the skin and bioluminescence are also due to skin activities which afford sexual recognition and other important purposes. These functions are under nervous and/or endocrine control. Barbels and flaps are the extensions of skins. Electric organs are also present in the skin of some fishes (*Malapterurus, Torpedo, Electrophorus* etc.). The skin also contains venomous glands in some fishes (*Noturus, Heteropneustes, Scorpaena* etc.).

The mucous glands are also present in the skin, the slimy secretion (mucous) of which contains fish odour. The skin colour and scales are of some use in classification.

Some notable contributions on the morpho-histology and histo-chemistry of skin in fishes are those of Bhatti (1938), Islam (1951), Kapoor (1965), Henrikson and Matolsky (1968), Asakawa (1970), Mittal and Munshi (1970, 1971) Roberts *et al.* (1972), Banerjee and Mittal (1975), Saxena and Kulshrestha (1979) and others.

Structure of Skin

The fish skin is mainly composed of two layers, an outer *epidermis* and an inner *dermis* (corium). The ectoderm consists of several layers of *stratified epithelial* cells of which the deepest layers are made up of Columnar cells. These cells form the *Stratum germinativum.* This layer is fertile and the cells always multiply in this area. *Stratum carneum* layer is mostly absent in fishes.

The *dermis* is composed of connective tissue, blood vessel, nerves and cutaneous sense organs. The upper layer is made up of loose connective tissue and is known as *Stratum spongiosum* and the lower layer which is thick and dense is known as *stratum compactum.* Several flask shaped or tubular muscular cells are scattered among the epidermal cells and may extend into the dermis. This is an indication of keratinization in certain fishes (*Periophthalamus, Bagarius bagarius* etc.)

The colouration in fishes is due to the presence of skin pigments. Two types of cells which are known as chromatophores and iridocytes are present in the dermis, which contain pigment granules.

Because, the fishes lead an aquatic life the epidermis is generally soft, cornification being a rare case. A peculiar pearl organ appears in the skin of some teleosts (minnows—cyprinidae) in the breeding season. Mucous glands of different shapes (both unicellular and multicellular) are present in the epidermis which secrete the slimy substance. Other types of glandular cells are also present, they are: Serous granulated cells and *Clavate* (Club-shaped) cells. In chondrichthyes mucous cells are

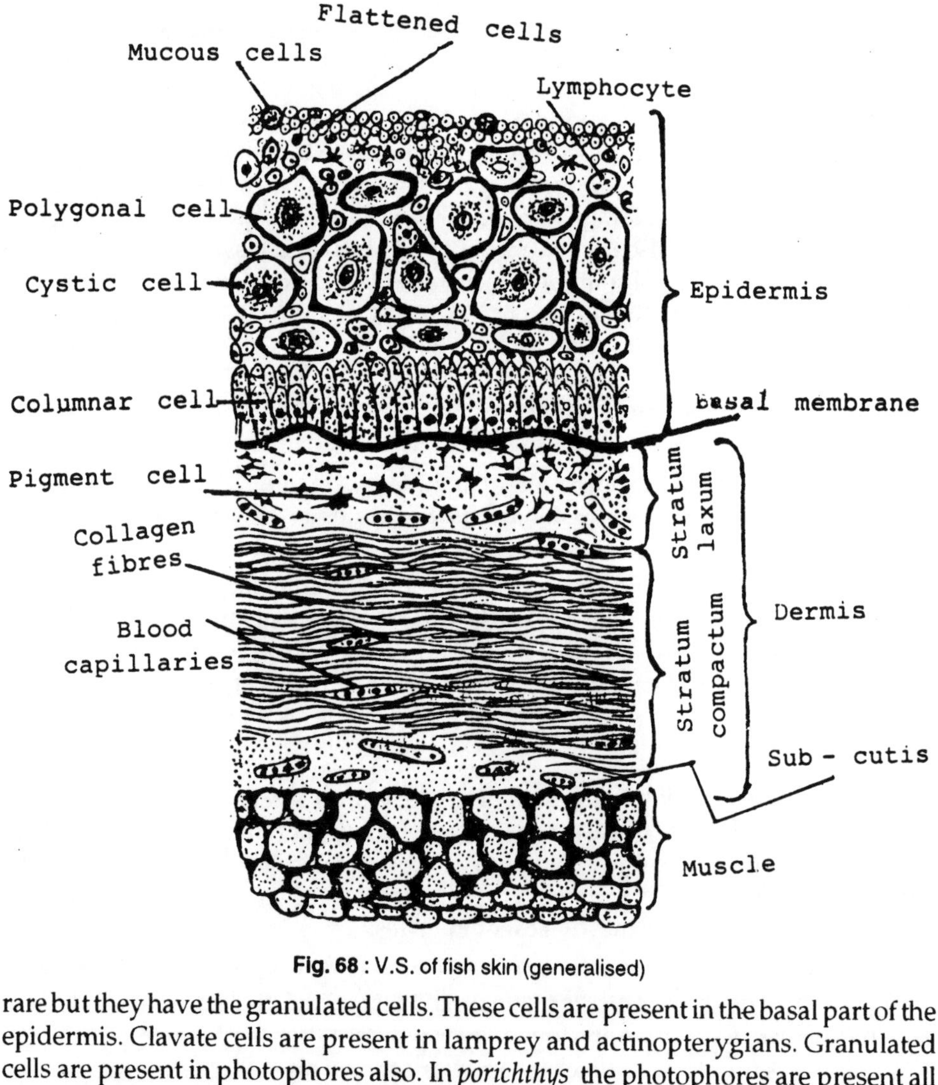

Fig. 68 : V.S. of fish skin (generalised)

rare but they have the granulated cells. These cells are present in the basal part of the epidermis. Clavate cells are present in lamprey and actinopterygians. Granulated cells are present in photophores also. In *porichthys* the photophores are present all over the body. In some teleosts (e.g. Trigla), the epidermis contains Chemoreceptor cells which resemble the taste buds. The excretory chloride cells occur in the epidermis of trigla. In elasmobranchs, *Pterygopodial* glands are present in the claspers of the males. In general, the skin in elasmobranch is very tough and rough to touch because of the presence of minute placoid scales.

Saxena and Kulshrestha (1979) have described the integument of *Mystus uittatus,* a non-scaly teleost fish. They have described three types of anchoring elements i.e. *anchoring filaments, anchoring fibrils* and *anchoring fibres* in the dermis of this fish. These structures provide firm anchorage to the integument on the underlying tissue and serve as pathways for nerves and blood vessels.

In *Bagarius bagarius,* the skin is scaleless, thick and rough in appearance owing to *keratinization.* There are three important layers: *epidermis, dermis* and *subcutis.* In the epidermis there is an outer layer of small, flat cells and sparsely distributed mucous cells. Then it is followed by small rounded *cystic cells* which are loosely distributed between the large polygonal cells. Several layers of vertically oriented columnar cells are supported by the basement membrane. Some pigment cells can be seen in the outer layer of the epidermis. The dermis is a thick layer (3-4 times thicker than epidermis). Its outer layer, the *Stratum laxum* is composed of blood vessels and nerves. The pigment cells of this area have a tendency to migrate to the epidermal region in the breeding season. At certain places there is aggregation of pigment cells in this zone. The lower part of dermis is known as *stratum compactum* which is a tough layer formed of cushion like pad of collagen fibres, blood vessels and nerves. Just below the dermis, lies the *sub-cutis* and the latter is attached to the underlying muscle layer. The subcutis layer is also provided with blood vessels and nerves.

Different Types of Scales

Scales are important exoskeleton in fishes. They have been divided into two basic types: *Placoid* and *Non-placoid.* The former is derived partly from the epidermis and partly from the dermis (as in elasmobranch), but the non-placoid scales are derived from the dermis (as in teleosts). From *annuli* on the scales, age of the fish can be determined in years. More than one type of scales may be present in one species, for example, the common basses (*Micropterus*) possess both Ctenoid and Cycloid scales.

(1) *Placoid Scale:* Placoid scales or dermal denticles are commonly found in sharks (Elasmobranchii). These are plate-like scales. The disc like broad basal plate is embedded in the dermis and the spine is projected out through the epidermis. The spine has a covering of enamel like material known as *vitrodentine.* Below this layer, there is a layer of *dentine* which encloses the pulp cavity. There is an aperture in centre of the basal plate which provides entrance to the blood vessels and nerves. Vitrodentine is epidermal in origin but the dentine is dermal in origin.

(2) *Cycloid Scale:* These scales are found in Carps. These are smooth, disc-like scales more or less circular in outline. The free margin of the scale is rounded and entire, not toothed. These scales have characteristic ridges alternating with grooves. The ridges are in the form of concentric rings. The central part of the scale is known as *focus.* According to some authors the living dipnoans possess cycloid scales because the basic cosmoid structure is highly modified.

(3) *Ctenoid Scales:* Ctenoid scales are present in several teleosts (perches). Grooves and ridges are alternately present. The posterior margin of the scale is comb-like or serrated. A nuclear, central zone can be recognized in this scale also which is called the *focus* of the scale. It is the first part of the scale to develop. In several species of fishes, grooves (radii) radiate from the focus towards the margin of the scale. The marginal denticulation is termed as teeth.

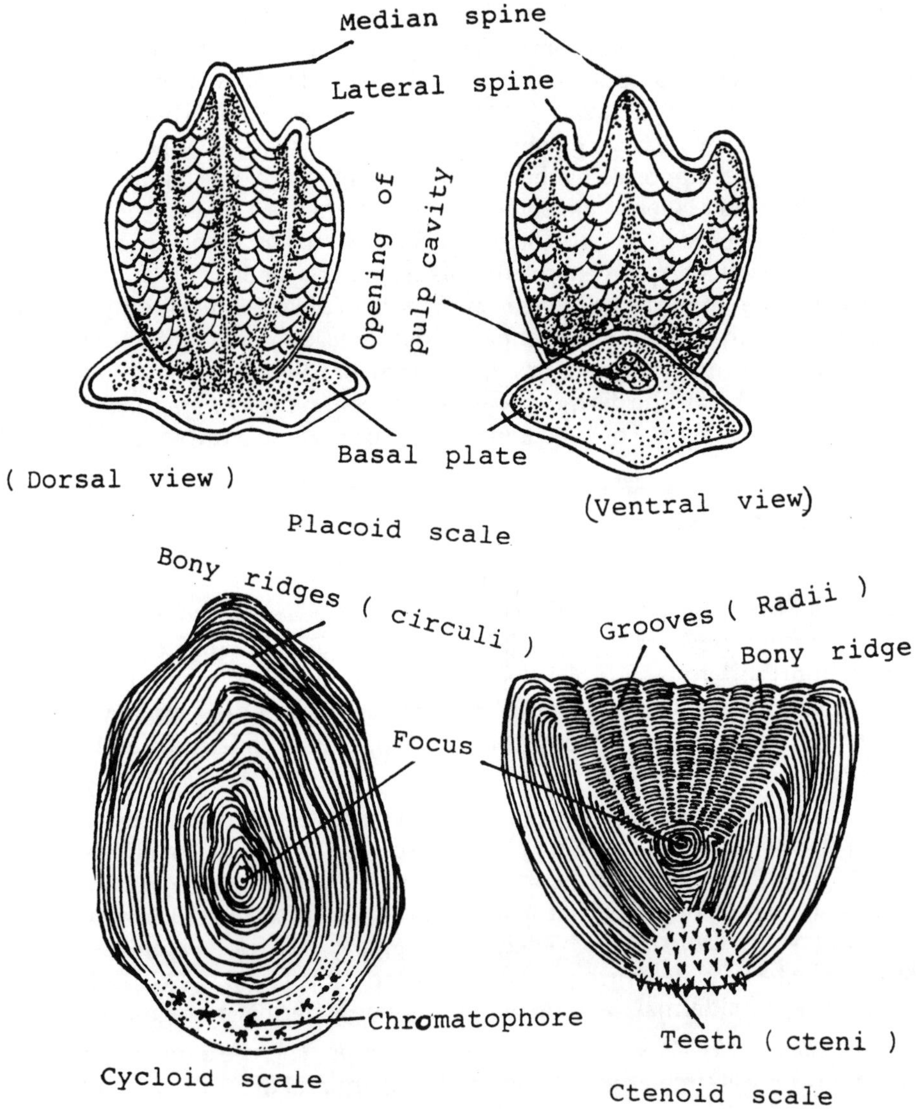

Fig.69 : Scales in Fishes

(4) *Ganoid Scale:* These are diamond-shaped scales. Ganoid scales are the characteristics of primitive forms e.g. Sturgeons, Bow fins, Gar pikes etc. The scales are bony plates, transversed centrally by canals. These are covered with thick enamel like substance, known as *ganoine.* Beneath this ganoine cap, there is a cosmine like layer. The inner most lamellar bony layer of the scale is known as *isopedine.* These scales are present in *polypterus.*

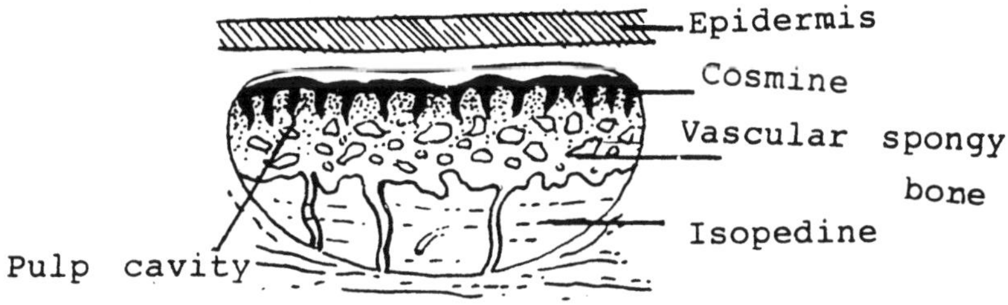

Cosmoid scale(Extinct crossopterygians)

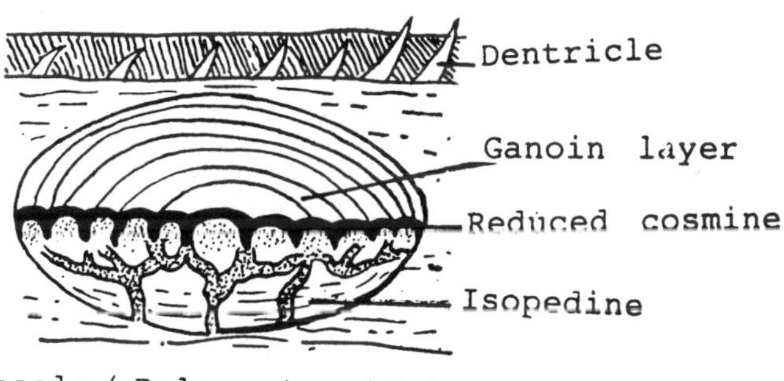

Ganoid scale (Palaeoniscoid)

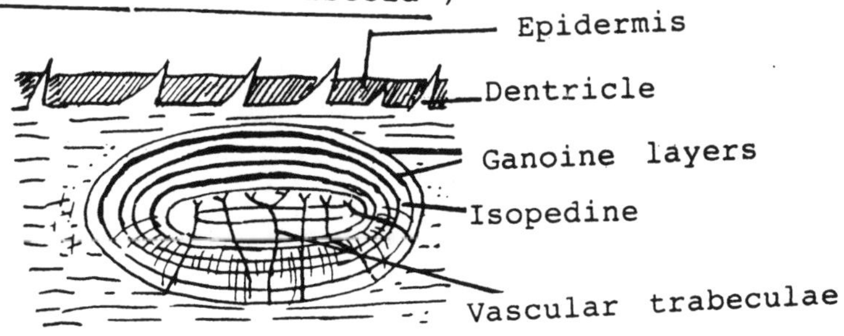

Ganoid scale (Lepisosteoid)

Fig. 70 : Some scales in T.S.

(5) *Cosmoid Scale:* Cosmoid scales are found in the living *(Latimeria)* and extinct Crossopterygians. The external layer is thin and enamel like known as *vitrodentine.* Below this layer there is the layer of dentine like material, the *cosmine.* This layer is hard hard and non-cellular having tubules and chambers. The inner-layer is made

up of bony substance called *isopedine*. It is a vascular layer (The lung fishes also have basically the cosmoid scale but the cosmoid nature is so modified that they have been considered as cycloid scale).

Scale Reading and Age Determination

There is a definite way of expressing the *scale count*. If the scale *formula* is given $100^{6}/_{8}$ it means that there are hundred scales in the lateral line, six scales above it and eight scales below it. The lateral line count always denotes the maximum number of scales (perforated) in the lateral line. All the scales that fall along the line starting from the origin of the dorsal fin are the scales of the lateral line. They run downward and backward to meet the lateral line. Similarly, the scales following along the line that starts from the origin of the anal fin, are scales below the lateral line. They run upward and forward to meet the lateral line.

A. Annuli of scale in a two-year old fish species

B. Abnormal growth showing false annulus (same age)

C. Abnormal growth in a three - year old fish (Skipped annulus at second Annulus)

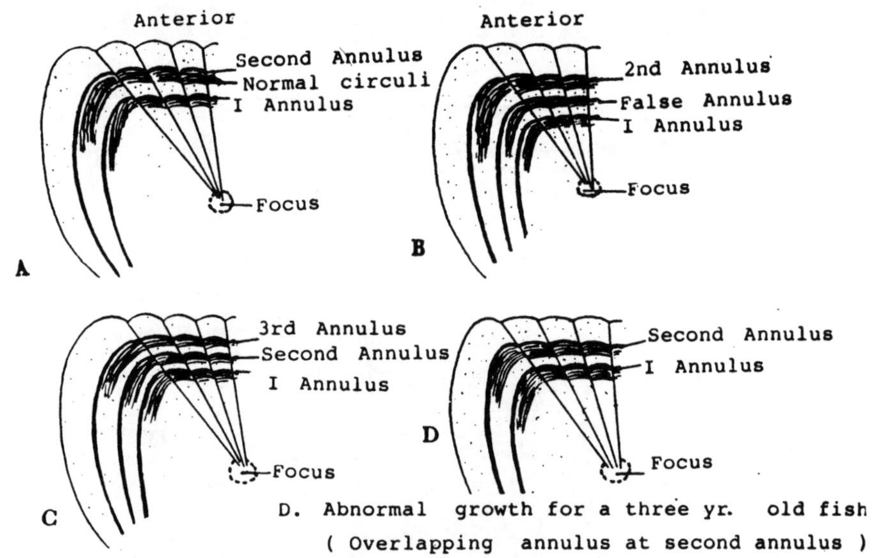

D. Abnormal growth for a three yr. old fish (Overlapping annulus at second annulus)

Fig. 71 : Four scales showing annuli

For the purpose of age determination, about 20 scales are removed from the side of the body just below the origin of the dorsal fin. In *soft-rayed fins* the scales are taken from the region above the lateral line but in the *spiny-rayed fins* the scales located below the lateral line are preferred. Large and symmetrical scales are taken for age determination. The scales are cleaned in water with the help of brush. Permanent mount of these scales may be prepared in the *glycerine-gelatin* mixture for study. The dry scales can also be studied under the microscope by keeping them in between the glass plates.

The true *annulus* can be marked on the scales as a thick and prominent lining in between the considerable number of ridges and grooves. The total number of *annuli* on the scale indicate the age in same number of years. A verification of weight and length, according with the age of the fish should be made by random sampling method. Annuli formation may be distorted sometimes by abnormal growth patterns and as such, it is essential to check and compare the result with normal standard growth pattern of fish species. The *false annulus, skipped annulus* (position coinciding with the annulus of the preceding year) and overlapping annulus are common abnormalities. Everything has been made clear in the sketch.

The Pigment-containing cells of the skin are known as chromatophores. The chromatophores comprise *melanophores* (brown or black), *xanthophores* (yellow), erythrophores (red), *leucophores* (white) *and iridophores* (reflecting). Pigments present in the leucophore and iridophore are colourless (basically guanine). More than one type of pigments may be present in one chromatophore. In the swordtail, *xanthoerythrophore* has been described by Goodrich *et al.* (1941). The *yellow carotinoid pigments* are present in the centre of the cell but *red pteridine* accumulation has been observed in the cellular processes. So,these cells are known as *'Chromatosomes'*. A very common chromatosome is the *melaniridosome,* which is formed by melanophore and iridophore.So, it may also be called a *compound chromatophore.*

The *melanocyte* is a cell which synthesizes a special *melanin* containing organelle, the *melanosome.* The *melanocyte* which participates with other chromatophores during quick process of colour changes are generally known as melanophore. In addition to all these terms there is one more term, the *melanoblast* which is considered as a precursor of melanocyte.

The melanophore is enclosed by a single cell membrane in *Fundulus heteroclitus* and other teleosts. The nucleus is quite prominent in these cells. Besides this, mitochondria, centrioles, melanosomes, ribosomes, vesicular smooth-surfaced endoplasmic reticulum and micropinocytotic vesicles are also present. A number of microtubules have also been reported in the melanophores of *F. heteroclitus.* Melanosomes are spherical or ellipsoidal bodies and they are surrounded by a limiting membrane. The enclosed melanin is very dense. The red pigment granules in *xiphophorus helleri* consists of outer limiting membrane and inner lamellae as reported Matsumoto (1965). According to Loud and Mishima (1963) the goldfish xanthophores contain large bodies and small vesicles are characteristic features of the cytoplasm.

Melanins, Carotenoids, Pteridines and *Purines* are the important pigments of the chromatophores. Melanins are the brown or black pigments derived from tyrosine. The study of biosynthetic pathway has revealed that tyrosine is oxidised to 3,4, dihydroxyphenylalanine (Dopa) and then to Dopa quinone. The enzyme tyrosinase is necessarily involved at this stage. Dopa quinone is then polymerised to form melanines. Melanin synthesis can take place in melanocytes and melalophores. Carotenoids are the yellow and red pigments of Xanthophores and erythrophores. They are unsaturated hydrocarbon compounds. Pteridines may be coloured or colourless. They are related to purines and flavins. They have both pyrimidine and an associated pyrazine rings. Xanthophores contain Pteridines and Carotinoids.

Silvery appearance of the skin is due to the presence of purines. Guanine is present in the form of crystals, granules and also platelets and is a predominating feature here.

Mechanism of Pigment Movement

When there is some modification in the distribution of Pigments in the chromatophores, physiological colour changes take place. There are several mechanisms explained by various workers, which are concerned with the movement of pigments in the pigment cells. Marsland (1944) studied the movement of pigments in *Fundulus*. The present studies are based on the pressue-temperature analysis on Melanophores. It has been revealed that the aggregation of Pigment granules is correlated with gelation of the protoplasm containing them, where as, melanin dispersal involves cytoplasmic solation. Activities of the fibrils present in the melanophores facilitate the aggregation and dispersion of pigment granules. Observations of Falk and Rhodin (1957) on *Lebistes* melanophores, it has been suggested that the contraction and relaxation of the fibrils between the two membranes (inner and outer) are responsible for aggregation or dispersion of pigment granules. But this has not been accepted by other workers. Another observation regarding the mechanism of pigment movement is that of Kinosita (1953, 1963) in *Oryzias latipes*. According to this worker, the melanosomes are negatively charged. The membrane potential increases on the processes of the melanophore but decreases in the central region. It may be recalled that the aggregation of pigment in the cell is caused under the influences of K^+ or epinephrine. After the application of physiological saline or atropine solution, reverse changes take place and melanin dispersion is observed. Thus in both the cases mentioned above, there is change in electric potentials. Thus it was concluded that the potential gradient was established along the cellular processes. Melanosomes must have migrated electrophoretically through the cytoplasm in the opposite direction of the intracellular current flow.

Under the electron microscope Bikle *et al.* (1956) have described the scale melanophores of *Fundulus*. Melanosomes are arranged in files or rows in a melanosphore processes. It was also pointed out that the microtubules are present between these rows and function as cytoskeletal elements maintaining the position of the melanosomes processes. They also define the channels in which the melanosomes move. This observation has been supported by Green (1968). There is now general agreement that receptors for melanin aggregating and dispersing stimuli are distributed along the cellular processes and the role of microtubules can not be ruled out.

It is well established that Melanocyte-stimulating hormone (MSH) affects pigment movements. Melanin dispersion by MSH requires, the presence of Na ions MSH increases the permeability of the melanophore membrane to sodium ions (Na^+). During the action of MSH, water entry has been pointed out which causes melanin dispersion.

Mechanism of Release of MSH

Melanocyte-stimulating hormone, the trophic hormone of the Pituitary is secreted from the Pars intermedia and is carried to the melamophores, where it promotes changes in skin colouration. As a result, the animals darkens. As suggested by Howe (1973), the mechanism of release of MSH from the pars intermedia is only partly understood and the whole process is very complex. In controlling the release of MSH,—adrenergic type receptors are necessarily involved. β-adrenergic type stimulation has also been pointed out. In *Anguilla anguilla*, melanin aggregation is an α-adrenergic response but the dispersion is a β-adrenergic responses. MSH-release-inhibiting hormones (MSH-R-IH) has been identified in the hypothalamus which is a peptide in its chemical nature. MSH-releasing hormone (MRH) may also be present in the hypothalamus. Thus, MSH exerts a negative feedback inhibition via the hypothalamus and further release is restricted which is evidenced from the presence of releasing hormone and inhibiting hormone.

Blood-borne hormones are mainly responsible for pigment movements. In certain cases, however, the pigment cells are regulated by nerves. Both humoral and neural control mechanisms have been described in several fishes. According to Baker (1968), both α-MSH and β-MSH are effective in dispersing eel melanophores *in vitro*.

Morphological and Physiological Colour Changes

Chondrichthyes and teleosts among cold blooded animals also undergo physiological colour changes. The levels of melanin increases in response to MSH stimulation. Chavin *et al.* (1963) have reported that *corticotrophin* increases the levels of melanin in the skin of *Carassius auratus*. But, Pickford and Kosto (1957) have informed that in *Fundulus heteroclitus*, MSH increases melanin synthesis in the skin and not the *corticotrophin*. So, a general conclusion can not be drawn at this stage. Wilson and Dodd (1973) suggested that MSH causes increased melanin synthesis in *Scyliorhinus canicula*.

Several hormones like MSH, sex hormones, *corticotrophin* and melatonin (Pineal hormone) are involved in colour change of the skin.

Melanin is formed from *tyrosin* by a complex process involving *tyrosinase* a copper containing enzyme. Increased levels of cutaneous melanin are associated with increased *hydrosinase* activity and it can be influenced by hormones. It has already been pointed out that dispersion of melanin in the melanophores is mediated by MSH and adrenaline. *Adenylcyclase* is associated with the melanophores. Melanin dispersion is regulated by the presence of cyclic AMP. Cyclic AMP stimulates a dispersion of melanosomes. Presence of Calcium is essential during this physiological activity of colour change. In various fishes both neural and humoral control of colour change have been described. The Pineal gland has also been implicated in the chromatophore control. Melatonin obtained from bovine pineal gland causes aggregation of melanophore in several fishes.

Colour Change in Teleosts: In teleosts, colour change can be mediated either by *humoral mechanism* or by *neural mechanism* or by combination of both. The response of melanophores to neural stimuli is very rapid but the humoral mechanism is a slow process. There are considerable interspecific difference in the control of colour change among diversed groups of teleosts. Aggregation of melanin and dispersion of melanin exhibit a colour change in fishes.

The colour change in *Anguilla anguilla* is humoral but neural control is also involved which becomes apparent after the removal of hypophysis. There is an aggregation of melanin in the melanophores in eels following adrenalin treatment. Thus a humoral mechanism which is predominant overrides a neural mechanism. In *Fundulus heteroclitus,* MSH of the pituitary gland becomes necessary for full expression of black essential background response. MSH treatment into pale fish does not affect the dispersion of melanin. The colour change in this killifish occurs in response to neural stimuli to the melanophores. There are melanin aggregating nerve fibres and probably also dispersing fibres. However, there is ability to respond to MSH also for complete darkening of the fish. In *Fundulus,* predominantly neural co-ordination overrides humoral one. In the European minnows (*Phoxinus phoxinus*) the aggregation of melanin is a result of nerve stimulation. It has been suggested that aggregating nerve fibres exist here in this case. Existence of Melanin dispersing fibres has also been suggested. The effect of endogenous MSH has not been described. Thus a neural co-ordinating mechanism is a dominant feature in *Phoxinus phoxinus.*

Colour Change in Chondrichthyes : Several sharks and rays exhibit colour change depending on the shade of the background. Analysis of the colour change in *Squalus, Scyliorhinus* and *Raja* has revealed that they exhibit white and black background responses that are mediated by MSH. There is no direct neural control of melanophores in chondrichthyes. Wilson and Dodd (1977) have advocated the presence of non-visual response. The pineal contributes to non-visual colour change.

CHAPTER 19

ENDOCRINE GLANDS IN FISHES

Fishes possess almost all the endocrine glands which are found in the higher vertebrates but, histophysiological details of all of them are not completely known. The important endocrine glands are: *Pituitary, Thyroid, Adrenal, Islets of Langerhans, Ovary, Testis* and *Ultimobranchial body* (Parathyroid). In addition to these organs the *Pineal body, Corpuscles of Stannius,* the *Urophysis* and *intestinal mucosa* are organs of doubtful nature however, they are considered alongwith the endocrine glands. The important endocrine glands have been discussed below separately in detail.

The Pituitary Gland (Hypophysis)

The study of pituitary gland and its hormones has attracted the attention of several workers and chief among them are Gorbman (1939), Olivereau (1954, 1963, 1967), Ramaswami and Sundararaj (1957), Pickford and Atz (1957), Porte (1961), Sathyanesan (1963), Fontaine (1964), Ball (1966), van Overbeeke and Ahsan (1966). Ibrahim and Chaudhuri (1970), Abraham (1974), Pandey and Pandey (1977), Sahai (1984, 1986), Rath (1991, 1993, 1996), Banerjee *et al.* (1992) and others. The pituitary gland in the case of European eel, *Anguilla anguilla* has been thoroughly investigated by Olivereau, in *Hilsa ilisha* by Sathyanesan (1963), and in *Poecilia* by Ball (1966) and Porte (1961).

Structure: The teleostean pituitary resembles more with the amphibian rather than any other group of vertebrates. It is located in *Sella turcica* of sphenoid bone. The *Adenohypophysis* and *Neurohypophysis* are the two major parts of the pituitary gland. The neurohypophysis is present in the ventral part of the brain just behind the optic chiasma. The Adenohypophysis is divided into two main parts. Anteriorly, the *pars distalis* is divisible into *rostral* and *Proximal Pars distalis* on the basis of cell types. The rostral pars distalis is also called the *Pro-adenohypophysis* and the proximal pars distalis is called the *mesoadenohypopysis.* Posteriorly, a *Pars intermedia* is present which is also known as *metaadenohypophysis.* The interdigitations of the centrally located neurohypophysis with the pars intermedia are deep and well marked but the neurohypophyseal pars distalis interdigitations are not so elaborate. Rostral Pars distalis comprises the anterior most region of the adenohypophysis but the proximal pars distalis is situated between the pars intermedia and the rostral pars distalis.

Histology of the Adenohypophysis: There are several types of cells present in the adenohypophysis and they take different stains.

1. *Prolactin Cells:* The Prolactin cells form a compact mass in the rostral pars distalis. These cells are columnar in appearance and their granules can be stained (red) with Azocarmine or Acid fuchsin. They are negative to PAS, Aldehyde fuchsin and Alcian blue stains. In the rostral pars distalis of eel the prolactin cells are arranged in follicles. Between these follicles the thyroid stimulating hormone cells are present, but towards the posterior border there is a layer of Adrenocorticotropic hormone cells. A large number of growth hormone cells are present in Proximal Pars distalis of eels which are arranged in cords.

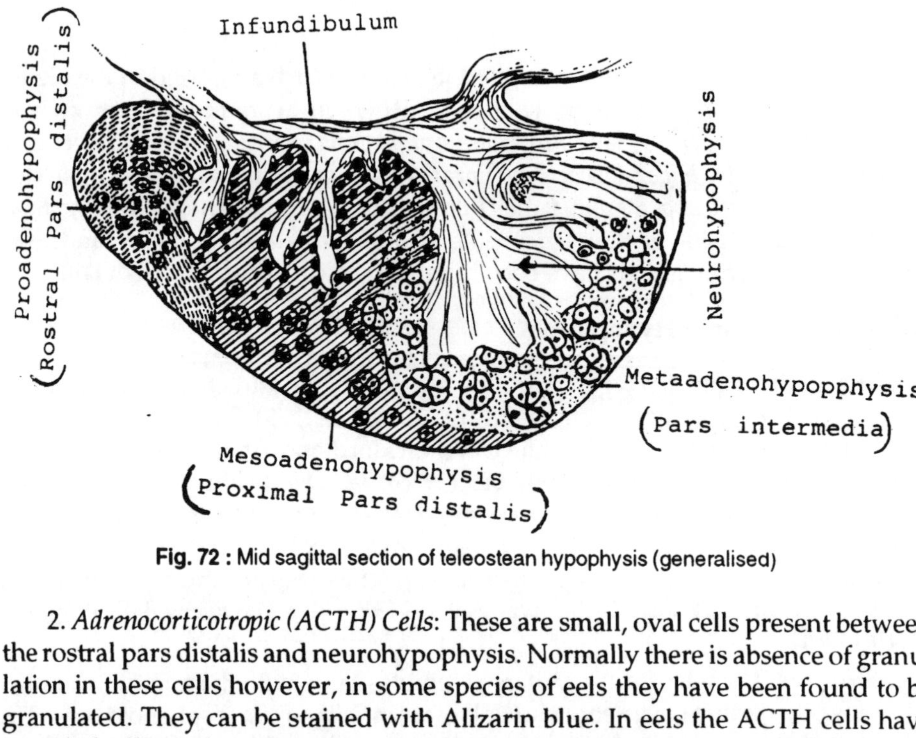

Fig. 72 : Mid sagittal section of teleostean hypophysis (generalised)

2. *Adrenocorticotropic (ACTH) Cells*: These are small, oval cells present between the rostral pars distalis and neurohypophysis. Normally there is absence of granulation in these cells however, in some species of eels they have been found to be granulated. They can be stained with Alizarin blue. In eels the ACTH cells have rounded, elliptical or pear shaped nucleus with distinct nucleolus. Diffuse endoplasmic reticulum, fine vesicles or microtubules are present in the cells.

3. *Growth hormone (GH) Cells*: They are also known as somatotropic cells. These are prominent acidophil cells in the Pars distalis, particularly in proximal pars distalis area. They can be easily stained with orange G.

In *anguilla* the somatotrops are intermingled with the thyrotrops. Somatotrops are negative to PAS, AF and Alcian blue stains.

4. *Gonadotrops:* The teleostean gonadotrops have been found located in the proximal pars distails but at sexual maturity they may spread into the rostral pars distalis as reported by Olivereau (1967), Baker (1967) and others. These are mucoid cells with granules and can be stained with PAS technique. The gonadotrops contain

glycoprotein. Variations in the shape and size of the cells may take place during the development period of gonad.

5. *Thyrotrops:* These are the basophil cells of the Pars distalis. In the immature male eel the thyroid stimulating hormone cells are small cells lying in the rostral pars distalis between the follicles of the Prolactin cells. Some of the cells may infiltrate into the follicle walls. The thyrotrops in the case of *Poecilia* lie in the finger like inner prolongations of the Proximal pars distalis. Some GH-cells may be present mixed with them.

6. *Pars Intermedia:* It occupies a smaller region in the hinder part of the hypophysis and surrounds the largest region of the neurohypophysial core partially or completely. With a few exceptions, it is usually invaded by neurohypophysial tracts. Olivereau and Ball (1964) have reported that Pars intermedia cells are sometimes found in the *Pars distalis.* Both basophilic and acidophilic cells have been identified in the Pars intermedia. The basophilic cell types can be stained with Aniline blue and the acidophilic with azocarmine or orange G. The amphiphilic cells take both stains in trichrome and tetrachrome techniques. In guppy, Follenius (1963, 1965) has described only one chromophilic cell types together with Chromophobes, Thus, variations can not be ruled out in different species of fishes.

Structure of Neurohypophysis: It has been already pointed out that there is a central neurohypophysis interdigitating with the adenohypophysis. The structure of the teleostean neurohypophysis has been fully investigated by a large number of workers (Scharrer, 1928, 1930, 1932; Lederis, 1962, 1964; Knowles and Vollrath, 1965, 1966; and Leatherland, 1967).

The neurosecretory axons penetrate throughout the various parts of the adenohypophysis. A large number of nerve fibres arise form the hypothalamus and enter into the substance of the neurohypophysis. The neurohypophysial nerve fibres contain pituicytes and droplets of neurosecretory material, and latter is referred to as "Herring bodies." Sometimes, lymphocytes and migrating cyanophils are also present.

The Preoptic nuclei usually lie almost dorsal to the optic chiasma on both sides of third ventricle. The two neurohypophysial hormones i.e. *oxytocin* and *vasopressin* are stored in the neurohypophysis though they are secreted in the hypothalamus.

Functions of Various Hormones

Hormones of the fish pituitary are mostly comparable with those of mammals with little variations. The functions of various hormones have been described below:

Hormones of Adenohypophysis

1. *Prolactin:* As there is no question of milk production in fishes, this hormone has got other functions. Prolactin is said to have important role in osmoregulation. Without Pituitary, some teleosts can not survive in freshwater, through they can continue for indefinite period in sea water e.g. *Betta splendens* and *Tilapia mossambica.* Prolactin, thus may be concerned with electrolyte balance.

However, a contradictory report has been given by Chavin (1956) that the gold fish (*Carassius auratus*) can survivie for a long time in freshwater even after hypophysectomy. According to Pickford and Kasto (1957), Prolactin is also concerned with melanogenesis. In *Gasterosteus,* as reported by Burden (1956), Prolactin is also concerned with the maintenance of epidermal mucous cells.

2. *Adrenocorticotropic hormone (ACTH):* This hormone is secreted by corticotrops and stimulates the adrenocortical cells to secrete glucocorticoids and mineralocorticoids like mammals. The release of this hormone is controlled through negative feedback with the adrenocorticosteroids. The structure of the teleostean ACTH is like that of the mammals.

3. *Gonadotropic hormone:* Gonadotropic hormones stimulate the gonads. According to Olivereau (1967) there is no physiological or biochemical evidence to show that two types of gonadotropins are secreted in teleosts. There is scarcity of definite information regarding this fact. Gonadotrops have been studied in several Indian teleosts in relation to sexual maturity by several workers (Sundararaj, 1959; Belsare, 1962; Khanna and Pant, 1969 and others). These workers have described characteristic secretory changes in them.

4. *Thyroid stimulating hormone (TSH):* Thyroid stimulating hormone is secreted by thyrotrops. This hormone stimulates the thyroid gland and controls the production of thyroxine.

5. *Somatotropic hormone (SH):* This hormone is produced by the GH-cells. It regulates the growth of various tissues of the body. It increases liner growth in fish in a number of ways. It increases protein synthesis, decreases nitrogen loss and stimulates oxidation.

Hormones of Pars Intermedia

Pars intermedia produces the Melanocyte stimulating hormone (MSH) and Melanocyte concentrating hormone (MCH). Pigment dispersion is controlled by the aforesaid hormones.

Hormones of Neurohypophysis

There are evidences that at least seven neurohypophysial peptides have been identified in teleosts. The first group of these peptides is associated with antidiuretic vasopressor principles and the second group with oxytocin-like principles. The first group is probably concerned with water balance including control of urine and also ionic regulation. The second group is responsible for the contraction of oviduct. The function of reproductive structures may be modulated by this group of peptides.

The neurohypophysial hormones are also concerned with the increase of GH, increase of glucose level, gill permeability and control of osmoregulation and some other functions.

Activities of the pituitary gland are controlled by Hypothalamic Release Hormone (secretions) conforming to the general vertebrate pattern. Use of Pituitary in fish culture has been described in a separate chapter of Induced Breeding.

Thyroid Gland

The thyroid gland is normally present in close association with the ventral aorta and branchial arteries in the teleosts, but sometimes unusual positions have been reported. There is great variation in its shape and anatomic position. The thyroid tissue can disperse from the pharyngeal region to eye, brain , kidney, spleen and other tissues of the body. The thyroid follicles have been reported in the head kidney

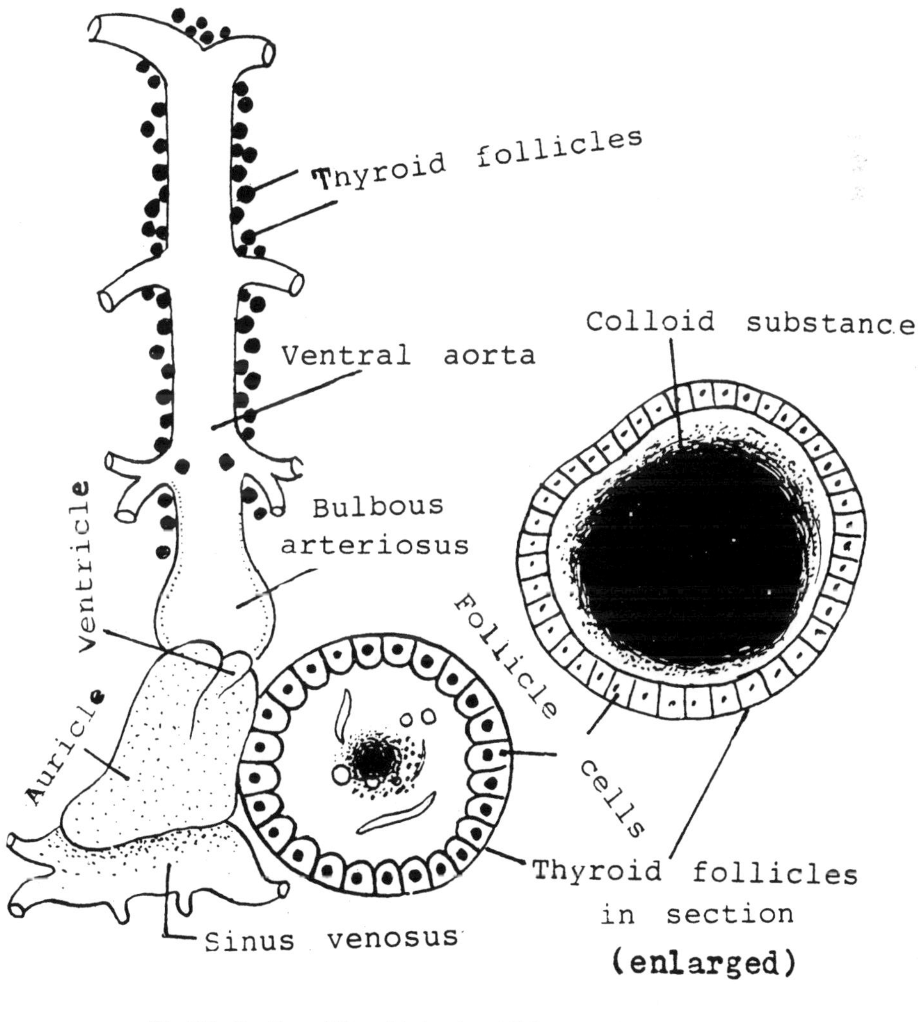

Fig. 73 : Position of Thyroid gland and T.S. of two thyroid follicles

of *Mystus vittatus* by Gurumani (1971). These heterotropic thyroid follicles have been considered to be functional and it has been supposed that they have migrated from the pharyngeal region. The author has revealed that the iodine content of the environmental water was not the reason for the migration of the follicles. When the gland is physiologically active there is decrease in the colloidal substance and increase in the follicular cell height.

The occurrence of thyroid follicles in head kidney has been reported by several workers like Chavin (1965), Sathyanesan and Prasad (1962), Sathyanesan and Chary (1962), Sathyanesan (1963), Nandi (1965), Srivastava and Sathyanesan (1967), Bose and Ahmad (1978), Alexandrino *et al.* (1985), Chakrabarti and Bhattacharya (1984), Brown and Stetson (1985), Graw *et al.* (1985) and others. These thyroid follicles have been found to be functional by Chavin, Sathyanesan and Srivastava and Sathyanesan.

The origin, occurrence , development and function of the heterotropic thyroid follicles in *Xiphophorus maculatus* have been studied by Baker *et. al.* (1955) and Baker (1958). Some air breathing fishes e.g. *Channa punctatus, C. gachua, C. marulius, C. striatus* and *Heteropneustes fossilis* have compact and encapsulated thyroid close to ventral aorta. In *clarias batrachus* the gland is condensed in three patches but is without a capsule. This is of course an intermediate condition. Ku. Sudha Sharma (1979) has described this gland in *Chela bacaila.* Here the follicles form compact bed around the anterior median extension of the ventral aorta. This thick bed of follicles extend in the same fashion upto the origin of second afferent branchial artery. Ectopic thyroid tissue was totally lacking in the fish. The dispersion of follicles was as usual.

On the morpho-histology and histophysiology of the thyroid gland in teleosts there are many important contributions. Some of them are those of Barrington (1954), Chavin (1956), Fortune (1956), Belsare (1959), Gorbman (1959), Robertson (1960), Baker-Cohen (1961), Eales (1964), Woodhead (1966), Pandey (1970) and others. There are evidences that cyclic structural changes in teleostean thyroids are correlated with annual environmental cycles, and this has been partially reviewed by Matty (1960), Fontaine and Leloup (1964), Singh (1967) and Jorgensen and Larsen (1967). They have been able to study the specific influence of temperature and photoperiod upon thyroid structure and function.

In several teleosts the thyroid follicles are not assembled into a single compact gland. They are scattered in the connective tissue of the sub-pharyngeal and parapharyngeal area. Baker *et al.* (1955) and Baker (1958) observed that in several species of teleosts, thyroid follicles migrate from the pharyngeal region into the head kidney but also to other places including even the eye. Chavin (1956) confirmed this phenomenon for the goldfish and showed that head kidney thyroid is more active than pharyngeal thyroid.

Thyroid-orientation in anterior-posterior axis has been observed by Belsare (1959) in *Clarias batrachus,* Rawat (1964) in *Barbus ticto,* Srivastava (1966) in *Notopterus notopterus* and by Pandey (1970) in *Rasbora daniconius.* The term "thyroid tissue" has been suggested by some authors (Gudernatsch, 1911 and Gorbman, 1959) instead of "thyroid gland" because of the prominence of follicular structure.

According to Bose and Ahmad (1975) the outstanding feature of teleostean thyroid is dispersed nature and its capability of extraordinary degree of mobility.

Several accounts of structure and function of teleostean thyroid have been discussed by Pickford and Atz (1957), Gorbman (1969) and Chester Jones *et al.* (1974),

Abdul Alim and S.S.Razi (1979) have reported the occurrence of the functional renal thyroid. The thyroid follicles were scattered and each follicle was surrounded by flat follicular epithelium and was filled with non-granular, eosinophilic and homogenous colloid.

Bose and Ahmad (1978) have made histopathological studies on the functional renal thyroid follicles in the freshwater fish *Mystus vittatus*. They have described the heterotropic renal thyroid follicles and their migartion in this fish. They reported that several heterotropic thyroid follicles are scattered throughout the kidney. These workers have described the presence of renal follicles as an adaptive response to a particular ecological condition. That, dispersion of the thyroid follicles in teleosts is under certain ecological factors, becomes more or less established. One of the follicles was observed in the lumen of the blood vessel. Thus the heterotropic follicels in teleosts might be formed by active migration of the folicles via blood vessels. Heterotropic thyroid follicles have been observed in *Barbus* (Sathyanesan and Prasad, 1962), *Engraulus* (Sathyanesan and Chari, 1962), *Catla* (Ahuja and Chandy, 1962) and *Amphipnous* (Srivastava and Sathyanesan, 1967). Baker (1958) favours the view that heterotropic follicles may arise by the active migration of thyroid cells of follicels from the pharyngeal area. Gudernatsch (1911) has already suggested that the blood vessels of the pharyngeal area during the embryonic period serve as substratum for the migration of follicles.

Srivastava and Sathyanesan (1971) have made a comparative study on the effects of thiourea and large doses of radioiodine on the thyroid and thyrotropes of *Mystus vittalus* (Bloch). They have reported certain marked histological changes following injections of heavy dose of ^{131}I. They noticed hypertrophy and hyperplasia of the follicular epithelium and hyperemia of the thyroid area. Later on, certain degenerative changes like follicular atrophy, nuclear necrosis, edema and perifollicular fibrosis were also observed.

Bose and Ahmad (1975) have discussed the structural details of the thyroid gland of *Lepidocephalichthys guntea* (Ham). The pharyngeal thyroid in *L.guntea* is in the form of a separate, unencapsulated follicles which are dispersed around the anterior most part of the ventral aorta in a connective tissue. The follicles are present in close association with the blood capillaries. The structure of the follicles resemble with that of other teleosts. The number of follicles is extremely low. Two types of follicles are there—the small follicles and the large follicles. The small follicles have thick wall and small lumen completely filled with acidophilic colloid. The large follicles have thin epithelium and the lumen of the tubule is not completely filled with colloidal substance. Heterotopic follicles were not encountered in their investigation.

Functions of the thyroid gland: Like other vertebrates iodine is trapped from the circulation and it is utilized by the thyroid follicles in the biosynthetis of thyroid hormone (thyroxine). Some stages of the biosynthetic pathway like *Monoiodotyrosine* and *Diiodotyrosine* have been identified in follicle extracts of several fishes. The secretion of thyroxine is under the control of thyroid stimulating hormone (TSH) of the Pituitary gland. Thyroid hormone is responsible for several metabolic activities in fishes including growth and development. It is responsible for Carbohydrate and

Protein metabolism, Calorigenesis and Calcium metabolism. It is also concerned with gestation in Elasmobranch, dermal thickening, changes in pigmentation and osmoregulation. Thyroxine also plays an important role in oxygen consumption as reported by Muller (1953). However, some contradictory reports have also been brought into light regarding oxygen consumption. The thyroid hormone has been considered important during fish migration. The thyroid gland seems to be active during migration period of the fish. Many authors have proposed a thyroid-gonad axis and a physiological link has been claimed between these two glands. *Calcitonin* is concerned with calcium regulation in fishes. It is definitely concerned with hydromineral metabolism in fishes. It increases clearance of calcium by the kidney. It is also concerned with reproductive function and it facilitates calcium supply during egg formation.

Adrenal Gland

Giacomini (1908) has already described that the adrenal gland of teleosts are situated within the anterior parts of the kidney. The adrenal gland is composed of interrenal and chromaffin tissues. The former is homologous to the adrenal cortex and the latter (chromaffin tissues) is homologous to the mammalian medullary cells. This region comprises the catecholamine (primary and secondary amines) containing cells. The interrenal cells are present in several layers. In *Puntius ticto,* these cells form thick glandular mass while in *Channa punctatus* they are arranged in the form of small lobules along the post cardinal veins. In *Heteropneustes fossilis* (Bloch), the interrenal tissue is arranged in lobules varying in thickness around the cardinal vein and its branches in the haemopoetic head kidney. The lobules of the adrenocortical tissue are so much packed together that there is hardly any interfollicular space left. The interrenal cells are generally columnar or polygonal with acidophilic cytoplasm and a distinct nucleus. The medullary cells in orth's preparation stand out clearly as

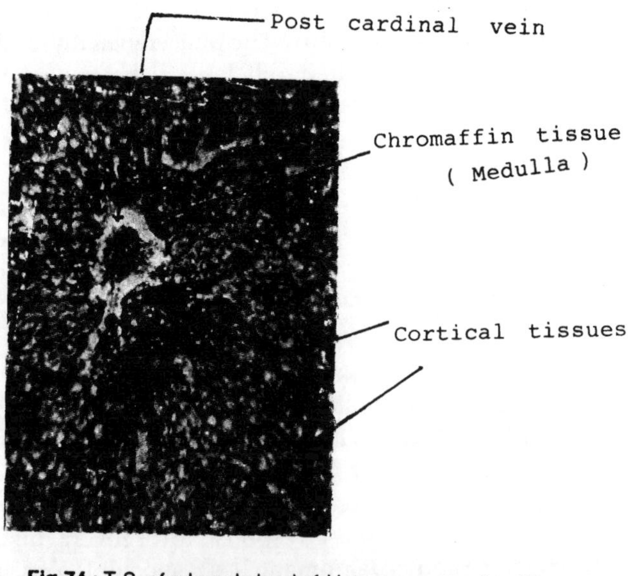

Fig.74 : T.S. of adrenal gland of *Heteropneustes fossilis*

dark brown entities. The cells are large and irregular, located near the wall surrounding the lumen of the cardinal vein. They intermingle with the interrenal tissue near the small blood capillaries. The nucleus may be oval, round or even irregular in outline. *Epinephrine* and *norepinephrine* secreting cells have separate entity.

Some important contributions regarding the structure and physiology of the adrenal gland in teleosts are those of Baecker (1928), Phillips and Chester-Jones (1957), Bondy *et al.* (1957), Chester Jones and Phillips (1960), van Overbeeke (1960), Chavin and Kovacevic (1961), Nandi (1962, 1965), Banerjee and Ghosh (1966), van Overbeeke and Ahsan (1966), Yadav Singh and Munshi (1970), Dixit (1971) and others.

Functions of the Adrenal gland: Adrenocortical secretions were isolated for the first time from the blood of fish by Phillips and Chester Jones (1957) and also by Bondy *et al.* (1957). The important hormones in the plasma were cortisol, cortisone and corticosterone. Aldosterone has also been reported by some workers in teleosts. Investigations suggest that the chromaffin cells secrete Epinephrine and Nor-epinephrine like the mammalian medullary cells.

Presence of mineralocorticoids, aldosterone has been pointed out in *Fundulus* and goldfish much earlier. The corticosteroid level varies at different physiological states of *Hippoglossus hippoglossus*. The corticoids in teleosts regulate the water and electrolyte balance and they are also concerned with protein and carbohydrate metabolism. Cortisol increases the uptake of sodium by the gills in several teleosts. Under experimental conditions also it has been observed that following cortisol adminstration, sodium turnover is increased in teleost gills. Renal sodium retention is increased and glomerular filtcration rate is reduced (as in trout). Cortisol can restore the rate of water absorption in the intestine of the fish, fresh water adapted eels. The interrenal also plays a role in osmotic adjustments of teleosts when the latter are subjected to salinity changes. Corticoids also promote gluconeogenesis. Hypoglycaemia and lowering of liver glycogen have been demonstrated in eels when the interrenal gland is removed. The association of 'stress' can be marked in several teleosts with increased plasma cortisol and glucose levels. The interrenal with the increased secretion of cortisol influences oocyte maturation in *Heteropneustes fossilis.*

Epinephrine and Nor-epinephrine have been found in the anterior kidney and the plasma of several bony fishes. When the fishes are disturbed for sometime, there is abnormal rise in the plasma concentration of Epinephrine (e.g. in rainbow trout). Epinephrine increases the plasma fatty acids of eels, scorpionfish and sea-bass but at the sametime it also decreases the plasma free fatty acids in some fishes like bream, gold fish and carp. Epinephrine is said to increase plasma cyclic AMP-levels in the trout. Catecholamine injection increases cyclic-AMP concentration in teleost muscles. Epinephrine causes a systemic vasoconstriction and a branchial vasodilation. Catecholamines have an excitatory effect and increase the rate of heart beating. According to Keys and Bateman (1932), catecholamines play an important role in the osmoregulations of teleosts. They do exert gill effects.

Islets of Langerhans

The endocrine tissues of the Pancreas are condensed into several islets which may have independent identity and may be present scattered in the pancreatic mass. Normally, they are present adjacent to the gill bladder, spleen or pyloric caecum. In different fishes the islets have definite locations.

In *Heteropneustes fossilis, Clarias batrachus* and *Mystus seenghala,* several pancreatic islets of different shapes and size are embedded within the exocrine mass of the Pancreas. The islets look like small protuberances within the pancreatic mass.

In *Channa punctatus* the islets present near the spleen and pylorus are exceptionally large, but some smaller islets are also present in the mesentery. A thin connective tissue layer surrounds each and every islet. It has also been reported that the exocrine cells invade the splenic islets. Islets and the surrounding tissues are richly supplied with blood capillaries.

In *Labeo rohita, Cirrhina mrigala, Schizothorax plagiostomus* and *Tor tor* the "Principal islet" (large islets visible with naked eye) is located on the surface of the alimentary canal near the entrance of the bile duct. Some small and large islets are present in the tissue of the mesentery, adjacent to gall bladder and the bile duct.

In *Mastacembelus armatus,* the principal islet is present in the loop of the duodenum and it is enclosed in a thick connective tissue capsule. It is situated anterior to the spleen. In *Wallago attu* small islets are scattered in the exocrine pancreatic mass and they are separated by connective tissue layer.

Some important contributions on the structure and function of the Islets of Langerhans in some teleosts have been made by Patel *et al.* (1966) Epple (1968), Khanna and Mehrotra (1968, 1969), Thomas (1970), Khanna and Singh (1971), Khanna and Rekhari (1972), Brinn (1973), Khanna and Gill (1973), Khanña and Bhatt (1974, 1975), Gill and Khanna (1975), Epple and Miller (1981) and others.

Histo-Physiology: In the islets of Langerhans three types of cells have been identified so far. β-cells (or B-cells) can be stained dark purple with the help of aldehyde fuchsin (AF) stain. Like mammals these cells secrete insulin. Another type of cells which are AF-negative are known as α-cells (or A-cells). They are of two types A_1 and A_2 cells. Silver stain selectively colours the A_1 cells but the A_2 cells are silver-negative. A_2 cells have been called D-cells by some authors. The presence of some granular cells have been pointed out in the islets, which have been called C-cells.

The β-cells are polyhedral in shape with centrally placed large round nucleus. The α-cells are almost triangular in shape and they have normally eccentric nucleus. The β-cells secrete *insulin* and *glucagon* is the product of the α-cells, particularly A_1 cells. The function of A_2 cells is still controversial.

Insulin is a hypoglycemic factor whereas glucagon is a hyperglycemic factor. Insulin facilitates the transport of a variety of substances e.g. glucose, monosaccharides, amino acids, Pot. ions, nucleosides and inorganic phosphates. The action of glucagon is glycogenolytic. The other functions of the hormones of islets of Langerhans are like that of mammals.

Pineal Organ

The Pineal, gland is present in the dorsal side of the brain and is a photoreceptor organ basically, but it is also considered to be an endocrine gland. The interest in Pineal morphology and histochemistry with a view to elucidate its function arose in different workers and the chief contributions are those of Hill (1891, 1894), Scharrer (1927), Holmgren (1958), Palayer (1958), Fenwick (1970) Steyn and Webb (1960), Bose (1961), Kelly (1962), Ariens Kappers (1965), Morita (1966), Hafeez and Ford (1967), Omura and Oguri (1969), Takahashi (1969), Saxena (1970), Hafeez (1971), Takahashi and Kasuga (1971), Sriwastava and Dubey (1975), Hafeez and Merhiga (1977), Mc Nulty (1978), Sriwastava *et. al.* (1980), Dubey *et al.* (1982), Khanna *et al.*, (1983), Hore and Alim (1989) and others.

Basically the pineal body is a hollow structure variously invaginated. It is divisible into *end bulb*, the *atrium* and the *nerve stalk* in cyclostomes. Pigment and sensory cells are present in the floor wall of the end bulb forming the so called retina. Projections arise from these sensory cells and they make contact with '*cones*' located in the roof of the end bulb commonly known as pellucida. The nerve stalk is dominated by cellular elements and only a few nerve fibres are present. It connects to the posterior commissure. The lumen of the pineal body connects with the third ventricle. The *pigment cells, sensory cells* and the *ganglionic cells* are well developed in the pineal retina. The Pineal body may be rudimentary in some fishes (e.g. *Hippocampus spinosus*), and it may be absent in certain elasmobranchs (e.g. *Torpedo ocellata*), and cyclostome (adult *Myxine glutinosa*).

Very little is known about the Pineal of Chondrichthyes. Photoreceptor capacity has been shown in *Scyliorhinus canicula*. Rudeberg (1969) made some light and electron microscope studies on the Pineal organ of this fish. The activities of the nerve fibres are influenced by the duration and intensity of the light. In the hitology of the cells, diurnal changes have not been observed so far. Munro and Dodd (1983) have revealed that in elasmobranch there is a well developed pineal and a parapineal, the latter being transitory. The pineal is associated with a cartilaginous window for transmission of light.

The Pineal organ of *Wallago attu* as described by Sriwastava *et al.* (1980) is hollow and consists of Pineal stalk, Pineal thalamus and conical elongated Pineal sac. It arises as a postero-mid-dorsal evagination of the epithalamus. The sac is conical with elongated narrow part and is attached to the under surface of the skin covering the pineal foramen. It is highly vascular and is also enclosed in a connective tissue capsule. The pineal stalk consists of low columnar epithelium. The Pineal parenchymatous villi produce into the lumen of the sac and consists of sensory, supporting and ganglion cells. On the basis of several staining techniques the sensory cells have been differentiated into Alfa cells, Beta cells, Gamma cells, Chromophobic cells, Aldehyde fuchsin Positive and negative cells etc.

Dubey *et al.* (1982) have described the Pineal organ of *Mystus aor*. It has Pineal sac, Pineal thalamus and Pineal stalk. The Pineal Parenchyma protrudes as pineal villi in the lumen whose magnitude reduces slowly towards the stalk. The ganglion cells are generally found in the lower half of the villi. The Parenchyma comprises the sensory, supporting and ganglion cells as usual. The dorsum of the sac has been found to be very thin. The sensory cell types are like that of *Wallago attu*.

Jose and Hore (1989) have described the pineal organ in an Indian Spiny eel, *Macrognathus aculeatus* (Bloch). The pineal organ as observed by them has a long and narrow stalk with an oval end vesicle of intermediate type. There is no pineal window in this case. The lumen of the end vesicle and pineal stalk communicates with the third vesicle. The end vesicle is situated on the roof of the brain in between the lateral eyes. The lumen of the stalk often possesses AB and PAS positive homogeneous coagulum. The dorsal sac is a well developed and compact projecting between habenular commissure and velum transversum as observed by them.

Hore and Alim (1989) have described the histophysiology of the pineal organs in mosquito fish, *Gambusia affinis*. In this fish as observed by these worker, the pineal body is club-shaped structure formed as an evagination from the roof of the diencephalon in between the hebenular and the posterior commissures. There is absence of Pineal window. The Pineal vesicle or the end vesicle is situated anteriorly and it is quite broad in appearance. The pineal stalk is located posteriorly and it is an elongated narrow portion. The lumen of the end vesicle and the pineal stalk is confluent with the third ventricle. The end vesicle has folded layer internally. The lumen of the end vesicle and pineal stalk is filled with PAS and AB positive homogeneous coagulum as reported by them. These authors did not find an influence over the apocrine secretion either by continuous darkness or by continuous illumination for ninety days.

The Pineal sac in most of the fishes is surrounded by collagen connective tissue forming a capsule. The sac is not always hollow but it may be solid in certain cases, as in the lantern fishes. There may be variation in the shape of the sac also. In *Wallago attu* it is conical but in *Bagarius bagarius* it is rosette like.

The cell bodies in the Pineal sac are not connected by means of duct or ducts. Naturally, the endocrine nature of the cell is indicated. Fenwick (1970) has already pointed out that the Pineal organ is an endocrine gland. The neurosecretory nature of pineal organ has been shown by several workers. Pinealectomy results in reduction of growth rate, and also some abnormalities appear in the skeleton. The pineal gland is physiologically linked with Thyroid, Pituitary and Corpuscles of Stannius. Recent experiments on *Mystus vittatus* have revealed that the pineal influences the maturation of gonads in fishes. Presence of *melatonin*, and neurosecretory substance containing mucopolysaccharides, basic protein, protein containing orginine and lysine, acidic lipids etc. are suggestive of the fact that the pineal body has definitely some endocrine role which is still controversial.

The pineal body in teleosts is really the site of synthesis and release of hormone *melatonin* as suggested by Fenwick (1970), Gern *et al.* (1978), Gern and Ralph (1979) and Kavaliers (1980). Oguri *et al.* (1968) demonstrated that the *5-hydroxytryptaphane* is taken up by the pineal organ in greater quantity. It is a precursor of melatonin. *Melatonin* is chemically an indole, *5-methoxy-N-acetyltryptamine*. This hormone is probably a chemical transducer of the photic environment and it regulates the reproductive functions also as reported by Reiter (1978, 1980). A pineal control of gonadal maturation has been shown in fishes (Urasaki, 1972; De Vlaming, 1975; De vlaming and Voldicnik, 1978). Endocrine function of the Pineal gland had also been suggested by Friedrich-Freksa (1932) who have claimed that its secretion is directly taken by the associated blood vessels.

Corpuscles of Stannius

Stannius for the first time discovered three nodular bodies in Sturgeon's kidney in the year 1839. These are small, oval or round in shape and are embedded partly or completely in the kidney of teleosts. They may be present on the dorsal, dorso-lateral or ventrolateral sides of the kidney. Normally, corpuscles of stannius are present in the posterior part of the kidney. Belsare (1973) has reported that these corpuscles originate from the pronephric or the mesonephric duct. The number and size of these bodies vary in different species of fish. In *Notopterus notopterus* there is only one corpuscle of stannius and it is 0.2 to 0.6 mm in size. In *Heteropneustes fossilis,* the number is two to four and the size 0.4 to 0.9 mm. In *Salmo salar* there are four to ten of these corpuscles of varying sizes (2-5 mm). In *Amia calva* there may be fifty or more corpuscles of stannius. *Clarias batrachus* has two to ten corpuscles whose size vary from 0.5 to 1.2mm. Large sized corpuscles are present in *Labeo rohita* which measure 3-6 mm and they are 2-3 in number. In this way, such reports are available on a large number of fishes.

Histology of Corpuscles of stannius

Some authors have described the structural details of corpuscles of stannius in several bony fishes. Important contributions are those of Rasquin (1956), Nadkarni and Gorbman (1966), Hanke and Chester Jones (1966), Heyl (1970), Belsare (1973), Pang (1973), Gill and Punetha (1977), Meats *et al.* (1978), Bhattacharya *et al.* (1982) and others.

The Corpuscles of Stannius are composed of parenhymatous cells, arranged in the form of follicles or irregular cords. These are separated by connective tissue layer and surrounded by fibrous capsule. Within the Parenchymatous cells or adjacent to them, is present a ganglionic unit having blood capillaries and nerve fibres. In *Anguilla anguilla* and *Salmon,* Aldehyde fuchsin positive and AF-negative cells have been identified. In the hill-stream fish, *Pseudoecheinis sulcatus,* only AF-positive secretory cells have been reported lying along the blood vessels. PAS-positive granules are present in the cells of corpuscles of stannius in the case of rainbow trout. Endoplasmic reticulum, Golgi apparatus and secretory granules are quite prominent. Two cell types contain large secretory granules and small secretory granules separately (e.g. *Anguilla anguilla* and *Gasterosteus aculeatus).* In the corpuscles of *Salmo salar,* there is only one cell type.

Function: It is thought that corpuscles of Stannius are concerned with electrolyte homeostasis in the fishes. When there is change in the salinity of water, increase or decrease in the granulation of cells can be seen. Hypophysectomy also affects granulation. In *Anguilla anguilla* when these corpuscles were removed, there was marked reduction in the plasma sodium, and increase in the concentration of Potassium and Calcium. The hypocalcaemic factor of the corpuscles is known as *hypocalcin.* The another factor *teleocalcin* is a glycopeptide (isolated from *Salmon)* and it has an inhibitory effect on Ca^{++}—ATPase. It is said to be hypocalcaemic in intact American eels.

According to some authors, the corpuscles of stannius is homologous with the adrenal gland. Thus calcium homeostasis is an important function of corpuscles of Stannius. The mian physiological role of the corpuscles is to maintain Ca^{++} to Na^{+} and Cl^{-} in the plasma.

Gonads

On the histomorphological, biochemical and physiological aspects of gonads of cyclostomes, there are some important contributions which include those of Sundararaj and Goswami (1969), Dodd (1972), Larson (1974, 1978), Weisbart and Youson (1975), Pickering (1976), Patzner (1978), Kime and Hews (1980), Kime *et. al.* (1980) Weisbart *et al.* (1980), York and McMillan (1980), Kime and Rafter (1981), Turner *et al.* (1981, 1982), Katz *et al.* (1982), Van Der Kraak and Donaldson (1983) and others.

Some more works devoted to reproduction and its regulation in cyclostomes are those of Schreiner (1966), Tsuneki and Gorbman (1977 a, b), Gorbman and Dickhoff (1978), Crim *et al.* (1979 a, b), Callard *et al.* (1980), Gorbman (1980), Larsen (1980), Nansen (1988) and others.

The gonad is unpaired in hagfishes and lampreys in both the male and female specimens. It is suspended from the dorsal body wall in the body cavity by means of mesentery. Testis consists of follicles containing male gametes which are liberated into the body cavity. In *Petromyzon,* the gonad extends the whole of the body cavity and there is no reproductive ducts. The sex cells are discharged in the body cavity through the abdominal pores present in the urinogenital sinus. The ovary is composed of eggs which are covered by a layer of follicular epithelium. The *microphagous larva* of a lamprey is known as the *Ammocoetes larva.* It spends burrowing periods of several years in the streams. During this period the growth is very slow. Later on, when metamorphosis takes place, there are rapid changes in the head region. In one type of lampreys gonadal differentiation and metamorphosis take place simultaneously. At the end of metamorphosis, spawning takes place and the lampreys die. This happens in the non-parasitic forms. In the parasitic forms however, sexually immature individuals are formed. They migrate into the marine water. Here they adhere to large fishes with the help of their newly formed oral sucker and oral disc of horny teeth. They grow rapidly in this *macrophagous phase* and after 1-2 years they return to freshwater spreams again. In *Lampetra planeri* ammocoetes, gonads are well differentiated. Oocytes are present in the immature ovaries,however in the tests, oocytes disappear and a few nests of so called presumptive spermatogenic cells are formed from the stem cells, already present. In lamprey females modified anal fins and cloacal swelling and in males, urinogenital papilla and modified dorsal fin are considered as the secondary sexual characters.

A mature *Lampetra fluviatilis* female may contain as many as 40000 eggs in its body cavity. All the eggs normally mature at a time. In the female *Eptatretus stouti* (a myxinoid) all stages of oogenesis are present in the ovary. In the hagfish *Myxine glutinosa* annual ovarian cycle has not been recognized. In lampreys the eggs are surrounded by an inner granulosa and an outer theca layer. In some species of *Myxine* and *Bdellostoma* ovotestis is present, the anterior part is the ovary and the posterior part is the testis.

Estradiol has been detected in the plasma of cyclostomes. *Testosterone, Dihydrotestosterone* and *Progesterone* have been found in the ovary of hagfish in very small amounts. In *Lampetra fluviatilis* there is evidence for estrogen induced vitellogenesis.

The sex in hagfishes can not be distinguished externally. In some species, seasonally synchronized reproductive cycle has been reported e.g. in a shallow water form, *Eptatretus burgeri.* In hagfish, the development is direct i.e. there is absence of a larval form. The breeding period in this species covers from June to October. The fish is hermaphrodite and the gonads are located anteroposteriorly. The ovarian mass is present lengthwise up to the end of coelomic cavity. The posterior section of the gonads is testicular. The male and female germinal cells are not mixed up together at any level.

The testis in cyclostomes (males) possesses several lobules containing some ampullae united. The lobules are connected by connective tissue sheets. The ampullae of this lobule are lined by germinal epithelium. In lampreys, this epithelium divides more or less synchronously in the whole gonad. In most of the hagfishes there is no regular breeding season. In *Eptatretus burgeri* regular gonadal cycle has been discovered by A.J. Matty and co-workers (Fish Endocrinology A.Matty). In lamprey, *interstitial cells* have been reported, though, these cells are absent in hagfish. The steroidogenic enzyme, 3 *β-hydroxysteroid dehydrogenase* has been reported in the interstitial tissue of lampreys. Testosterone has been detected in the plasma of cyclostomes.

The physiological role of these hormone in cyclostomes is not very clear and *gonadotropin-sex hormone axis* is well established in cyclostomes.

There are several reviews dealing with the histomorphology and physiology of gonads and some reproductive processes in elasmobranchs. These contributions include those of Mahadevan (1940), Matthews (1950), Kudo (1956), Simpson *et al.* (1964), Sathyanesan (1966), Stanley (1966), Lance and Callard (1969), Guraya (1972), Te Winkel (1972), Dobson and Dodd (1977a, 1977b), Dodd (1977), Dodd *et al.* (1982), Wourms (1977), Kime (1978), Dodd and Dodd (1980), Jenkins and Dodd (1980), Dodd and Duggan (1982), Dodd *et al.* (1982) and others.

The Ovary in several species (e.g.*Dasyatis*) is a single structure of variable size in the body cavity and it is naked (gymnovarian). It is not continuous with the oviducts. It is suspended by the connective tissue, *mesovarium.* In scoliodon however, the ovaries are paired structures. In elasmobranchs round follicles are present in the ovary which contain the ovum. The germ cells become primary oocytes before sexual maturity. In mature Ovary, *'Corpora lutea'* and *Corpora atresia* are present in certain cases. There is seasonal variation in the vitellogenic oocytes of various species. The theca externa of the maturing follicles consists a single layer of cuboidal or flattened cells having endoplasmic reticulum and lipid droplets, mitochondria and prominent vasicles. Below the *theca externa layer*, *theca interna* is present which is characterised by the presence of several rows of flattened elongated cells. There is an interlocking meshwork of collagen fibres and collagenocytes in between these cells. Rough endoplasmic reticulum, abundance of mitochondria and contractile microfibrils are associated with these cells.

The blood plasma of mature female contains a calcium-binding *lipophosphoprotein,* known as *vitellogenin.* As in other vertebrates, it is synthesized in the liver under the influence of female sex steroids. It passes into the oocytes, and there, it gives rise to the yolk proteins, *lipovitellin* and *phosvitin.*

Testes are elongated and subcylindrical, extending throughout the full length of the body cavity. The unit of structure in testis is *ampulla* or *follicle* and the arrangement of this structure is zonate. The division of the germ cells are synchronous. There is seasonal variation in the weight of the testis. All *Spermatogenetic stages (Primary and Secondary Spermatogonia, Primary and Secondary Spermatocytes, Spermatids and Spermatozoa)* are present in the maturing testis. *Sertoli cells* are well developed in elasmobranchs.

Testosterone, androsterone-4-ene-3, 17-dione, *androsterone* and *dehydroepiandrosterone* are present in the rays and sharks and male sex hormones. Unlike other hormones *testosterone* appears in plasma also. The sperms of *Squalus acanthias* have large quantities of Steroid (C_{21} and C_{19} compounds). It has been shown that in *Raja radiata,* plasma concentrations of testosterone is lower in the evening than in the morning. In *Scyliorhinus canicula, dehydroepiandrosterone* appears to be the active precursor of testosterone. So, this compound definitely comes in the biosynthetic pathway of the formation of testosterone from pregnenolone.

Estradiol-17 β is present in the ovary of *Squalus suckleii.* It induces the secretion of *Vitellogenin* by the liver. Presence of *Oestriol* and *Progesterone* has been detected in the ovary of *Torpedo marmorata.* Oestrone is present in the ovary of some elasmobranchs. *Oestrone* and *Oestriol* have been detected in the plasma also. The process of sex steroid biosynthesis in elasmobranch is not very clear.

The problem of reproduction and the histophysiological studies of the gonads and their seasonal changes have been the subject of investigation by a large number of workers. Most of the fishes are seasonal breeders and spawn mainly in June and July. It is well established that in most teleosts the *ovary* undergoes fairly regular seasonal changes and it has been demonstrated in a number of teleosts by a series of investigations (Sathyanesasn, 1962; Belsare, 1962; Rai, 1967; Khanna and Pant, 1967; Lehri, 1968; Rastogi and Saxena, 1968; Bisht and Joshi, 1975; Guraya *et al.* 1975; Sahu *et al.* 1985; and others). There are several internal and external factors which are responsible for certain variations in spawning behaviour.

There is one pair of ovary in female. It is covered by a ovarian wall and encloses a cavity the ovocoel. During the spawning period the tunica albuginea is a thin layer but during the rest period it is a thick layer. The germinal epithelium consists of a single layer of cuboidal cells which possess very little amount of cytoplasm. During the breeding period, the gonosomatic-index rises much. There is increase in the ova diameter. During October to February ovigerous lamellae are the prominent structure and these are the seats of production of new crops of oogonia. There is reduction in the size of ovary. Oogonia are in stage I. In January and February oocytes are

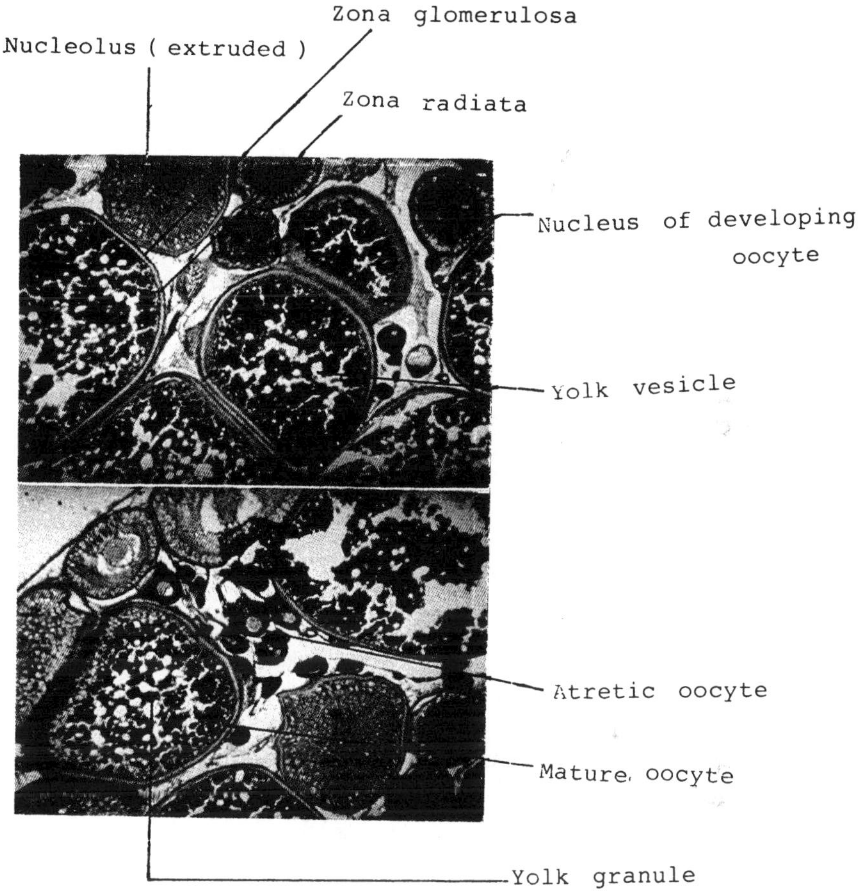

Fig. 75 : Parts of section of ovary of Amphipnous cuchia

formed and the wall of the ovary becomes thick and vascular. In February, 10 to 20 per cent of the oocytes are in stage II of the international stage of maturity. In this month perinucleus stage is reached. During the period March to May, the ovary becomes pale yellow and reaches stage III. Yolk nucleus appears and nucleolar extrusions can be seen. In April, the margins of the oocytes mostly become undulating and wavy. The yolk vesicles appear along the periphery in the form of vacuoles arranged peripherally in the oocytes, but gradually, they occupy the whole ooplasm. In the month of May only 15 per cent oocytes belong to stage V and rest are in stage-IV of the international stage of maturity . During the period June to mid of August the ovary becomes deep yellow in colour. Most of the oocytes are in stage VI and only a few belong to stage V. In the month of June the *Zona granulosa* (outer layer) and *Zona radiata* (inner layer) become clear. The ripe ovum is full of yolk granules and is surrounded by the fibroelastic layer 'theca'. The nucleoli of the oocytes accumulate in the centre of the nucleus. June to July, is the real breeding season in several fishes. In certain cases, it continues upto mid of August. The oocytes acquire the largest size during the spawning phase. From August, the post-spawning period starts. The ovaries at this stage are very much shrunken and the whole structure almost collapses. It is reddish in colour. Several atretic oocytes and post-ovulatory follicles are observed in this phase. Oestradiol-17 β has been identified in the ovaries of *Salmo irideus* and *cyprinus carpio.* It is actually a major ovarian steroid hormone of most teleosts. It has been proposed that pregnenolone is converted into progesterone, 17α-hydroxyprogesterone, androstenedione, testosterone, 17 α-hydroxypregnenolone, dehydroepiandrosterone and a little of corticosteroids. During steroid hormone metabolism in teleost ovary, certain enzymes like *7α-steroid reluctase* and 7α *hydroxysteroid dehydrogenase* have been detected.

Some of the important contributions on the testicular activities in teleosts are those of Nair (1965, 66), Khanna and Pant (1966), Rai (1966), Lehri (1967), Ruby and Mc Millan (1970), Sehgal (1971), Sanwall and Khanna (1972), Sakari and Igarashi (1974), Shrestha and Khanna (1976), Patzner (1977), Bhatti and Al-Daham (1978), Lite Wellys (1979), Chan and Chua (1980), Hoffman *et al.* (1980) Pandey and Mishra (1981), Pollock (1982) and others.

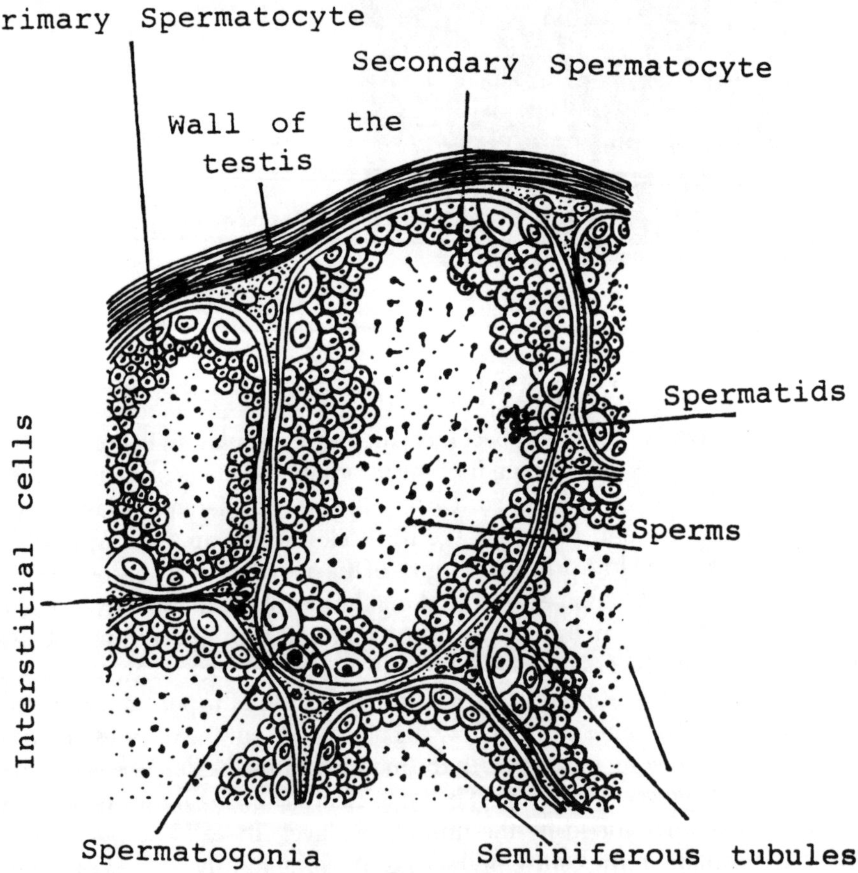

Fig. 76 : T.S. of mature testis

There is one pair of testis (in male) which is transparent when immature, but with maturity its colour becomes creamy white. The testis is richly supplied with blood capillaries, particularly during the breeding season. When the testis becomes matured *tunica albuginea* becomes thin. The testis is fully packed up with seminiferous tubules whose wall becomes thin and the lumen enlarged during the breeding season. In between the seminiferous tubules are present the interstitial cells in the same fashion as in tetrapods.

There are very few works devoted to the cyclic changes of the activity of the Leydig cells or the lobule boundary cells. Some worth mentioning contributions in this regard are those of Ahsan (1966), Hyder (1972), Wiebe (1969), Dodd (1962), Donaldson (1973), Lofts and Bern (1972), de Vlaming (1974), and Sultana Yasin *et al.* (1980).

The testis undergoes cyclic changes throughout the year and there is variation in its appearance, weight and developmental stages of various spermatogenetic cells. The developmental activities initiate in the month of February. The peak of the activities is seen in the month of June and July. The spermatogonia attached to the boundary wall of the lobule are the largest. They are spherical and with rounded nucleus, which has diffuse chromatin materials. Spermatocytes are rounded and small with lesser amount of cytoplasm. Gonosomatic index is lowest in the month of December and it rises in June-July. In the month of February the thread like testis enlarges to attain a thicker appearance and occupy nearly half of the body cavity. It is the phase of growth. In March, the testis becomes morphologically larger having a large number of Primary and Secondary Spermatocytes. It is the maturation phase. In June and July the testis covers the entire body cavity and a large number of spermatozoa are ready for spawning. The testicular lobules are fully packed up with mature spermatozoa. The post-spawning phase of the testis is reached between the period mid of August to November.

The event of spermatogenesis has been divided by several authors (Sanwal and Khanna, 1972; Davis, 1977; Chan and Chua, 1980; Hoffmann *et al.* 1980; Sinha and Mondal, 1981; Mukhopadhyay and Sinha 1986) into various stages.

Testosterone is the main important androgenic hormone in fishes. In certain fishes (*onchorhynchus nerka*) testosterone is conjugated with glucuronic acid. *Testosterone, androstenedione* and *androsterone* have been identified in certain teleosts. Progesterone has been isolated from the gonads of teleosts.

Intestinal Mucosa

Endocrine activities have been described in the epithelial cells of the intestine. Several hormones are produced by the gastrointestinal tracts and they can act either on gastrointestinal organs themselves or on other organs of the body. A large number of peptides have been identified in the endocrine cells or nerves of the gastrointestinal tracts and they have marked biological effects.

There is no evidence of gastrin-like hormone in the gut of cyclostomes.

Comparatively, very few investigations have been made of the gastrointestinal activities in fish. In fishes only three hormones/hormone like substances have been demonstrated. They are *Cholecystokinin, gastrin* and *secretin.* There is no information of gastrointestinal glucagon as stated by Unger *et al.* (1968).

Gastrin-like activity has not been demonstrated in cyclostomes. However, in elasmobranchs and teleosts, this hormone is present. Presence of gastrin-like activity has been reported from *Coho salmon, Squalus acanthias, Lepomis macrochirus, Rhinobatus productus* etc. Gastrin-like activity has not been reported in the hagfish *Eptatretus stouti.* Secretion of gastric acid has been observed in *Gadus morhua* following histamin administration (intramuscular). The main physiological action of gastrin is to stimulate the secretion of acid in the stomach. Gastrin-like several gastrointestinal peptides have different pharmacological effects including tropic action stimulating the growth of the stomach and intestinal mucosa.

Cholecystokinin-like hormone is present in cyclostomes, elasmobranchs and teleosts. This hormone has been isolated from the intestine of *Lampetra fluviatilis* and *Petromyzon marinus, Anguilla anguilla* and *Chimaera monstrosa.* In mammals, this hormone stimulates the contraction of gall bladder. Similarly extracts of river lamprey *Lampetra fluviatilis* causes contraction of rabbit gall bladder. Extracts of the intestine of *Eptatrelus stouti* also causes contraction of gall bladder of guinea pig. This hormone also stimulates the secretion of enzymes from the exocrine pancreatic tissues.

This hormone evokes production of pancreatic fluid. Bayliss and Starling prepared active extracts of secretin from Salmon, dogfish and skate intestine. Crude extracts have been prepared from time to time from cyclostomes, holocephali, elasmobranchs and some teleosts. This hormone stimulates the pancreatic enzymes also and induces gall bladder contraction like CCK. This hormone stimulates the rate of pancreatic juice flow. The secretion of *Esox lucius* resembles vasoactive intestinal polypeptide (VIP) more closely in comparison to that of porcine secretin.

Urophysis

The urophysis is present in both elasmobranchs and teleosts on the spinal cord of the tail region (neurosecretory and neurohaemal area). It is present in the form of a prominent swelling. A well developed neurohaemal urophysis is seen only in teleost fishes. Definite neurosecretory cells have not been identified in the caudal nerve cord of cyclostomes and holocephalians. Valuable contributions on the caudal neurosecretory system in fishes are those of Dahelgren (1914), Enami *et al.* (1956), Enami (1959), Sano (1961), Bern and Takasugi (1962), Maetz *et al.* (1964), Gabe (1966), Lahtou (1966), Bern *et al.* (1967), Hiran *et al.* (1967), Fridberg and Bern (1968), Lederis (1969, 77), Loretz and Bern (1981), Marshall and Bern (1981) and others. In elasmobranchs the neurosecretory cells which are called *Dahelgren* cells, have cell bodies about twenty times larger than ordinary motor neurons. The axons of these cells terminate at the blood vessels of the lateroventral side of the spinal cord. The axons of the neurosecretory cells in teleosts concentrate with blood vessels to form a neurohaemal function just like that of neurohypophysis. In certain cases stalk may be present (e.g. *Fundulus* and *Oryzias*) but in others the stalk is absent (e.g. eel). The Urophysis may be paired or unpaired structures and may project ventrally or laterally.

The neurosecretory cells are characterised by the presence of polymorphic nuclei and a basohilic cytoplasm. The unmyelinated axons of these neurosecretory cells pass into the haemal region and terminate on the capillaries to discharge their secretion into the capillary endothellum. They give rise to *Herring bodies* also. Sometimes *glial elements* and *ependymal* processes are also seen among the axon terminals. *Urophysins* which are the intracellular carrier proteins are present in elasmobranchs and teleosts. The neurosecretory cells possess electrophysiological properties of neurous but with longer action potential in comparison to motor neurous.

Functions of Urophysis

The following are the important functions of Urophysis secretions—

1. It elevates blood pressure in fishes.
2. It is responsible for the contraction of several smooth muscles.
3. It increases the urine flow.
4. It is directly or indirectly concerned with osmoregulation, salt balance.
5. It plays an important role in the reproduction (oviposition and spawning) of some fishes (e.g. *Gillichthys* and *Lebistes*).
6. It is also concerned with gas metabolism and buoyancy.
7. It is probably concerned with corticotropin release also as proposed by some workers.

Ultimobranchial Organ

There are some important contributions on the structure and function of *Ultimobranchial organ* in various groups of fishes. Worth mentioning contributions are those of Camp (1917), Watzka (1933), Krawarik (1936), Rasquin and Rosenbloom (1954), Urist (1962, 1964, 1966), Cooper *et al.* (1967), Flemming (1967), Urist and Van de Putte (1967), Copp (1969), Pang (1971), McMillan *et al.* (1976), Wen dellar Bonga (1980) and others.

The ultimobranchial organ is present as a band like structure below the oesophagus and is derived from the last branchial pouch area in the embryonic conditions. During the course of development of the fish, backward migration of this tissue takes place. It comes to lie over the pericardium. In elasmobranch, it develops from one side of the Pharynx only. In cyclostomes no outgrowths of Pharynx comparable to ultimobranchial tissue has been identified. As a matter of fact ultimobranchial body has not been demonstrated in cyclostomes.

The position of this gland varies in different species of fishes. In *Squalus acanthias,* the gland is present in the left side between the pericardium and the ventral surface of the pharynx, just anterior to the beginning of the oesophagus. In

Scyliorhinus caniculus, the gland lies ventral to the pharynx., medial to the 5th gill arch. In certain specimens of this fish the gland may be bilateral but in others it is present only on the left side of the pharynx. In teleosts, it is generally located on the septum between the abdominal cavity and the sinus venosus. The gland in holocephalians is bilateral.

The gland consists of several follicles which enclose granular materials, and the surrounding epithelium comprises columnar cells. Some of the cells are *mitochondrial* rich cells but others are poor in mitochondrial content. In rainbow trout the gland is solid without follicles. It is composed of secreting cells and non-granular irregularly shaped cells. The ultimobranchial gland resembles the porathyroid of higher vertebrates.

Functions

This gland contains *Calcitonin* in all fishes. It is believed that secretion of this gland regulates calcium in the body. The gland is involved in controlling hypercalcaemia like terrestrial vertebrates. In chimaeroids and elasmobranchs also, the ultimobranchial glands contain calcitonin as suggested by Copp *et al.* (1967). This hormone has been implicated in Calcium regulation in teleosts also. According to Fontaine (1964), this gland is involved in ion regulation, and removal of this gland in *Anguilla anguilla*, the plasma calcium level was raised. Thus, it lowers the plasma calcium level like mammals. The gland is probably also concerned with hydromineral metabolism, migration and reproductive behaviour of fishes. It facilitates mobilisation of calcium during egg formation. However, definite roles of this hormone are to be ascertained.

CHAPTER 20

INDIAN FISHERIES

The production of fish in India is low as compared to other countries of the world though it has enormous potential resources. India has really all ideal conditions for the improvement of fisheries. It is surrounded by sea on its three sides and besides this it has many big rivers, bays, lakes, canals, reservoirs, ponds, tanks and many water loggings at various places. There is great scope for further expansion of fisheries in our country and as such, the Govt. is paying much attention to it now. *Pisciculture* is an important aspect which can supplement not only for solving the food problem to a great extent but it will be a source of employment for the unemployed also. Development of fisheries means an increase in production and also exploitation of production potential. (The statistics of the catches have been mentioned below):

World Fish Catch-1994

As per record of the *"Fishing News international"* published from London in 1996 and incorporated in *"Fishing Chimes"* of June 1996, the world record of fish catches in 1993 and 1994 were 102.184 million mt. and 109.585 million mt. respectively. The country-wise data have been given below in detail:

Country or area	*1993 Tonnes*	*1993 Place*	*1994 Tonnes*	*1994 Place*
China	17567907	1	20718903	1
Peru	8452476	2	11587339	2
Chile	6036005	4	7841031	3
Japan	8128121	3	7363314	4
USA	5948242	5	5940737	5
India	4337730	7	4540180	6
Indonesia	3676360	8	3954228	7
Russian Fed.	4461375	6	3780538	8
Thailand	3330827	9	3432000	9
South Korea	2648977	10	2700037	10
Norway	2561771	11	2551476	11

(Continued)

Country or area	1993 Tonnes	1993 Place	1994 Tonnes	1994 Place
Philippines	2263789	12	2276197	12
Denmark	1656285	15	1886851	13
North Korea	1780000	13	1800000	14
Iceland	1718498	14	1560184	15
Spain	1290000	17	1380000	16
Mexico	1200686	18	1260015	17
Taiwan	1415834	16	1248895	18
Malaysia	1154562	27	1173480	19
Vietnam	1100000	20	1150000	20
Bangladesh	1047170	21	1090596	21
Canada	1172017	19	1010582	22
Argentina	932206	22	949344	23
United Kingdom	872460	23	923404	24
France	831178	25	838332	25
Myanmar	836878	24	824468	26
Brazil	780000	26	820000	27
Morocco	622441	28	750088	28
Turkey	559234	32	604104	29
Pakistan	621695	29	551899	30
Italy	551794	31	547281	31
Netherlands	530529	33	526091	32
South Africa	563076	30	521062	33
New Zealand	470383	34	493239	34
Poland	423029	35	460229	35
Venezuela	390333	36	423979	36
Sweden	347820	40	394242	37
Senegal	377676	37	388042	38
Tanzania	331467	41	342932	39
Ecuador	331000	43	339915	40
Ghana	375162	39	336269	41
Iran	318055	42	314268	42
Ireland	307800	46	314072	43
Ukraine	371343	38	310722	44
Egypt	302829	47	305727	45
Namibia	329990	44	300833	46
Nigeria	255499	50	282089	47
Germany	316374	45	270837	48
Portugal	272605	48	253927	49
Faeroeis	261274	49	249927	50
Sri Lanka	220900	-	224000	51
Greece	199108	-	223081	52
Hong Kong	226843	-	220120	53
Uganda	219814	-	213145	54
Australia	244700	-	210500	55
Kenya	183091	-	203517	56
Countries	97727200		105178300	
Other countries	4456900		4406900	
World Total	102184100		109585200	

Kinds of Fisheries

(1) *Inland Fisheries:* Inland fishery resources in India are very rich. About 30 per cent of the total fish production is contributed by the inland capture fisheries alone. Inland fishery can be conveniently divided into two categories: *fresh waters* and *brackish waters.* The fresh water fishery comprises the great river system, fresh water lakes, irrigation canals, tanks, ponds and reservoir, and the brackish water fishery includes the estuaries (river mouths), lagoons, backwaters, and brackish water lakes. The managements of *Capture fisheries* are provided by the rivers (riverine), estuaries (esturine) and the lakes (lacustrine) but the *Culture fisheries* are provided by tanks, ponds and jheels etc.

(a) *Fresh water fisheries*: Besides extensive river system there is a variety of inland water ranging from-icy-cold tanks to tropical fresh water ponds. There are various species of fishes suitable for cultivation in ponds and confined waters. The major fresh water inland water bodies are the *Ganges system,* the *Brahmaputra system* and the *Indus system* in the northern part of India and the *East coast river system* and the *West coast river system* in the southern India. Lakes situated at higher altitudes support cold water fisheries of both indigenous and exotic fishes. The *Ganga system* is one of the largest river system in the world. The river Ganges takes its origin from Gangotri in the Himalayas and finally joins the Bay of Bengal. The Ganga system has a total length of about 8000 Km. The river Ganges comprises the range of Himalayas in the beginning and then covers the states of Haryana, Uttar Pradesh, Bihar, Bengal and also a part of Rajasthan and Madhya Pradesh. The river Yamuna is a major component of the Ganga system, and it borders the states of Punjab and Haryana and also flows through the territory of Delhi. Other principal tributaries of the Ganga system are the rivers Ramganga, Gomati, Ghaghara, Kosi, Gandak, Tons and Sone. The important tributaries of the river Yamuna are the rivers Chambal, Betwa and Ken.

The *Brahmaputra system* has a total length of about 4000 Km. and covers Arunachal, Assam, Bhutan, Sikkim and parts of North-West Bengal besides the Himalayan slopes. The river Brahmaputra originates from a glacier-mass near Mansarovar lake and passes through Tibet where it is known as *Tsangpo.* The principal tributaries of Brahmaputra in Assam are Jiodhal, Subansiri, Dihrong, Burai, Bargang, Ranganadi, Dhansiri, Pulhamari, Jaibhareli, Manas, Aie, Pagladya, Champamati, Sankosh and Gangadhar along the north bank and along the South bank are Dibru, Disang, Dihang, Dikhu, Jhangi, Kalong, Digru, Dudhnai, Kulsi, Krishnai and Jinari. The *Indus system* comprises the rivers Beas and Sutlej.

The main constituents of the *East coast* system are the Mahanadi, the Krishna, the Godavari and the Cauvery, having a length of nearly 6430 Km. The river Mahanadi is the largest river of Orissa. The fish and fisheries of the river has been intensively surveyed between Sambalpur and Cuttack. Other less important rivers of Orissa are the Brahmani, Daya, Bhargavi and Subernrekha. Tributaries of the river Cauvery from the Nilgiri have some cold water fishes (trout and tench). Majira, Indravati and Wainyunga are the main tributaries of the river Godavari. Some minor tributaries are the Purna, Maner and Sabari. Paingunga and Wardha are the secondary tributaries of Waingunga. The main tributaries of Krishna are the Bhima and the Tungbhadra. The tributaries of Cauvery are the Bhawani, the Noyil and Amaravati.

The *West Coast river system* has a length of 3380 Km. and includes the basins of the Narmada and Tapti rivers mainly. Other short rivers are just like the terrestrial streams. The river Narmada has as many as 18 tributaries. The river Tapti flows through the states of Madhya Pradesh, Maharashtra and Gujarat before joining the Arabian sea. The river Narmada originates from the Amarkantak hills in M.P. and covers the states of Madhya Pradesh and Gujarat, finally joining the Gulf of Cambay.

Fish Production Data of Bihar

(Made available by the Directorate of Fisheries, Govt. of Bihar, Patna)

Fish Production in mt.

S.N.	*Name of District*	*Year 1993-94*	*Year 1994-95*	*Year 1995-96*
1.	Patna	6500	5300	5670
2.	Nalanda	3000	5650	5200
3.	Bhojpur	4500	5170	3550
4.	Buxar	-	-	3000
5.	Rohtas	3600	4800	5800
6.	Gaya	3000	3500	5500
7.	Aurangabad	5300	4250	5000
8.	Nawada	5710	4560	5300
9.	Jehanabad	5050	4800	4800
10.	Muzaffarpur	4200	3500	5600
11.	Vaishali	5050	2150	5500
12.	Sitamarhi	5050	1000	5300
13.	Saran	2000	4000	5700
14.	Siwan	-	1970	4000
15.	Gopalganj	4150	4900	4250
16.	East Champaran	3900	4790	5690
17.	West Champaran	3170	5000	5500
18.	Khagaria	6500	7300	7200
19.	Saharsa	5500	5760	7250
20.	Madhepura	4810	5300	3990
21.	Purnea	6500	6500	5220
22.	Katihar	3450	6100	5820
23.	Bhagalpur	5500	4000	110
24.	Munger	5850	5920	5000
25.	Deoghar	4900	1300	5020
26.	Dumka	4700	6100	3900
27.	Sahebganj	5700	3300	6900

(Continued)

S.N.	Name of District	Year 1993-94	Year 1994-95	Year 1995-96
28.	Godda	4350	3450	760
29.	Darbhanga	7250	7900	8300
30.	Madhubani	6400	6490	9290
31.	Samastipur	4190	5510	6155
32.	Begusarai	4400	6000	6075
33.	Hazaribagh	6970	7020	6500
34.	Giridih	4300	4750	5050
35.	Dhanbad	5000	2900	12000
36.	Bokaro	-	-	1590
37.	Ranchi	12000	13000	13000
38.	Lohardagga	5140	3650	5010
39.	Gumla	9020	7750	11400
40.	Palamau	7100	5550	7000
41.	Garhwa	-	-	2930
42.	Singhbhum	7000	4500	8750
	Total	200710	195370	239580

The riverine fishery of the plains supports the fisheries of the following fishes:

(i) Major carps: *Catla catla, Labeo rohita, L.bata, L.fimbriatus, L. calbasu, Cirrhinus mrigala, Schizothorax* spp. and also *Tor* and *Puntius* spp. etc.

(ii) Cat fishes: *Mystus seenghala, Mystus aor, Wallago attu, Bagarius bagarius, Pangasius pangasius, Silonia silondia, Ompok bimaculatus, Rita rita, Heteropneustes fossilis, Clarias batrachus, Anabas testudineus, Channa gachua, C. punctatus, Channa striatus, Eutropiichthys vacha* etc.

(iii) Clupeids: *Hilsa ilisha, Notopterus notopterus, N. chitala, Setipinna phasa, Gadusi chapra* etc.

(iv) *Eels: Anguilla bengalensis, Amphipnous cuchia* and *Mastacembelus armatus* etc.

(b) *Estuarine Fisheries:* The important sources of estuarine or river mouths fishes in India are the vast estuarine areas of the rivers Ganges, Mahanadi, Godavari, Krishna, Cauvery, Narmada and Tapti, brackish water lakes of Chilka and Pulicat and the backwaters of Travancore-Cochin in Kerala are also its resources of estuarine fisheries. The estuaries may be open estuaries or embanked brackish waters. The large Chilka lake and backwaters of Kerala have perennial connections with the sea.

Most of the fishes constituting the estuarine fisheries in India are marine species capable of tolerating salinity changes. Important species are:

Hilsa ilisha, Liza corsula, Mugil cephalus, Anchoviella, Mystus, Lates calcarifer, Eutroplus suratensis, Setipinna phasa, Tachysurus, Pangasius, Nematalosa and *Osteogeniosus* etc.

There are certain important species which are reared in confined saline waters (or embanked brackish waters). These are —Milk fish (*Chanos chanos*), mullets (*Mugil cephalus,*), Pearl spot (*Etroplus suratensis*), Bhekti (*Lates calcarifer*), *Tilapia mossambica, Hilsa ilisha* and *Osphronemus goramy*.

Chilka Lake: The Chika lake of Orissa is shallow brackish water lake with an area of 906 sq. km. in Summer and 1165 sq. km during the rainy season. It is joined with the sea by a 23 km long channel. Water from the river Daya, a deltaic branch of river Mahanadi flows into the lake. The lake receives water frớm certain local streams also. The total annual production of fish from this lake has been estimated to be 3285 metric tons. The important fish fauna of this lake comprises the species of the genera—*Ambassis, Strongylura, Xenentodon, Therapon* and *Gerres.* Other fishes are *Sillago sihama, Glossogobius giruis, Megalops cyprinoides* etc. Fresh water carps, murrels and catfishes comprise less than 10 per cent population of the fish fauna of this lake. There is great scope of exploitation of the resources for the development of estuarine fisheries in India. The Central Inland Fisheries Research Institute, Barrackpore (West Bengal) has undertaken many research projects for the development of estuarine fishery.

(c) *Reservoir Fisheries:* Reservior fisheries has attracted much attention these days. A large number of reservoirs are associated with various river systems all over the country. This great water mass is now exploited for developing the fisheries of a large number of local and exotic species. Several carps and *tilapia* contribute much in developing fisheries of the reservoirs. Reservoir conditions are such that natural hybridization is greatly favoured. A catla-rohu hybrid of the Rihand reservoir in U.P. is a good example of hybridization (Prasad, 1976; Natrajan *et al.* '76). There are more than 100 man-made reservoirs in Andhra Pradesh alone. Breeding grounds have been located in several reservoirs. Catla, rohu and mrigal spawn in the tail ends of the Tilaiya reservoir. Some fishes breed in the Kotwal reservoir of Madhya Pradesh also.

Table of a few important reservoirs

States	*Name of the Reservoirs/Dams*	*River*
Bihar	Maithan Dam	Barakar
	Tilaiya Dam	Barakar
	Panchet Dam	Damodar
	Konar	Konar
U.P.	Rihand	Rend (Sone)
	Dhandraul	Bhakar
	Dhora	Dhora
	Sardasagar Dam	Chuka Sanda
	etc.	
West Bengal	Kangasabati	—
Punjab and H.P.	Govind Sagar	Sutlej
	Beas Dam	Beas

(Continued)

States	Name of the Reservoirs/Dams	River
Maharashtra	Shivaji Sagar	Koyna
	Darwa Dam	Darwa
Orissa	Hirakund	Mahanadi
Rajasthan	Rana Pratap Sagar	Chambal
	Bajaj Sagar	
Madhya Pradesh	Gandhisagar	Chambal
	Kotwas	—
Tamil Nadu	Mettur (Stanley)	Cauvery
	Bhavani Sagar	Bhavani
	Poondi	Koraliyar
Gujarat	Ukai	—
Kerala	Periyar	Periyar
	Neyyar	Neyyar
Karnataka	Tungbhadra	Tungbhadra (Krishna)
	Vanivilas Sagar	Vedavathi
	Linganamakki	Sharavathi
	Krishnaraj Sagar	Cauvery
Jammu and Kashmir	Lidder Project	
Andhra Pradesh	Nagarjuna Sagar Dam	Krishna
	Osman Sagar Dam	Musi
	Nizamsagar Dam	Mowgina
	Himayat Sagar Dam	Issi

(Other reservoirs of Andhra Pradesh are—Hussian Sagar, Kadam, Mopad Dam, Mannair, Cumbum, Pocharam, Kolisagar etc.).

Data on Fish Catches in the Important Reservoirs of U.P.

S.N.	Districts		Name of reservoirs	Fish Production (in Quintals)	
				1993-1994	1994-1995
1.	Varanasi	1.	Musakhand	38.77	65.13
		2.	Latifshah	37.19	—
		3.	Chandra Prabha	39.19	55.92
2.	Sonbhadra	4.	Dhandraul	26.43	—
		5.	Rihand	533.71	586.43
3.	Mirzapur	6.	Arhaura	6.70	57.10
		7.	Mauza	77.95	2.53
		8.	Upper Khajuri	7.85	34.09
		9.	Sukhda	0.21	3.14
		10.	Ghauri	—	28.00
4.	Jhansi	11.	Pariksha	64.90	68.56
		12.	Pahadi	159.17	129.26
		13.	Lahchura	121.43	100.31

(Continued)

S.N.	Districts		Name of reservoirs	Fish Production (in Quintals)	
				1993-1994	1994-1995
		14.	Barwar	20.90	108.66
		15.	Pahunj	137.64	79.13
5.	Banda	16.	Barua	109.98	110.00
		17.	Ohan	21.46	40.00
		18.	Rangwa	221.82	256.00
		19.	Bariarpur	40.20	11.85
6.	Hamirpur	20.	Arjun	277.64	179.99
		21.	Majhgawa	80.92	28.57
		22.	Raimura	15.35	26.61
		23.	Kewalari	33.00	14.93
		24.	Kabrai	101.45	119.07
		25.	Salarpur	18.29	11.36
		26.	Kamalpur	15.35	-
7.	Gonda	27.	Koharagaddi	176.36	214.11
		28.	Ganeshpur	17.65	59.75
8.	Bahraich	29.	Dahaura	20.27	99.86
9.	Allahabad	30.	Gularia	90.43	46.80
		31.	Badhana	15.60	53.20
10.	Etah	32.	Dariawganj	49.42	39.14
11.	Bijnaur	33.	Pili	129.69	78.71
12.	Siddharthnagar	34.	Majhauli	30.00	33.00
		35.	Bajhasagar	89.75	83.65

(Data made available by Sri Mohan Gupta, Joint Director, Fisheries, on behalf of Govt. of U.P., Lucknow)

Data on fish-catch (in kg) from departmental reservoirs in Bihar

Sl. No.	Names of reservoirs	Year 1993-94	Year 1994-95
1.	Badua reservoir	986.00	1070.100
2.	Amhara reservoir	584.00	683.500
3.	Belharma reservoir	412.00	517.250
4.	Chandan reservoir	322.00	372.100
5.	Nagi reservoir	44.00	196.00
6.	Nakti reservoir	280.00	279.900
7.	Morbay reservoir	150.00	223.600
8.	Amriti Sikhandi reservoir	110.0	140.00
9.	Getal Sud reservoir	4112.00	6589.00
10.	Hatia	434.125	763.400
11.	Nandani	26.575	63.00
12.	Lalmatia	86.600	102.900

(As per information from Directorate of Fisheries, Bihar).

(d) *Cold Water Fisheries:* The cold water masses comprise hill streams with rapids and pools, lakes and man-made reservoirs. Fishes of the plains do not survive in cold hilly waters. Cold water fishes have low temperature tolerance (0°C to 4°C). Severe cold water bodies are present in Kashmir, Himachal Pradesh, Uttar Pradesh, Northern Bengal, Meghalaya, Bhutan, Sikkim, Arunachal Pradesh, Tamil Nadu, Kerala and also Bihar. Cold water bodies are fed by streams, rain water and melting snow. Some of the important cold water fishes are: *Labeo derio, Labeo dyocheilus, Barilus* spp., *Tor tor, Tor putitora, T.khudree, Acrossocheilus hexagonolepis, Schizothorax* spp., *Garra gotyla, Salmo trutta fario, Salmo gairdneri, Cyprinus carpio, Carassius carassius, Noemacheilus rupicola, Puntius ticto, Glyptothorax pectinopterus* and *Tinca tinca.*

Table showing important cold-water lakes and streams

States	*Cold water lakes and streams*
Uttar Pradesh	Nainital
	Bhintal
	Devariatal
	Naukuchiatal
	Sattal
Himachal Pradesh	Renuka
Kashmir	Wular
	Dal
	Kishensar
Tamil Nadu	Ootacamund (Ooty)
	Shevaroy
	Kodai Kanal
Kerala	Devicolam
	Elephant
Bihar	Kakolat (in Nawadah district).

(2) *Marine Fisheries*: Marine water offers lucrative fishing and includes the Indian ocean, the Bay of Bengal, Arabian sea, many gulfs, backwaters, lagoons, coral reef, swamps etc. Coastal fishing forms the bulk of the marine fish production. The fish production is higher on the west coast particularly during September to February. With a coast-line of about 3600 miles, a continental shelf extends over a distance of nearly 100 miles from the shore on the western coast. About 75 per cent of the total sea fish landings are from the west coast alone. The sardine fishery, the mackerel fishery and the prawn fishery are the special features of the west coast.

(i) *Coastal Fisheries:* There are twelve bio-geographical zones along the coast line:

(a) Kerala and South Malabar

(b) Malabar and South Manara

(c) Bombay and Gujarat

(d) Konkan

(e) Palk Bay and Gulf of Manaar

(f) Kathiawar

(g) Coromandel South

(h) Coromandel North

(i) West Bengal and Orissa

(j) Andhra South

(k) Andhra North

(I) Andhra Middle

Important fishing areas on the west coast from north to south are Gujarat area, Konkan area, North Canara area, South Canara area and Malabar area. Similarly the east coast includes (from North to South) Deltaic area, Telgu area, Coramandel coast area and Gulf of Manaar area. There is considerable variation in the nature and composition of fisheries in different coastal zones already mentioned. The Sardines, Anchovies and Clupeoids are landed on the West Bengal coast. Clupeoids are also landed on the North Andhra and Orissa coasts. Pulicat lake has abundance of ribbon fish (*Trichurus* spp.). Flying fishes (*Cypselurus* spp.) are found in the Nagapatnam area. Seer fishes (*Scomberomorus*) are caught in most parts of the coromandel coast. The Palk Bay is rich in small sardines, silver bellies, white fish (*Lactarius lactarius*) and *Hemirhamphus*. In the Cape of Comorin and Gulf of Manaar area, rudder fishes (*Lethrinus* spp.) and rock perches (*Epinephelus*) are available. Malabar coast is the ground for carangid (*Caranx*), *Cynoglossus semifaciatus, Sardinella longiceps*, Pomprets (*Stromateus*), many cat fishes, sharks and rays. Oil Sardines (*Sardinella longiceps*), are also present on the Canara coasts. The Konkan coast is a good ground for the mackerel, *Rostrelliger kanagurta*. This coast is also known for shoals. Bombay and Saurashtra coasts are very rich in Bombay Duck (*Harpodon nehereus).* The ghol (Sciaena), dara (*Polydactylus indicus)* and rewas (*Polynemus)* are important fishes of both North and South coasts of Kathiawar.

(3) *Offshore and Deep-Sea Fisheries:* For augmented fish production, fishing offshore and distant waters seemed to be essential. Deep sea fishing stations have been set up at Bombay, Travancore, Calcutta, Cochin, Tuticorin, Visakhapatnam and some other places. Norway, Japan and United States Governments have shown all cooperations. Bombay, Cambay, Veraval, Porbandar and Dwarka regions have different compositional features of the fisheries. The commercial fishes of the above regions are: rewa *(Eleutheronema tetradactylus*), dara (*Polydactylus indicus),* ghol *(Pseudosciaena diacanthus),* wam *(Muraenesox talabon),* Karkara *(Pomadasys* spp.), Pomfrets (*Stromateus*) and koth (*Otolithoides brunneus*), some cat-fishes and rays and sharks. Dwarka region is quite good for dara koth and karkara fisheries. The karkara fishery is best in Porbandar region and warm fishery in Cambay and Veraval regions. Catfishes, rays and sharks are found in appreciable quantity in Bombay and also Cambay regions. The trawler catches are better during the day time. Bull-trawling, the Japanese method of fishing is quite profitable in comparison to other trawling. The important fishes that are caught during the offshore fishing experiments on the Kerala coast are: *Lutianus malabarius, Epinephelus* spp, *Latianus argentimaculata, Pristis cuspidatus* and *Carcharhinus limbatus.* Some other fishes

which are obtained from the trawling grounds comprise—*Lethrinus reticulatus, L. ornatus, L. nebulosus, Epinephelus areolatus, Parupeneus trifasciatus* and *Lutianus johnii* etc.

The Deep sea fishing centres at Calcutta include Tiger Point, Black Pagoda, Sand Head, False Bay Point, off the Prachi river mouth, off the Devi river mouth and off the Baitarani river mouth. *Kurtus indicus* is found in abundance in these regions. Pomfrets, sciaenids, ribbon fishes, perches, eels and some elasmobranchs are also found in these regions.

Principal Capture Fisheries of India

Hilsa ilisha (Clupeide) is an oblong compressed fish with both profiles equally convex. Males are about 30 cm. long and the length of the female is 35 cm. They become mature at the age of 1 to $1^1/_2$ years. They are widely distributed over the Indo-Pacific region. It is a fast swimming fish. It feeds on both phytoplankton and zooplankton. It is deep water euryhaline fish. They are marine fish but lay their eggs in fresh water. Thus its migration is of anadromous type. They used to migrate from the Bay of Bengal and regularly reached as far as Allahabad through the river Ganges. But now it is becoming more and more scarce with the construction of Farraka barrage on the Ganges in Bengal. The zone from Murshidabad to Allahabad which was considered to be the spawning ground has been denied to this migratory fish. In the recent years the decline in the catches of *hilsa* in the lower stretches of rivers are because of barrage and dam construction at many places e.g. Krishna river, on Cauvery river, on Indus river, on Godavari and Damodar rivers.

The *hilsa* fish is richly distributed in Arabian sea, Persian gulf and Bay of Bengal. Various areas e.g. Saurashtra coast, Palk Bay, Madras coast, Vishakhapatnam coast, Orissa coast and Bengal (Midnapore) coast support hilsa-fishery.

Backwaters of Kerala coast, Chilka lake and Hooghly estuary also support hilsa fishery. Similarly some fresh water areas of certain rivers like Ganges, Brahmaputra, Padma, Mahanadi, Daya, Krishna, Cauvery, Godavari, Narmada,Tapti, Purna, Ulhas and Kali also support hilsa-fishery. There is variation in the fishing activities in the different regions of the inland waters. The hilsa is the permanent resident of the Chilka lake. Also, there are evidences that some of the fishes live in the fresh water of the river Ganges in Bihar and Uttar Pradesh throughout the year. They never migrate to the sea. Annual production of hilsa is more than 16 thousand metric tons. These fishes may spawn several times during the spawning season. Eggs are 2.0 to 2.3 mm. in diameter. Hatching takes place in 12-24 hours after fertilization. When the larva becomes 20mm. in length it assumes the shape and characters of the adult.

Various gears are employed for the capture of *hilsa*. In the upper stretches of estuaries and the riverine area purse net and dip-nets are of great use but in the lower estuaries large gill-nets and encircling nets are extensively used. On the coastal area of W.Bengal and Orissa bag-nets and Stake-nets are used. In Chilka lake, seine-nets and drag-nets are mostly used. In the Mahanadi estuary, drift-nets are generally used after the winter months. Cast-nets can also be operated from small platforms in the upper stretches of the river. Rangoon-nets, Stake-nets and Cast-nets are used in Godavari and Krishna rivers, drift-nets in Narmada, Gill-nets and drift nets on Saurashtra coast and drag-nets and purse nets are employed in the Ganges in Bihar and U.P.

In view of the depleting fish stock in rivers, there is need for reviving hilsa-fishery. For this purpose rivers should be restocked with young hilsa.

(1) *Oil Sardine Fisheries:* Sardines (Clupeidae) constitute about one-third of the marine fishes of the Indian waters. They are chiefly represented by *Sardinella* spp., *Dussumieria* spp., *Kowala* sp. and others. There are ten species which constitute an important fishery along the West and South-east coasts of India. These species are *Sardinella fimbriata, S. longiceps, S. gibbosa, S. albella, S. dayi, S. clupeoides, S. melanura, S.perforate, S.sidensis* and *S.sirm.* But, the oil Sardine, *Sardinella longiceps* is one of the best known fishes which are commercially important. The fishery of *Kowala coval* and *S. fimbriata* comes next to oil Sardine fishery.

These fishes are not only used as food in fresh and cured conditions but its oil is extensively used in leather, jute and soap industries. Also, guano is used as fertilizer for tobacco, coffee and tea crops. In India oil Sardine fishery is a commercially important regular fishery along the west coast, however, on the east coast it is irregular and not so important. The oil Sardine fishery on the Malabar coast is very old one. *Fragilaria oceanica* (a diatom) is a favourtie food of the *Sardinella* juveniles. Population of Sardine is greatly affected by water temperature and availability of food. The peak fishery season on the Malabar coast is September to January.

The oil Sardines can attain a length of 22-23 cm. However the length of commercial catches is only 12-15 cms. The life span of oil Sardines is 3-4 years.

The fishing gears generally used on the Malabar coast consists of Seine-nets (*mathi Kolli vala*) and gill-nets (*mathi chala Vala*). The eco-sounding apparatus and fast moving power craft equipped with radio telephones has been proved to be of great advantage.

(2) *Bombay Duck Fishery:* Bombay Duck Fishery is a local but commercially important fishery of the Bombay Coast from Ratnagiri to Broach. Here the fishery is mainly a single species fishery of *Harpodon nehereus* (Synodidae). This fish is however, also present on the West Bengal , Orissa and Coromandel coasts. The fishery season starts from September and lasts in the month of January. Large bag-nets (dol-nets) are the main fishing gear. About 20 per cent of the total landing is marketed in the fresh condition but the rest 80 per cent is sun-dried and preserved for packing and marketing. Temporary preservation may be done with ice. The flesh is white in the beginning but later on after preservation it becomes straw-coloured and acquires a pleasant smoky flavour. The spawning grounds normally lie in off shore water.

(3) *Mackerel Fishery:* Mackerel (*Scombridae*) is found all along the coast of India, excepting the northern part of the West Coast. Mackerel forms a good proportion of the total marine fish landing in the country and more than 95 per cent of the total landings come from the west coast. The main mackerel fishery is confined between Quilon and Ratnagiri. *Rostrelliger kanagurta* is the only species which supports the mackerel fishery. They feed on both Zooplankton and Phytoplankton.

The chief mackerel fishery centres on the west coast are Ratnagiri, Karwar, Malpe, Malvan, Goa, Tellicherry, Kozhikode, Cochin and Alleppey. On the east coast, sporadic appearance of mackerel shoals have been reported from Mandapam, Nagapatnam, Kakinada, Madras and Visakhapatnam. They appear on certain parts of Orissa also.

On the basis of the intensity of fishing, types of gears used and seasons of fishery, the west coast has been divided into three regions: The first region (Cape Comorin to Ponnani river) is marked by moderate fishing where they are caught during August to February. Boat-seines and dugout canoes are used for fishing.

In the second region (Ponnani river to Mangalore) the fishing season starts from August-September and continues till March-April. Boat-seines (*Odom Vala, Paithu Vala,* and *Ayila Kolli Vala)* and gill-nets (*Avila Chala Vala*) are used with dugout canoes for fishing.

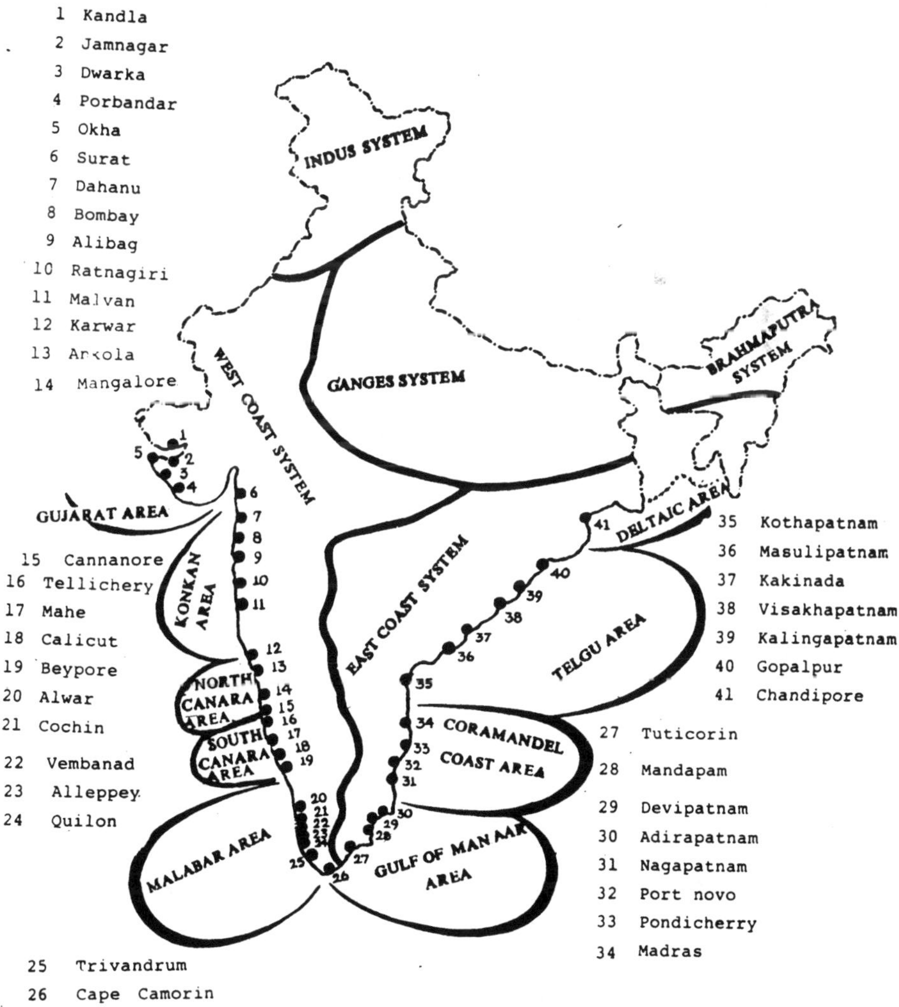

Fig. 77: Map of India showing various fishing zones and centres

In the third region (Mangalore to Ratnagiri) mackerel fishery starts from October-November and it lasts till February- March. Gill-nets (*Patta bale)* and Shore-seines (rampani) are used as gears.

Mackerel Spawns from April to September. The minimum size of the fish at the first spawning is about 22 cm. The fish is only 10 cm. in the first year but it gradually attains 18 cm. at the end of the second year.

Mackerel is in great demand for food in the fresh condition. But for the lack of transport and storage facilities its supply to the consuming centres is very much limited. It is sent to Bombay market for consumption. More than 50 per cent of the catches are salt-cured and prickled and canned. The cured fish is also exported to Ceylon.

(4) *Ribbon fish-Fishery:* Ribbon fishes are voracious omnivorous fishes. They support the fishery of the Coasts of Tamil Nadu, Andhra Pradesh and Orissa on the east coast and the coasts of Kerala, Konkan and Bombay on the west coast. Ribbon fishes (*Trichuridae*) are represented in Indian waters by three important species. i.e.*Trichiurus haumela, T. savala* and *T. muticus.*

They have strong lashing bodies and their sharp teeth can damage the nets. They measure from 16 to 80 cm. They come inshore regularly after spawning. They appear in inshore waters from June to October. Spawning takes place before June, only once in a year. These fish can be easily sun-dried owing to its ribbon like shape. Gears used for catching these fishes include seines and cast-nets.

(5) *Sole Fishery:* Soles are also called the flat fishes. Commercial sole fishery is contributed by the Malabar sole, *Cynoglossus semifaciatus* (Cynoglossidae). It attains a length of 17 cm. Some of the major species are *Cynoglossus dubius, C. semifaciatus, C. puncticeps, C. biliniatus* and *C. lida.* They are bottom feeders. They feed on polychaete worms, crustaceans and bivalves. Spawning occurs during monsoon period. Eggs appear in October and the larvae metamorphose to form adult-like young ones appearing in January. Catches of August-September consist of Pre-spawners mostly. Fully mature specimens can be obtained only in late October and November.

The sole fishery is a major fishery of the West coast. It is confined to the Kerala and S. Kanara zones. The important sole fishing centres include Baikampady, Ullal, Kanhangad, Hosdurg, Cannanore, Tellicherry, Quilandy, Kozhikode, Chowghat, Ponnani, Narakhal and Alleppey-Purakkad. On the Andhra coast sole fishery exists in the South of Visakhapatnam.

Commonly used gears in sole fishing are shore-seines (*noona vala*), boat-seines (*Paithu Vala*) and cast-nets (*Veechu Vala* or *beesu bala*) which are operated from canoes. Sun-drying of soles is the main method of preserving them. They may not be salted before subjecting them to above processing.

(6) *Shark and Ray Fishery:* Elasmobranchs have great demand for the reason that their big livers give a higher oil yield. Commercially important species of shark are the genera *Scoliodon, Carcharhinus, Galeocerdo, Sphyrna, Nebrius* and *Stegostoma.* In the coastal waters of India, they are found in abundance. Important rays and skates include the genera *Rhinobatus, Rhynchobatus, Pristis, Trygon, Dasyatis, Aetobatus,*

Aetomylus and *Rhinoptera.* These fishes are present on the east as well as the west coasts. The landings of sharks and rays go upto 15 to 40 thousand tons annually. Main season of fishery extends from July to March and May to January respectively on the West and East Coasts.

The important fishing centres on the east coast are Tuticorin, Point Calimere, Adirampatnam, Nagapatnam, Kakinada, Masulipatnam, Contai and Visakhapatnam.

On the West Coast large scale commercial catches are landed at Bombay, Kathiawar, Trivandrum, Calicut, Tellicherry, Mangalore, Karwar, Veraval and Kodinar.

Active fishing is however carrid out along the coast of Tamil Nadu and West Bengal on the east coast and at Bombay, Kathiawar, Kanara, Travancore and Malabar on the West Coast.

Sharks are voracious carnivores. Rays and Skates are caught in shallow waters (upto 10m deep) but the sharks are caught from waters 45 to 54 m. deep. Fishing gears include gill-nets, drift nets, wall-nets, seines and long lines with hooks. Hooks are baited with tainted fish or chunks of beef.

(7) *Other fisheries:* There are various fishes which support the fisheries at different places. They are not very significant however, they have been mentioned below with very short descriptions.

(A) Gizzard shad (Clupeidae): *Anodontostoma chacunda* is a very common example. They are plankton feeders. Mature specimens are 13 cm. in length. They are available throughout the year except from June to August. The spawning season is from Nov. to Feb. They are captured by gill nets, seine-nets and cast-nets.

(B) Flying fishes (Exocoetidae): It includes *Cypselurus* species. Fishery is confined to west coast and also Coramandel coast. They become the food fishes from June to August. Madras city, Nagapatnam, Kadapakkam and Krusadai Island are the main landing centres.

(C) Indian Salmon (Polynemidae): *Eleutheronema tetradactylus* is a very common fish. They are common rewas of Bombay. Spawning takes place from January to March and also from July to September. They are very common in Hooghly river at Calcutta and on the Coramandel coast. On the West they are found in N.Canara, Kozhikode and Valapad. These fishes can be sun-dried.

(D) Carangids (Carangidae): They are found on the Malabar coast. They inhabit all warm seas. They feed on macrozooplankton. These fishes are either salted or sun-dried.

(E) Snappers (Lutianidae): They support the fishery at various places. These are carnivorous fishes. The fishery season comes from June to July. These fishes are good for eating flesh. They can also be dried.

(F) Silver bellies (Leiognathidae): *Leiognathus* is a very common species. They are found in abundance in the gulf of Manaar. Fishing season varies in different zones. Bag-nets and gill-nets are the main gears for catching these fishes.

(G) Sciaenids (Scieaenidae): *Pseudosciaena coibor* is a very common example found in Bombay and Kathiawar waters and Gangetic delta. Air bladders are of much economic importance. They are known as *maws* used for making isinglass.

(H) Sail and Spear fishes (Istiophoridae): The common example is *Istiophorus gladius.* It is sold fresh and is liked as food. It is treated in the same way as seer.

(I) Seer fishes (Cybiidae): *Scomberomorus* spp. are very common. They are found all around the coast of India. They are closely allied to mackerel. They are sold at Bombay and Madras. Its reddish flesh has very high fat content. These fishes can be dried or packed in ice.

(J) Pomfrets (Stromateidae): Several species of pomfrets are available in Calcutta and Bombay markets. They are caught at many centres on the east and west coasts. These are highly priced marine fishes. There are white pomfrets (*Chondroplites* spp.), Grey promfrest (*Stromateus* sp.) and black pomfrets (*Formio* sp.)

(K) Tunnies (Thunnidae): These are very timid fishes caught with hooks. Also, Japanese boats are used for catching these fishes. The tuna fisheries off the Maldives and Laccadives are to be developed.

(L) Anchovies (Engraulidae): It includes the *Anchoviella* species, abundant on the west coast. Fishing takes place from August to December.

Fresh Water Pond Culture

The importance of fish culture (*Pisciculture)* in rural economy has been realised now. The major fish farming areas comprise fresh water pond culture, paddy-cum-fish culture, culture in sewage-fed waters, culture in reservoirs, cage-culture, brackish water culture, coastal marine culture (*mariculture),* Salt-pan culture and culture in clod waters. But, here only the fresh water pond culture is being dealt with. The aim of pond culture is to obtain maximum yield of fish to get nutritive flesh and by-products of fishing industries which may be of great economical value. India has a total potential of about 3-6 million hectares, of which fresh water ponds cover more than 1(one) million hectares.

Fresh water fish culture in ponds and tanks has been an age-old practice in many states. For example, Bihar, Bengal and Orissa are definitely credited with age old practices in this trade. Intensity of stocking cultivable waters with fast growing fish seed i.e. major carp seed and other exotic varieties have much to do with the development of inland fisheries as a whole. It also depends upon the production of large quantities of fish seed (fish fry and fingerlings) in fish farm and nurseries following traditional and composite fish culture technique. Fish seed can be obtained from natural water resources like rivers, lakes and reservoirs.

Cultivable fishes: It is advisable to have a comprehensive idea about the cultivable fishes with regard to their food, disease resistance, climatic preference, growth rate and ecological considerations for their survival etc. Cultivable fishes should have ability to feed on both natural and artificial diet and should be of nutritive value. They should be fast growing herbivorous fishes which can withstand changes in climatic conditions. They should be resistant against diseases. Cultivable fishes should have amicable nature to live with other fishes. Also, they should be profile breeders. They should tolerate variation in O_2 content of water and occasional turbidity.

Major carps, Chanos, Mullets (acclimatised to fresh water) and some exotic fish i.e. Mirror carps, Chinese carps,. Crucian carps are good cultivable fishes which are suitable for fresh water ponds. Carps are much profitable to culture. Much attention has been paid to the culture of *Labeo rohita, L.calbasu, Catla catla* and *Cirrhina mrigala.* Besides them, *Notopterus chitala,* *Labeo boga* and *Mugil corsula* are aslo cultured.

Carps do not breed in stagnant water, and so their spawn (fertilized eggs) or fries are procured from streams or rivers. These are reared in the tanks of small size known as nursery tanks and then finally they are transported to the stocking tanks. For the culture of *Heteropneustes fossilis, Clarias batrachus, Anabas scandens* and *Channa punctatus,* even impure and muddy waters are suitable. But these fishes should not be cultured with carps in the same pond.

Factors affecting fish culture: Many environmental factors affect the fish culture. Though the temperature and intensity of light are the most important factors, however, rain water, flood water currents, turbidity, diseases, toxic pollutants, hardness and salinity of water, oxygen content and pH of water also play an important role in fish culture.

Management of fish culture: Management of pond has been discussed in Chapter 26. Management has to be tackled from viewpoint of breeding, hatching, nursing, rearing and stocking ponds. Various stages of the fish are cultured in the ponds having different properties. Following types of ponds have been recommended to manage them.

Breeding Pond: Breeding of fishes is the first stage in fish culture. Breeding ponds are prepared adjacent to rivers and other natural water resources. After the beginning of monsoon, the spawning of carps takes place in the flood regions of the great rivers.

Breeding can be of two types: Natural breeding (Bundh breeding) and Induced breeding. The natural bundhs are particular types of ponds where riverine conditions or natural water resources conditions are created for the breeding of fishes taken for culture purpose. Low- lying area are most suitable for the construction of these bundhs. Large quantity of rain water can easily be accommodated in this area. These bundhs have an outlet which can function as an exit for excess of rain water. The shallow area of these specially designed bundhs are used as spawning ground.

When there is water throughout the year the bundhs are called the *wet bundh* or *Perennial bundhs.* For the entrance of water there is an inlent and similarly for the exit of water there is an outlet at suitable place. The water flow is controlled with the help of bamboo fencing. Sometimes the constructed pond is seasonal. It is surrounded by three walls (made of clay or soil) and one side is open. Rain water flows towards the bundh and fills the pond. Water is always present in the shallow area and it dries up after the monsoon is over. This type of bundh is known as *dry bundh.* Another type of bundh is known as *Pucca bundh* or *Modern bundh.* Here, after each spawning bundh can be cleared of water. It is a masonry construction having a sluice gate at the lower most level and thus the total exit of water is possible.

Fish Seed and Fry: Spawn embraces eggs and larvae younger than the fingerling stage. In Bengal and some parts of Bihar, the terms *dim* is used for eggs; *dimpoma* for early larvae with yolk sac and *dhanipona* for older fry which are about 4 cm long. Fine dhanipona are also known as *phuldhani.* The term *Chara* is used for young fish usually 10-23 cm. long. The term *nala* is in use for larger fish (more than 23 cm. long) for transplanting. The term fish seed is applied to all grades of fish traded for stocking purpose.

Carps breed near confluences of rivers and streams but they are known to breed in *bundhs* regularly. The eggs are collected 12-14 hours after fertilization and are allowed to hatch under protected conditions. The fry are collected with the help of *benchi jal* in Bengal and some other places. *Benchi jal* is 5-7 m long with a mouth 8-10 m circumference. It is a funnel shaped structure with closed mesh. The mouth is strengthend with a rope and it is provided with two wings. Both ends (anterior and posterior) are open. *Gamcha* is a tailed rectangular structure at the posterior end. All stages can be collected in *gamcha* and then they are transferred to the *hatching pit.* The fry are transported in earthware containers (hundies) which may have a capacity to carry as many as 70000 larvae. Seed collecting nets vary at different places. In Bihar, Orissa, U.P. and Delhi some fish fry are collected by gear which slightly differs from *benchi jal.* In Madras fingerlings are captured for stocking.

Induced Breeding: For the progress of fish culture induced breeding has been made practicable. Induced breeding stimulates breeders to release eggs and sperms finely from the ripe gonads The spawn collected from riverine and other resources are never pure because in natural condition it is always mixed with the spawn of other undesirable species. A pure spawn of desired species of fish can be made available by induced breeding only.

Types of Induced Breeding

Inducing in pond breeding fishes: Fishes which commonly breed in ponds can also be induced to some extent. They are allowed to breed under the influence of some spawning stimulants. For the purpose, the old (original) water is replaced by fresh rain water. Suitable temperature and light intensity can also act as stimulant. Only selected species should remain in the pond and suitable site for the attachment of eggs should be provided. Also, wild spawning is provided by sex-wise segregation.

Inducing in fishes not commonly breeding in Ponds: Carps and some other fishes do not breed in confined waters and so some stimulant is necessarily needed for breeding. Spawning in bundhs occurs after continuous raining. Eggs and sperms are released in water following sexual display. Fertilization takes place in water. So, heavy monsoon water current, higher temperature (24°C-30°C) and cloudy weather followed by thunderstorm are some of the stimulants which brings about spawning of fishes.

Induced breeding has also been successfully applied in the case of Indian major carps through pituitary hormones. The gonadotropic hormones (FSH and LH) of the pituitary gland stimulates maturation of gonads and the process of spawning in fishes. The method of induced breeding has been fully discussed in separate chapter.

Hatching Pit: When eggs are fertilized, they are kept into hatching pits. Hatching pits are nearer to the breeding grounds. Hatching pits are of two types—*Hatcheries* and *Hatching hapas.* Hatcheries are small ponds in which fertilized eggs are transferred and the latter hatch after 2 to 15 hours. The *hatching hapa* is a rectangular case of fine netting held on four bamboo poles, one at each corner of the rectangular case in the river. The hapa is made up of a close meshed mosquito net-cloth. A good circulation of water is maintained in the hapa. For large fishes its size is 8′ × 3′ × 3′ but for the smaller fishes it is 5′× 3′ × 3′.

Hapa may be *fixed* or *floating* type. Several floating hapa are arranged in series attached with the bamboo and floated on the surface of the river. In order to avoid over-crowding of eggs, only one layer of eggs is spread in each of the hatching hapas. The hatching of eggs takes place in the outer hapas. The hatchlings are kept for 36-48 hours in hapas and then they are carefully transferred to nursery ponds.

Transport of Fry to Nursery Ponds

At many places fish fry are transported to nurseries in earthen *'hundies'* and as such, heavy mortality is caused. The obvious reasons for mortality are decreased in oxygen content, toxicity caused by waste products, increased CO_2 concentration, strain and injury to fry during transport, etc. Now, fry are subjected to conditioning before transportation as a precautionary measure. They are kept in a fixed volume of water for a definite period and then transported in vessels, open or closed around which wet cloth is placed. They are also transported in sealed metallic vessels provided with sufficient oxygen gas. They are also transported in polythene bag which ensures good oxygenation. Several types of receptacles with additional arrangement for the supply of oxygen are also used now a days for transportation.

Nursery Pond: It is always advisable that the nursery ponds should be near the hatching hapas so that the newly hatched delicate fry may be conveniently transferred to the nursery ponds. These ponds are shallow water reservoirs not more than 3 to 5 feet in depth. The ideal nursery ponds are 50 to 60′ × 30 to 40′ × 4 to 5′. The entrance and exit of water is kept under control. Predatory fishes are removed from the pond. Chemical fertilizers alongwith cowdung should be provided in the pond before the release of fry into it. Sufficient zooplankton and phytoplankton grow within 15 to 20 days. Sometimes, heavy casualty is caused in the nursery pond. The probable reasons are sudden change in the quality of water, lack of suitable food, over growth of plankton, decreased oxygen content of water, presence of predatory insects and fishes and cannibolism. When the fry attains a length of 10 to 15 cm., they should be immediately transferred into the rearing ponds.

Rearing Ponds: These are longer and narrower ponds in which the fingerlings are reared. These ponds are convenient for swimming. These ponds may be seasonal but they are free from predators. These ponds are about 6′ deep. When fingerlings attain a length of 20 cm. they are generally transferred to the stocking ponds.

Transport of Fingerlings: The fingerlings are transported to stocking ponds in a container which is internally lined with foam which protects the fingerlings from physical injury. During transport, aeration of the tank is essential. Also, for less consumption of dissolved oxygen during transport the fingerlings are kept inactive by the use of sedatives, i.e.Sodium amylate and barbiturate. Before transferring these fingerlings to rearing ponds they are perfectly washed. For washing, antibiotics, methyl blue, copper sulphate, potassium permanganate, formaline, common salt have been recommended in definite concentration. Thus, finally the fingerlings are transferred to the stocking ponds.

Stoking Ponds: The stocking ponds should be completely free from weeds and predatory fishes. Now for the proper growth of the fishes, sufficient food is essential. 20000 to 25000 kg/hactare of cowdung and 1000 to 1500 kg/hectare of fertilizers (super phosphate, ammonium nitrate and ammonium sulphate) are recommended annually for this pond so that proper growth of zooplankton and phytoplankton may take place. Artificial food like powdered rice, oil cakes, paddy, mustard, ground nut etc. may also be added. Quantity of fishes, types of fishes, nature of soil etc. are also taken into consideration. When the fishes attain normal size, they are harvested for use. Smaller fishes should be again released into the stocking ponds for further growth. *Notopterus chitala* is also a predatory fish and it should not be there in the nursery tank at least.

Sewage and its Utility in Fish Culture

Sewage is considered as a valuable organic fertilizer and is utilized in fish culture. It is very rich in nutrients. Sufficient quantities of Nitrogen and Phosphorus are present in the municipal sewage. Efforts are being made to treat the domestic sewage to make the effluents suitable for discharging into natural waters. Important contributions related to this topic are those of Banerjee *et al.* (1989) and Verma *et al.* (1991).

Sewage is also responsible for primary production in water. Co_2 liberated from the decomposing sewage is picked up by the primary producers in the process of photosynthesis. Thus sewage-fed water can promote the growth of algal bloom and the latter causes the first tropic level of consumers—the Zooplankton. Zooplankton are utilized as food by several groups of fishes, certain worms, insects and larvae which form the food materials for the fish, are produced in sewage sediments. Sewage is definitely a pollutant and does harm to the fish. It is a sources of several bacterial and microbial pathogenic infections. The ratio of carbon and nitrogen in the municipal sewage has been estimated to be 1: 3 roughly. Municipal sewage contains some faecal matters also. For fish culture practices it has been suggested to treat sewage in a scientific way. Raw sewage is subjected to sedimentation, dilution and putrefaction for controlling pollutional hazards. The process of sedimentation involves mechanical treatment by which heavier solids are separated from water. The process is conducted in sewage channel under high velocity of water. It is dropped suddenly into a large pond. In this process the BOD value is greatly reduced. By applying the process of dilution with freshwater, the effects of harmful substances are greatly minimised.

High concentrations of CO_2, ammonia and hydrogen sulphide are brought to sublethal levels as a result of the process of dilution. Long storage of sewage in a natural condition causes putrefaction.

In India, Germany, USSR, Poland, Israel, Hungary, China and Indonesia, sewage is widely used in fish culture. Several data are on record regarding sewage-fed fisheries.

Some important contributions regarding sewage-fed fish culture are those of Choudhuri (1976), Ganapati (1977), Ghose *et al.* (1979), Sen (1986), Sukumaran *et al.* (1987) and others.

Fingerlings of Labeo, Catla and Mrigala are raised with an annual yield of 1200 kg/hac. The fingerlings of Indian major carps are stocked and they attain a definite marketable size in six months with an yield of approximately 1000-5000 kg/hac. annually. Ponds with low dissolved O_2 content are used for raising some air breathing fish like *Anabas, Clarias, Heteropneustes* and *Channa*. By using sewage, very high yield of *Cyprinus carpio* has been reported from Java in cage culture. The yield has been estimated to be at least 10 times greater in compariosn to the above data. Sewage-fed fish culture has become very popular at certain places of Tamil Nadu, West Bengal and Orissa.

Integrated Fish Farming

Integrated fish farming is gaining momentum in different parts of India and other countries. High economic return and reduced marginal cost of production have attracted persons of various disciplines to the concept of integrated fish culture. The operational expenditure on sewage fisheries is less as compared to that of other ways of freshwater fish culture. Fish farmers can obtain an estimate of higher income by developing this method. Live stock and Poultry manures are good organic fertilizers for integrated fish farming. Integrated fish farming is actually the development of structural network in line with local condition involving recycling of waste products as manure, biogas, crop production, feed and other useful items.

Some review articles on integrated fish farming in India are those of Jhingran and Sharma (1980), Natarajan and Sharma (1980), Tripathi and Mishra (1986), Rath (1989), Sharma (1990) and others.

Now-a-days, integrated culture system has been introduced with a view to produce fish, meat, egg, milk, vegetables and other food materials of nutritional values within the farm itself on economic scale.

Accumulation of waste products which can pollute the environment should be disposed of and for this purpose recycling of the waste/by products for food production through integrated system of fish culture must be encouraged as suggested by Sharma and Das (1988). Thus integrated fish farming is a model of recycling wastes/by products for food production. It is a great energy saving attempt which can utilize the natural resources and maintain the ecological balance as suggested by Rath (1990).

The intensive carp culture in our country is dependent on supplemental feed and inorganic fertilizers mainly. The integrated fish farming system is divisible into:

(a) Fish cum crop integration
(b) Fish cum livestock integration
(c) Fish, crop and livestock integration.

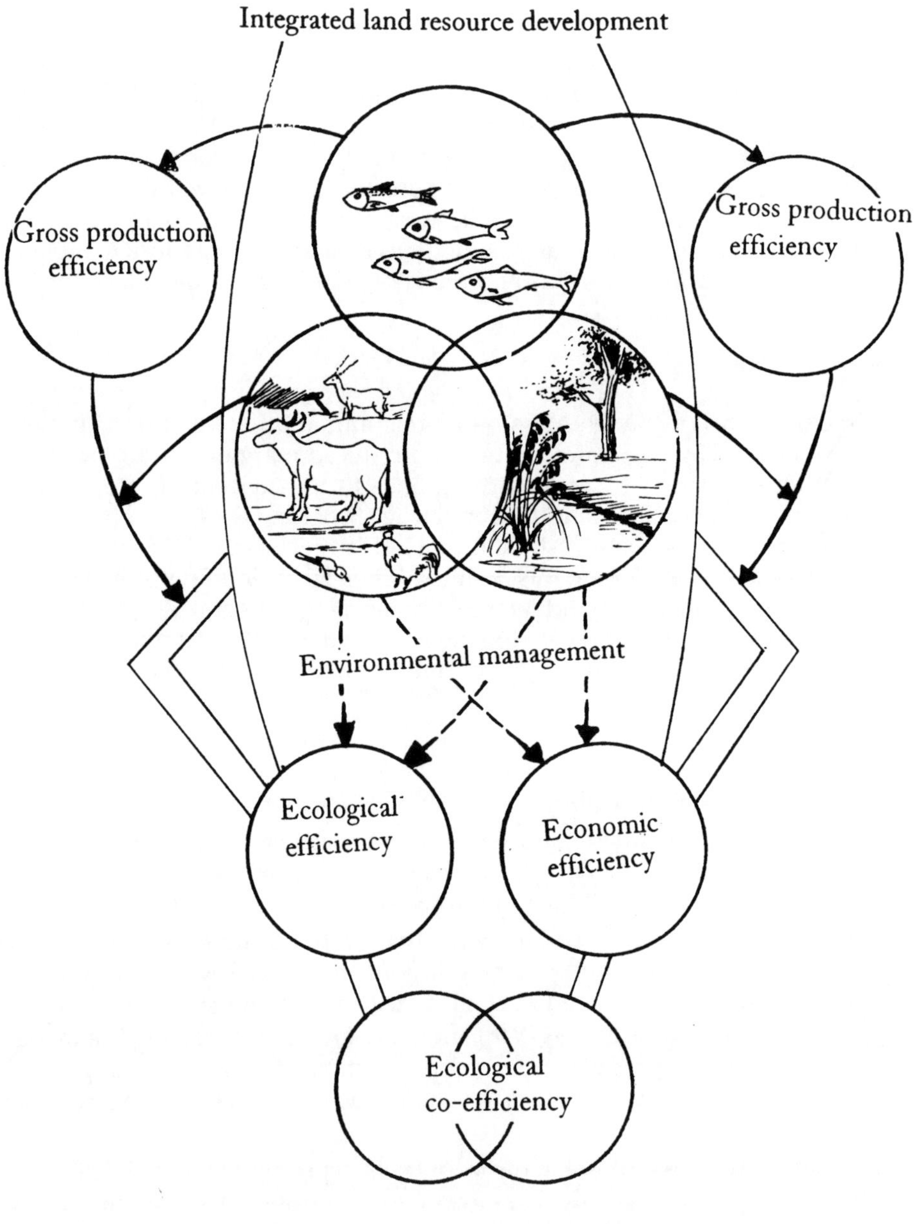

Fig. 78: Integrated farming system and efficiencies (Partly based on Rath)

Some agricultural components which are generally incorporated in the integrated system must be palatable, resistant to diseases, and nutritious and there should be well developed root system of the plants. They generate feed for fish culture and also generate potentiality of organic fertilizer, energy and fish production. *Alfa alfa, Romain lettuce,* Bunch grass, *Lactua tentaculata, Zea mays,* sweet potato, cucurbita, Banana, Bamboo, Papaya, Sugar cane, Wheat, Paddy, Coconut, Tomato, Makhana, Mulberry, Brinjal are important components (Plants) supposed to be much useful in fish farming. Cows, Goats, Sheep, Pig, Ducks, Chick, Goose etc. are livestock components for intergrated fish farming system.

The ecological concept in the integrated farming system necessarily involves—reception and fixation of solar energy and subsequent production of organic substances by the primary producers by the use of solar energy and substances. In the next stage consumption of primary producers by the macroconsumers takes place. After that, decomposition of primary producers and macroconsumers by microconsumers is a normal feature. Finally, transformation to form suitable for nutrition of the producers takes place. Animal waste is used as direct feed, autotrophic production and heterotrophic production. The mineralized fraction of the wastes provides nutrients for phytoplankton and the non-mineralized fraction is used as food base for bacteria and protozoans. Zooplankton ingest small manure particles coated with bacteria. They can digest bacteria.

Fish Seed (Details)

To-day fish culture has spread to most of the states and it is of great commercial value these days. Traditional aquaculture methods are being replaced by modern scientific methods. According to Jhingran (1976) the country at present is on the threshold of equaplosion. Bengal, Bihar and Orissa are credited with old practices in this trade. That the availability of fish seed is an essential prerequisite for fish culture. For fish culture the demand of fish seed is increasing.

Fishes have very high fecundity but only two per cent eggs become adults in the natural condition. The term fish seed is used to denote all stages of life cycle of a desirable fish species from egg to young ones that are traded for stocking to fish culture ponds. Though there are several stages but the fish seed is traditionally classified into *Spawn, fry* and *fingerlings.* Various stags in the development of fish are:

1. Spawn (fertilized eggs which are in the process of development)
2. Hatchlings (hatched stages)
3. Prolarvae or Sac fry (Larvae with Yolk Sac)
4. Fry (Larvae with Yolk absorbed -16 to 50 mm in length)
5. Post larvae (Alevin).
6. Juveniles (young one looking like adults).
7. Fingerlings (Young ones of larger fishes 51-100 mm in length).
8. Yearlings etc.

The success of fish culture depends on the availability of desired quality and quantity of fish seed. There should be standard sizes of various fish seed as recommended by the Second Fish Seed Congress at Calcutta in 1986.

Collection and trade of fish seed in India: There are three principal sources of collection of fish seed, which are:

1. *Rivers* } from natural breeding of fish
2. *Bundhs* }
3. Techniques of induced breeding in ponds—from artificial breeding of fish.

Though, there is a great success in the technique of induced breeding of major carps but collection of seeds from rivers and bundhs has become very popular now. About 90 per cent of the total spawn collected are taken from rivers.

Collection of fish seed from rivers: The rivers in India, support a rich commercial fishery. There is greater abundance of major carps in the rivers of northern India, but in the rivers of Peninsular India, there is poor availability of Indian major carps. There is great potentiality for collection of fish seed from rivers because of enormous size of rivers and their tributaries (estimated to be about 27000 K.M.) Bihar and West Bengal are noted for their contribution towards riverine collection of seeds.

The important rivers of India which contribute fish seed for fish culture are Ganga, Kosi, Mahanadi, Burhi Gandak, Yamuna, Betwa, Ramganga, Narmada, Rapti, Sone, Godawari, Ghaghara, Brahmaputra, Satluj, Cauvery, Gomati, Mahananda, Banas, Padma, Bhagrathi etc.

Collection of fish seed is made both from breeding grounds wherever known, and downstreams near them. During the monsoon periods when rivers are flooded, millions of fish eggs and fry drift in surface water alongwith the current. For fish culture the spawns of the Indian major carps are collected on large scales in Bihar and Bengal. Howrah (W.B) is a very important trading centre in fish seed taken from rivers. Trading is however restricted to fry and fingerlings only. When eggs are collected from rivers they hatch out within a short period. These are reared in thousands of nursery tanks situated in and around Calcutta. Fry and fingerlings of carps taken from rivers are raised in nursery tanks and they are brought by rail to Calcutta and Howrah market (between middle of May to middle of August).

Collection of eggs from breeding grounds and downstreams have been reported from certain places in Madhya Pradesh particularly from Banmore (Gwalior) and Jharoni fields (Morena) which are linked with the tributaries of the river Chambal. Eggs are collected from 1-2′ deep water by scooping with a *gamcha.* Drifting eggs are collected with the help of shooting nets in Garuanala tributary of Betwa river. In Bihar also egg collection has been reported at certain sites of the river Mahananda. Normally good quality of eggs are collected at the breeding ground.

Spawn Collection is a very popular operation in Bihar, West Bengal and U.P. In Uttar Pradesh alone there are about 80-85 registered centres on the Ganga, Yamuna, Gomati, Betwa, Ramganga, Ghaghara and Rapti rivers. The spawning period of the major carps in the Gangaes system is from May to September. Spawns appear in the rivers Kosi, Ganga and their tributaries during the rainy season when several areas are overflooded. Some of the centres of quality spawns on various river systems in

Bihar are— Kursela (Below the confluence of Kosi and Ganga), Babuaghat (on the Kosi), Mehdi Jhajha (on Badua), Tilauthu (on Sone), Dingrahaghat (on the Mahananda), Khagaria (on Burhi Gandak), Sultanganj (on Ganga), Mokamahghat (on Ganga), Karhagola (on Ganga), Dighwara (on Ganga), Buxar (on Ganga), Japhaha (on Burhi Gandak), Dhundhua (on Sone), Ahirauli (on Ganga), Bahiara (on Sone), and Balwa (on Kosi).

In west Bengal the important Centres are: Nimtita (on Ganga), Dhuliyan (on Ganga) and Pairachali (on Kangasabati).

In Uttar Pradesh the important centres of Spawn collection include Mehewa-Jamunapur (on Yamuna), Mehawapatti (on Yamuna), Anwar (on Yamuna), Dhumanpur (on Yamuna), Kishanpur (on Yamuna), Salempur (on Gomati), Tajpur (on Ramganga), Nethla (on Yamuna), Maut (on Yamuna), Deolan (on Yamuna), Ghagraghat (on Ghaghara), Jhansi (on Betwa), Rajghat Nanora (on Betwa), Muzaffarnagar (on Ganga and Yamuna), Saharanpur (on Ganga and Yamuna), Bansi (on Rapti), Bijnor (on Ganga and Yamuna), Kishanpur (on Yamuna), Sardanagar (on Ramganga), Balaha (on Tons) and Nanamau (on Ganga).

In Orissa these centres are Bhagipur (on Mahanadi), Naraj (on Mahanadi), Ravipui (on Mahanadi), and Tikkerpara (on Mahanadi).

In Madhya Pradesh the important centres for Spawn Collection is Pidrai (on Betwa).

In Rajasthan the centres are Sopari (on Banas), Negria(on Banas), and Baretha Barrier (on Uttangan).

In Gujarat, Sisodra (on Narmada) and Rania (on Mahi) are the important centres for collection. Nanded (on Godavari) is the important centre in Maharashtra.

In Punjab the important centres of collection are Wazir Bhullar (on Beas) and Loduwal (On Satluj).

In Tamil Nadu, Kulithalai (on Cauvery) and Nirathanallur (on Coleroon) are the main Centres of collection.

In Andhra Pradesh, Dharamapuri (on Godavari) is an important Centre of collection. In Assam, North Guahati (on Brahmaputra) and Hamidabad (on Brahmaputra) are the centres of Seed Collection.

In Mysore the important centre is Sosale (on Cauvery). In Haryana, Majhawali (on Yamuna) is a very important centre of Spawn collection. It will not be out of place to mention that in Haryana there are several large, median and small fish farms on record. These fish farms are located at Dadupur (Ambala), Damdama (Gurgaon), Jyotisar (Kurukshetra), Kalengu (Gurgaon), Lahli (Rohtak), Sampla (Rohtak), and Kavroi (Sonepat). Median farms include Badkhal farm (Faridabad), Jhajjar farm (Rohtak), Rohat farm (Sonepat), Saidpura farm (Karnal) and Ottu farm (Sirsa). The small farms are there at Bishangarh (Ambala), Mundri (Kurukshetra), Sohna (Gurgaon) and Sultanpur (Gurgaon).

Fry and fingerling collection centres are comparatively few. In Haryana the important centres are Dhobiawala, Khalog, Biblipur lake (all in Karnal) and Majhawali (Gurgaon). In Delhi Ali, Chilla, Okhala, Razapur and Wazirabad are the important centres. In Madhya Pradesh, Jharoni (Morena), Susera (Gwaliar) and Pilua Ketwal (Gwalior) are such centres. In Uttar Pradesh, Keethani (Agra), Bithoor, Gangaghat and Golaghat (Kanpur), Lamti (Gonda), Chopan (Mirzapur) and Jarwal Katli (Bahraich) are the important centres for fry and fingerling collection. In Rajasthan also there are some centres associated with Bhadrawati, Banas, Kalisindh, Dai and Ruparail rivers.

Collection of fish seed from Bundhs: During monsoon period water, accumulates in the low lying fields. These are blocked off by strong embankment or earthen *bundhs* across the outflow. There is rise in water level, which inundate adjoining shallow areas also. Several bundhs are located in Bankura and Midnapore of West Bengal and Chhattarpur of Madhya Pradesh.

Desirable species are obtained by microscopical studies and sieving of spawns. Sieving of spawn, using selective sieve, is helpful in segregating the spawn of the desirable species from the undesirable ones.

The most desirable species include the four Indian major carps, i.e. *Catla catla, Labeo rohita, Labeo calbasu* and *Cirrhinus mrigala*. If the fry is less than 3 cm in size, identification can be made only under microscopical examination. Fry of *Cirrhinus* and *Catla* can however be separated from the mixture of the four by using the Chinese method using dissolved oxygen requirement. When there is depletion of Oxygen *Cirrhinus* and *Catla* fry prefer different layers in the jars. Spawn is categorized in three groups (i) Major Carps, (ii) Minor Carps and (iii) others. A percentage ratio reveals the idea of spawn quality.

CHAPTER 21

RESERVOIR FISHERY MANAGEMENT

Reservoirs are created by impoundment of river water or the water of the stream i.e. they are freshwater impoundments. It is primarily meant for irrigation, power generation, flood control, navigation and water supply. It is one of the great potential fishery resources in India. They are located both in hilly regions and in plains. Reservoirs may be connected with river system also. The size and design of the reservoir vary according to local conditions. The fishery potential of reservoirs in India is underdeveloped. The surface water area of existing reservoirs in India is estimated to be more than three million hectares. But the present fish yield from reservoirs is not more than 10 Kg per hactare per year. It can be augmented however. Government intervention is essential for making the reservoir fishery management effective so that the economic returns may be maximised. The range of water area of a reservoir can be from 10 Sq. Kms. to 500 Sq. Kms. and the perimeter can be from 10 Kms to 100 Kms.

Analysis of the Major Policy Issues Relevant to Reservoir Fishery Management

(1) *Impoundment issues* : First of all the *hydrobiological survey* of the water system should be conducted in the area where the reservoir is to be constructed. The survey should include the seasonality of water flow relative population of fish species, study of plankton, physical and chemical nature of water and other ecological requirements including nature of terrain etc. *Clearance of all the obstructions* at the site is very much essential so that it may be a good fishing ground in future, clearance of obstructions facilitate easy fishing and light penetration in the reservoir. Also, the growth of benthic fauna is not suppressed. Aquatic vegetation is really a menace for many reservoirs. Obstructions also include the submerged rocks, boulders etc. If necessary, the difficulties should be solved with the help of other related Govt. departments. The construction of *fish escape screens* is also essential so that the fish should not escape through the sluice gates. It may be electrical screen or any other mechanical device. There is the need of a *fish seed farm* for the reservoir for the supply of fish seed in time which can be of great economical value. Arrangement should be made for timely *supply of water* to the reservoir if needed, and also to the seed farm. This point is very crucial for seed stocking purpose.

(2) *Post-impoundment issues* : There are certain post-impoundment issues which are taken into consideration for better prospect of reservoir fishery management. It is essential *to collect necessary scientific data* so that the technical recommendations may be fruitful. The collection of data should include Physico-Chemical Characteristics of the soil and water, seasonal water levels, meteorological observations, aquatic flora and fauna with special reference to plankton concentration, fish fauna and population dynamics, location of breeding grounds for different fish species etc.

Survey of fish stocks should be done in the different parts of the reservoir in order to know which type of aquatic habitat suits a particular fish species. Such study helps in sustained production of economically valuable fishes.

Fish Seed Stocking Operations are also necessary. Fingerlings should be reared adjacent to reservoir site. It will be an economic venture. The purpose should be to stock the desirable size of the fingerlings in the reservoirs. There is need for the development of *gear technology* for efficient capturing of fish in the reservoir. There should be selective fishing only by choice of appropriate gear and craft. Fingerlings of size of 15-20 cm. length are most suitable for stocking. In smaller reservoirs fingerlings numbering 3500 to 5000/hac. can be stocked.

(3) *Administrative issues* : There are several basic administrative issues, crucial for reservoir fishery management. Fishing rights in a resevoir are normally vested in certain Government bodies like State Fisheries Department, the State Fisheries Corporation and the Irrigation Department etc. Corruption and false reporting create serious management problem. Sometimes organised theft is also committed. Restriction like minimum catch size, minimum mesh size are not properly observed. Memberrs of the fishery, staff do not collect correct relevant data including fish seed stock. The reporting is generally false and manipulated. Fishing should be done by labour intensive methods with simple craft and gear. This will provide employment opportunity to poors. Authority should develop systems to overcome corruption and false reporting practices. Government has to take *policy decision* not only for creating employment opportunities but also for collecting revenue through this resource. The fishermen should be given *proper training* so that they may have skill necessary for taking up fishing in the reservoirs. Poaching of fish from the reservoir is also problematic. It can be controlled only at the government level, by making provisions in the State fisheries act so that poachers, if caught can be prosecuted. *Mechanised boats for patrolling* will be of great use. Time to time, the *economic viability* of the reservoirs should be assessed. There is wide variation in the basic policy for leasing rights in different states. There can be *direct fishing* by a government authority. *Lease by auction* which is open to all is also a common feature sometimes. A *royalty basis* is also adopted sometimes. In addition to all these, *multiple licenses* to fishermen or *fishermen's co-operative societies* is also there in practice. All these leasing policies have some merits and demerits. The policy should be such as to incorporate the following qualities :

(1) The fishermen should enjoy fair wages and the profit of the contractors and middlemen should be considerably reduced.

(2) All sorts of corruption including poaching should be controlled.

(3) Investment should be minimum so that the fishermen and co-operative Societies should be encouraged.

(4) Fishermen should be provided economic and social security.

(5) Necessary fish seed stock should always be maintained and the seed producing agency should be separate.

(6) Contractors can be made responsible for fish seed stocking under the lease agrement.

Some measures for improvement of Reservoir fishery : Discharge of effluents into a reservoir of the water system feeling the reservoir can be sometimes very harmful for reservoir fishery management and as such, legal measures should be taken to control water pollution. There should be frequent applications of latest technological developments to improve reservoir fishery. Precaution should be taken to eradicate the predatory fishes from the reservoirs. Fishing should not be done during the breeding season. A dense stock of commercially important species of fish should be maintained in the reservoir. The minimum mesh size for nets should be 30 mm.

Concluding remarks : The intervention of the state government is necessary for the improvement of reservoir fisheries. The Central Inland Fisheries Research Institute (CIFRI) can contribute much in this regard by providing consultancy and technological assistance to the State Governments. The CIFRI should make technological recommendations on the basis of all-India Co-ordinated research projects on ecology and fisheries of reservoirs. The ratio of fingerlings of different species of fishes in a reservoir polyculture practices should be recommended. For example 10 fingerlings of the size of 15 to 20 cm in the ratio of 6 catla : 4 rohu per hectare area have been recommended for Govind Sagar reservoir of Punjab. The CIFRI conducts short term training programmes for field level fishery staff. There is need for creating an effective and functional institutional framework to promote exchange knowledge of latest technological developments between the CIFRI and the State Fisheries Departments. Such attempts will definitely increase the productivity of resevoirs. The fishermen based Cooperative Societies should be productive and not only marketing oriented. There should be adequate transport infrastructure for local and outside sales. Fish production in Indian reservoirs varies from water to water depending on the fishery development activities.

Reservoir Management in U.S.S.R.

Large number of reservoirs are located over different climatic regions of USSR. The total reservoir area in USSR is between 5 to 10 million hectares. Several dams are under construction. The present annual fish production from reservoirs have reached nearly 10,00,000 tonnes. Some of the very large reservoires of USSR are Kakhovskoya, Kuibyshevskye, Phy Rybinskoye, Tzimljanskoye and Volgogradskoya. These are probably the larget reservoirs of the world.

For ensuring high productivity, several measures have been adopted. Spawners of valuable food fishes like *Abramis brama* (Linnaeus), *Cyprinus carpio* (L.) and *Lucioperca lucioperca* (L.) are transplanted to spawning stocks. Next, the fish hatcheries are constructed at the reservoir site to raise fingerlings of desirable fishes.

Food reserves of the reservoirs are enriched with feed organisms. Hydro-biological regimes are suitably altered for sustaining large fish population. There is mass development of phytoplankton in many reservoirs. For some period the fishing efforts are banned which increases the strength, particularly of the food fishes in the reservoirs. Thus huge stocks of the fry of desirable fish is obtained. Measures are also taken to prevent trash fishes like *Perca fluviatalis* (L.), *Rutilus rutilus* (L.), *Acerina cernika* (L) etc. Predators are destroyed by all means.

The soviet fishery scientists, in collaboration with engineers make suitable preparation and levelling of the reservoir bottom for commercial fishes. They prepare hauling areas for the operation of Seines. Not only that, they also develop artificial spawning areas and work out the optimum water level regime for the success of breeding and survival.

Bacteriological studies in USSR have revealed that role of bacteria in food conversion from one farm to another is of great use for many species of fish. Supplying of detrius facilitates development of rich saprophytic microflora. Several methods have also been developed for increasing the population of zooplankton which include several species of rotifers, cladocerans and copepods. Various food invertebrates have also been acclimatised in certain reservoirs. Some exotic fishes particularly imported from China have also been introduced into the reservoirs for better fish production. These fishes included *Ctenopharyngodon idella* (val.), *Hypophthalmichthys molitrix* (Val.) and *Aristichthys nobilis* (Rich.).

The construction of dams across certain rivers restricted the migration of some anadromous fishes like *Huso huso* (L.), *Acipenser stellatus* (Pallas) and some other fishes. Also the resident fishes are prevented from local migratory activities. Now the Soviet Scientists have evolved fish locks which are incorporated in the dams. Fish locks have several merits. There is possibility of wide entrance, because, a large volume of water can pass through fish lock. Also, fishes of different size and behaviour can pass through these locks. These fishes do not get wearied even in tail to head water. Originally the fish locks were on the Tymyla Hydro-electric station on the Don River and at theVolgogard Dam on River Volga.

The fish lock system contains :

(a) Inlet Chutes—which are also known as twin fish collectors and are placed in the tail water.

(b) Outlet Chute—which is located at the head water.

(c) Twin lock chambers—for lifting up.

(d) A turbine with a generator—for supplying water with particular velocity at various spots in the fish collection chamber.

The whole system operates by the principle of impelling latices which consist of screens, moving horizontally in the inlet and outlet chutes and in the lock chambers it moves in the vertical plane. Fishes are attracted and accumulated in the fish collectors for two hours and often that passage from tail to head water takes place only 40 minutes in all the three chambers of the fish locks.

Reservoir Management in U.S.A.

In U.S.A. there are about 300 impoundments which have a capacity of 1700000 ha. of water surface. Reservoirs were basically constructed for flood control and also generation of hydro-electric power. Bennet (1962) has reviewed the progress of reservoir management in U.S.A. Lake Keokuk, a low-dam impoundment on the Mississippi river was studied earlier in 1920's. Number of reservoirs increased in 1930 and in the beginning, studies were confined to plankton, bottom fauna and fish. Ellis (1937) came to conclude that when there was decay of organic matter in the impoundment, productivity became higher for sometime but later on it was deserted. Some of the biologists conceived that when undesirable populations were removed either by chemical treatment or by draining, there was remarkable improvement in productivity. Thus, gradually, the reservoir fishery was taken up with interest. Now, several measures have been adopted for the improvement of the reservoir productivity.

The water levels preferred are favourable for selected species only and other undesirable species are suppressed. Fishermen are made aware of suitable time and place to catch fishes. Some more species of fishes are also introduced which contribute directly to the fishing baskets. These fishes include *Roccus chrysops, R. sexualitis* and some other species. In addition to the fish spp. some desirable organisms are also introduced to fill some vacant ecological nitches. Over population of some fishes e.g. *Carpoides* spp., *Dorosoma*, spp., *Aplodinotus grunniens* and even *Cyprinus carpio* is controlled for reducing competition and making better scope for food and space to all the fishes in the reservoir. Many devices are developed to attract the fish to fish docks.

Some Important Reservoirs of the States

1. *Stanley* : This reservoir is located on River Cauvery at Mettur in Tamil Nadu. The dam was constructed in 1934. *Hogenakal* water falls form the northern limit of this reservoir. Three tributaries are there : *Palar* (on west), and *chinnar* and *Thoppiar* (on east) enter this reservoir above Mettur. From Mettur the river Cauvery takes its course towards south upto Bhavania town.

The important centres for fishing in this reservoir are :

(a) Keerakaranur

(b) Kunandiyar

(c) Masilapalayam

(d) Pannavadi, and

(e) Hogenakal.

The fisheries of this reservoir has been described by Rangnathan and Natarajan (1969) and Sreenivasan (1976). The fishes of major commercial importance of this reservoir are—*Cirrhinus cirrhosa, Labeo kontius, Lebeo ariza L., fimbriatus, Mystus aor, M. seenghala, Pangasius pangasius, Puntius dubius, Silonia silondia* and *Wallago attu.*

Various developmental stages of *Catla catla* have been stocked in various stretches of the river Cauvery. *Cyprinus carpio, Labeo calbasu, Cirrhina mrigala, Osphronemus goramy* and *Eutroplus suratensis* have also been transferred from time to time. Fishing is done with *Uduvalai drift nets, Oosavalai, perch traps, long lines, hooks and lines, Rhagoon net, Catla nets* etc. Several nets are made of Synthetic twine now. The average annual total landing comes to be around 400 tonnes with slight fluctuations every year. The highest percentage in the landing is that of *Catla catla, Wallago attu* and *Cirrhinus cirrhosa*.

(2) *Govind Ballav Pant Sagar (Rehand Reservoir)* : This reservoir was created in 1962. Here, the dam has been constructed on the river Rend near the village Pipri of the Mirzapur district of U.P. It is a water spread area of 46,620 ha. The average annual fish landing is round about 3000 quintals. *Catla catla* is among the dominating carps in this reservoir. Natarajan *et al.* (1977) distinguished three types of intra-specific populations based on the characters of the length of Pectoral fin. They have reported the natural occurrence of *Catla rohu* hybrids from Rehand reservoir. The hybrid preferred *ceratium* for their food. The hybrid is supposed to be useful substitute for *Labeo* species as latter exhibit a poor performance.

(3) *Damodar-Valley Corporation Reservoirs (Tilaiya and Konar)* : Today the Damodar Valley Corporation is a well known multipurpose project in Bihar. It contains the Damodar and its two main tributaries e.g. Barakar and Konar. The Damodar is itself the tributary of the river Ganges. Dams were constructed during the period 1952 to 1958. The four dams included two on Barakar, viz., one each at Tilaiya and Maithon, one on Konar and one on Damodar at Panchet. The Central Inland Fisheries Research Institute (CIFRI) was established later on at Hazaribagh for various scientific assessment at Tilaiya and Konar reservoirs particularly. As these reservoirs are built on seasonal rivers they are live during the monsoon period only. Some data based on Jhingran (1982) are as follows:

The substratum of Tilaiya is acidic (pH 5.5-6.0) in nature and it is silty-clay-loam to loam. The substratum of Konar is also acidic in nature within the same range but is sandy-loam to clay. There is very low percentage of organic carbon (0.3 to 0.9) and also that of phosphorus (1.2–8.0) in both the cases. Organic nitrogen ranges from 0.069 to 0.104 per cent. The value of Ca ion is medium which is 13.2–16.2 ppm. The concentration of nitrate is 0.25-0.28 ppm and that of phosphate it is 0.024-0.03 ppm. Both these values are satisfactory. The plankton crop as estimated by Jhingran was 100 kg/ha for Tilaiya and 240 kg/ha for Konar. Blue green algae dominated the phytoplankton though they were not utilised by the fishes which were economically important. Periphyton mainly formed the food of *Labeo calbasu, Cirrihina mrigala* and *Puntius* spp. *Ambassis nama* is most important among the thrash fishes. Also, the predatory fishes like *Wallago attu, Notopterus chitala* and *Barilius bola* are in abundance in both the reservoirs. The average annual yield per ha production of fish in both the reservoirs is about 15 tonnes.

(4) *Rana Pratap Sagar* : It is the biggest reservoir of Rajasthan covering an area of 2,00,00 ha at full reservoir level. It was built in as early as 1968 on river Chambal in

the district of Chittorgarh. As reported by Chaudhury (1978) there is more than required submerged vegetation which include *Vallisnaria, Hydrilla* and *Potamogeton*. In this reservoir, *Labeo calbasu, L. rohita, Catla catla, Cirrhina mrigala* and *Tor* sp. are the dominating fish. In addition to these fish, some cat fishes are also there. Natarajan *et al.* (1975) conceived that thrash fishes like *Ambassis nama, A. ranga, Amblypharyngodon mola, Esonus danrica, Osteobrama cotio, Puntius sophore* and *Puntius ticto* are harmful to the productivity of major carps owing to overlapping food spectra. The average annual production of fish from this reservoir is about 125 tonnes now.

Under the integrated Chambal Valley Scheme were also constructed Gandhi Sagar, Jawahar Sagar and Kota Barrage.

CHAPTER 22

ECONOMIC IMPORTANCE OF FISH

(By-Products)

Fishes are very rich in protein, carbohydrate, vitamins (A,D and E), iron, calcium and other minerals. Fishes are used as food either cooked, salted, smoked or preserved in other ways. In one pound of fish the food values come to be 300-600 calories, which is much higher in comparison to other food materials for human consumption. Fresh and preserved fishes are used as food, also protein, fat and other useful contents in the body of fish are processed into a number of valuable products and by-products which have been discussed later on in this chapter.

Government of India is now paying much attention to the development of fish and fisheries for the improvement of quality and quantity of fishes. Fisheries research stations have been set up at Mandapam (T.N.) Barrackpore (W.B.), Kakinada (T.N.) Visakhapatnam (Andh.P.), where developmental programmes of fish and fisheries are carried out.

There is abundance of marine and inland resources of fish, however, there is scarcity of suitable carft and gears and also inadequacy of transport and preservation facilities.

By-Products of Fish and Other Uses

Fish Liver Oil: This is a very important poduct of fish. Fish liver contains protein, fat and water mainly. The percentage of fat is between 55 to 75. Vitamin A (A_1 and A_2), Vit. D, and Vit. E are present in the fatty substance. Some of them may be partly associated with the proteins of the liver also. There is great variation in the quantities of fat and vitamins from fish to fish. Cod (*Gadus morrhua* and *G. callarium*) liver is very rich in its fat content but poor in vitamin A content (1000-3000 I.U./g). On the other hand some sharks (*Galeocerdo tigrinus, Sphyrna blochii, Pristis cuspidatus* etc.) have the highest fat and vitamin A content (15000 to 1000000 I. U./g.) The ratio of vitamin A and D is such in the liver, that it is much suitable for human needs. Fish liver oil is not only manufactured in big factories but also in cottage industries. There are various methods by which the oil can be extracted. These methods are : method of boiling, method of autofermentation, method of steaming, and method of chemical digestion. The chemical digestion comprises *aquacide digestion, alkali digestion, enzyme-alkali digestion* and *method of solvent extraction* etc. Standardisation of vitamin A is done by several methods like *Biological estimation* (by using vitamin A deficient food), Calorimetric estimation (by adding chloroformic solution of antimony trichloride), and *Spectrophotometric method* (by ultraviolet ray absorption). In cottage industry the extraction is done by a simple model of fish liver oil extractor, a model proposed by Saha (1956).

Fish Body Oil : Oil can also be obtained from the entire body of certain fishes (e.g. oil sardines, herrings and salmon) by dry or wet methods, but this oil is different from the liver oil. Body oil is however poor in vitamin A and D contents. Glycerides of fatty acids are present in the body oil in varied proportions. There is trace of iodine in this oil. Body oil is used for various purposes as given below :

(i) To make paints and varnishes.
(ii) Dressing of Leather and tanning of skin.
(iii) For steel tempering in industries.
(iv) For making cheap soap (Laundry soap and insecticidal soap).
(v) For manufacturing certain chemicals (alkyl halides, ammonium salts etc.)
(vi) For making cosmetics, lubricants, candles etc.
(vii) Use as fungicides for citrus trees.
(viii) Use in manufacturing printing ink and plastics.
(ix) Used on the surface of boat for preservation.
(x) It is also used as cooking medium.

Fish Meal : The nutritional value of fish meal is higher than the meat of cattle. Nutritional value of raw fish is greater in comparison to that of preserved and processed fish and fishery products. Fish meal is ground, cooked and dried preparation of the fresh fishes. It contains about 55-70 per cent protein, 2-15 per cent oil/fat and 10-20 per cent minerals (Ca, P, I) as per many reports. The protein contains all the essential amino acids. Vitamins like B_{12} B, A, D, K and E are also there in the fish meal. Sardines, Mackerels, Ribbonfish, Silver bellies and some sharks are used as raw material for fish meal preparation. By-products of canneries and fish oil industries may serve as fish meal. *Fish flour* is a hydrolysed protein and is supposed to be superior quality food. It is of great use for human consumption. It is prepared by a sophisticated solvent extraction process. It may be mixed with wheat or maize flour and is used in bakery products (bread, biscuits and cakes etc.) It is manufactured in India, South Africa, tropical Africa, U.S.A, Morocco and Chile.

Fish Silage : The physical nature of this product is either semisolid or liquid. Fresh fishes are minced and mixed with sulphuric acid (pH2) or formic acid (pH 4-5) or in both (one after another). Fish silage is highly nutritive and is manufactured in Norway, Denmark and some other countries.

Fish manure and guano : These are inferior quality of fish meal products. They are not fit for animal consumption. Fish manure is a by-product of curing yards, fish glue industries and oil extraction plants. This manure mainly contains nitrogen (5-7 per cent), phosphates (4-6 per cent) and lime (4-6 per cent). It is very useful for coffee, tea and tobacco crops. Fish guano is the by-product of body oil extraction plants. The product quickly decomposes in oil and mixes well. Its nitrogen content is very high (8-10 per cent) and it is an effective manure.

Fish Sausage and ham : These are spiced pasted fish meat preparations and are popular in several countries like Japan, U.S.S.R., and U.S.A. Fish ham are small pieces (1 sq. cm.) of solid fish meat. The fish is cooked at a temperature between 85°-90°C. Spices include salt, chillies, coriander, onion, glutaminate, sugar, egg-white and vegetable oils etc. Some antiseptics (nitrofurazon, ascorbic acid etc.) are added to it. They are helpful in preventing rancidity.

Fish Glue : Fish glue is prepared from trimmings, bones and skin. The latter substances are washed, ground and charged into steam-jacketed cookers. The charge is covered with water and the medium is made acidic with the addition of acetic acid. Then it is cooked for 6-10 hours. The liquor is extracted from the residue. The liquor when concentrated is used as glue but the residue serves as poultry feed and manure. Residue consists of protein (53.0 per cent), fat (1.5 per cent), crude fibre (0.8 per cent), calcium and magnesium phosphates (27 per cent and other constituents. Fish glue is a good adhesive and is extensively used in the manufacture of court plaster, backing for labels, and book binding, and stamps. The glue prepared from the skins of cod is of very high quality and is very usful in photo-engraving work.

Isinglass : Isinglass was formerly used as a substitute for gelation but now it is used for the clarification of wines, beer and vinegar. It may also be used for the preparation of plasters and special cements. Isinglass is a collagen produced from the inner part of the air bladder of certain fishes (catfishes and carps). It is insoluble in cold water. Russian isinglass containing less than 0.5 per cent ash and about 3 per cent matter insoluble in hot water, is supposed to be a high grade isinglass. The air bladders of perches and Indian Salmon also provide very good materials for isinglass manufacture.

Fish Leather : The skin of cod, salmon, halibut, some sharks and rays and other fishes are tanned and marketed as ornamental leather. The skin is detached from the fresh and soaked in brine for a day. Then it is treated with salt solution containing 10 per cent hydrochloric acid. They are drained and the surface of the skin is scraped with a knife in order to remove denticles. Then they are lined and tanned by usual process. The shark skin is durable and is used in the manufacture of shoes, hand bags tobacco pouches etc.

Fish Caviar (Fish roe) : Caviar is a processed and salted form of fish roe. It has great value as food. U.S.S.R. manufactures caviar from sturgeons which is a high esteemed delicious food. Fish roe is a good appetizer also. It contains all essential amino acids and some vitamins (B, C, D, and E). It has very high lecithin (upto 59 per cent) and cholesterol (upto 14 per cent) contents.

Shark fins : Fins (excluding caudals) are cut near the root and are washed in sea water. They are dusted with a mixture of wood ashes and lime and dried in the sun. They are also smoked sometimes. This cured product is brittle. Shark fins are important items of food and are much popular in China and Philippines.

Insulin : Fish can also provide raw materials for the manufacture of insulin. Shark pancreas is rich in insulin.

Fish Macaroni : This product is manufactured in India also. The fish *Barbus carnaticus* is minced and mixed with tapioca or sorghum flour. After gelatinizing with hot water some wheat semoline is added to this preparation. It is also spiced with salt, chilies and tamarind. The paste is finally dried.

Fish Biscuits: Fish biscuits are prepared in Chile and Morocco. Fish flour (already described) is blended with biscuit mixture before baking.

Controllers of disease : Certain species of fish are used in controlling some diseases. In India, a large number of exotic and indigeneous species of fish are larvivorous and feed at one stage or the other on mosquito larvae and thereby control malaria, yellow fever and other dreadful diseases. These fishes are *Gambusia affinis, Lebistes reticulatus, Carassius auratus, Oxygaster, Notopterus, Rasbora, Danio, Puntius sophore, Glossogobius, Ambassis, Channa orientalis, Mystus vittatus* etc. Naturally, their contribution in controlling certain diseases is important.

Scavengers : Certain freshwater fishes like *Clarias batrachus, Heteroneustes fossilis* and *Bagarius bagarius* feed on excreta. Many fishes are omnivorous feeding on decaying matters and thus they are true scavengers.

As Bait : Several fishes are employed as bait for catching large fishes and other animals. Flying fishes are employed as bait for catching turtles in the sea. Larval forms of Lamprey, Puntius, Rasbora and some other fishes are also used as baits for catching game fishes and species of large fishes.

Aquarium : Fishes are kept in aquarium by many people for decoration and also for scientific studies. Some fishes like Gold fish, Globe fish, Angel fish, *Puntius ticto* etc. are common aquarium fishes.

CHAPTER 23

FISHING TECHNOLOGY

(Crafts and Gears)

In fishing technology, crafts and gears are the real means of production. Fishing method actually means the way in which fish can be captured. Gears are the instrument used for fish catching and the crafts provide platform for the fishing operations carrying the crew and fishing gear. There are several types of crafts and gears operated in sea and inland waters. There are some gears which can be operated without the aid of craft. Crafts and gears used in the different parts of the country are mostly indigenous, non-mechanized and locally built, however, mechanized crafts have also been introduced in certain parts of India.

The farm fish can be captured in two ways-drying out (emptying the ponds or farm) or not drying out. Ponds which can not be completely dried out are not the real farm ponds. To reduce considerable losses, following precautions should be taken at the time of capture:

1. Feeding should be stopped 2 or 3 days before capturing.
2. Harvesting should be done in the cool weather preferably in the morning. It should be avoided when it is raining or thundering.
3. Normally, long transportation is avoided.
4. Young fishes, Salmonids or other delicate fishes should not be heaped up in scoop nets or any other receptacle.

Fishing can be practised with various equipments. Several devices and equipments are used for capture. Equipments differ according to the nature of water bodies, the age of the fish and their species etc.

Principal Equipments for Capture

Following are the important sea-fishing crafts :

Catamaran: The use of Catamaran is confined to the east coast from Orissa to Cape Comorin with a little extension towards north on the Kerala Coast. It is the most rudimentary craft used by any group of traditional fishermen all over the world. The fisheries sector is predominated by small scale traditional craft and gear. It is a very economical and efficient craft evolved for surf beaten coasts.

The word 'Catamaran' is derived from the Tamil "Kattumaram" which describes the nature of craft. It is a Keelless craft formed by lashing together 3 to 7 pieces of light rough-hewn wood. A loose rubber is hung between the logs. It is known as 'teppa'. Catamarans have a length of 5-12 m, width 0.7 m to 1.4 m, and depth 0.3 to 0.7 m. It is constructed with logs of woods.

Generally the Catamaran consists of 2 main loge and two side logs. They are cut into boat shape and tied together with a rope. There are four types of catamarans :

(a) *Orissa and Ganjam type* : These are boat shaped catamarans made up of five logs which are pegged with wood instead of being tied together.

(b) *Andhra type* : It is slightly large than the above type. It has heavy wood. There are strong median lögs used in fitting the sides.

(c) *Coromandel type* : It is commonly used around Madras. It is made up of 3-5 logs, with considerable variations in pattern. In the flying fish fishery off Nagapanam, *Kolamaram* (seven-logged catamaran) is used.

(d) *Boat Catamaran* : It is used on the coast around Mandapam. It has three logs fitted into a regular boat shape. There are variations of this type in the Tuticorin, Cape Comorin and some other areas.

Masula boat : It is a frameless, double ended, keel-less boat constructed from mango planks stitched together with palm leaf fibres. It can withstand the severe knocking of the surfs. Masula boats are 8-12m in length and are of weak construction. It can be used in fair weather only. It is operated near the shore. The smaller

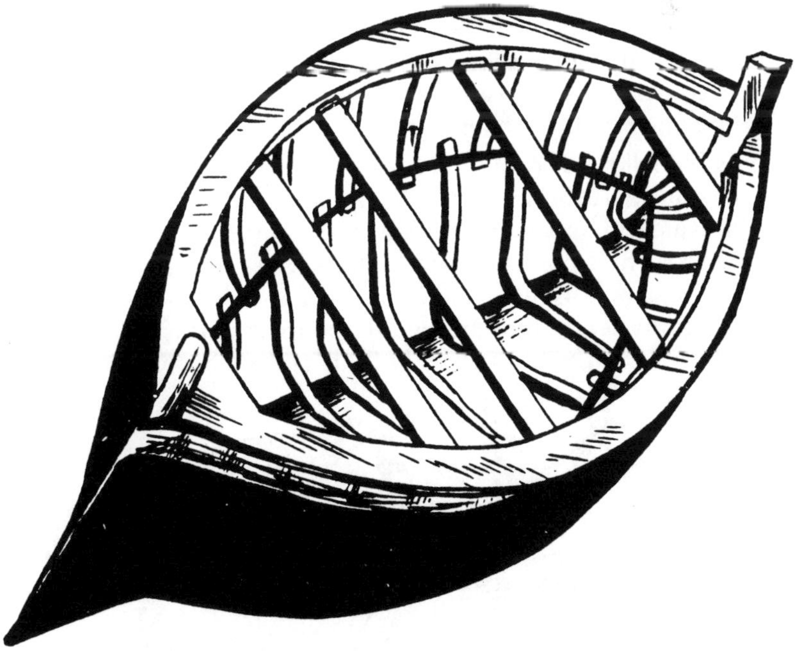

Fig. 79 : Dinghi-A Carvel boat of Orissa

masula boat are extensively used in gill net fishing. *Bar* boats of Orissa and *Padava* or *padagu* on the Andhra coast are the examples of masula boats.

Dinghi and Nauka : These are carvel boats commonly operated in West Bengal and Orissa. Naukas (12-13m x 3m x 2m) are also used for fishing and other purposes.

Tuticorin boats: These are also called the fishing luggers. These carvel boats upto a size of 10-11m x 2m x 1m are operated in inshore waters. They are also used as mother-ships and cargo boats.

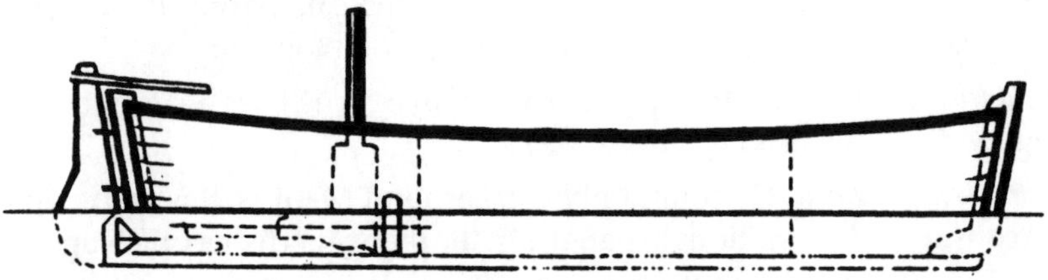

Fig. 80 : Tuticorin type fishing boat

Dugout Canoes : These are made from the hollowed trunk of the Palmyran tree. They are used on the Kerala and Kanara coasts and also near Kathiawar. The large dugouts (*Vanchi, Odams)* comprise the main fishing crafts of the Malabar coast. These are 10-20m long boats which can be operated by one or two fishermen. It can also be used for fishing in rivers and canals. The smaller dugouts are known as *thonies* and are used for drift fishing and for seining.

Plank-built Canoes: Here, dugouts are further enlarged with planks on the sides. These are used in Kerala, North Bombay and Kathiawar.

Outrigger Canoes : These are large (up to 15m. long) in size with a narrow keel and more spread out planks. Canoes with single outrigger are used on the Kanara and Konkan coasts. These are also known as *rampani* boats because they are used for mackerel operations with the *rampani* net.

Built-up boats : These boats can be seen on the west coats along the Bombay-Cambay coast and north of Ratnagiri. It has a pointed bow, straight and narrow keel and low gunwale. This is particularly known as Ratnagiri type of boat. The Bassein type having broad hull, pointed bow and straight keel is locally known as *machwa*. The *Satpati* type known as *galbat*, has a broad beam, median-pointed bow, straight keel and high gunwale. The Broach type is flat bottomed and is of great use in inshore and estuarine waters. The *Satpati* type built-up boats can be easily mechanized.

Fig. 81: Rampani boat—An outrigger canoe of Karwar

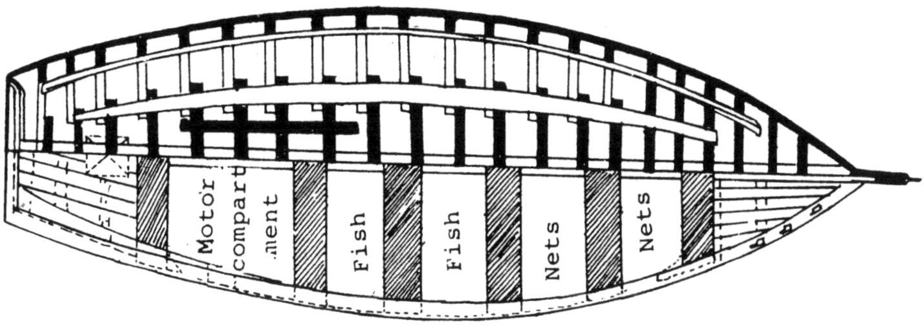

Fig. 82 : Satpati type fishing boat

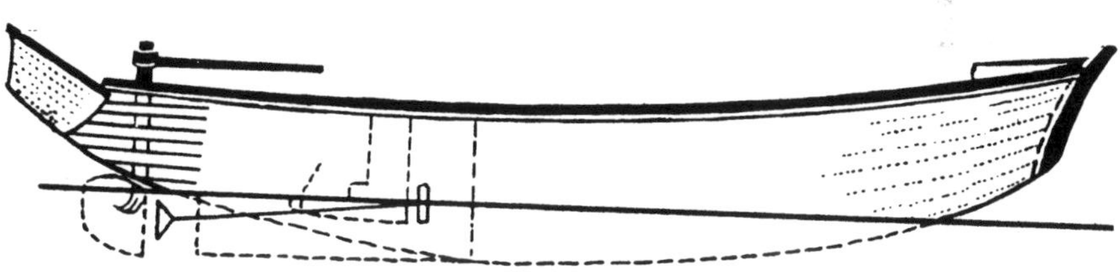

Fig. 83 : Kakinada Nava (Andhra State)

Shoe Dhonie : The shape of this craft resembles a shoe and it is used in rivers and sea. It is very common in Godavari. It is made up of teak wood and is constructed with planks grooved with ribs and frames. Nails are also used. It is wide and flat forward. 3 to 4 persons can operate this craft for fishing with gill nets.

Coracle : A coracle is like a round basin. Its frame is constructed with split bamboos, the outer being covered with leather. It can be operated in rivers, canals and reservoirs with a stout, short stick by 2 to 3 fishermen.

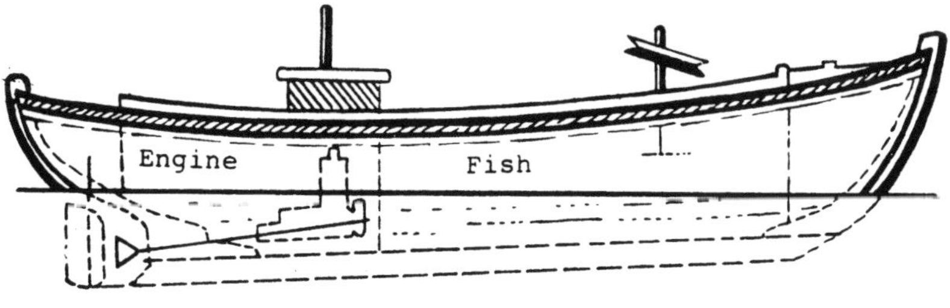

Fig. 84 : Pablo type fishing boat of Madras

Kakinada Nava : This craft is very common for inshore fishing. It is a keel-less boat of about 9.5m length, made of teak wood and carvel built. They are constructed with frames and ribs. Nails are also used in their construction. It is of the open type with a little space decked. They can be used in rivers, lakes and reservoirs also.

Sea fishing gears : Sea-fishing gears are of various types. Nets, the main gears are made of cotton yarns, hemp or other special yarns. They can be prepared by the fishermen themselves or they are the products of cottage industries.

Fixed nets : Fixed or stationary nets are conical or rectangular in shape. These are of various sizes and meshes. *Panch, Kathia-Kool jal, behundi* or *ghurni jal* and *panch-Kathiaber jal* are conical nets used in W. Bengal and Orissa. *Jadi* or *mtagh jal* of Gujrat and Kathiawar coasts, *Kalam-katti valai* of the Gulf of Manaar and some parts of the Palk Bay, Bayd or *mal jal* of W. Bengal and Orissa, *barnada jal* of N. Orissa, *Kala valai* of Tanjore district, and *Konda vala, Thorku vala, Waghol jal, bangda jal* (or *Patta bale)* of the Kanara coast are some of the important examples of rectangular nets.

All these nets may be fixed in the tidal regions of inshore waters during the low tide with the help of floats, stakes or sinkers. The high tide brings the fish in the net which are subsequently trapped. *Behundi* or *ghurni jal* when fixed, turns around the pole with the change in the direction of the tide and as such, operations become convenient at different times of the day. A variety of fish species going against the current are grilled in the *Kala valai* nets.

Seines : These are very large nets for active fishing. It encircles a large part of water believed to contain a lot of fish. A seine is often used in running water. It is generally rectangular in shape and is mounted between a wire or balk provided with leads. The net is kept stretched out vertically in the water. Seines are of two types. These are known as *Shore seines* and *Boat seines.*

Shore seines are operated from the sea-shore. Each net contains a bag with wings and scarelines are used for driving the fish into the bag. The net is kept in position by wooden floats and stone sinkers held in the head and foot ropes. One end of the net remains on the shore and the other extremity carries the rest of the net and places it in the semicircular way. Finally the two ends are slowly dragged by groups of fishermen.

Boat seines are conical bags with wings. The mesh increases from the bag position towards the outer end of the flanks. This boat is operated in the sea by boats or catamarans. The fishes are trapped in the bag. Coir ropes are used for the purpose of towing. Floats and weights are also used.

Beach Seine (haul seine) : It consists of two walls of net webbing of strong twines which are known as wings. The wings are joined to a central bag of net-webbing. The wings may be equal or unequal in size tapering at the ends. At the ends they are connected to the warps either directly or by means of brail (Spreader) of stout pole. At regular intervals, spreaders are present which run from float-line to lead-line. The size of the mesh is large in the wing than in the bag. The float-line carries suitable

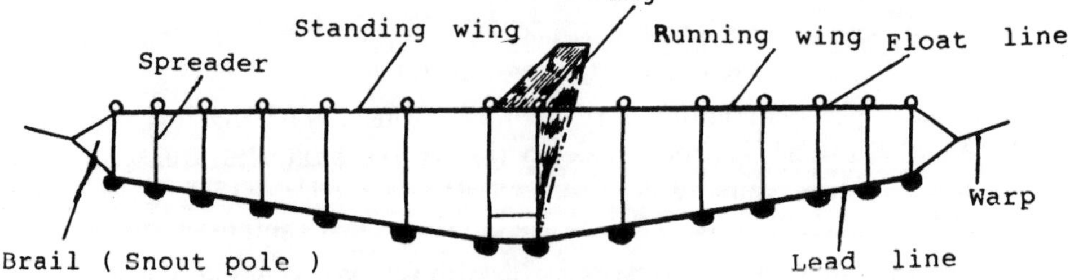

Fig. 85: Beach Seine : The net

floats and the leadline has sinkers. The net is laid out in such a way that its one wing (standing wing) remains at the beach. The running wing is shot, at right angles to the shore. This end is again brought back to the beach. As a result, a large arc is formed and it encircles a particular section of water. The float line and the lead line do not allow the fish to escape. Hauling is carried out by pulling the two warps and assembling the wings.

Danish seine (Drag seine): A Danish seine is used in deep water. Here the float line remains in side water and never reaches the surface. The wings are smaller, replaced by warps. Principle of operation is like that of the beach seine.

Purse Seine : Purse seine is in use for catching mostly pelagic fishes and some migratory fishes. It is operated from the vessel. In the hanging condition, the floatline of the net wall remains at the surface, the lead-line is at certain depth from the surface and does not touch the bottom. The fish can not escape below the lead-line by the net being pursed during the process of hatching. For this purpose a purse line of strong cable is also there. The net has a single wall and there is no bag. The central part which acts as the bunt, has the thickest twines. During operation, one end of the net is held on a small boat. The net is laid out by the vessel cruising at a higher speed and making a circle so that it comes back to the small boat. The purse line is handed on board the vessel. The net then takes the shape of a purse. The pull on the purse line increases at the end of the operation and it equals the weight of the lower half of the net. The entire net is hauled aboard alongwith the catch.

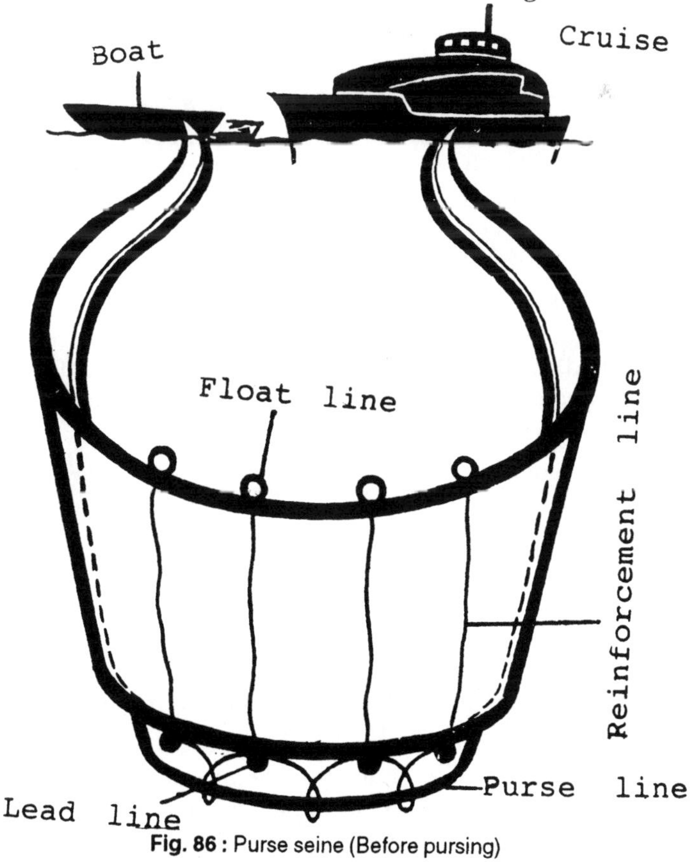

Fig. 86 : Purse seine (Before pursing)

Scoop Nets (Dip nets) : Scoop nets are round in shape. When delicate fish are handled the net is shallow. Mesh is proportionate to the size of the fish. The net is fixed inside the frame. The shape of this net is like that of a finger-bowl. It consists of a piece of net-webbing set on a rigid frame. The net can be moved swiftly in a scooping manner, lifting the fish out of water.

Trap Nets and Nets : This equipment may be rigid or pliable, mobile or fixed. They are passively operated nets. These equipments are used in shallow waters. Trap net are rigid, made in wicker and vary in shape, size and handling. In the lower part they are cylindrical and in the upper part they are like a truncated cone. One or two cone-shaped necks are present in the interior of the trap net. These form a funnel which stops the escape of the fish caught. The interior opening has a diameter close to the size of the most fish. Fish are let into an enclosure through guarded entrance from where they can not escape. Fyke nets or hoop nets and pound nets are of different varieties. Pound nets are larger types of trap nets. There is a main chamber (heart) opening with a wide gate guarded by slot like entrance. The hearts are connected to one or more pockets called *cribes*. The opening of the cribe is also guarded by slot like entrances. The leader used in front of the gate is a wall of net webbing. The enclosure of the net is either roofed or open. Anchors and stakes are also used.

Fyke net : They are supple and formed by a net fixed to rigid wooden hoops. They have roofed enclosure in the form of cylindrical bag of net webbing. The net is blind at one end and open at the other end. Fykes are cone-shaped. The opening (mouth) and the hoops are guarded with funnel-like entrances which are directed towards the blind end. The blind end is also called the cod end or the last pocket. On each side of the mouth there is an extension of a wing known as diverging wings. This wing is set at an inclined angle. The mouth and the wings are held on stakes. The net is used in shallow water to catch catfishes and pike spawners. The catch can be collected from the last pocket. A cylindrical fyke net with an opening provided with a neck at each end is know as a *drum*.

A drop net : In this case, there is a net mounted squarely and suspended at its corners by two supple hoops, which are tied in a cross at the top and attached to a pole. It can be pulled up, and down from the banks of the water or from a boat. When the drop net is pulled up the net forms a deep pocket which holds the fish. There is variation in its dimensions.

Cast net : It is a cone-shaped net cast from the edges of the water. It is made of a circular piece of net webbing. The circumference is inwardly curved when it opens it forms a circular sheet which imprisons the fish. The cloth is bordered with a large hem and leads are attached to it. The net is thrown over water and is held by a rope (handling line) attached to its centre. The net spreads like an umbrella over a group of fishes. Sinkers are present along the perimeter which increase the weight and facilitate sinking of net towards the bottom. When perimeter touches the bottom, hauling line is pulled to raise the net on board. Fish are thus collected. These are hand operated nets with string or without string.

Drift-net and Gill-nets : Gill-net are passive nets of enmeshing or entangling types. Here the fish get entangled in the fabric mesh and they are dead by the time of hauling. Nylon is the best material for the twines of these nets. Suitable colour (less

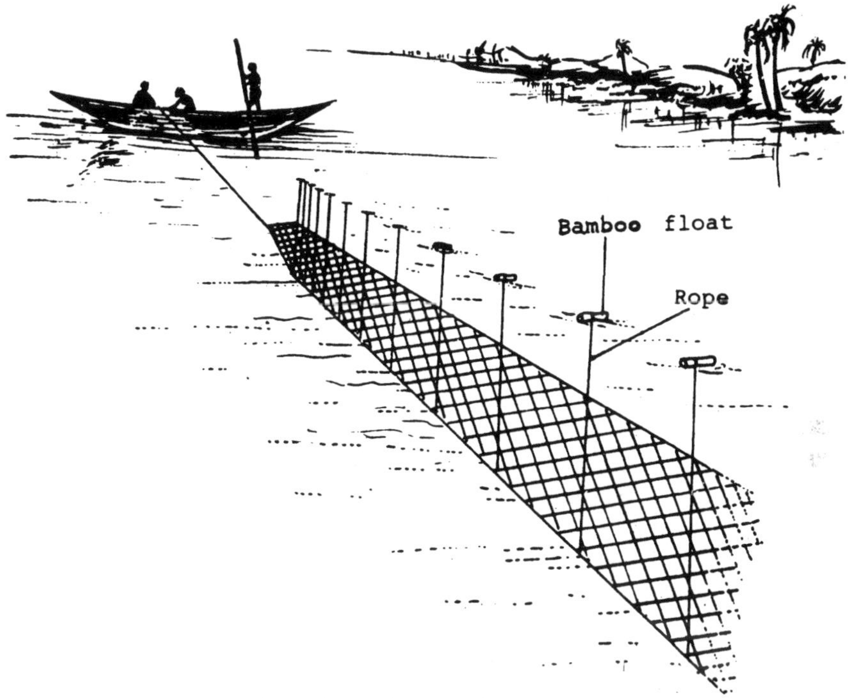

Fig. 87 : Karal or Katla Jal–A Drift-net

conspicuous) of the net enhances the success in fishing. These nets are left over night and then hauled. Reinforcement to net-webbing is done by lacing several rows of meshes of heavier twines (selvage.) There are two principal types : *Simple gill nets* and *trammel nets*. In case of *Simple gill nets* a loose net-webbing is set in the path of movement. When the fish tries to swim through a mesh, only its head passes through the mesh, but its large body can not pass through it. When fish tries to withdraw its head, twines slip under the gill cover and the fish is entangled. Thus, they can not escape. The fish is thus gilled (caught by the gill) and hence the name gill nets.

The gill nets are generally set in three ways : floating, anchored and staked. The floating type (drift net) is simply a vertically suspended wall of net with a float line and a lead line. In the anchored type, there is an anchor with the help of which the net is held stationary. It does not permit free drifting. In the staked types, the net is fixed at the bottom with the help of stakes or anchors. The gill nets are generally rigged with vertical snoods and frames. Snoods are twines attached at intervals between the floatline and lead line. Snoods increase fishing efficiency and frame provide reinforcement.

Trammel net are two or three walled. The walls are joined above at the float line and below at the deadline. A small-mesh webbing (lint) is loosely hung between two tightly hung walls with the help of these nets a wide size range of fishes can be caught. Small size fishes are gilled at the lint. Large size fish pushes a bag of the loosely hung lint and get entangled.

Hooks and Lines : Hooks and line fishing consists of two types : handlines and longlines. Line fishing is operated in a variety of ways using baited hooks, chain hooks, both revolving and non-revolving are used for catching large fishes.

In hand line fishing the gear consists of a single vertical line, sinkers and baited hooks in series. Long line fishing consists of a long horizontal main line having vertical branch spaced at uniform intervals. Each branch bears a series of baited hooks. In its operation anchors, anchorlines and floats are used.

A hook is a metallic equipment with several parts like eye, shank, bend and spear. The spear end has an inclined barb with outer and inner points.

Trawls : Trawls are large towed nets or dragging type nets. They work on the principle of catching fish by filtering water. It is just like a bag of net-webbing, with a mouth and a tapering blind cod end. The upper margin of the mouth is lined with a float line and the lower one with a foot rope. The floatline keeps the mouth open. Hydrostatic floats are also used. Foot rope is rigged with a number of wooden or metallic bobbins (thread wound cylinder) and is connected to the fishing line (lower margin of mouth). The cod end is reinforced with toothed chafing gear and cow-hide chafer. The bag carries splitting strops at considerable intervals and they prevent the bag from collapsing. Wing like net webbings extend from the side angles of the mouth. There is gradual decrase in the size of the mesh size from the wing to the cod end. The mainlines extend as base-ends (legs of lines) and the additional lines (lastridges) provide longitudinal strength to the trawl net. Other boards, sweeplines and spreaders assist in towing and dragging. Special rigging may be carried out between the warps and the legs of line of the net. *Otter trawls* are operated with the help of other boards. Trawls with beams are called the *beam trawls*. During operation, the otter boards (one on each side) keep the mouth of the trawl net open.

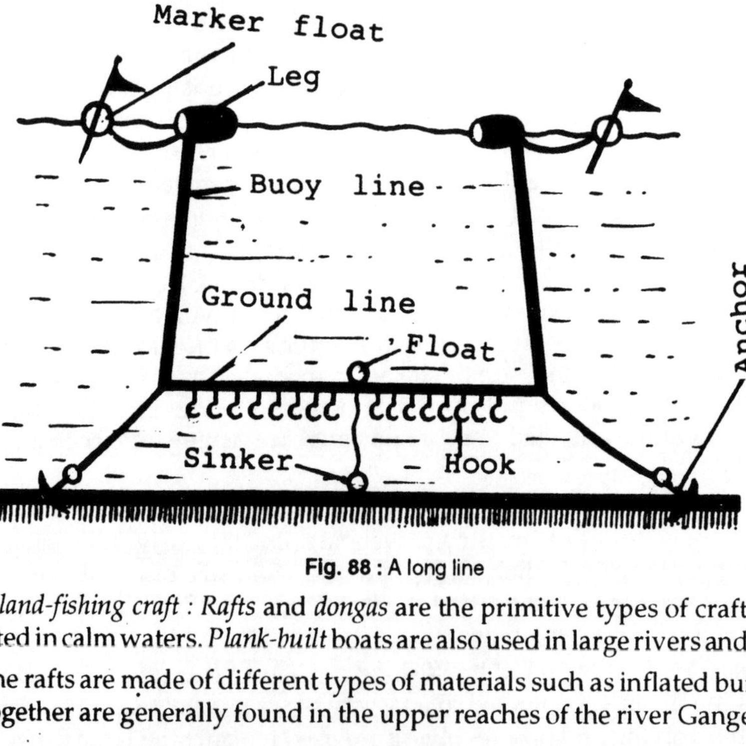

Fig. 88 : A long line

Inland-fishing craft : *Rafts* and *dongas* are the primitive types of craft. They are operated in calm waters. *Plank-built* boats are also used in large rivers and estuaries.

The rafts are made of different types of materials such as inflated buffalo skins tied together are generally found in the upper reaches of the river Ganges. Banana

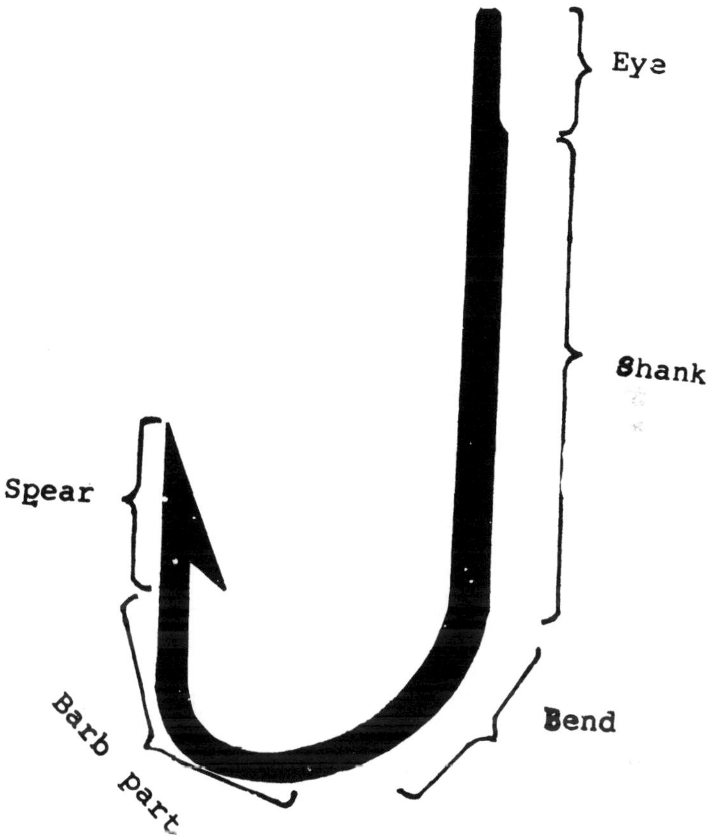

Fig. 89 : A simple hook

stems or shola bundles are tied together to form a floating platform. Several inverted earthenware pots laced together in a bamboo frame work are also used as platform in some marshy areas, ponds and jheels. Dug-out canoes called *dongas* in Bengal, *ekhta* in Bihar and *odam* in Malabar, are also common on the shallow waters of the tributaries. *Vallam* is a sturdier dugout used in the backwaters and estuaries of Kerala. *Chatty* rafts (earthen pot raft) are also commonly used in Tanjore dist. (Madras), in the river Cauvery in Tiruchirapalli. The *coracle* which has been already described is used in the rivers Cauvery and Tungbhadra and also in some reservoirs. *Tigarni* or *gamla,* which is very similar to Coracle is used as craft in W. Bengal.

There are different types of *plank-built boats* used for fishing in rivers with strong currents and tides. Small riverine and estuarine crafts are called *dinghis.* They are employed in W. Bengal for operation of purse-nets and dip-nets. *Dinghis* have narrow tapering bows and sterns but they have no keels. The *Chhandi nauka* used for operating drift-nets are upto 18m. long and 3m.wide. These are used in drift-nets fishing in the lower and wider reaches of the deltaic area. *Bachari* is another type of large boat like *Chandi nauka.* It is slightly longer but is narrower than the Chhandi boat. *Mechho bachari* is a medium sized boat used for transporting live fish in Calcutta area of W. Bengal. In the Chilka lake and the river Mahanadi, *nava,* a plank-built boat is used. *Machwa* type boat is used for operating large nets in the estuaries of Gujarat.

Khulnawa : Banerjee *et al.* (1981) have described a special type of craft used in the river Ganges.

It is a special fishing device for Minnows in the river Ganges at Patna (Bihar). *Khulnawa* is a local name which means an open wale boat . It is said to have been introduced here from the *tarai* area of Nepal. This device is operated at night in calm weather particularly from February to April. Certain species of fishes like *Oxygaster bacaila, Setipinna phasa, Aspidoparia morar, Gadusia chapra* and species of *Puntius* are easily caught in a moonless night.

Khulnawa has three components in its structure :

(1) Boat with one of the wales open

(2) Screen platform, and

(3) a frilled pole.

In the construction of the boat, kathal (*Artocarpus integriofolia*) or sal (*Shorea robusta*) wood is used. The boat is a keelless dinghy with equipointed bow and stern. It is about 7.5m in length. The wale on one side has a cut opening which is 5m long and 12 cm. deep. The boat is kept dark in colour by coaltar coatings.

The *screen platform* is a closely knit screen of bamboo splinters measuring 5m x 0.5m. Fine flat stripes of bamboo are oven by interlacing them with 5 rows of plastic cords. The screen is supported and reinforced by broader splinters of bamboo 70 cm long at intervals of 50 cm. Over the width of the screen, the extra length of the splinters project inwards. Here they are attached to the boat providing room for fastening, with strings to pegs which are fixed on floor of the boat. The free margin of the screen is constantly immersed in water. The screen is always kept sparkling white by coatings of enamel paint.

The frilled pole has a piece of 4 to 6 m long bamboo pole with tufts of dry save grass (*Pollinidium anguistifolium*) drooping as frill along 3/4th of its length. A tuft of 4 to 6 dry blades of the grass is tied to the narrower end of the pole. Now half of the length of the tuft is twisted into string and the rest half is left loose. The nest tuft is tied to the first tuft and similar initial half of it is twisted into string, the remaining part drooping as frill. Series of the tufts of grass are wrought to make a drooping frill along the length of the pole. The last tuft is twisted into string and fastened to the pole. The whole frill is tied at intervals (50 to 60cm) and it hangs from the pole. *Khulnawa* is operated by two fishermen. The boat is always kept parallel to the bank of the river. The side of the boat with open wale and the screen faces the bank of the river. The free edge of the drooping grass is kept overhanging the surface of the water. In the dark the sparkling light of the screen platform gives the fishes an illusion of flowing stream. Minnows happen to be schooling in between the boat and the bank.

Inland Fishing gears : Because of highly diverse nature of inland water areas, there is great variation in the methods of fish catching technology. Methods range from catching with the hand to the operation of large and cleverly contrived nets for fishing. Cast-nets of both the stringed and stringless varieties are suitable for operation in inland waters of all types. Individual fishermen operate some implements like spears, bows and arrows, small traps and also rod and line. Important fishing gears used for capturing fish on a commercial scale have been described below :

Gear used in estuaries, lagoons and back waters

In the deltaic areas of some rivers, various types of *bag-nets* are set against the tidal currents. They are operated with the help of heavy anchors and floats. They may be tied to stakes or may be operated from boats with the help of wooden frameworks. Mostly small fish are caught in this case.

By means of bamboo screen or walls of netting, some parts of lagoons of estuaries are enclosed. Fish are captured by draining the enclosed areas or by operating cast-net or dip nets. *Khal patta jal* and *char patta jal* (Sundarbans), *thattu vala* (Kerala) and *Janos* (Chilka) are used on the same principle. Bush fishing is also practised in the Sunderbans. Here bamboo screens are used to enclose areas piled with bushes for attracting fishes. Cat fishes form the most important catch of such gears.

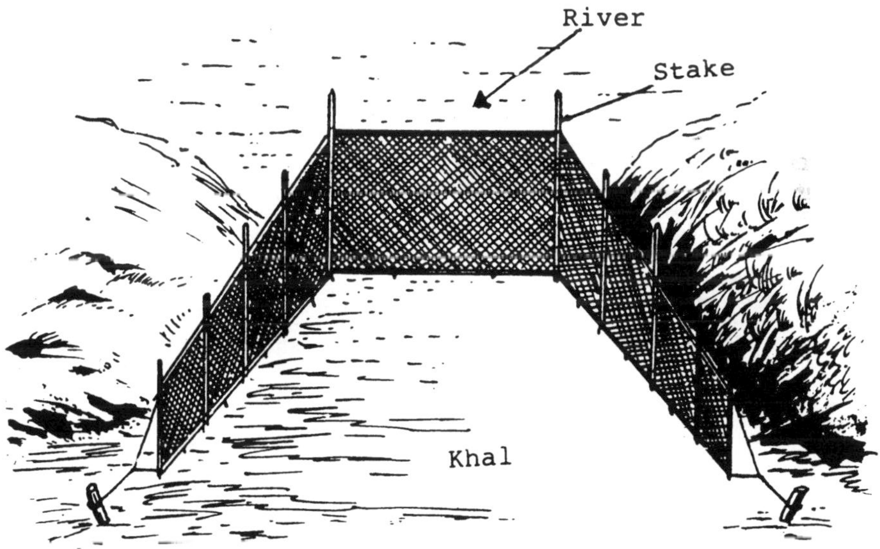

Fig. 90 : Khal Patta Jal of Sunderbans

In the Chilka lake several types of bamboo traps with a large *patta* are employed. For capturing *Hilsa,* varied types of nets are also operated in the deltaic area of the river Ganges. The purse nets, *Shanglo jal* and *Kharki jal* are very commonly employed in the upper reaches of the estuaries. Also, seine-nets, *Kona jal* and *moi jal* are used in the upper reaches of the estuaries. In the Chilka lake, the drag-nets, *bekti* or *mori jalo, Khadi jalo, Sahalo jalo, Patua jalo* and *mani jalo,* are also commonly operated. In the estuaries areas of the river Ganges, particularly for capturing large fish, the drag-nets, *ber jal* and *jagat ber jal* are frequently employed.

Fig. 91 : Ber Jal-in the Ganges

Fig. 92 : Shanglo Jal–A Purse net

In the Sunderbans, a deep seine net, *Kochal jal* is operated with the help of 4 or 5 boats by about 24 fishermen. *Jangla jal* is also used in the Sunderbans. The operation of *Kochal jal* is slightly different. The ends are drawn together and the lower end is turned up to form a pocket in which the fish are caught. The net is never dragged to the shore.

For *Hilsa* fishing in the estuarine areas of W. Bengal *Chhandi jal* (a drift gill-net) is in operation. It may be more than 300m. long and about 3m. wide. In the Chilka lake *Menjia jalo* and *noli jalo* are the important gill-nets which are commonly used. Rangoon nets are also used in the estuaries of Godavari and Krishna for capturing *Hilsa*. In the back-waters of Travancore and Cochin (Kerala) the Chinese dip-net is used. This net is locally known as *Cheena vala* or *Kambu vala*. It is a large dip-net measuring 9-11m. square.

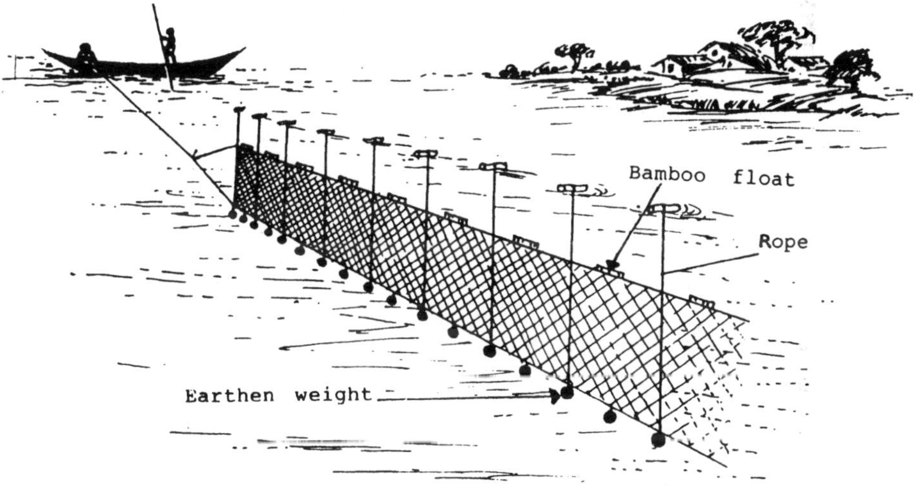

Fig. 93 : Chandi Jal—A Drift Gill-net of West Bengal

In the backwaters of Cochin and N-Travancore a specialised type of fishing gear is used for mullet fishing. This is known as *Changalapayilal* or *Changadam*. Two connecting poles hold two long and narrow dugout canoes of equal length. A net runs the whole length of the outer side of each canoe. The net extends out board upon slanting sticks. A long scare line which is made of short pieces of chain, is conveniently streched from bow to bow of the dugouts. The mullets are frightened by the scare line, leap into the air, and are easily caught in the net or in the tangle of twigs in the canoes. Handlining and rod and line fishing from small dugouts are also in practice in the backwaters of Kerala.

Gears used in ponds, jheels, lakes and reservoirs : Seine and dragnets are commonly used commercial fishing gears. Seines are operated from boats or by wading in water. Large seines known as *Jagat ber* or *mahajal* are occasionally used for fishing in extensive jheels. These seines can be frequently seen in the Gangetic areas. Simple drag-nets are also used in ponds and jheels. In some lakes and reservoirs where operation of seines and drag-nets are not convenient, Rangoon-net and the *uduvalai* are employed. The Rangoon-net is made of fine cotton. It consists of a number of rectangular pieces of netting tied and to end so as to form a wall. It is buoyed up by floats which are normally spindle shaped. The fish get easily gilled or entangled in the net. *Uduvalai* can be operated at a greater depth. It has small sized sinkers which are attached to the foot rope. For catching catfishes, longlining is employed at some places in the lakes and reservoirs.

Gear used in the hill-streams : Various types of traps and cast-nets are used in the hilly areas. Some parts of the streams are bunded off and basket traps are kept in the narrow gaps in the bunds. During the breeding season, considerable catches have been recorded. Explosives and poisons are used for capturing fish on large scale.

Gear used in rivers : Seines and drag-nets are commonly used gears in the rivers; *Ber jals* of different dimensions and varying mesh size are also used in the Ganges system. They are characterized by the presence of a stout foot rope and absence of a bag at the midlength. Also there is no sinker at all. The net may be loaded upon more than one boats and then hauled ashore by several fishermen.

Kona jal or *bhasa gulli* (91m x 9m) is specialized type of large cotton seine-net extensively used for *Hilsa* fishing. Small-meshed pockets which are conical in shape are attached all along the net at intervals of about 9-12m. Fish can not escape out from the pockets because of the presence of valve like arrangements. *Jagat ber* or *Maha jal* is also popular in the riverine areas. It is used all around the year except July, August and September only. *Moi* or *moia jal* a simple type of drag-net is used in shallow waters. *Chunti jal* of Bihar is a pocketed drag-net (4 x 2m) and is operated by two fishermen. *Karal* or *Katla jal* is an important drift net for carp and *Katla* capture in the river Narbada. *Hela jal* is a dip-net used for capturing catfishes. It consists of two bamboo poles which cross each other near the two long sides. *Karra jal* is operated from a bomboo stage. It is almost like *Hela jal*. *Bhesal jal* and *firki jal* are operated with the help of boats. *Firki jal* is very often used for catching *Hilsa* in the rivers Brahmaputra and Padma.

Kuriar net is a small net used in shallow waters where the fishes migrate along the current. This net is used for catching big carps, and is also used for *Hilsa* fishing now, though it was not used for *Hilsa* fishing originally. The net is kept in inverted position and dipped and taken out of water. This net can also be operated single handed.

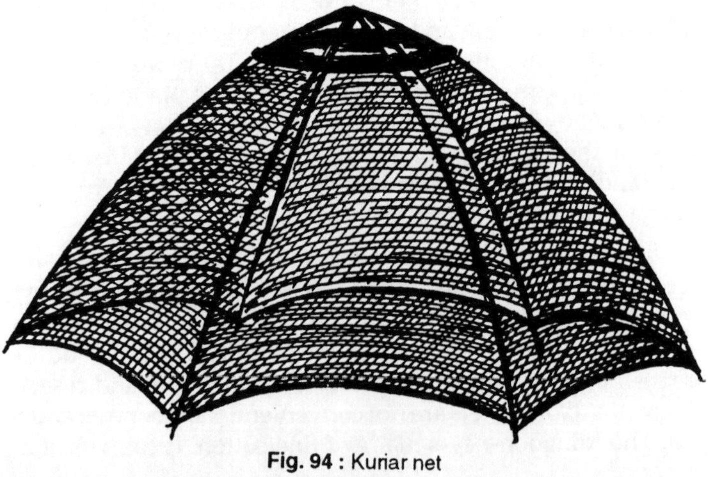

Fig. 94 : Kuriar net

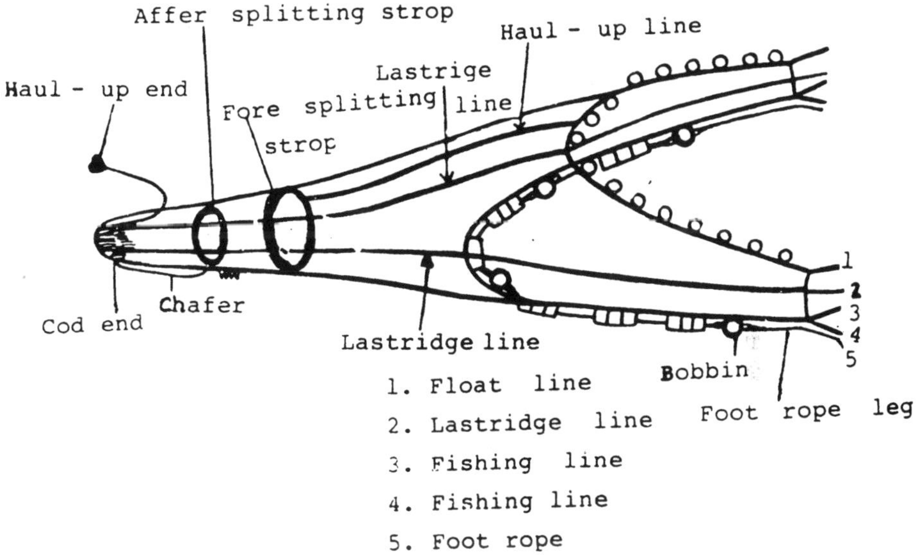

Fig. 95 : Trawl : the gear

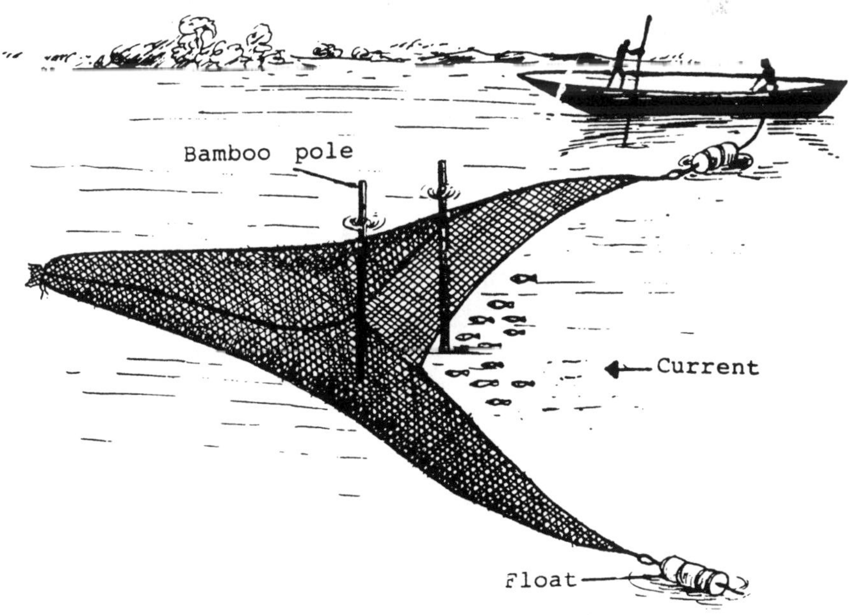

Fig. 96 : Been Jal of West Bengal

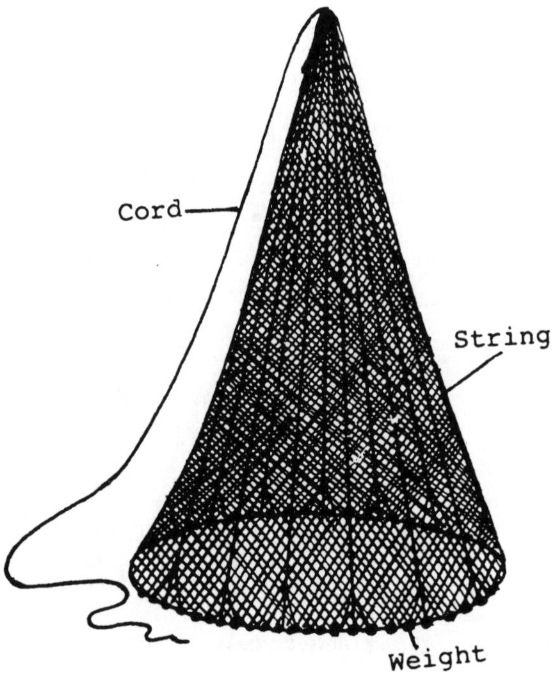

Fig. 97 : Stringed cast-net

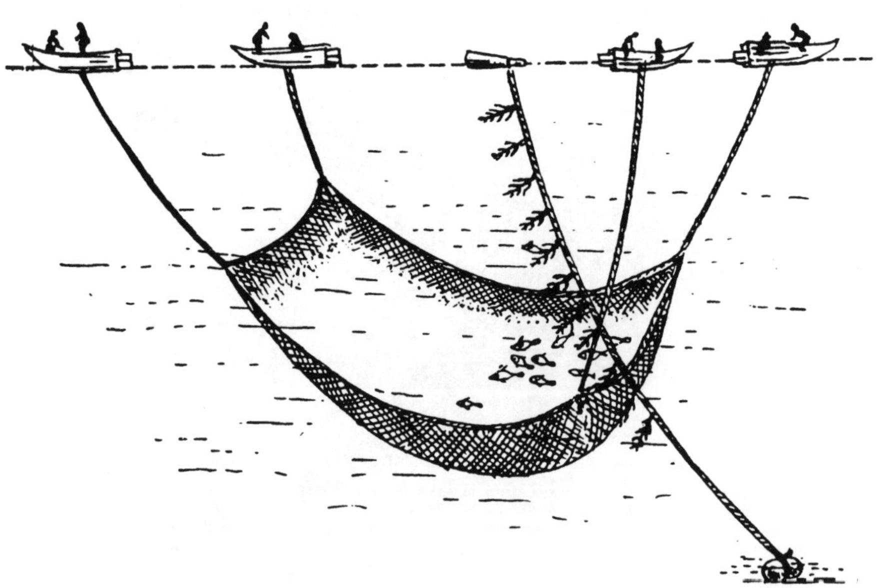

Fig 98 : Mada valai—A shore-seine of Coramandel Coast

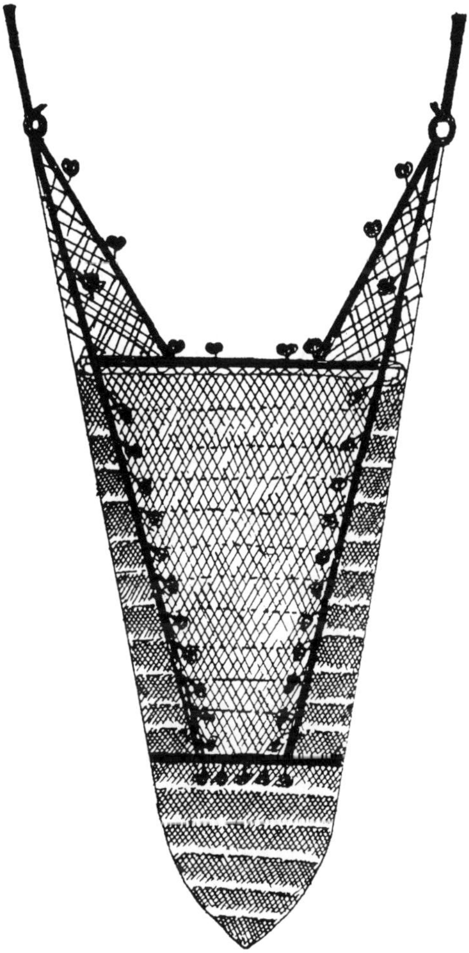

Fig. 99 : Kolli vala—A Boat-Seine of Kerala Coast

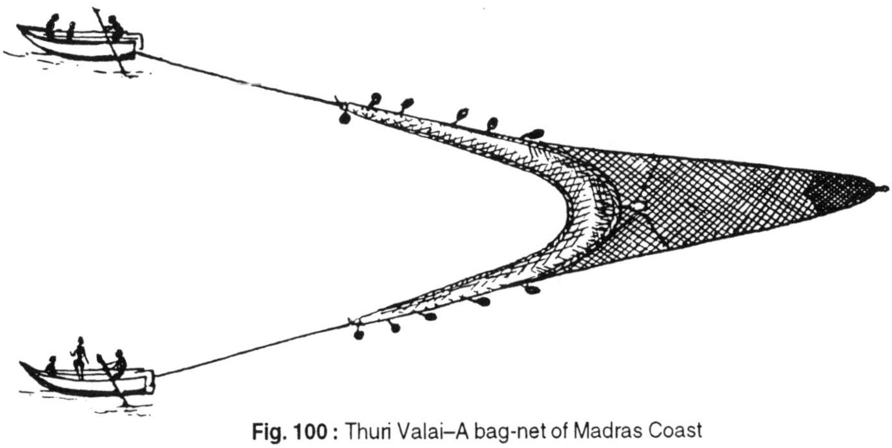

Fig. 100 : Thuri Valai–A bag-net of Madras Coast

Grey mullets (*Liza corsula*) are caught with the help of *Koila jal* of *Khorsula jal*, a special type of dip-net. This net is small-meshed and rectangular in shape measuring not more than 2.5 x 2m. The net is suspended by a bamboo frame. It is operated in shallow waters. *Jamda* which resembles an open bag is practised in Narmada by *bhil* fishermen. It is also a dip-net. It is used to capture migrating *Hilsa*. *Suti jal* is a stationary bag-net. It has a long tubular bag with a long wing (1-15 m high nearly) of wide-meshed netting on both sides of the mouth. The wings are well supported on stakes. *Bada jal*, a variation of *Suti jal* has a wide mouth which is kept open by a vertical rod. Purse-nets are also used for the capture of *Hilsa*. *Kharki jal* and the *Shanglo jal* or *Sharki jal* are purse-nets. In *Shangla jal* the purse is opened or closed with a weighted cord but in *Kharki jal* a vertical bamboo rod is attached to the lower margin of the mouth serving the same purpose. *Bachari* or *othar jal* is a cast-net commonly used for the capture of *Katla*, *Rohu* and *Pungas*. The peripheral area of this net is more than 55m. the cone being 15m and the mesh size 2.5-8.9 cm. Three or four fishermen can operate this net from boats.

Bamboo Screen : A bamboo screen is used in shallow ponds and small rivers. It is manipulated and handled like a seine. A bamboo screen and a drop net are sometimes combined for operation.

Electric equipment : Electric equipments are also used for fishing in ponds. Current is provided by generator or batteries. Fish within the electric field receive shock and they are made numb for a few moments. During this period they are seized.

Mechanization of Indian Crafts

It is a fact that fisheries sector is predominated by small scale traditional crafts and gears. Nets are made of natural fibres mainly cotton and hemp. But now, mechanised boats have been introduced in large number. Also, durable nylon yarn of synthetic fibres is imported from Japan and other countries for this purpose. Nylon fibres are manufactured in India, (Garware Nylon Ltd. Bombay) also. For increased fish production, higher economic return to the industry, and greater safety to the fishermen, craft motorization and production of specialized boats seemed to be essential. Specialized boats are constructed at various boat building yards with different construction materials. Diesel engines are now obtained and are utilized for motorization of *navas* and even *catamarans* and they are put into operation. Price of the specialized boats depends on the operational efficiency and economic viability. Improved trawlers are very costly and not within the reach of the fishermen. The Andhra Pradesh, West Bengal and Tamil Nadu Governments are doing their best for the improvement of fishing crafts and gears. Motorization of craft in Bombay was started in 1952.

Machwa and *Lodhia* type boats in Saurashtra are quite suited for motorization. *Satpati*, *Nava* and *Pablo* types of boats are also fit for mechanization.

CHAPTER 24

PRESERVATION AND PROCESSING OF FISH

For the marketing of fish, proper conservation seems to be very much important. Fish marketing is a race against time to bring the fish to the consumers before the quality is deteriorated. When the fish dies, glycogen of the muscle is converted into lactic acid and *rigor mortis* sets in. As a result of this, stiffening of flesh takes place. With the increase of pH of the flesh the fish becomes gradually alkaline and finally it is spoiled. Intense and rapid decomposition takes place. Its pH rises to about 7.6 as compared to 6.4 in a fresh fish. Three types of deteriorative changes have been observed in the landed fish. These changes are *bacterial, enzymatic* and *oxidative*. Bacterial spoilage proceeds quickly but autolytic and chemical changes are comparatively slow. Proteins and other nitrogenous substances are split up into ammonia, carbondioxide, amino acids etc. As a result of putrefaction, foul smelling end-products (for example—hydrogen sulphide and indole) are produced. In marine teleosts, when *trimethylamine oxidase* is reduced to *trimethylamine*, a sharp characteristic odour of the spoiled fish can be felt.

Before preservation, fish are properly cleaned. The slime, faeces, blood stains and foreign materials are washed with water. Body cavity of the large fishes is also properly washed. The methods used for the preservation of fish include conservation by cold (refrigeration and deep freezing), and also salting, drying, smoking, canning etc. The product obtained by drying, salting and smoking is popularly known as *cured fish*.

Cold permits the process of conservation of dead fish in a fresh condition for a long time. Refrigeration permits fish for preservation not more than two weeks, however, deep freezing allows conservation for several months.

Methods for Conservation

1. *Refrigeration* : Low temperature definitely retards autolysis, bacterial action and putrefaction, when the fishes are to be preserved for only a few days they are chilled in ice. When they are conserved at around 0°C, decomposition is prevented for a limited time. The fish and the ice are mixed (in alternative layers of fish and

crushed ice) in small case, baskets or barrels. Water from the melted ice flows easily. In larger fishes, ice may be put in the body cavity.

2. *Deep Freezing* : This process is also known as quick freezing. Deep freezing permits preservation for a long time. In deep freezing, bacterial action is inhibited. The fish retains its physical properties and nutritive value for several months. The temperature in deep freezing is-18°C to-20°C. Before freezing the fish are washed and the heads of large fishes are removed. Also, they are gutted. Fillets are also frozen. Cold storage preservation of fish is practised only at limited places in India. In Bombay and Calcutta also little cold storage facilities are available. Fish are kept overnight in the cold storage and then they are sent for marketing the next day.

3. *Salting* : Sodium Chloride acts as a preservative and prevents bacterial growth and also inactivate most of the enzymes. During salting partial dehydration of fish by osmosis also takes place. Salting can be dry (alternate layers of fish and salt) or wet or brine (16 to 20 per cent salt). Salt and crushed ice are also spread on the fishes (10 to 20 Kg of salt and 100 Kg of ice). For light and cold salting conservation should take place in a cold room (2 to 3°C). For average salting the temperature should be around 16°C but for strong salting, normal atmospheric conditions are quite suitable.

Heads and viscera of the large fish are removed. Also, deep longitudinal scores are made with knives on the flesh. Large sharks are cut into several pieces before salting.

For dry salting fish are packed in tubs or tanks. They are kept in layers between which salt is sprinkled. Before packing, rubbing must continue for some time. The proportion of salt to fish varies from 1:3 to 1:8, however, oily fish require more salt. The fish are removed from the container after 10-24 hr. They are washed in self-brine and dried in the sun for 2-3 days.

In the wet salting process the fish are gutted, slit-incised and cleaned. They are packed in large vats containing concentrated salt solution. It is regularly stirred daily till properly pickled. Ratnagiri method of preservation is very common in Maharashtra, and Tamil Nadu. Black pomprets, sharks, salmon and seer are mostly treated in this method. The fish are split, gutted and cleaned as described already. For 3 Kgs of fish 1 Kg of salt has been prescribed. About half the quantity of this salt is perfectly rubbed on the cut surfaces first day. These are then stacked on the floor of the curing shed. Next day, the fish are restacked with top layer moved to the bottom. The remaining salt is also utilized in the same way. On the third day rest of the salt is rubbed and the fish are again restacked. They remain in this condition for about 8 days. Liquor formed is allowed to flow. Then they are removed. They are not sundried. Wet salted fish become ready for marketing without drying. In the "pit curing" method the fish treated with salt are buried in pits lined with the leaves of *Cadjan*. Fish are removed from the pits after 2-3 days.

4. *Drying* : Sun-drying is the simplest method of curing fish and is extensively practised in India. More than 35 per cent of the total catch of sea fish is estimated to be cured by drying in the sun. Bombay Duck, ribbon fish, silver bellies and some other small marine fishes are subjected to sun drying. Fresh water fish (*Labeo Catla, Puntius* etc.) are also dried in some parts of Bengal, Assam and Bihar but in very

small quantities as compared to marine fish. Fish are spread on the mat or in the field or on the sand and are periodically turned over. They are also spread in *Cadjan* leaves. They are kept in the sun for 2-3 days. At certain places, fish are dried by hanging on bamboo or wooden rods or on ropes stretched horizontally between two poles. Some fish may be split and salted before drying. A dry weather with sun-shine which is not too hot is suitable for drying. In sun-drying fish are dried uniformly, however they develop peculiar flavour which is not acceptable to most of the consumers. Drying of fish can be carried out artificially also when dehydration can be done by mechanical driers which can provide a continuous current of hot air. Products of mechanical drying are better than that of sun-drying. Thus removal of moisture from the tissue inhibits bacterial and enzymatic putrefaction of fish.

5. *Smoking* : Fish are also submitted to the action of wood smoke. Thus, they can be preserved with the help of hot or cold smoke, but smoked fishes are very popular in India. This method of preservation is used in some parts of Orissa and Madras. Sardines, pomprets, jew fishes, ribbon fishes, mackerel and small seer, *hilsa* and some other fishes are subjected to this process. When the flesh of the fish is impregnated with smoke, preservation takes place because of its phenolic constituents which have a mild antiseptic action. Heat of the smoke also contributes in this process to some extent. Composition of smoke depends on the wood. Conifer wood should not be used. After brining, fish are suspended on rods in a kiln and are brought in contact with smokes, hot or cold, heavy or light, long or short depending on the product desired.

For cold smoking the fish should be dried and then lightly salted and finally exposed to a smokeless fire (temperature should not exceed 38°C). After this, real smoking takes place at a temperature below 28°C. Fresh fish or fish rapidly salted in brine, are subjected to this process. The fish are kept at a high temperature (130°C) first near a strong fire but the smoking should follow at a temperature around 40°C.

6. *Canning* : There are some difficulties in this process because of irregular supplies of desired fish, scarcity of good and cheap containers and limited canning season. Canning does not affect the nutritional value of protein and fat and some vitamins (Vit. A, Vit. D, Vit. B_2, B_{12} and Pyrodoxine etc). Fish canning in India is not prospering though Sardines and Mackerels are canned in some factories. Import of canned fish has been encouraged. In the process of canning the original flavour of the fish is retained.

Canning method is costly. After cleaning, the fish is cut into pieces in some filleting plants. Pieces are then brined or pickled. After preliminary cooking pieces are put in cans. These are then sterilized with steam and high temperature (around 110°C). The cans are sealed as canneries. Vacuum created in the sealed cans adds to preservation for longer period.

7. *Pasting, Pickling and Spicing:* Pasting is a domestic process employed in certain parts of India. The fish are cut into slices which are subjected to salting and drying. Then they are treated with a spicy paste and the latter is prepared by mixing ghee with vinegar, mustard, chillies, garlic, tamarind, turmeric etc. The colombo method of curing fish by picling is very common in Malabar and S.Canara districts. Mackerel and sardines are gutted, washed and salted and little of fleshy covering of the fruits

Garcinia cambogia is thrust into the abdominal cavity of the fish. Fish treated in this way are arranged in barrels made of wood. Salt and fruits (*Garcinia cambogia*) are sprinkled between each layer and allowed to cure. It is exported to Ceylon. Use of tamarind in place of above fruit has been successfully tried at Mandapam (Central Marine Fisheries Research Institute).

8. *Preservation with Chemicals:* Some chemicals in different concentrations have been tried as fish preservatives. Preserving the Pacific salmon with salicylic acid and boric acid is an old practice. Sodium benzoate, sodium hypochlorite, carbondioxide, sulphurdioxide and sodium-bisulfate, mixture of sodium acid phosphate and sodium benzoate, hydrogen peroxide are also in use as preservatives. Most of them have not been preferred for industrial use. Only sodium nitrite and soidum chloride are extensively used for industrial applications. In Canada and some other countries, nitrites of sodium or potassium are used as fish preservatives. They suppress the formation of trimethylamine in marine fish and they are also bacteriostatic. Effect of nitrite on bacterial growth is pH dependent. Nitrite at 200 $\mu g/ml$ concentration stops bacterial growth at pH 5.7 to 6.2. At higher pH (6.5 and above) it becomes ineffective.

Sodium nitrite (0.02 per cent) and sodium chloride (5 per cent) in ice are very much effective.

Some antibiotics are also used as preservatives. Aureomycin (Chlorotetracycline, Terramycin (oxytetracycline) and chloromycetin are important antibiotics. A fish when dipped in a solution of 50 ppm concentration of aureomycin remains fresh for several hours. This antibiotic is effective even when 1 ppm in concentration. A concentration of 5-7 ppm is recommended in many countries. In cooking process 50 per cent of this antibiotic is destroyed.

Besides the above chemical preservatives, ascorbic acid, sodium ricinoleate (0.2 to 0.5 per cent), cresol and some other phenolic components are also used as preservatives.

9. *Preservation by Exposure of gamma rays:* An exposure of low radiation of gamma rays helps in destroying both bacteria and the pseudomonas group of microbes. Thus gamma rays can act as preservative.

Food poisoning: Mild or severe illness may be caused by eating fish, raw or preserved. Some fishes (sardines, mackerels, herrings etc.) are rich in histidine, an important amino acid. Because of poor preservation decarboxylation of histidine takes place and it is converted into histamine. Breakdown of flesh starts by the action of bacteria, *Proteus morganii.* Histamine and some related substances known as "Saurine" are responsible for food poisoning. The aforesaid fish may cause severe allergic effects (gastrointestinal upsets, utricaria, edema, asthma etc.) upon sensitive individuals. Toxin produced by bacterial pathogen infecting the fish causes biotoxication. *Puffer-poisoning* is caused by eating some members of the family tetraodontidae and Lagocephalidae (for example—*Tetraodon* sp., *Diodon* sp. *Liosaccus* sp. etc.). Puffer poisoning may cause gastrointestinal disorders, neurological disorders and respiratory failure.

Spoiling fish carries bacteria or their toxins or both. The nature of food poisoning depends on the species of the pathogens and quality of toxin. Important types of poisoning are:

(i) *Poisoning due to Salmonella and Shigella:* These bacteria are not normally fish pathogen but can attack fish of polluted water. Fish are the intermediate host and man is the final host.

(ii) *Poisoning due to Staphylococcus:* These bacteria enter fish by contamination during handling and processing. Pathogens are present in the nose and throat of a large number of fish. Bacteria may be found in all types of preserved fishes. They multiply and produce toxin causing serious problems.

(iii) *Poisoning (Botulism) due to Clostridium batulinum:* Botulism is very dangerous type of food poisoning taking place as a result of consuming smoked, salted, spices or pickled fish products. It has been reported from Canada, U.S.A., Europe, Russia and Japan. Toxin is produced by the above mentioned bacteria which causes death. Muscle paralysis is a marked sympton which causes immediate death. Administration of antitoxins is the only treatment.

(iv) *Poisoning due to halophilic (rods and Cocci) bacteria:* 'Pink' spoilage develops pink patches. Pathogens are present in the salt used for curing 'Pink'. It develops characteristic offensive odour. When the products are consumed they cause food poisoning. The spoilage may however, be controlled by cold storage (below 5°C) of the salted fish. In 'Dun' spoilage of salted fish the patches are either brown or black instead of pink.

CHAPTER 25

TRANSPORT AND MARKETING OF FISH

Transportation of fish is one of the important aspects of fish culture and marketing. Both live and dead fishes can be transported from one place to another as per requirements. There is inadequate transport and storage facilities, however, in certain states of India, for example, Tamil Nadu, Bihar, Orissa, M.P., W. Bengal and Maharashtra it is being much improved. Tamil Nadu Govt. has also set up some freezing and cold storage plants at Kazhikode and Mangalore. Several ice and cold storage plants are under construction at some places in Bombay, Madras, Travancore, Cochin, Andhra Pradesh and Orissa etc. Bombay, Calcutta and Madras are some of the large centres of fish consumption in India. Large quantities of fish are transported from the Chilka lake area to Calcutta and from Kazikode to Madras and Bangalore. Carrier motor launches also transport iced fish from various fishing centres to Bombay.

During transportation, several factors are taken into consideration for example— the species of fish, size, water temperature, length of time taken, atmospheric pressure and length of stops etc. Transport of fry is carried out very carefully. Fish spawn and fry are also transported by aeroplane from Calcutta to some other states. Otherwise, they will die when released and in that case it will be a waste of efforts, time and money.

1. *Transport of Live fishes* : Resistant fish can be transported dry in buckets without water or in baskets. Other fishes can be carried in cans, pans, vats and other receptacles carried by hand or vehicles of all sorts like, barrows, wheel barrows, motor lorries, different types of vans or trailers, railways and even aeroplanes. Transport by aeroplanes provides excellent service particularly for brood fish, eggs or fry of species which are introduced to new surroundings quite different from the original habitat. Transport problem is of particular importance in fish culture.

(i) *Receptacles of transport* : The receptacles are adapted not only to the size of the fish but also to the species and the quantity of fishes which are to be transported from one place to another.

(a) *Dry transport* : When the large resistant fishes are to be carried to short distances, baskets and buckets with perforated bottoms are used. There is no need to carry the fishes in water.

(b) *Cans* : When small quantities of fry or average size fishes are to be transported over a short distance, small cans are generally used. These are known as "Goujonnieres". But for the transportation of large quantities of fry and fish of average size, cans with flat bottom are preferred. Cans are either oval or circular with a capacity of 20 to 40 litres. These cans are in metal or plastic sheets. Zinc cans are lined inside with a protective layer in order to avoid poisoning of the fry. The can is provided with two apertures which have stoppers. It can be emptied with the help of lower stopper and water can be renewed with the help of upper stopper. A special model of can is used in mountains for carrying the fishes by a man on his back. It is of about 15 litres capacity and is more useful. Fish fry and fishes are also transported by bamboo receptacles in the far east countries.

(c) *Polythene Bags* : Because of reduced weight, the polythene bags are extensively used for carrying small quantities over land or aeroplane. About one third of this bag is filled with water and the fishes are kept in the bag. Oxygen is introduced into the bag with the help of a rubber pipe or a bottle. The upper part of the bag is twisted and closed with a solid elastic band. One or more bags are placed in a carton and then they are transported. The oxygen above the water diffuses slowly during transport and a balanced oxygenation is ensured.

(d) *Barrels and Vats* : Fishes are also carried in barrels and vats. Barrels are now less used and old type wooden vats have been almost replaced by metal or plastic of the same design. These are conveniently carried by vans.

Wooden barrels have solid handles on either side. They have oval section and lie lengthwise on one side. The shape of the barrel is such that they facilitate oxygenation and automatic aeration goes on when they are carried. The opening of the barrel is quite large. The covers are truncated pyramid like. They are hollow to enclose ice. The bottom is pierced with holes for flowing water from the melting ice.

Vats are like turncated cans or cylinders resting on flat end with round or oval circumference. Vats are of varying capacities (50-150 litres) containing a bottle of compressed O_2 (3-7 litres at 130 to 150 atm.) inserted vertically fixed with collars. Sometimes, the bottle can also be fixed outside the vat. A pressure reducing valve with a tube carries the oxygen to a spray which is well protected by a cover. Precaution is taken to protect the handles and hoops of barrels and vats against rust.

(e) *Special Vehicles* : For transporting fishes in larges quantities fish farms have motor lorries, mounted with metallic tanks of different shapes. Tanks are provided with an aeration system. Often bottles of oxygen or compressed air are in use. There is installation of sprays at the bottom of these tanks which ensures the distribution of gas. Sprays are in hard porous materials or a simple plastic perforated tube generally fixed to a metal frame on the bottom of the tank. Air pumps are also used which functions on the battery system or with the help of motor of the lorry. Some vehicles are equipped with hydraulic pumps sucking water from the bottom of the top and spraying the same in atomized form from the top. Large quantities of fishes are also shipped by railways.

2. *General rules for transportation* : For successful transport of fish and fry in particular, supply of sufficient oxygen in the receptacle should be ensured. For this purpose water must be kept at a low temperature. There should be arrangement to

renew water at different stops, movement of receptacle should be moderate, there should be adequate aeration by a supply of air or oxygen. There are some important factors which influence transport of living fishes. These factors have been described below.

(a) *The species of fish* : Oxygen requirements vary considerably according to species of fishes. For Salmonids there is sufficient need of oxygen.

(b) *Age and Size of the Fish* : Breathing requirement is higher not only in the large fishes but the small fishes also require greater amount of oxygen corresponding to their total body weight.

(c) *Relative resistance of the fish* : Fishes depending on artificial food are less resistant in comparison to fishes having natural food. Spawning fishes feel difficulty during transportation.

(d) *Length of time of transport* : It has been observed that when the time taken is comparatively short the stocking rate is greater.

(e) *The Temperature of water* : Low water temperature is more suitable during transportation. Oxygen content at low temperature is higher. The best range of temperature is 4 to 10°C in most of the cases.

(f) *The nature of the transport receptacles* : The wooden transport receptacle warm up more slowly in comparison to metal, however, the latter can be thermically insulated.

(g) *Means of transport and lengths of Stops* : Faster transport and shorter stops provide a better chance of success.

(h) *Climatic conditions* : The temperature of the receptacles and also its oxygen content are greatly influenced by climatic conditions. To reduce the metabolism of the fishes and their oxygen intake, tranquillizers (e.g. MS 222) have been used. Lamarque (1962) has described an experiment in this connection which is as follows :

Before placing the Salmonids in polythene bags they are shifted to a bath in MS 222, the concentration being 1 / 10000 until the fishes lose equilibrium and rest on the bottom. Before placing in the bags, they are washed when they are removed from the above solution. Two litres of water are needed for 1 kg of fish. After this test the fish can conveniently stay in the bag for 6 hrs. Lamarque has also suggested that tranquillizer can be placed in the transport receptacles also. In this case the concentration should not exceed 1 / 100000.

3. *Preparation of Transport* : A cool weather is suitable for transportation. In warm weather, night is the best time for transportation. It can be carried out in the early morning also. If the railway is used for transportation, then it should be carefully watched that the time taken is minimum. Cans or barrels, receptacles etc. should not be completely filled. At least 20-30 per cent space should be left for aeration.

4. *Transportation* : (i) Rapid warming of water should always be avoided. For this, receptacles should not be placed in direct rays of the sun. In a hot weather the cans or barrels should be kept in contact with the ice blocks. Ice is never placed in the water directly. Cans can also be covered with cloth, soaked with water. Evaporation of this cloth can maintain freshness to some extent inside the can.

(ii) There should be frequent change of water over a long journey. Entire water should not be changed atonce before it will lead to temperature difference, harmful for the fishes. Water should be changed slowly. First half of the original water should be replaced with freshwater first and then after 5 or 10 minutes, whole water should be changed. Freshwater should be unpolluted and well aerated. Sometimes air is pumped into the water for aeration when urgently needed.

(iii) Jolting throws the fishes against the side of the carrier and shocks of this kind will injure the fishes and the latter will gradually die, so, jerking should be avoided.

(iv) When the fishes are transferred to a new environment, they must be acclimatized slowly and progressively.

(v) Quantities of fish should vary according to type of transport i.e. with diffused oxygen or without diffused oxygen. Excessive oxygen can be harmful for the fishes particularly to the health of the fry. Several experimental data have been given by a large number of researchers (Charpy, 1945; Schaperclaus, 1933, 1961; Hofmann, 1967) with regard to transportation of fishes without diffused oxygen. Wohlfarth *et al.* (1961) have described that in Israel 1 kg of carps with an average weight of 30 gm. can be transported in a polythene bag with oxygen in 2 to 2.5 litres of water for 4 hours.

Transport of Freshy killed fish : Even the dead fishes should be transported at a low temperature to avoid the danger of decomposition of their flesh. The temperature should be between 0 and 4°C and as such, the fishes are placed in crushed ice. This method stops the development of bacteria and also enzymatic and oxidative changes.

Fish Marketing

Fish marketing system plays an important role in the fishery trade. Fish market is a place inside or outside the country where the fishes and fish products of commercial importance are subjected to sale. So, it seems as a link between the trader and the consumer. A good market always serves to safeguard the interest of the trader and the consumer. A trader also cares for maximum production, best possible quality of commodity and their timely supply to consumers at reasonable cost. Fishes are directly associated with the economy of the country, it earns foreign exchange also, by the disposal of the commodities in the international market. Some important points related to the success of this trade are :

1. The demand position of the consumer market should always be assessed.

2. Sudden price rise and also fall of price should be prevented. Prices should be stabilised irrespective of bumper or poor landing of fish or fish products. Creation of artificial scarcity leads to dangerous consequences.

3. A preliminary statistics on catches should be collected prior to diversion of the fish to various agencies dealing with storage, preservation, canning industries and manufacturing units of various products and by products. Statistics on fresh consumption should also be collected.

4. There is great need for quality control at various levels as per requirements of the local and foreign markets.

5. All precautions should be taken to prevent losses of fish and fish products due to wastage.

6. There is need to be attentive to even small points of conscience against the harmful activities and functioning of the middle men, money lenders, hoarders, retailers and even co-operative societies involved in this trade.

7. That the fishes have very high food value being rich in protein, carbohydrates, vitamins and minerals, should be given wide publicity.

Co-operative movements have also gained importance in fishery trade. It can safeguard the interest of the small entrepreneurs and stops their exploitation by the middlemen. The fishery trade is also promoted by this movement. There is need for collective efforts by the fishermen, consumers, industrialists and Govt. authorities. In several countries (Canada, Japan, Italy, Norway, Denmark etc.) there is much more mechanization and sophistication in fishery operations at all stages, right from capture to marketing. Fishery trade can solve many socio-economic problems of poverty-hit fishermen. They can be provided many credit facilities for various expensive purposes involved in fisheries improvement. In many foreign countries (e.g. Canada) also there is provision for granting loan to the poor fishermen. Heavy amounts in the form of loans are granted under "Fisheries Improvement Loan Act".

The poor fishermen are being exploited in many Asian and African countries by the middlemen in this trade. These middlemen lend money to the fishermen on very high interest, particularly at the time when there is fall in catches. But, now the picture has changed and the credit-facilities have been extended to them by co-operative societies at a low interest. Now the fishermen can get education and training at several centres under extension services and rural integration programmes. Through co-operative societies the fisherman can be benefitted in several ways as given below :

(a) Facilities for credit, finance and loan.

(b) Facilities for distribution, transport and marketing.

(c) Facilities for processing and preservation of fishes.

(d) Facilities for equipments (crafts and gears).

(e) Facilities for making them aware of the socio-economic facts for the welfare of the fishermen and their family members. The socio-economic facts include rights of fishing, lease of water, insurance against risk of life and property, unprecedented poor catches etc.

In India, marketing requires much improvement. Fisherman do not get actual price of their produce because of the interference of the powerful rings of the businessmen. Efforts are being made to prepare schemes for the marketing of fish and fish products throughout India in co-operation with the state Government. In Calcutta, Bombay and Madras, fishes are sold by auction under the regulations enforced by municipal authorities but still the influence of the middlemen is there. Bulk of the fishes landed are marketed through the co-operative agencies or affiliated societies in Orissa, Saurashtra, Uttar Pradesh and Bombay.

Concluding Remarks

India is among the ten fish producing countries of the world with regard to sea-food production and export. It is keeping pace with other nations in fish production. But the fish markets in different parts of India are not well organized. There is need to reform the markets by modernizing the traditional fish marketing methods by introducing new management techniques. For improving fish marketing the major segments of study should be (a) Demand, (b) supply (c) Attractive marketing and (d) Economics. The demand and consumption of fish depends on the availability and also the fish eating population in India. There are several factors which affect the price of the fish. These factors include elasticity of demand, weight and quality of fish, distance of procuring centres to fish markets and structure and location of fish markets. The strategy of fish market management should be analysed in the light of the present pattern of marketing, setting of objectives, development of fish demand, formulation of new plan and marketing operation and control etc.

CHAPTER 26

POND, ITS MANAGEMENT AND PRODUCTIVITY

Pond is an artificially constructed shallow body of water where there is abundance of aquatic plants. Ponds are generally rectangular in shape. An ideal pond has a depth between 6-7 feet for better productivity. Several ponds are 1/3-1/2 acre in area. The source of water supply to the pond may be from a river or from a spring or rain water. At certain places where the water level is low, pond gets water from its bottom in a particular season of the year. A pond must be manageable for controlled farming. A fisheries pond should have suitable bottom (for the development of flora and fauna for fish feeding), pond wall, dike, outlet (monk or sluice), inlet (with screen) by pass channel and drains or ditches. Calm and limnophil water, muddy-clay bottoms and rain water have rich biogenic capacity. A *eutropic* pond is a water resource which has sufficient nutritional substances. Rearing of fishes in localized water is known as *Pisciculture* . The physico-chemical nature of pond has much to do with the productivity of pond. These parameters have been discussed in detail below :

1. *Light* : Light is a complex environmental factor and its penetration into pond water can produce diverse ecological effects. It supplies energy for the process of photosynthesis in plants. The Phytoplankton, Zooplankton, organic and inorganic particles and turbidity of water either reflect or absorb the light rays. Light controls several aspects of plant life like structure, shape, physiology, growth, and their local distribution etc. Production of chlorophyll and stomatal movement are also controlled by light. Light has far reaching effects on the animal also. It affects a large number of biological processes like reproduction, development, growth, locomotion, migration and many physiological processes. *Salmon* larvae undergo normal development only when there is sufficient light. Migration in eels and Salmons are affected by photoperiodism. Sundararaj (1973) reported that in *Heteropneustes fossilis,* longer days induce early maturity. Penetration of light in water also affects the temperature of pond water.

2. *Temperature* : Temperature has multisided effects on plants and animals comprising aquatic life. Different species of plants and animals vary greatly in the limits of temperature tolerance. Fishes are *Stenothermal* i.e. they can tolerate small

variation in temperature. Several examples can be cited in favour of the fact that temperature governs the distribution of plants and animals to a great extent. The variation in water temperature has a great effect on the productivity of pond. For metabolism, growth and reproduction of the fishes, an optimum temperature is always essential. Suitable temperature for *Salmon* is 10°C, for *Tilapia* 20-30°C and for major carps it is 20-37°C. *Tilapia* can not survive at a temperature less than 8°C. Indian carps can not survive at a temperature less than 16°C. Indian major carps, chinese grass carps and silver carp can not survive when water temperature is raised above 40°C.

3. *Turbidity* : The river water of the pond water sometimes looks cloudy. It is simply because of turbidity. Turbidity may be because of suspension of silt or clay particles or it may be due to excessive plankton growth or some other reasons. Turbidity of flooded water is higher in comparison to the water of lakes. Penetration of sun light depends definitely on the degrees of turbidity. Turbidity is very harmful for many fishes, however, some fishes can tolerate a certain range of turbidity. Some fishes can live in turbid water also. Turbidity can affect penetration of sunlight and thereby affects the photosynthetic activities of aquatic plants. Productivity of the pond can thus be affected. Turbidity can affect water temperature also.

4. *Dissolved O_2 Content* : Dissolved O_2 is also important for the productivity of the pond. Different quantities of dissolved oxygen is suitable for different fishes. Photosynthetic plants also provide O_2 to the medium. At 20°C, salmonids require 9 mg/litre of dissolved oxygen for aquatic breathing whereas carps need 6-7 mg/litre only. During day, the oxygen concentration of water becomes higher but during night it goes considerably down. Fishes may die asphyxia when there is depletion of dissolved O_2.

5. *Carbondioxide* : CO_2 comes into the pond-water through decomposition of organic materials, respiration of various organisms and from the atmosphere when dissolved in water. Carbondioxide is useful for the green plants in the synthesis of carbohydrates mainly.

6. *Hydrogen-Ion-Concentration (pH) and Alkalinity* : Hydrogen ion concentration of water has marked impact on the growth of the fishes and also on its healthy or unhealthy conditions. When the pH of water is 7, it is said to be neutral. When pH is lower than 7, it is supposed to be acidic. When pH is higher than 7, it is supposed to be alkaline. pH, above 9 and below 4.5 is injurious to fishes. The pH of water between 8-9 is suitable for almost all fishes. If necessary, lime can be added to it. Sudden fluctuation in pH is harmful for fishes. Thus quality of water depends on the bicarbonate content of water. The following chemical reactions are often seen taking place in the pond water maintaining equilibrium.

$$Ca(HCO_3)_2 + 2HCl \longrightarrow CaCl_2 + H_2O + 2CO_2$$

$$Ca(HCO_3)_2 + KOH \longrightarrow CaCO_3 + KHCO_3 + H_2O$$

$$Ca(HCO_3)_2 \rightleftharpoons CaCO_3 + H_2O + CO_2$$

$$CO_2 \text{ (atmospheric)} + H_2O \text{ (rain water)} \longrightarrow H_2CO_3$$

$$H_2CO_3 + CaCO_3 \longrightarrow Ca(HCO_3)_2$$

Thus when there is excess of CO_2 in water, bicarbonate is reproduced. Bicarbonate also increases with the help of rain water, as shown in the last two reactions. Alkalinities between 10-15 ppm give best results in fish culture.

7. *Nitrogen and Phosphorus* : Average 0.2 ppm of dissolved nitrogen is considered favourable for better productivity. The optimum limit of Nitrogen can be in the range of 0.3 to 1.3 ppm. 60-120 ppm of Phosphorus (P_2O_5) is supposed to be ideal for high productivity.

8. *Aquatic Fauna and Flora* : Pond should be rich in aquatic fauna and flora which will definitely increase the productivity of the pond. Phytoplankton and Zooplankton are consumed by the fishes and as such, their presence is always necessary in all seasons. The submerged plants are also of great use. They serve not only as food for some fishes but they harbour a host for small animals (snails, insect larvae etc.) The bottom fauna, feeding on the bottom debris also serve as food for many fishes.

9. *Depth of the Pond* : The depth of water is also an important factor. Penetration of light, and temperature of water depend on the depth of water. Photosynthetic activity, and several physico-chemical conditions of pond are thus affected. Sustaining of required amount of biota depends on the depth of the pond. The light is modified by water medium in respect to intensity and spectral composition. Different rays penetrate upto a definite depth of water. Distribution of Phytoplankton and Zooplankton also depends on the depth of the pond.

Management of Pond

Under normal conditions the pond has a limited capacity for holding the fish crop and its productivity, which is almost constant. But, management practices can greatly increase its capacity. Management includes the use of fertilizers and supplementary food, control of noxious vegetation, polyculture and skimming, improvement of physical factors, control of fish enemies etc. Management of pond increases both qualitative and quantitative production of fish. Some of the important measures for increasing fish production have been discussed below :

1. *Control of Weeds* : Weed control is one of the important aspects of pond management. Some of the common weeds of the pond are :

Microcystis, Oscillatoria, Ceratium, Volvox, Eudorina, Nostoc, Anabaena, Chara, Spirogyra, Oedogonium, Cledophora, Marsilea, Pistia, Eichhornia, Azolla, Salvinia, Hydrilla, Vallisneria, etc. Some of the weeds serve as food for the fishes but most of them cause hindrance to movement of fish and create problem during fishing operations. Some of them may be poisonous for the fishes also.

Blue green alga *Microcystis* covers the pond surface and forms a thick, blackish green scum which cuts off air and sunlight from the plankton below. The secretion of *microcystis* and its allies are pisonous for the fishes. *Anabaena* and *Nostoc* also form a blanket over the surface when grow in excess later on. During the rainy season Chara also creates problem by forming a thick mat (8-10cm) on the surface. *Spirogyra* is also troublesome for young fishes. Some *Eichhornia* species are troublesome weeds. Weeds can be controlled in many ways and some of them have been described below :

(i) *Chemical Control* : Copper sulphate in the concentration of 0.5 to 1.0 ppm kills *nostoc* and some other filamentous algae. A mixture of Copper sulphate (3.63-5.44 kg/acre) and ammonium sulphate (9-13.6 Kg/acre) has been recommended for the removal of *Chara*. Some herbicides which are commonly used, include calcium cyanide, sodium chlorate, quick lime, amitrol, methoxane etc. Dicotox is effective in controlling submerged weed like *Hydrilla* and *Vallisneria* etc.

(ii) *Mechanical Control* : Some weeds are also mechanically removed. Spirogyra can not be removed so easily by delicate copper sulphate spray and as such its mechanical removal becomes necessary. *Eichhornia* is skimmed off the surface with the help of a rope. Floating and submerged algae are removed by filtering method. Some large weeds are cut into pieces and are finally removed. Some ponds which have been neglected must be filled up with mud, aquatic plants will grow in abundance which will be controlled later on.

(iii) *Biological Control* : Introduction of herbivorous fish (*Ctenopharyngodon idella*) and birds (e.g. Swan) eat up some aquatic weeds which are not desirable for many fishes. Use of some fertilizer (e.g. Cowdung and Compost) cause good growth of phytoplankton which can easily cut off sunlight to deeper parts of the pond, thereby causing disadvantages to the larger plants. Also less harmful weeds should be introduced into the pond.

2. *Control of fish enemies* : There are various animals preferring only the adult fish but also the eggs and fry as their food. These animals are insects (notonectids, dragonfly, nymphs, bugs, beetles and stick insects), reptiles (snakes, crocodiles, turtles), birds (Cormorants, Pelicans, herones gulls, ducks) and mammals (otters, cetaceans, pinnipedes). Even carnivorous fishes of large size become the enemies of other smaller fishes. Frequent drainage of pond is essential. At least once in a year the pond should remain dry. In this way, pond bottom can be kept dry for a considerable period and as such most insects and their larvae will be destroyed. Quicklime should be sprayed on the bottom. Periodical shooting of Predatory birds is also effective. Occasional spray of toxic substances in dilute concentration should also be practised. Scoop-nets and trap-nets may be used for the removal of unwanted organisms.

3. *Control over the species cultivated* : For increasing production, the choice of a suitable fish is an important consideration. Genetically improved varieties will definitely yield more. Monosex cultivation increases fish production. Males of *Tilapia nilotica* and females of pike and eel have higher growth rate in comparison to opposite sex. Mixing of different age groups of a particular fish in pond may be preferred for better production. Polyculture (composite culture) can yield higher production. They can make better use of the food resources and ecological potentials of the pond. They should not be predatory and should tolerate each other. Sometimes, for qualitative production prey and predators are mixed together. For example, *Tilapia* may be mixed *Lates niloticus*. Predators check excessive growth of the principal fish. Composite culture is practised in China, Japan, India, Pakistan, Europe, Israel, U.S.A. and other countries. Different combinations of fishes are preferred at different places. Combination of *Catla catla*, *Labeo rohita* and *Cirrhinus mrigala* in the ratio of 3:3:4 is an old practice in W.Bengal. *Labeo calbasu* may also be added to the above combination and catla, rohu, mrigal and calbasu are in the ratio of 3:3:3:1, in that case. In West Bengal, Andhra Predesh, U.P., Haryana, Tamil Nadu

and Maharashtra a new combination of three indigenous species and three exotic species have been successfully attempted. Indigenous species include catala, rohu, mrigal and the exotic species included common carp (*C.carpio*), grass carp (*Ctenopharyngodon idella*) and silver carp *Hypothalmichthys molitrix*. All these fishes have different feeding habits.

4. *Skimming or Successive intermediate fishing throughout a year* : Intermediate fishing increases total fish production in a year. By intermediate fishing operations the population of fishes in the pond should be reduced. It provides better scope for individual growth. When a fish attains marketable size it should be removed. Successive multiple production in one year should also be attempted if climatic condition favours.

5. *Use of fertilizers* : Fish production can be increased in the pond by the use of fertilizers. It facilitates the decomposition of food residues and excreta, increases the quality of natural food in the pond and stops dietary diseases also. Thus it encourages higher production. The fertilizers include phosphate, lime, potash, magnesium, nitrogenous compounds and manures of plant and animal origin. Sewage is also a highly valuable organic fertilizer which is rich in nutrients. Phosphorus and nitrogen are present in great quantities. When sewage decomposes, CO_2 is liberated and the latter is picked up by primary producers for synthesis. The fertilizers favour better production of zooplankton and phytoplankton which serve as food for all categories of fishes.

6. *Supplementary feeding and artificial food* : For certain fishes (tilapia, trouts and eels) the natural food is of only little significance. Natural productivity is not so important for these fishes. When natural food is supplemented with some artificial food, production of fish in the pond can be enhanced. Both vegetable foods and animal foods can be provided for the various fish crop in the pond. Pulses, cereals, tubers and roots, meals and brans of grains, oil seeds and several miscellaneous items, particularly of kitchen wastes are some of the vegetable foods. Among the animal food are the cultivated insects (silkworm pupae, larvae, chironomous larvae etc.) liver, lungs, spleen blood shrimps, fishes, snails, frog meat, several fish foods are prepared in the factories which can also be used occasionally.

7. *Control of diseases* : The fish can be subject to many diseases particulary when the farming is intensive. Many fungal, bacterial, viral, parasitic, environmental, dietary and other types of diseases have been encountered in the fish crop. So, all precautions should be taken to save the fishes from all hazards. Pond water must be of good quality in order to aviod dangers from lack of O_2, and pollution. Infected ponds and the material used must be disinfected. Sometimes the diseases may take the form of epidemics and large scale mortality may ba caused. Ponds should be hygienically maintained. Frequent use of benzalkonium chloride (100-600 ppm strength). Potassium permanganate (0.5 gr/100 litre) disinfects the pond. Use of lime is also good for this purpose. Fishes should always be supplied with rich food. Curative measures should be taken for the treatment of individual fish also as described in the fish diseases chapter.

Composite Fish Culture

Composite culture or Polyculture or mixed fish farming is the culture of more than one species of fish in the same water body. It mainly comprises carp Polyculture which has attained the status of organised industries. It is a system of pond management. Polyculture is an old-age practice for India also. "Indian Freshwater Aquaculture has been largely organic based , with inputs derived from activities of agriculture and animal husbandry, with plant and animal residues forming the major component of feeds and fertilizes in carp polyculture" (Ayyappan, 1996). There is a very common combination of Catla, Rohu and Mrigala normally in the ratio of 3:3:4 (Alikunhi, 1957). Sometimes only one species of Calbasu (*Labeo calbasu*) is also added to this combination and then the ratio becomes 3:3:4:1. In southern India, *Labeo fimbriatus, Labeo kontius, Cirrhinus cirrhosa* and *Catla catla* are cultured together in varied ratios. A mixed farming has been encourged on the basis of various ecological considerations now in several states like U.P., Bihar, West Bengal, Haryana, Andhra Pradesh, Maharashtra and Tamil Nadu. In this full fledged co-ordinated research project which was started in 1971, three indigenous major carps and three exotic carps have been chosen. The combination includes :

	Indigenous Species	*Species Ratio*	*Habit*
1.	*Labeo rohita*	2.5	A column feeder feeding on decaying plants
2.	*Cirrhinus mrigala*	1.0	A bottom feeder consuming decaying plant, detrius mainly
3.	*Catla catla*	1.0	A surface feeder which consumes zooplankton
	Exotic Species		
4.	*Cyprinus carpio*	2.0	An omnivorous habit, scavenger on plants and animals
5.	*Ctenopharyngodon idella*	1.0	Feeding on coarse macrovegetation
6.	*Hyophthalmichthys molitrix*	2.5	A surface feeder on Phytoplankton

The Polyculture ponds are frequently cropped also with regard to the size of the fish. The average yield of indigenous major carps in the mixed farming has been estimated to be 4000 kg. per hectare annually. The same estimated value for exotic carps is 3000 kg. per hectare annually. The average yield of both indigenous and exotic species cultured together has been estimated to be 8000 kg per hectare annually.

Stocking density of six species has now been increased to 8000 per hectare with the help of intermediary input technology and to 10000 per hectare with the help of high input technology. For a much more higher density (upto 25000 fingerlings/ hac.) is being experimented at CIFA (ICAR), Bhubaneswar (Orissa).

As per report of several workers in the field of fish culture and breeding some more fishes on the ground of several suitable ecological sub-nitches have been preferred. These suitable fish species recommended for addition to the above mentioned carp culture combination are - *Ompok bimaculatus, Notopterus chitála, Pangassius pangassius, Mugil cephalus, Osphronemus gorami* and *Labeo calbasu.*

CHAPTER 27

COMMON BIOTA OF FISH PONDS OF INDIA

Fish ponds of India are very rich in their biota comprising Plankton (Zooplankton and Phytoplankton), and various types of weeds described in this Chapter. Plankton include both animals and plants of small (microplankton) and large size (macroplankton) The plankton occur in all natural waters and artificial impoundments like tanks, ponds, reservoirs and irrigation channels. Zooplankton are exclusively animals and the phytoplankton are of plant origin.

Certain plankters grow very quickly and under favourable conditions they attain enormous densities. Such organisms which grow and multiply into exceptionally dense community with much higher concentration form the *blooms*. Blooms of both phytoplankters and Zooplankters may be harmful for fish farms. At night they cause oxygen depletion in water of the ponds because of respiration and as such, may cause large fish kills. Certain plankters like *Microcystis* sometimes show a remarkable population explosion in the pond. Pond biota belonging to both plant and animal communities, either *litoral* or *benthic* affect the productivity of the pond.

Important contributions covering various informations on the biota of fish ponds of India are those of Pruthi (1933), Iyenger (1939), Philipose (1940, '48, '58, '59, '67, '70), Thomas and Srinivasan (1949), Chatopadhyay (1951) Alikunhi (1952), Ahmad (1954), Chacko and (Krishnamurty (1954), Biswas and Calder (1955), Lawrence (1955), Alikunhi *et al.* (1955), Das and Srivastava (1955-59), Singh (1956), Pruginin and Lipshitz (1957), Mitra (1959), Ramchandran (1960), Hickling (1962), George (1962), Alikunhi and Sukmaran (1964), Zafar (1964), Moitra and Bhattacharya (1966), Moitra and Bhowmick (1967), Verma (1967), Bhowmick (1968), George Michael (1968, 1969), Ramchandran and Prabhu (1968), Philipose *et al.* (1970), Saha *et al.* (1971), Khan and Siddiqi (1974), Ramchandran *et al.* (1975) and others.

Weeds : Excessive growth of aquatic plants becomes menacing to fish culture. Only moderate growth of plants is useful for fish cultivaton. Various types of weeds have been described below :

(1) *Filamentous algae* : They form 'mats' or 'scums'. The floating masses are sometimes referred to as 'hairweeds'. They obstruct free movement of the fishes.

Important filamentous algae include *Spirogyra* spp. *Oedogonium* spp., *Microcystis aeruginosa, Oscillatoria, Anabaena, Pithophora polymorpha Cladophora, Chlamydomonas* etc. and they are present in the main body of water.

(2) *Emergent weeds and marginal Weeds* : These are rooted in the bottom but they have their foliage and flowers above the water surface. The important emergent weeds are *Eleocharis plantaginea, Typha elephantiana, Euryale, Iporroea aquatica, Marsilea, Scirpus articulatus, Jussiaea, repens, Neptunia olereacea, Cyperus* spp. *Nymphaea* spp., *Nelumbo nucifera, Trapa bispinosa, Colocasia* spp., *Panicm repens, Nymphoides cristatum, Phragmites harka, Hydriophyllum tuberculatum* etc. They serve not only as hiding places but also breeding places for some predator aquatic insects.

(3) *Submerged Weeds* : These weeds may or may not be rooted i.e. some of them have roots but others are devoid of roots. Some of the important examples of submerged weeds are *Hydrilla verticellata, Vallisneria, Najas, Ceratophyllum, Utricularia, Eleocharis, Otellia, Ceratopteries, Potamogeton, Chara zeylanica, Sagittaria, Lagarosiphon, Nymphea, Panium, Neptunia* etc. They definitely cause hindrance to fish movement but some of these are great source of oxygen.

(4) *Surface floating weeds* : They form matlike structure on the surface of the water and reduce light penetration and atmospheric gas contact with the water body. These weeds include *Echhornia grassipes, Pistia stratiestes, Spirodela polyrhiza, Azolla pinneta, Lemna minor, Salvinia cucullata, Wolffia arrhiza, Nymphaea, Nelumb* etc. *Salvinia* spp.

Control of weeds : When a new pond is under construction, precaution should be taken that the weeds should not establish there in the very beginning. For this, the depth of water should always be higher than 0.5m. shaping and sodding of the pond edge above the water level accounts much for reducing the marginal and shallow water weeds. There should be no muddy water swampy area around the pond. There should be no scope for the growth of luxuriant vegetation. There should be balanced aquatic vegetation requisite for pond ecology.

Control of weeds is a very important part of pond management. It involves removal of undesirable vegetation which is harmful in many ways for fish culture. There should be always moderate growth of aquatic plants so that they may be useful for fish culture. The various measures used to control the weeds have been discussed below in detail:

(1) *Manual and Mechanical Control methods* : Sometimes manual methods are also employed for the removal of the weeds. Methods of hand picking and up rooting of certain emergent and marginal weeds are also there in practice. Labourers cut them with forks, sickles and other suitable tools. There are some diesel operated machines also to cut and remove them from the ponds. Sometimes liquid cow dung is used to control the algal blooms (tides). Grazing of marginal weeds also prevents their excessive growth. Always less harmful aquatic plants should be introduced.

(2) *Chemical Control* : Suitable herbicides should be used particularly for controlling the emergent plants. There are several herbicides now available in the markets for controlling the aquatic weeds. But, precaution should always be taken that they

are used at a very low rate (less than 10 ppm). They should be cheap and non-toxic to human beings and stock animals. In no case, water of the pond should be polluted.

Echhornia grassipes is supposed to be the most noxious weed. The well known chemical 2, 4–dichlorophenoxy acetic acid is generally used to control this weed as it is not harmful for the fish (Saha *et al.*, 1958). It has effective herbicidal actions. If it is brought in direct contact of the leaves or it is absorbed by the roots, the plants can be easily destroyed. 4.5 to 6.7 Kg of this chemical in per hectare area of the pond is normally sufficient to destroy this floating weed. Philipose (1957) has advised to repeat its application if the weeds are not completely destroyed. *Simazine* is also an important herbicide for this purpose and is used as spray at the rate of 5 Kg per hectare in the form of aqueous emulsion. For damaging and killing the *Pistia stratiestes* and *Salvinia* spp. foliar spray of *Paraquat* at the rate of 0.02 Kg per hectare in aqueous solution has been advised by Patnaik (1968). They can also be killed by the use of 1-2% aqueous ammonia. Ramchandran and Rama Prabhu (1968) have suggested the use of 2,4-D sodium and *simazine* both at the rate of 5 Kg per hectare.

For killing the young *Cyperus* and *Eleocharis plantaginea* which are common weeds, foliar spray of 2, 4-D sodium and 2,2-dichloropropionic sodium in aqueous solution has been found to be suitable. 10 to 12 Kg of this combination per hectare is generally used in a wetting agent for quick effect. *Calocasia* and *Ipomea* spp. can also be controlled by the use of aqueous solution of 2, 4-D sodium at the rate of 5 Kg per hectare of the pond. The aquatic grasses *Panicum* spp. can be controlled by the spray of 2, 2-dichloropropionic acid at the rate of 10-15 Kg per hectare. But, it requires longer time for complete eradication.

As suggested by Srinivasan and Chako (1952), Singh (1962) and Ramchandran and Prabhu (1968), foliar spray with various formulations of 2,4-D herbicides are effective in controlling the emergent weeds like *Nymphaea, Nelumbo, Euryale* and *Nymphoides* spp. Calcium cyanide, amitrol, Sodium Chlorate and quick lime are also effective weedicides. Copper sulphate, sodium arsenite, superphosphate and ammonia in aqueous solution have been found to be much suitable for eradication of submerged weeds. Various concentrations of these chemicals as recommended by some workers have been given below. Banerjea and Mitra (1954) have recommended the application of Copper sulphate with H_2SO_4 at a concentration of 10 ppm for controlling *Ottelia* in alkaline ponds. For controlling *chara*, copper sulphate can be applied either alone or with the combination of *Ammonium sulphate* as advised by Chatopadhyay (1951). According to Philipose (1963), Sodium arsenite at a concentration of 5-6 ppm is effective in clearing several submerged weeds. This concentration of sodium arsenite is not harmful for the fish community as a whole. Mitra (1959) has reported that superphosphate at 500 ppm can be effective in eradicating several weeds. Ramchandran (1963) has suggested the use of ammonia in aqueous solution for controlling certain weeds.

For controlling the soil-rooted aquatic weeds, use of 2,4-D herbicide, simazine and aquattol has been suggested. Simazine and aquattol have been found to be effective against *Hydrilla verticillata*. 40 ppm of SO_2 in the form of bisulphite in acid medium can also kill *Hydrilla vercillata* as suggested by Ramchandran and Prabhu (1968). Application of 2, 4-D herbicide soaked in brick pellets to the root-zone of soil-rooted aquatic weeds had been found to be effective by Ramchandran and Prabhu (1976). Dicotox is also effective in controlling Hydrilla.

Some chemicals have been suggested for eradication of algal blooms and mats which cause oxygen depletion in water. *Microcystis aeruginosa* can be controlled by the use of simazine at a concentration of 0.5 to 1.0 ppm. Diuron can also control this noxious alga at a slightly lower concentration (0.1 to 0.3 ppm.) Repeated spray of copper sulphate (0.3 ppm) can also control algal blooms.

(3) *Biological Control* : Some weeds can be controlled by herbivorous fishes like *Ctenopharyngodon idella, Puntius javanicus, Tilapia mossambica, Cyprinus carpio, Osphronemus goramy* etc. They can eat up the aquatic vegetation. Even advanced fry and fingerlings can consume certain types of weeds as reported by Alikunhi and Sukumaran (1964). *Ctenopharyngodon idella* has been quite effective in controlling *Hydrilla, Azolla, Salvinia* and *Ceratophyllum, Ottelia, Vallisneria, Utricularia* etc. Even in Russia and China the grass carps are stocked in large reservoirs for utilization of weeds. Common carps help in uprooting of the weeds during the process of burrowing, while searching food. Avault *et al.* (1968) controlled *Pithophora* with the help of common carps. Philipose (1968) has reported that *Tilapia mossambica* can control submerged vegetation and filamentous algae also. They can be useful in controlling *Chara, Najas* and other soft vegetation. Aquatic vegetations can also be controlled to some extent by employing ducks and geese.

Plankton

The term 'plankton' has already been explained in this chapter. Plankton has great food value even for the mankind. It is also the food for fish and several other aquatic animals. Fishes are both Phytoplankter-feeding as well as Zooplankter-feeding in habit. Phytoplankton produce oxygen during Photosynthesis and thus help in the purification of water making the latter suitable for fish respiration. They are also used for clearing utensils directly or indirectly. Several products are prepared from plankton in the industries for the use of mankind.

Common Plankters of Indian Waters as reported by various workers are as follows :

1. *Phytoplankters : Diatom Peridinium* spp., *Volvox, Euglena, Cyclotella menenghiniana, Ceratium, Pinnularia* spp. *Anabaena spiroides, Actiniatrum, Oscillatoria* spp., *Milosira granulata, Closterum, Synedra ulna, Eudorina elegans, Microcystis aeruginosa, Pediastrum simplex, Nitzschia* spp., *Raphidiopsis, Synura uvella, Arthrospira platensis, Navicula* spp., *Cyclostella, Dinobryon sertularia, Chlamydomonas, Trachelomonas, Chlorogonium, Pandorina, Gambella* species, *Scenedesus quadricauda, Tetraedron minimum, Botrycoccus braunii, Spirulena gigantea, Phacus* spp. *Hirundinella* etc.

2. *Zooplankters : Actinosphaerium, Diffugia, Arcella, Vorticella, Keratella, Polvarthra, Polyarthra, Epistylis, Pedalia, Padophrya, Brachionus rubens, Colochilus, Tokophrya, Filinia, Saurophrya, Asplachna, Hexarthra, Cladocerans, Diaptomus, Daphnia, Ceriodaph-*

nia, Bosmina, Moina, Simocephalus, Dipahanosoma, Aplanchna, Cyclopes, Cypris, Neuplius, Mesocyclopes, etc.

In addition to the above mentioned Zooplankters, there are several members of benthic macrofauna in ponds which are associated with the roots of larger weeds. They comprise several molluscs, arthropods and annelids both adults and larval forms. Several harmful plankton are controlled by the use of ammonia (2-3 mg/litre), lime and Chrotoxyphos (0.1 to 1 mg/litre) separately.

CHAPTER 28

INDUCED BREEDING

Carps normally breed in running waters of rivers and streams where they have ample space for movement. The water in the breeding season becomes dirty brown but it is rich in minerals and other natural resources including higher O_2 content. During this period sufficient materials are available. Such environment provides stimulus for spawning. Carps never breed in captivity though their gonads may be matured and ovulation might have taken place in natural habitat. For the development of fish culture it is essential that the carps should breed in confined water so that it may be dependable source of quality fish seed.

Induced breeding is that technique by which ripe fish breed in confined water when stimulated by pituitary hormone administration. This hormone is a gonadotropin, extracted from the hypophysis of a mammal or a fish. Chorionic gonadotropin (CG) is equally effective. Induced breeding of fish in confined water through pituitary hormone injection has been attempted in carps (indigenous and exotic species) and some other fishes. It has really provided opportunities for the progress of fish culture in India and abroad. Several researches regarding the use of pituitary extract in induced breeding are on record. Some of the important contributions are those of Khan (1937), Choudhury (1955), Fontenele (1955), Ramaswamy and Sundararaj (1956-57), Pickford and Atz (1957), Combs and Burrows (1959), Choudhari and Alikunhi (1957), Alikunhi and Parmeswaran (1963), Ahsan and Hoar (1963) Lee *et al.* (1987), Rath (1987, 1988), Rao and Ram (1991), Sahu and Rao (1991), Rajyalakshmi *et al.* (1991) Abraham *et al.* (1995) and others.

In the past, fish culture depended on the natural reproduction and growth of the fish in the ponds and other enclosures of water bodies. Today, fish culture has been paid much attention and it is enjoying the privilege of several techniques of modern science and technology. The recent association of hormones and aquaculture is considered as a proper domain of investigation by fish endocrinologists. This sort of work was started in 1934 for the first time in Brazil and the fish pituitary glands were injected to induce ovulation. Later on this method became popular in Russia, Europe,North America, India, China and other countries. Houssay (1930) of Argentina injected pituitary gland to some small-sized viviparous fish and brought about premature birth of the young ones. von Ihering (1934) developed proper techique for inducing ovulation using fish pituitary. The technique was known as *hypophysation*.

Later on, Gerbil'skii (1937-1938) a Russian Scientist performed experiments on *Acipenser stellatus* and injected intraperitoneally one or two fresh pituitaries taken out from individuals of the same species. The fish spawned near the mouth of the river.

Inducing spawning of carps in China and India is a common practice now. Experiments on induced spawning Pituitary injections were performed in early 1950s in China gradually on *Molopharyngodon piceus, Aristichthys nobilis, Hypophthalmichthys molitrix* and *Ctenopharyngodon idellus*. In India, Pituitary hormones were sucessfully administered to *Catla catla, Labeo rohita* and *cirrhinus mrigala*, and spawning was observed. Thus the hormones initiated ovulation. Recently, experiments were successfully performed on *Exomus danricus, Pseudeutropipus atherinoides clarias batrachus, Heteropneustes fossilis, cirrhinus reba, Labeo bata, Puntius sarana, Ctenopharyngodon idella* and *Hypophthalmichthys molitrix* by several workers.

For facilitating artificial reproduction and selective breedings procedures gamete preservation had become a very popular step these days. For gamete preservation, some important works have been devoted which include those of Yamamoto (1939), Yanagimachi (1956), Wither and Morley (1968), Clemens and Hill (1969), Ott and Horton (1971 a, b), Dushkina (1975), Billard *et al.* (1977), Billard (1978 a,b), Carpentier and Billard (1978), Arai *et al.* (1979), Ashwoodsmith (1980), Benau and Terner (1980), Baynes *et al.* (1981), Billard (1981), Baynes and Scott (1982), Chao (1982), Hara *et al.* (1982), Harvey (1982), Stoss and Donaldson (1982, 1983), and others.

Pituitary banks are likely to be installed for the purpose of induced breeding in order to meet the demand of Pituitary extract in various parts of the country. Researches are going on to make improvements of induced breeding techniques. The whole process of induced breeding can be described under several heads as given below. Some more experiments have been performed on induced breeding by Ramaswami and Lakshman (1959), Ibrahim and Chaudhuri (1976), Donaldson and Shehadeh (1972), Pandey and Hoar (1972), Carreon *et al.* (1976), Chaudhuri (1976), Brandt and Schoonbee (1980), Juario and Natividal (1980), Kagawa and Nagahama (1981), Donaldson *et al.* (1981 a,b), Donaldson and Hunter (1982), Crim *et al.* (1983) and others.

Induced Breeding of Carps

1. *Preparation of the Pituitary extract for injection*: Pituitary gland is collected from a ripe fish which is known as a donar fish. The common carp *Cyprinus carpio* is chosen donar in most of the countries. The piturary extract is normally prepared during May and June. The Indian Major carps i.e. *Labeo rohita, Catla catla, Labeo calbasu, Labeo gonius* and *Cirrhina mrigala* do not breed in confined water and as such they are subjected to induced breeding experiments.

The pituitary gland can be carefully removed through foramen magnum with the help of a forcep in a cut fish-head. The gland can also be removed by dissecting the head and using a butcher's knife. A freshly caught fish or a fish well preserved in ice may be used for this purpose. The gland, immediately after its removal from the brain is frozen and stored in a refrigerator. It may be preserved in acetone at 10°C.

It is however, easy to preserve the gland in absolute alcohol at room temperature. The preserved gland is macerated in a tissue homogenizer with a small quantity of distilled water. The solution is centrifuged and suspended particles are removed. Then 0.3 per cent sodium chloride solution is added to it. Now it is ready for injection. For longer storage the extract can be preserved in glycerine instead of sodium chloride. Sometimes, trichloro-acetic is also used instead of glycerine for the preservation of pituitary extract.

2. *Selection of breeders* : Large-sized breeder should not be preferred. Medium-sized fully ripe and healthy fish between the age group of 2 to 4 yrs and weighing only 1 to 5 kg. are supposed to be ideal breeders.

Male and female fishes exhibit sexual dimorphism in the breeding season and they can be easily recognized. They should be netted out before the breeding season and the potential breeders should be kept in separate pools under care. Breeders should not be injured at the time of either netting or transportation. They should be provided with supplementary food. About 2000 breeders can be stocked in a tank of one acre.

3. *Injection technique and doses of extract* : For higher percentage of fertilization, there should be synchronization between ovulation and milt shedding. For this purpose generally two males and one female are taken in every set. Doses depend on the age, sex size and state of maturity of both the donar and the recipient. A dose of 2 to 3 mg of the gland per kg of bodyweight is given to the female. There is no need of administering the dose to a male fish if it is in the state of milt oozing. After 6 hrs. a second injection of 5-8mg of the gland per kg of body weight should be given to the female fish if needed. For the male fish the dose is 2-3 mg per kg of body weight. More than two injections should not be administered. The injection may be intra-muscular (in the caudal peduncle or shoulder) or intraperitoneal (at the bases of paired fins). Second injection should be given in the evening and the first one should be given in the early hours of the day. A cool, rainy or cloudy weather is better for an early spawning. The fishes should be transferred to the breeding *hapa* after injecting the pituitary hormone.

4. *Spawning in breeding hapa* : A set of breeders is released into the breeding hapa for spawning following administration of the pituitary extract. The breeding hapa is a rectangular case of fine netting. For larger fishes its size is 8′x3′x3', but for the smaller fishes it is 5′x4′x3'. It is held on four bamboo poles, one at each corner of the rectangular case. The roof of the hapa may be open or closed. The hapa is made up of a close-meshed mosquito net-cloth. Meshes can not allow the laid eggs and milt to escape and maintains a good circulation of water. 3/4 of the hapa is always under water and the rest part is in the air. Spawning takes place within 3-6 hours after injection. The unfertilized eggs are pearl like and transparent but the fertilized eggs are white and opaque. A hatching hapa is also rectangular and made of muslin or malmal cloth. The mosquito net hapa is present inside it. The hatching hapa is open from above.

5. *Treatment of Parasites and diseases of breeders* : Breeders should be treated with $KMnO_4$ solution (0.5g in 100 litres of water) for a few minutes. The treatment should be followed by formaline (200 mg/1 litre of water) for one hour at least. Any

mechanical injury to an individual fish may be cured by using stronger solution (20 per cent) of $KMnO_4$ with the help of cotton (dipped in the solution). If this much care is taken, fish can get rid of certain diseases.

6. *Factors influencing induced breeding* : For successful breeding certain factors are taken into consideration. Climatic and hydrological conditions should be favourable. Cool weather (temperature 24°C-31°C), cloudy and rainy day have been proved to be better. Turbidity of water should be between 100 to 1000 ppm. Flowing water with higher O_2 content is of great use. The intensity and duration of light also affect the induced breeding and spawning. Pituitary glands taken from the same or related species as the recipient species are said to be more effective.

Use of Ovaprim in Induced Breeding

Ovaprim is a new hormonal approach for the breeding of carps and some other fish. Ovaprim is a product of Syndel Laboratory, Canada. It is a ready-to-use drug in solution form and contains *Salmon Gonadotropin Releasing Harmone* (Gn RH) and *Domperidone.* This drug is now marketed in India by M/S Glaxo. Domperidone is dopamine antagonist and can be dissolved in organic solvent. In one ml of Ovaprim there is 20 ug of gonadotropin releasing harmone and 10 mg of domperidone.

Successful breeding has been demonstrated with Ovaprim which is potent at room temperature. Several teleosts (Carps and Catfish) respond to induced breeding following administration of Ovaprim.

Ovaprim is much superior in comparison to carp pituitary extract in inducing spawning. In male fish the dose is 0.1 to 0.2 ml/kg and in the female it varies from 0.25 to 0.8 ml/kg depending on the indviduals of different fish species. Some workers have tried to administer both the pituitary extract and the ovaprim simultaneously and they have revealed satisfactory results.

Advantages of Induced Breeding

There are manifold advantages of induced breeding and some of them have been mentioned below :

1. The seed spawn is timely available, its availability from natural sources is quite uncertain.
2. A pure spawn of a desired species is made available. The spawn obtained from the rivers are not pure. They are mixed with the spawns of other species and sorting of pure seed from the mixed spawn is not possible.
3. Any quantity of pure spawn can be made available.
4. Several carps attain sexual maturity in ponds but they do not breed in confined water. Such fish can be subjected to induced breeding and spawn can be collected.
5. It is economical to obtain a spawn from induced breeding experiments in comparison to its collection from the riverine sources.
6. The induced breeding technique is very simple and can be learnt even by a layman.

CHAPTER 29

PREPARATION AND MAINTENANCE OF AQUARIUM

Fishes are controlled and maintained sometimes in a small tank either in a personal house or in the laboratory. Its purpose may be commercial, decorative, or it may also be a hobby. Fishes are also maintained in the aquarium for scientific studies. The tank (rectangular), partly filled with water should be equipped with a heater (thermostatically controlled), a reflector, scavengers (cat fishes, snails etc.) and some sort of vegetation. These are essential requirements of an aquarium. A dozen or more tropical fishes can be provided plenty of room even in a small aquarium. An aquarium is always provided with a cover.

Tank (Aquarium) and Its Size

For tropical fishes the tank should have the bottom of slate or wired glass, with sides of thick glass set in an angle iron framework. Aluminium frame-work can also be used in place of iron. The glass should be held with special aquarium cement. The aquarium can be prepared in three different sizes i.e. 21″ × 12″ × 15″ or 24″ × 12″ × 15″ or 36″ × 12″ × 15″ (in all the cases the depth of the aquarium is 15″ normally, and the base size can be of three different measurements as indicated above). Fine aquarium gravel is mixed with sand and spread over the floor of the tank. The metallic frame should be painted with suitable paints. The tank should have a tank cover in which there is a hole for fitting an electric lamp holder. An ordinary bulb of 60 watt is enough for an aquarium. The aquarium may be placed on a table near a window. The inside of the cover should be painted to avoid condensation and subsequent rusting. The sand and gravel should not be disturbed while introducing water in the tank. The sand should be covered with a piece of paper and water should be gently poured until the tank is about one-third full.

The Aquatic Plants for the Aquarium

Some sort of vegetation is essential for the aquarium. Some plants are slightly better oxygenators than others. The under water plants in an aquarium produce oxygen, the amount of which depends on the number of particular plants. Some important plants are :

(a) Fanwort (*Cabomba caroliniana*)
(b) Tape Grass (*Vallisneria americana*)
(c) Sagittaria (*Sagittaria gigantea*)
(d) Hygrophila (*Hygrophila polysperma*)
(e) Elodea (*Anacharis canadensis*)
(f) Milfoil (*Myriophyllum spicatum*)

Aquarium Fishes

Generally, small-sized fishes are preferred for aquarium. Both live bearers and egg laying fishes are kept in the aquarium. The important fishes among the live bearers are :

(a) *Lebistes reticulatus* (Guppy)
(b) *Gambusia affinis*, and
(c) *Mollienesia latipinna* (Mollies)

The egg layers include

(a) *Betta Splendens*
(b) *Colisa latia*
(c) *Tilapia macrocephala*
(d) *Pterophyllum eimekei* (Angel fish)
(e) *Symphysodon discus*
(f) *Macropodus opercularis*
(g) *Trichogaster trichopterus*
(h) *Hemichromis bimaculatus*
(i) *Barbus ticto*
(j) *Danio melabaricus*
(k) *Brachydanio rerio*, and other fishes

Collichthys collichthys and *Malapterurus electricus* are typical scavengers.

Some More Equipments, and Maintenance of Aquarium

A thermometer is always required to test water temperature. As temperature fluctuation should be minimum, it is always advisable to check water temperature frequently. A floating thermometer is quite useful for this purpose.

Sometimes it becomes necessary to catch a fish in the aquarium and transfer it to elsewhere. For this purpose a *handier rectangular net* is essential. With the help of this equipment the fish is netted in the corner of the aquarium and it can not make a dash for freedom during which it might be injured.

A large *glass siphon tube* is also essential to remove the debris and uneaten food by sucking them up. A piece of hollow glass tube which is longer than the depth of the tank is supposed to be satisfactory for this purpose. Thus, undesirable substances should be siphoned out after considerable intervals.

The *aerator* or aquarium pump is also an equipment which is electrically operated. It can pump a continuous stream of bubbles through water of the aquarium. If it is filled inside the water of the aquarium, more fish can be kept in a given volume of water. The bubbles produced by the aerator facilitate the movement of water from the bottom towards the top and thus the water comes in contact with the atmospheric air, and is oxygenated. *Diffuser stones* are also used with aerators. These artificial stones have a number of holes through which air can bubble out.

With the help of "feeding ring", which is made up of plastic, dried foods are sprinkled in particular area of the aquarium. This equipment is made to float on the surface of the water. For feeding microworms, there is a plastic container, open at the top and has a suction cap. It can be fitted inside the aquarium. The worms can easily escape into the tank through the minute holes present at the base of the container.

To clear the glass of the aquarium, fine *steel wool* is held in the fingers by some fish-keepers. An ordinary *razor blade* is also clipped at the end of a wooden handle to serve the same purpose. The water of the aquarium should be at a constant heat and so the *electric heater* is of much use for this purpose. These heaters are made up of an element perfectly set in a glass tube and is thermostatically controlled. The heater is usually set at a temperature of 72 °F. It functions automatically. When the water temperature falls, particularly at night hours, the heater switches on but when the water is held steady at 72 °F temperature, it switches off automatically.

For the growth of vegetation in the tank, sufficient light is needed. So, the aquarium is always placed near the window in order to enable it to get direct sunlight at least for a period of two hours every day. Sometimes, electric bulb is also used to get light when sun light is not available.

A temperature round about 72° is ideal for the tropical fishes in the aquarium. There should not be much fluctuation and it should be strictly observed.

Fishes should be regularly supplied with food but excess of food should be avoided. Also, same type of food should not be always used. There should be frequent change in the nature of the food materials.

Live food in addition to plants available in the aquarium, includes daphnia, infusoria, tubifex, mosquito larvae, earthworms, brine shrimps, drosophila, microworms (e.g. *anguillula sillusiae*) etc. There are some prepared foods also e.g. eggs, potato (pieces), fish, ant eggs, cereals, shrimps (cut into pieces) and other substances. Prepared foods are also available in the form of fish food at the shops. Live food is always better in comparison to other types of food.

Precautions for an Ideal Aquarium

When the aquarium is carefully prepared, very little maintenance is required. The aquarium should not be left uncared for a long time. When the level of water falls, fresh water should be immediately added to it. Waste products should be carefully siphoned out without disturbing the fishes. Overcrowding in the aquarium should always be avoided. Minimum temperature fluctuation and sufficient light are the basic needs of the aquarium and should always be maintained. For the tropical fishes, pH of water should be about 7.0 (but for the marine forms a pH of 8.0 is suitable). The specific gravity should be 1 only. In changing the water of the aquarium a constant flow should be maintained with the help of tubes. Aerator should also be used frequently. Predators should not be allowed to enter into the aquarium. The fishes should be subjected to potassium permanganate or copper sulphate bath before keeping in the aquarium.

CHAPTER 30

SHAPES OF TAIL, MEDIAN AND PAIRED FINS

In case of fish the tail is primarily a locomotory organ and it acts effectively while the fish is moving in water and goes from one place to another. Fins are also counterbalancing organ in a few fishes. These are either paired or single and median. The pectorals and the pelvics or ventrals are the paired fins. There is great variation in shape and position of these fins in different fishes. The fin rays of bony fishes may be hard and spiny or soft. Spiny rays are seldom branched.

The unpaired fins probably arose from a primitive median fold of skin which gradually became strengthened by skeletal structures. Parts of the fold disappeared to give rise to several varieties of unpaired fins found in a large number of modern fishes. The continuous laternal body folds which later on broke up to give the broad based primitive paired fins, might have contributed in the origin of paired fins. The skeletal elements of the median and paired fins became more and more complex with the evolution of fins in fishes.

There is great variation in the endoskeleton of the paired fins in different groups of fishes. But, probably they have been derived phylogenetically from originally separate segmentally arranged *radials.* These radials of the paired fins were also originally joined like the radials of the median fin. But, they were gradually simplified and reduced to one piece as in teleost.

There are several pioneer contributions on the phylogenetic origin of fins and their skeleton, and chief among them are those of—Gegenbaur (1872, 1895), Traquair (1874, 1897), Huxley (1876), Thacher (1877), Mivart (1879), Balfour (1881), Haswell (1883), Fritsch (1883-1901), Howes (1887, 1890), Cope (1890), Woodward (1898), Mollier (1893, 1897), Goodrich (1901), Regan (1904), Budget (1902), Vogel (1909), Sewertzoff (1926), Nikolajs (1963) and others.

The shape of the tail is definitely correlated with the terminal part of the notochord or vertebral column. There are various types of Caudal fins in fishes which have been described below :

1. *Protocercal :* It is considered as ancestral type which encloses notochord or vertebral column. The fin is equally extended above and below as shown in the

figure, moreover it ends straight. This type of fin can be seen in the young larval stages of fish and adult cyclostomes.

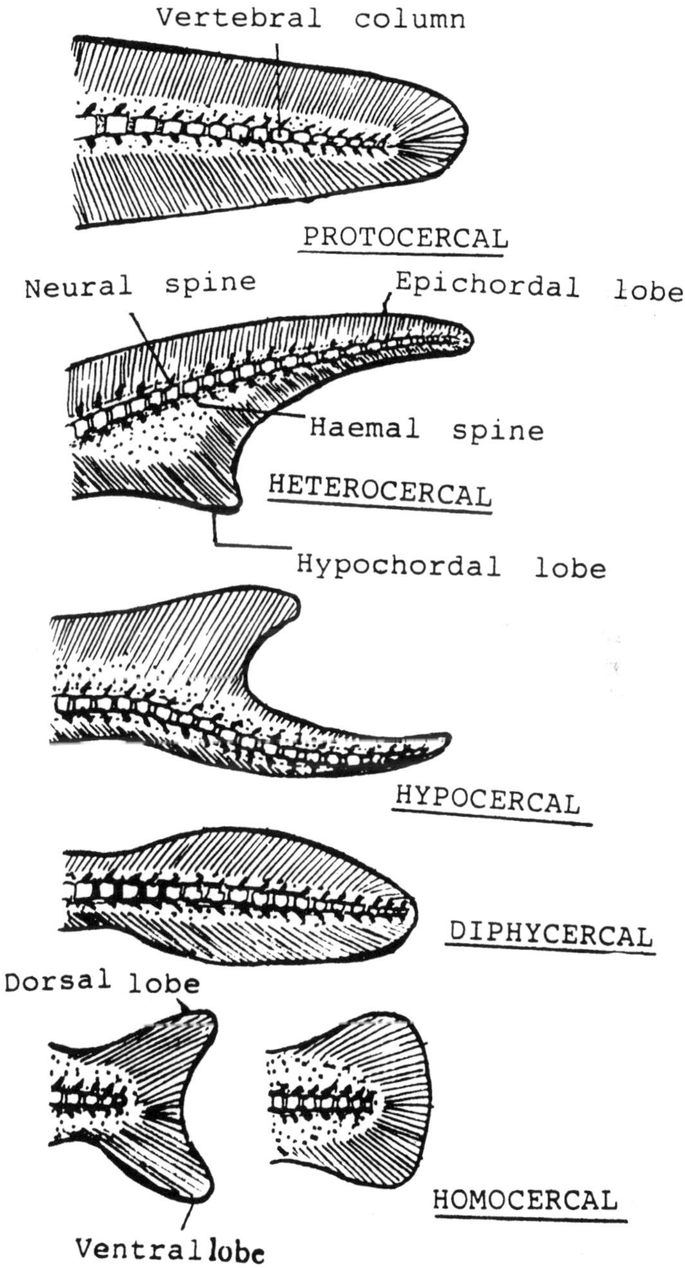

Fig. 101 : Shapes of tail and caudal fin

2. *Heterocercal* : Here the vertebral column is bent upwards and ends in the elongated upper lobe which is always longer than the lower lobe. The fishes of older groups had this type of fin (e.g. ostracoderms, but also in elasmobranchs).

3. *Hypocercal* : These are also known as *"reversed heterocercal"*. Here also, the lobes are unequal. The vertebral column ends in the lower lobe which is always longer than the upper lobe (e.g. Anaspida and some ostracoderms).

4. *Diphycercal* : The vertebral column is bent downwards. It reaches at the tip of the tail fin and both the upper and lower parts are equally developed. This type of tail fin is present in *Holocephali,* Lung fishes and some crossopterygian fishes. When a continuous median fin is formed by the union of *dorsal, anal* and *caudal* fins, the tail is spoken as *gephyrocercal.*

5. *Homocercal* : It is a symmetrical caudal fin beyond the end of the vertebral column. It is probably the lower lobe of the ancestral heterocercal tail. It can be seen in the larval stage of several teleost fishes. During development the dorsal lobe is lost, naturally, it is formed from the lower lobe.

Dermal Fin Rays : Fins are supported by rod like structure mostly parallel beneath the epidermis. These are dermal rays which may not be joined. In elasmobranch fins and rays are non-jointed flexible rods which are generally known as *Ceratotrichia.* In ray-finned fishes (actinopterygii) jointed rays are present which are derived from the rows of scales. These are called *Lepidotrichia.*

Pterygiophores : These are deeply situated bones or cartilages on which dermal rays rest. It may consist of one to three pieces but in advanced forms, fusion may take place. The separate elements are called *radials,* larger ones are called *basals.*

Paired Fins : Paired appendages of vertebrates have arisen independently as vertebrate novelties. Paired fins of lungfishes (Dipnoi) called *archipterygia* have a central axis of several bones from which corresponding sets of radials diverge towards both the margins. Many opinions have been proposed with regard to possible phylogenetic origin of fin skeleton. In the crossopterygian fins one primary radial and one or two secondary radials are present.

As revealed by Gegenbaur the original type resembled the skeleton of the pectoral and pelvic fins of *ceratodus,* the fossil dipnoan. In this *archipterygium,* the median jointed tapering axis articulated with the girdle. It was provided with a preaxial and a post axial series of fewer radials. The radials were arranged in pairs on the segments of the axis and diminished in size towards the distal extremity of the leaf like fin. Such a biserial *archipterygium* has been described as *mesorachic* and *rachistichous.* The Devonian Crossopterygii also possessed this but here the axis is short and the segments are few in number. Moreover, the post axial radials in the pectoral fin are much more reduced. Separate post axial radials are absent in *Eusthenopteron* (Goodrich, 1901). A perfect archipterygial type of endoskeleton is present in the pectoral fin of carboniferous *Pleuracanthodii.* But, the Pelvic fin had only preaxial radials attached to the axis.

As suggested by Gegenbaur the various types of paired fin skeleton found in the teleostomi may be derived from the archipterygium where, axis became shortened and finally lost and the radials were reduced in number. The post axial radials completely disappeared.

In Elasmobranch, the *rhipidostichous* type of Pectoral fin skeleton, having a fin like arrangement of radials was also deduced from *archipterygium*. It is supposed that there has been marked reduction in the axis represented by the posterior basal *metapterygium*. Large number of Preaxial radials and only few vestigial post axial radials are present. That the *archipterygium* is a very ancient type of fin skeleton is correct. Originally segmented separate and parallel radials of the paired longitudinal fin-folds became concentrated and fused at their base and thus a *'pleurorachic'* and *'monostichous'* or uniserial type of skeleton was formed.

In *Cladoselache*, the peripheral radials are parallel and unfused and the basal elements combine to form a longitudinal axis. Pelvic fin elements are quite differentiated from the girdle. In the modern *chondrostei* the pectoral fin skeleton has a posterior axis and some preaxial radials most of which are articulated in front of the girdle. There is some similarities in the Pectoral fin skeleton of *Amia* and *Acipenser*, however in the former the axis is very short and also radii are ossified. There has been much reduction in *Lepidosteus*. Thus is teleostei the axis disappeared and the radii articulate on the girdle.

In the Dipnoi both Pectoral and Pelvic fins have become biserial but in other fishes the pelvic fin is of uniserial type, the axis being freed from the body wall at the posterior end.

In *pleurocanth*, the basal pieces are separate and the girdle bears many radials. In the pelvic fin of Selachians, axial elements fuse to form *basipterygium* (exception–*Chlamydoselachus*). Very few anterior radials rest directly on the girdle.

Many theories have been proposed to explain the origin of paired fins in fishes but among them the *Gill arch theory* of Gegenbaur, *Fin fold theory* of Goodrich and *Dermal spine theory* of Gregory and Raven are important. These theories have been described in detail below :

1. *Gill Arch Theory* : This theory was proposed by Gegenbaur. According to this theory the paired fins are the modified gill structures. The Pectoral fins were formed from the anterior gill arches and the pelvic fins have been formed by posterior shifting of some of the gill arches. It has been also suggested that the girdles represent the arches, the fin fold represents the gill flap and the fin skeleton represented the gill rays. The following are the main objections raised against this theory:

(a) In the ontogeny, a paired fin is a longitudinal ridge, never making its appearance as a dorso-ventral fold.

(b) The position of the Pelvic fin is attributed to their backward shifting (migration). There is no evidence about the Pelvic fins to be more anterior, either in the primitive fishes or in their earlier fossil representatives. In certain teleosts, the pelvic fins are situated far forwards, thus the position is considered as secondary.

(c) The gill arch theory does not give satisfactory explanation for participation of large number of segments in musculature formation and nerve supply of the paired limbs.

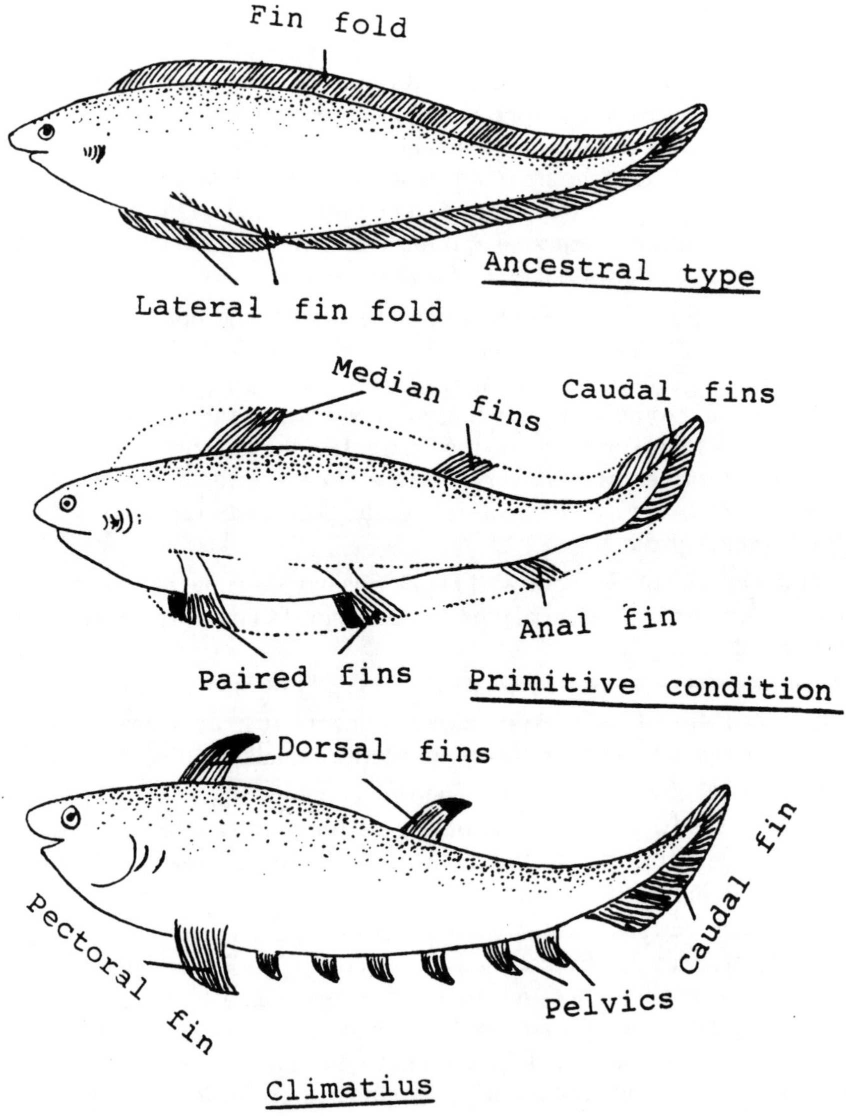

Fig. 102 : Diagrams to show origin of paired fins

(d) The rudimentary muscle buds and the presence of nerve plexus are also found at the posterior end which is not a case of backward migration.

(e) If the gill rays contribute in the formation of the skeleton of the paired fins, their muscle supply is expected from the lateral plate musculature innervated from dorsal root.

(f) The visceral arches lie in the gut wall but the girdle lies in the outer body wall.

Thus the gill arch theory has not got general acceptance.

2. *Fin-Fold Theory* : The idea of fin fold theory has been supported by Goodrich, Balfour, Thacher and Mivart. That the median and paired fins originated in early ancestors from a continuous median and two ventrolateral folds along the body is supported by the following evidences :

(a) Several muscles which are responsible for the movement of the fins are derived from many segments of the body covering towards the limb bud. Of course, original fins were extensive and some time they were continuous. Segmental muscle and nerves converge towards the growing limb from points from and behind its base.

(b) *In Cladoselache* the paired fins were broader at the base. The skeletal supports emerged parallel and quite uniformly from the base. This indicates a departure from a once continuous fold on each side. It is an additional support to the fin fold theory.

(c) Among the ancient acanthodians there were up to seven pairs of ventrolateral fins. In *Parexus* there were seven pairs of ventral fins. This suggests break up of two continuous folds.

(d) Traces of lateral fin folds may be observed in embryos of certain elasmobranchs (*scyllium*).

(e) The metapleural folds of *Branchiostoma* seem to match the aforesaid hypothetical plan. Here, a single dorsal fin continues around the tail to the ventral side as far as forward as the atriopore. Metapleural fold extends anteriorly on other side. Gaps in the dorsal fin and the metapleural folds might have resulted in the formation of median and paired fins.

(f) In the fossil *Jamoytius* the paired fins are more or less in the form of continuous folds on each side of the body.

There are some contrary arguments also, which are as follows :

(a) It is difficult to find truly primitive group where fins are continuous. In several cases (e.g. Pleurocanth Sharks and Lamprey) they fuse and make continuous median folds. But according to fossil evidence they are quite specialized and come from earlier kinds, having separate fins.

(b) In ostracoderms, the median and paired fins were spine like and short based. In acanthodians they are considered as a special multiplication of defensive spines which are not always supported by fin membrane.

(c) The idea that the broad-based fins of *Cladoselache* were specialized and not primitive was proposed by Gregory and Raven (1941). Also, they were analogous to those of rays.

(d) It is difficult to explain the change of position of the Pectoral and Pelvic fins, there is no support from ontogeny.

(e) Metapleural folds of Amphioxus develop in correlation with, and outside of the atrium; moreover, Amphioxus is no longer considered as ancestral chordate by many authors. Amphioxus has no other skeletal structure other than notochord.

(f) That the segmental muscles and the convergence of nerves towards the growing limb may be supposed to be an illusion. When the limb bud appears, it is quite large. It receives muscles from the adjacent body segments. The muscle buds and their nerves enter the limb bud adjust their rate and direction of growth to the limb. In shark, there is no question of convergence towards the limb base rather a divergence of nerves and muscles segments within the body takes place.

Thus there is an indication that fins arose in connection with median and paired spines, already established in ostracoderms. The function of the spines were defensive but later on it became locomotory. The pectoral spines acted as props in keeping the body upright at the time of resting on the bottom. A membrane or fold of skin extended out between the spine and the adjacent wall of the body later on. For effective locomotory action the internal structure of rays was essential.

3. *Dermal Spine Theory of Gregory and Raven (1941)* : According to them the paired appendages of Gnathostomes have originated from the paired appendages of ostracoderm ancestors. These archaic creatures possessed a paired row of dermal spines on the ventral side of the body. Loss of spines in other regions of the body and their retention in pectoral region and pelvic region could account for the origin of paired fins. Spiny fins were provided with muscles which helped in their movement. So, paired fins were separate elements supported by spines. The view has also been supported by Weichert (1951). The Dermal spine theory explains some anatomical facts.

There are some difficulties in accepting this hypothesis. These are :

(a) There is no embryological support to this theory. That the spines appeared first in ontogeny and then muscles, is not a suitable explanation. There is no satisfactory argument for the fact why so many buds should appear for the formation of paired median fins.

(b) That the dermal spines are regarded as a special feature developed in ostracoderms, out of necessity because they are not present in cyclostomes.

(c) The presence of spines in Pectoral and Pelvic fin is a specialized feature. Primitive teleosts and mostly soft rayed fins and dermal spines have developed in certain specialized fishes (e.g. Siluroids). If presence of spine is a primitive feature, it should have been represented in primitive teleosts and also elasmobranch.

Conclusion

Out of all the above mentioned theories the *Lateral fin fold theory* seems to be more satisfactory. It has been supported by Goodrich. Recently, Nikolajs (1963) has also supported this view, while describing the 'Evolution of Limbs in Vertebrates' (Journal of Anatomy Vol. 97, Part I).

The position of the girdles, the fins, the fin skeleton, the derivation of musculature and nerve supply from several segments are some of the evidences in favour of Lateral fin fold Theory. Also, the correlation between development and adult structure of paired and unpaired fins, and similar dermal fin rays are natural explanations in favour of this theory. The basal parts of the joined rays converge and fuse together to form larger bones but the distal rays remain separate.

CHAPTER 31

FISH AND PESTICIDES

Several pesticides create enormous pollutional problems, and there are many reports regarding their impact on fishes. Toxicity effects of several pollutants have been described by Konar (1970), Ahsan and Ahsan (1974), Chakrabarty and Konar (1974), Obeser (1975), Basak and Konar (1976), Krishna Gopal (1976), Sarkar and Das-Mahapatra (1977), Agrawal *et al.* (1978), Agrawal and Srivastava (1980), Shukla *et al.* (1981), Dawson (1982), Singh and Singh (1982), Kulshrestha and Arora (1984), Bhattacharya *et al.* (1985), Chakravarty *et al.* (1986), Agrawal and Tyagi (1987), Sarkar and Mukherjee (1989) and others.

The important pesticides which have been commonly used by various workers are Aldrin, Lead nitrate, Cadmium chloride, Zinc sulphate, Mercuric chloride, Lead arsenate, Malathion, DDT, Endosulfan, Sevin, Lithium, Manganese etc. Toxicity data are available on both lethal and sublethal concentrations. Reports are also there on the toxicity of industrial wastes. Today lethal dose (LD) and tolerance limit (TLm) for many fish species to different pesticides are also known. Observations have been made on several species of fishes (e.g. *Channa punctatus, Heteropneustes fossilis, Peecilia latipinna, Scyliorhinus canicula, Clarias batrachus, Mystus vittatus, Salmo gairdneri, Amphipnous cuchia, Tilapia mossambica,* Rainbow trout, *Fundulus heteroclitus,* Guppies etc.) under normal and experimental conditions by various workers.

Specific effects of Pesticides : Histopathological effects induced by different concentrations are on record. Pesticides effect various organs of the fish including stomach, intestine, skin, gills, liver, kidney, brain, ovary and testis. In the oesophagus, the mucosa and submucosa gradually start losing their cellular structure. Dilation and congestion of the blood vessels, infiltration of lymphocytes in the submucosa have been reported. Degenerative changes in the longitudinal muscles and extensive fibrosis of circular muscle fibres have also been reported by some workers.

In the stomach the mucous folds become flat and the epithelial lining becomes homogenous and necrosed. Superficial ulceration and glandular atrophy have also been reported. Inflammatory cell response in the submucosa and muscular area have been observed. There are clear signs of degeneration of the gastric glands.

Marked increase in the number of pepsinogen granules are also on record. Loss of serosa at certain places has been reported. Ulceration of the pyloric stomach and almost complete denudation of the columnar epithelial lining of mucosal fold have also been reported in certain cases. Sometimes, particularly in the higher concentration of the pollutant, the mucosa, submucosa and muscularis become homogenous, losing all the cellular details. Haemorrhage at certain places may be seen. Also, increase in the number of mucous secreting goblet cells in the beginning, following the treatment of lower concentration of the pollutants have also been reported.

In the intestine also, partial atrophy is very common following treatment of the pollutants. There may be some reduction in the size of the villi. In certain cases, swelling of the villi has also been reported. Necrosis of mucosa and inflammatory cell response have been marked in the submucosa. Degenerative changes at several places have been seen.

In the liver, hyperplasia, fatty infiltration, vascular dilation and congestion, extrusion of nuclear materials loss of cell boundaries, displacement, disintegration and degeneration of nucleus, vacuolation, and glycogen depletion are important effects of pollutants.

Some changes have been reported in the testis and ovary of the fish following treatment of various concentrations of the pollutants which are evident from the histological picture of the glands. Damage of the endothelium of the capillaries, degeneration of the spermatogenetic stages, vacuolation of cytoplasm, testicular necrosis and fibrosis of testicular components have been reported. Androgen synthesis is much affected. In the ovary also, the oocytes show clumping of cytoplasmic materials, atrophy in the oocytes, fibrosis of the ovarian mass and retardation of developmental processes have also been observed.

The toxicants can affect the kidneys of the fish also. Shrinkage of glomerular tuft, reduction in the diameter of the kidney tubules, vacuolation of the cells of the tubules, necrosis and rupturing of glomerular wall and tubules are also on record.

In the skin, disappearance of mucous cells, destruction of epidermal cells, detachment of epidermis, reduction in the melanophore area and some other types of deformities have been reported.

In the gills also, several histophysiological effects have been observed following their contact with the pollutants. Some of these effects are disintegration of epidermal cells, coagulation of blood cells, necrosis of epithelial and most cells, excessive mucous secretion etc. All these effects gradually decrease the respiratory efficiency of the fish.

Organochlorinated pesticides can produce more severe effects on the gills than carbamate or organophosphorus pesticides. Because of continuous pollution of water bodies, fishes become sluggish and the rate of respiration becomes low, and as a result fishes ultimately die in certain cases.

Concluding remarks : The use of pesticides has become a controversial matter today. Some of them have been declared as 'hazardous' by WHO. Some of the pesticides have been banned in many countries e.g. *Methyl parathion* and *Hepatochlor* have been banned in U.S.A. and U.K. To impose a total ban on the pesticides is not possible, because, they are largely used for agricultural purposes. Fish can be used to determine the quality of water and the farmers can be benefited with the idea of pollutions caused by pesticides. This concept may be of some use in paddy-cum-fish culture.

CHAPTER 32

SOME PRELIMINARY METHODS IN FISHERY SCIENCE STUDY

Fresh fishes are first fixed in 10 per cent formaline i.e. one part 40 per cent commercial formaline and nine parts water. Small and delicate specimens can be fixed in 5 per cent formaline also. Sometimes ethyl alcohol (70 per cent) is also used as fixative for such types of fishes.

For the purpose of measuring different parts of the fish accurately, fine needle-like dividers, dial reading callipers, stainless steel ruler (with millimeter measurements), measuring boards or meters etc. are often used. If the measurement is not correct all calculations will give wrong results which may offend international acceptance with regard to certain parameters.

Body Measurements of a Fish

Total length of the fish : The total length means the maximum elongation of the body from end to end. Thus, from the most anterior projecting part of the head to the posterior most tip (or caudal fin) is included in the total length. When the jaws are unequal, mouth is first closed and then the longer jaw is included in the measurement. When the caudal fin is forked, the tip of the lower lobe is used in measuring the distance. The measurement is a straight line and it is never taken over the curves of the body.

Standard Length : This is the distance from the anteriormost part of the head to the end of the vertebral column i.e. up to the base of the caudal fin where the median fin rays meet the hypural plate.

Body depth : The distance between the dorsal surface where its height is greatest, to a straight line to the ventral surface or profile excluding the fleshy or scaly parts pertaining to fin bases.

Head length : It is a straight measurement of the distance from the tip of the snout up to the posteriormost edge of the opercular bone. But, the spinous projection, if any, is excluded.

Head depth (height of head) : It is the perpendicular distance which is measured from the midline at the back of head vertically downwards to the vertical contour of the head. It is never taken up to ventral profile line.

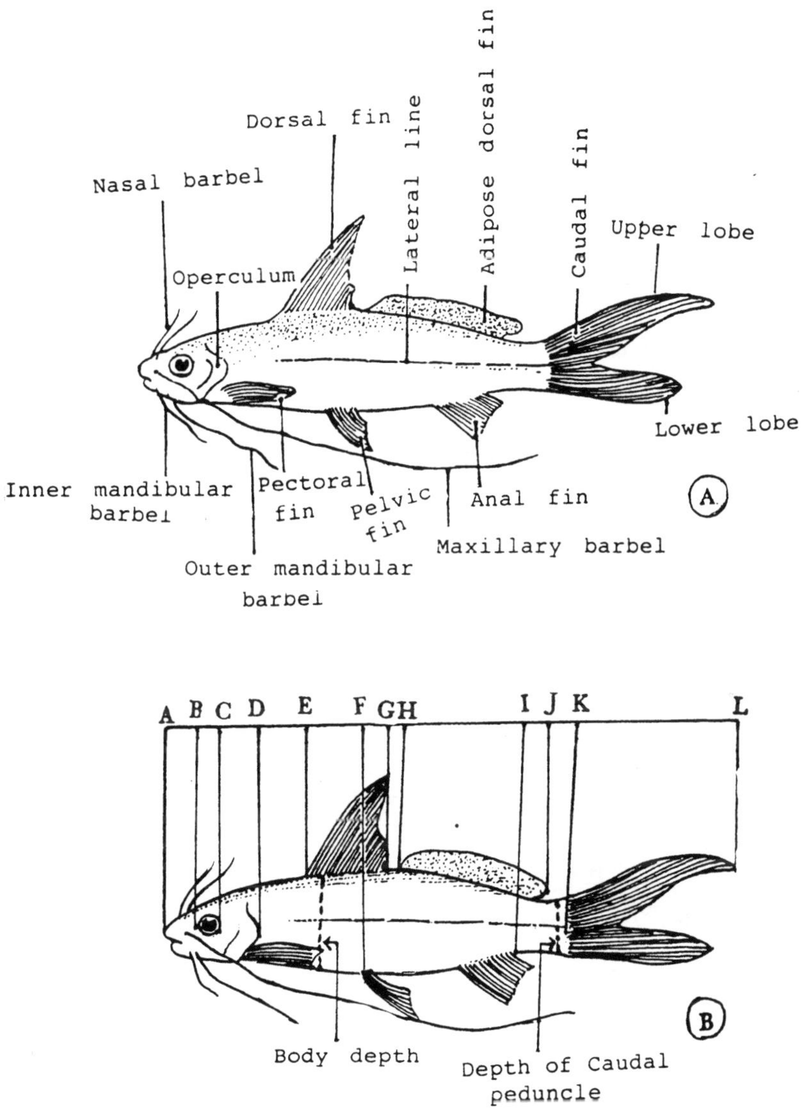

Fig. 103 : Mystus cavasius

(A) showing important parts (B) showing body measurements

AB—Snout length, CD—Postorbital length AD—Head length,

AE—Predorsal length, AF—Prepelvic distance, AK—Standard length,

AL—Total length, BC—Eye diameter

EG—Width of dorsal fin (Length of base of dorsal fin),

GH—Distance between rayed dorsal fin and adipose dorsal fin,

HJ—Length of base of adipose dorsal fin.

Head width: It is the greatest distance across the head with gill covers held in the normal position.

Eye diameter: It is the distance between margins of the eye ball across the cornea.

Snout length: Straight distance between the anteriormost part of the snout or the upper lip (whichever is extending farthest forward) to the front hard margin of the orbit.

Interorbital width : It is the least distance between the two orbits.

Gape width : The greatest distance of the mouth opening when the mouth is closed—is called the gape width.

Predorsal length : It is the straight measurement from the mid-point of the anteriormost part of the head or tip of the snout or upper lip to the base of the first dorsal fin ray.

Postdorsal Length : It is a straight measurement from the structural base of the dorsal fin to the end of the vertebral column.

Pelvic distance : It is a straight distance from the mid-point of the anteriormost part of the head to the base of the pelvic fin (anterior point).

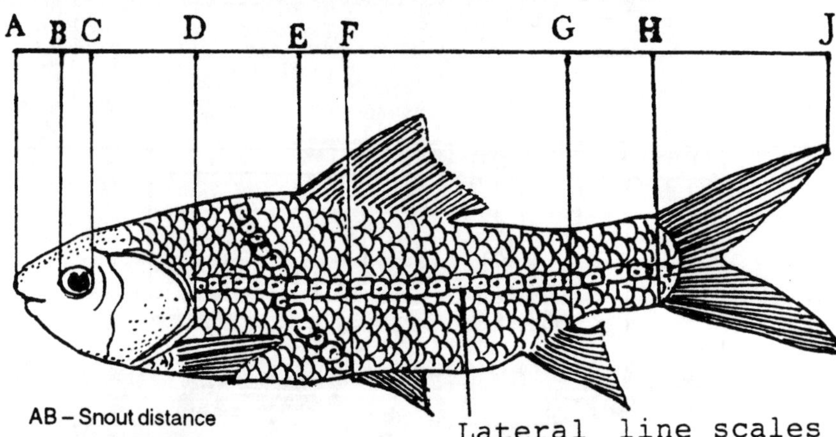

AB – Snout distance
GH – Length of the Caudal peduncle
AJ – Total length
AE – Predorsal length
EH – Post-dorsal length
AF – Prepelvic distance
CD – Post-orbital length

Fig. 104 : Different body measurements of *Labeo rohita*

Length of Pectoral and Pelvic fins : It is the distance from the origin or point of insertion into the body, to the extreme tip of the fins.

Depth of Caudal peduncle : It is the straight measurement of the least vertical distance from the dorsal to ventral profile at the narrowest part of the caudal peduncle.

Length of the Caudal Peduncle : It is the measurement of the area extending between the base (Posterior) of the anal fin up to the end of the vertebral column i.e. base of the caudal fin.

Important Counts

Fin rays : Long and mobile filamentous prolongations in all the paired and median fins of the bony fishes are called rays. Movements of the fins depend on the articulations and flexibility of the rays. The term 'ray' also applies to spines irrespective of its inclusion within the membrane. There are three different types of fin rays :

Soft ray :	These are very thin, flexible and often branched.
Hard ray :	These are formed by solid union of soft rays. Hard rays are rigid and they may be sharply pointed. They are cartilaginous in nature. In sisorids, the rays are very hard.
Spinous rays :	These are bony in nature and they are much harder and stronger than rays. They lack membranous covering. They possess serrations or teeth. These are commonly found in cat-fishes.

Simple ray : There is no branching either at the tip or at any other place. In the anal fin they have membranous covering and are teased out for study.

Branched ray : These rays are branched either at the base or in the middle or at the tip.

Rudimentary ray : These rays are not properly developed.

Caudal fin rays : They have principal and branched rays which are separately counted.

Pectoral and Pelvic fin rays : Even the smallest one at the inner end of the fin base is counted. At the time of counting, magnification is required.

Branchiostegal rays : Right from the lower edge of the opercle to the ventral surface of the head, there are several tiny thin bones arranged fanwise. These are branchiostegal rays covered by the branchiostegal membrane. The most anterior branchiostegal rays are very short.

Fin ray count : The fin ray formulae express counting of fin rays in different fins of the body. Dorsal fin is generally expressed by the symbol D, anal fin by A, Pectoral fin by P, Ventral fin by V, and Caudal fin by C. The number of spines is expressed by the roman numerals and for expressing the number of soft rays, arabic numerals are used. If we write D XI, 12 then it means that the dorsal fin has eleven spines and twelve soft rays.

Scale Counts : The number of scales along the lateral line and also in the transverse row above and below it on each side is expressed by the scale formula. If we write $80^5/_7$, it would mean that there are eighty scales in the lateral line, five scales above it and seven scales below it. The lateral line count expresses the maximum number of scales in the lateral line. The scales are distinguished by their perforated nature. Scales above the lateral line scales fall along the line which starts from the origin of the dorsal fin and runs downward and backward to meet the lateral line. Similarly the scales below the lateral line fall along the line which starts from the origin of the anal fin and runs upward and forward to reach the lateral line.

Trunk circumference scale count : It denotes the number of scale rows that will cross the circumference line of the body at the level of the dorsal fin.

Caudal peduncle scale count : It expresses the number of scale rows crossing the circumference line of the body at the level of the narrowest part of the caudal peduncle.

Condition Factor

Condition factor of fish is expressed by relating the length of the fish to its weight. The condition factor is calculated in a simple way by the formula :

$$K = \frac{W}{L^3} \times 100$$

(Here K is the Coefficient of Condition, W = weight of fish in gm; and L = standard length of fish in cm).

Higher values of K always indicate well being of the fish. Lower values will mean that the fish are in poor condition. Lower values always reflect overpopulation, diseased condition and scarcity of suitable food.

According to 'Cube *Law*' the weight of the fish equals the cube of length times a constant. Mathematically, $W = aL^3$, where W = weight, L = length and 'a' is constant. Le Cren (1951) has reviewed this cube parabola. The general parabolic equation is mathematically expressed as :

$$W = cL^n$$

Here, W = weight of the fish (gm)

L = length of the fish (mm)

c = a constant

n = an exponent

The equation $W = cL^n$ is calculated in its logarithmic forms as :

$$\log W = \log c + n \log L.$$

Fecundity : Fecundity is considered as the number of eggs produced in one year. Fecundity is high where the eggs are liberated in to open marine waters, but it is lower in freshwater forms and also, where there is parental care. Fecundity and egg size tend to be inversely related. *Absolute fecundity* is defined as the number of eggs in the ovaries of an individual fish that are ripening for the ensuing spawning period. The term *relative* fecundity expresses the number of eggs per unit length or weight of fish. Several authors believe that fecundity increases with length, weight or age. In the formula $F = aL^b$; F is fecundity, L is the length and 'a' and 'b' are constants.

Estimation of number of eggs : Mature ovary (entire) is taken and carefully preserved in 5 per cent formaline. The volume of the ovarian mass is determined by water displacement method. The ovary is then cut into, say, three segments. The volume of each segment is determined. The mature eggs are then segregated from other eggs and ovarian tissues. The volumes of the latter two are measured separately and the volume of the mature eggs is determined as such. The matured eggs are counted. This experiment is done with the two remaining sample segments. Thus the number of eggs can be calculated. When the ovary is voluminous, it may be divided into desired number of segments for convenience.

The methods are generally employed for counting of laid eggs :

Volumetric method : A sample of say 100 eggs (n) from the unknown lot of eggs is taken. Excess of water is removed by blotting and the total volume (v) of these eggs is determined by water displacement method. The whole lot of eggs including the sample are dried and the total volume (V) is obtained. The total number of eggs in the lot (X) is now estimated as follows :

$$X : n = V : v$$

Von Bayer's method : In this method, first of all, average diameter of eggs is obtained with the help of graduated trough. Now, the number of eggs per c.c. of the lot is directly read from the Von Bayer's table. The total number of eggs for the whole lot is estimated after finding out the total volume of the lot.

Related Terminology

Oviparous : Those fishes which lay eggs are called oviparous fishes. Fertilization may be external or internal but the eggs hatch externally.

Ovoviviparous : When the eggs hatch internally and the young ones are not nourished by the mother, the fishes are called ovoviviparous.

Viviparous : Fishes in which eggs hatch internally and the young ones get nourishment from the mother till their expulsion from the uterus, are known as viviparous. These fishes are also known as live bearers.

Planktonic eggs : These are passively floating and drifting eggs, as in the case of mackerel and sardine.

Semibuoyant eggs : These eggs neither float nor perfectly settle on the bottom, as in shad.

Demersal eggs : When the eggs sink to the bottom and settle near the bottom, they are known as demersal eggs.

There are five important terms related to spawning manner which have been suggested by Kryzhanovsky (1949). These are :

Phytophils : Those fishes which lay their eggs in aquatic vegetation are known as Phytophils (e.g. Carp).

Lithophils : Fishes which spawn on hard surfaces, particularly that of stones (e.g. Salmon).

Ostracophils: Fishes which deposit their eggs inside a bivalve (mollusc), for example — Bitterling.

Psammophils : Those fishes which deposit their eggs in sandy surfaces are known as Psammophils (e.g. Loaches).

Pelagophils : Those fishes which spawn freely in column of water and the eggs usually float—are known as Pelagophils (e.g. Cod).

Spent individuals : Fishes which have spawned are known as spend individuals. Gonads in these fishes become almost empty, however, residual gamets may be present.

Gonosomatic Index : The development of gonads is estimated by determining its weight relative to the body weight of the fish. This can be expressed as follows :

$$G.S.I. = \frac{\text{Weight of the gonad}}{\text{Weight of the fish}} \times 100$$

Prominent Discoverers of Fish Species

Annandale	Jordon	Rechardson
Bleeker	Kulkarni	Schneider
Bloch	Lacépéde	Scopoli
Blyth	Le Sueur	Silas
Chaudhuri	Linnaeus	Shaw
Cuvier	Mc Clelland	Smith
Davis	Muller	Steindachner
Day	Misra	Swainson
Deraniyagala	Mirza	Sykes
Filippi	Mukherji	Tilak
Fowler	Nalbant	Vandeli
Gray	Nilsson	Van Hasselt
Gill	Oshima	Valenciennes
Gunther	Pallas	Vinciguerra
Hamilton	Peters	Walker
Heckel	Raj	Whitley
Hora	Rao	Wu
Jayaram	Regan	Yazdani
Jerdon		

CHAPTER 33

SOME COMMON FRESH WATER FISHES OF INDIA

In this chapter some very common freshwater fishes of India have been described with their latest classification, diagnostic features, distribution and fin formula in most of the cases. 41 genera and 57 species have been taken into consideration. Some of the fishes are originally marine forms but they have now adapted freshwater habitat. Such fishes have also been described. Some of the exotic fishes have also been described in this chapter. Name of the discoverer has been mentioned in each case along with the name of the fish species.

Description

No. 1 *Channa punctatus* (Bloch)
Channa marulius (Hamilton)
Channa striatus (Bloch)

Systematic position:

Phylum	—	Chordata
Sub-Phylum	—	Vertebrata
Class	—	Pisces
Sub-Class	—	Teleostomi
Super-order	—	Acanthopterygii
Order	—	Channiformes
Family	—	Channidae

Diagnosis: They are commonly known as *"snake heads"*. These are elongated scaly fishes, the head having large shield like scales above. Abdomen is rounded and the head is slightly depressed. Mouth is large and protractile extending below orbit sometimes. Dorsal and anal fins are elongated but these are spineless. The caudal fin is separate and round in shape. Eyes are lateral and moderate in size. Jaws are equal. Teeth are present on jaws and palate. Accessory respiratory organs are present in the form of folded linings in the paired cavities on the roof of the pharynx.

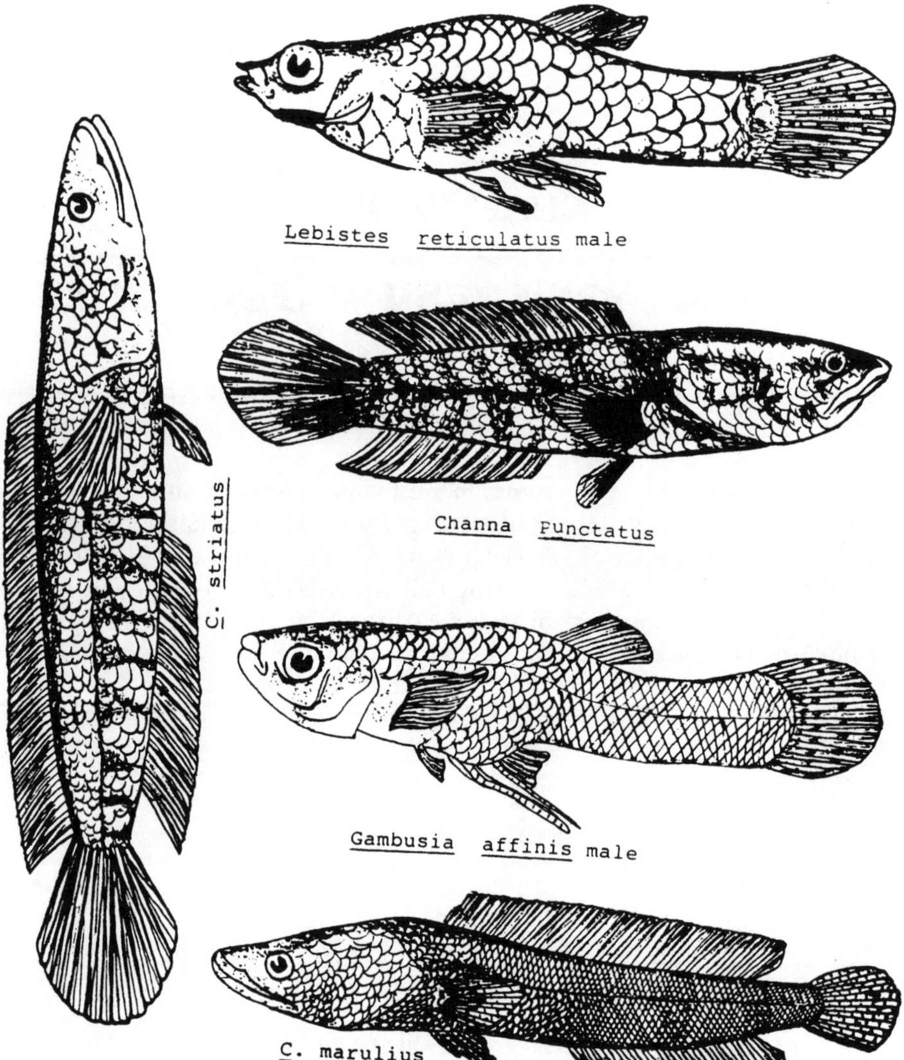

Fig. 105 : Fishes of the Orders: Channiformes and Atheriniformes

Channa punctatus of the muddly streams are greenish brown above and yellowish below in colour. In brackish waters they may exhibit purple colour. A dark variety with black spots are also present. In this species, Pelvic fin has more than half length of Pectoral fin. Also, 15-16 predorsal scales are present. The length is 11-31 cms. These are carnivorous.

Channa marulius can be stocked in wells. They feed on kitchen refuse, frog and dead animals. They attend a length of 30 cm. in one year. On the basal portion of the caudal fin a white-edged ocellus is present.

The pelvic is less than half in length of pectoral fin. Pectoral fins have darker and lighter patches at certain zones.

Channa striatus has dark-brown or black colour in the upper part of the body but in the lower part the colour is orange or yellowish. They are carnivorous fishes. There are 18-29 Predorsal scales. The length is 30-35 cms.

Distribution: These species are distributed throughout India, Nepal, Bangladesh, Pakistan, Sri Lanka, China, Burma, Malaya, Thailand, Philippines and some other places.

Fin Formula

C. punctatus:

$D_{29\text{-}30'}$ $P_{16\text{-}17}$ $V_{6'}$ $A_{20\text{-}22'}$ $C_{12'}$ $LI_{35\text{-}37'}$ $Ltr_{4\text{-}5/7}$

C. marulius:

$D_{46'}$ $P_{18'}$ $V_{6'}$ $A_{32'}$ $LI_{65\text{-}66'}$ $Ltr_{6/11}$

C. striatus:

$D_{41\text{-}43'}$ $P_{16\text{-}18'}$ $V_{6'}$ $A_{24\text{-}25'}$ C_{10} $LI_{56\text{-}60'}$ $Ltr_{7/10}$

Note

Channa gachua is a synonym of the species *C.orientalis*. Here, the anal fin has 21-23 rays. There is no black spots on scales. Dorsal fin has 32-37 rays. Lateral line curves downwards after *12th* scale.

Fin formula

$D_{32\text{-}37'}$ $P_{15\text{-}16'}$ $A_{21\text{-}23'}$ $C_{12'}$ $LI_{41\text{-}45'}$ $Ltr_{4/7}$

Other important species of the family *Channidae* are:

C. leucopunctatus (Sykes), *C. stewartii* (Playfair), and *C. pseudomarulius* (Günther).

No. 2 *Gambusia affinis patruelis* (Baird and Girard)

Systematic Position

Phylum	—	Chordata
Sub-Phylum	—	Vertebrata
Class	—	Pisces
Sub-Class	—	Teleostomi
Super-Order	—	Atherinomorpha
Order	—	Atheriniformes
Family	—	Poecilidae

Diagnosis: It is a larvivorous exotic fish with cylindrical and compressed body. The abdomen is rounded. The head is short and the snout is pointed. The mouth is small and oblique. The cleft does not extend to the orbit. The eyes are present in the centre of the head. Upper jaw is short and the lower jaw is slightly turned upwards. There is absence of teeth on the palate. In case of male the dorsal fin is present in the middle of the body. In females, this fin is present mid-way between the front margin of the eye and tip of the caudal fin. The dorsal fin has 6-12 rays and the anal fin has 8-10 rays. The anal fin in male has a longer process which distinguishes it from the female.

The shape of the Caudal fin is round and the number of lateral line scales varies from 28-32 only. This fish is also known as mosquito fish because of its liking for mosquito-larvae. This fish is generally $2^1/_2$-3" in length.

Gambusia punctata (Poey) is another important species.

Distribution: Now it is found in India, Pakistan, Sri Lanka, Bangladesh, Thailand, Burma, Philippines, Malaya, Hawai, Coastal waters of United States and Formosa.

No. 3 *Lebistes reticulatus* (Peters)

Systematic Position

Phylum	—	Chordata
Sub-Phylum	—	Vertebrata
Class	—	Pisces
Sub-class	—	Teleostomi
Super Order	—	Atherinomorpha
Order	—	Atheriniformes
Family	—	Poecilidae

Diagnosis: This fish resembles very much with *Gambusia* but in this case the *movable spatuliform teeth* are present. Eyes are big and situated on the dorsal profile of the head. Caudal fin is elongated. The length of the anal fin rays is almost equal to the length of gonopodium (in males). Black spots or some other brilliant coloured patches are present on the body. Functional hermaphroditism has been reported in *Lebistes*. *Lebistes* has been reported to be self-fertilizing. This fish was introduced in India from South Africa in as early as 1908. It is also a larvivorous fish like *Gambusia*.

Distribution: Originally it was found only in tropical America but now it has been introduced into India. It is now well established in certain parts of Tamil Nadu and Maharashtra.

No. 4 *Xenentodon cancila* (Hamilton)

Systematic Position

Phylum	—	Chordata
Sub-Phylum	—	Vertebrata
Class	—	Pisces
Sub-class	—	Teleostomi
Super Order	—	Atherinomorpha
Order	—	Atheriniformes
Family	—	Belonidae

Diagnosis: Body is sub-cylindrical, stout and compressed. The abdomen is rounded and the head is pointed. Snout is also sharply pointed. The fish is greenish grey above but whitish below. Silvery streak with dark margin extends along the body from orbit to middle of caudal base. The upper part of the body is distinct by the presence of black dots. Eyes are moderate but superior in position. In the adult fish, both the jaws are prolonged into a beak. Along the upper surface of the head, there is a deep longitudinal groove. The lower jaw is slightly larger in size. Jaws are provided with a row of sharp and widely separated teeth which are larger in size. An external row of numerous fine teeth are also present particularly on the lower jaw. Dorsal fin is inserted just above the anal fin and there are 15-18 rays and no spine. Anal fin has 15-19 rays. Caudal fin is truncate. The lateral line is visible on the posterior half of the body. The scales are irregularly arranged. The fish is good for eating.

Distribution: They are found in India, Pakistan, Nepal, Sri Lanka, Bangladesh, Malaya, Burma and Thailand.

Fin Formula

$D_{16\text{-}17'}\ P_{11'}\ V_{6'}\ A_{17'}\ C_{15}$

No. 5 *Zenarchopterus* (Hemiramphus) *dispar* (Valenciennes)
Z.ectuntio (Hamilton)

Systematic Position

Phylum	—	Chordata
Sub-Phylum	—	Vertebrata
Class	—	Pisces
Sub-class	—	Teleostomi
Super Order	—	Atherinomorpha
Order	—	Atheriniformes
Family	—	Hemiramphidae

Diagnosis: Fishes have much elongated body, sub-cylindrical and laterally compressed. The lower jaw is prolonged into long slender beak bearing a sensitive fringe. The upper jaw is short and more or less triangular. The head and snout are pointed. The mouth is superior and wide. Teeth are villiform on jaws. Dorsal fin is inserted for back and has 11 to 14 rays and no spine. Anal fin has 10-12 rays. In males, 6th and other rays may be modified. They are much elongated. The anal fin may be separated into 1-3 distinct parts. The caudal fin is rounded and truncate. It is nerve forked. The lateral line is complete with up to 50 scales. In Z. *ectuntio,* the triangular part of upper jaw is longer than wide. In Z.*dispar,* the snout is uniformly brown in colour. In males of this species one or two dorsal rays are thick and elongated. Also in males, either in 3rd and 4th or 4th and 5th, 6th and 7th anal rays are much elongated. It is an important food fish.

Distribution: They are found in India, Sri Lanka, Philippines, Burma, Thailand and Malay.

Other important species are:

Z. *brachynotopterus* (Bleeker), Z. *buffonis* (Valenciennes).

No. 6 *Macrognathus aculeatus* (Bloch)

Systematic Position

Phylum	—	Chordata
Sub-Phylum	—	Vertebrata
Class	—	Pisces
Sub-Class	—	Teleostomi
Super Order	—	Acanthopterygii
Order	—	Mastacembeliformes
Family	—	Mastacembelidae

Diagnosis: It is generally greenish or brownish grey in colour but in the ventral side it is yellowish or lighter. The body is eel-like, elongated and compressed. The head is long and pointed. Jaws are unequal, the lower jaw being shorter. The snout is long and fleshy and it accommodates a concave prolongation of the upper jaw. Mouth is inferior, eyes are small and superior. Small teeth are present on both jaws and also on the extension of the upper jaw, particularly at the segmented area. Teeth are also present on the palate and vomer. Preorbital spines are absent. There is no gill-racker. The dorsal fin is inserted far behind. Caudal fin is rounded. Dorsal and anal fins are not confluent. Spines are present in the first dorsal fin. The last spine is as long as first to third spines. Pectoral fin is very short and the ventral fin is absent. There are three anal spines, second one being the longest and the strongest. Scales are cycloid. These are smaller in size, present between and around eyes and posterior nostril. Air bladder is elongated and the lateral line is present. This fish is edible.

Distribution: India, Pakistan, Bangladesh, Sri Lanka, Nepal, Thailand, Vietnam and Malay Archipelago.

Fin formula

$D_{18\text{-}22/47\text{-}48}$, P_{19}, $A_{3/46\text{-}50}$, C_{15}, $Vert_{18/30}$

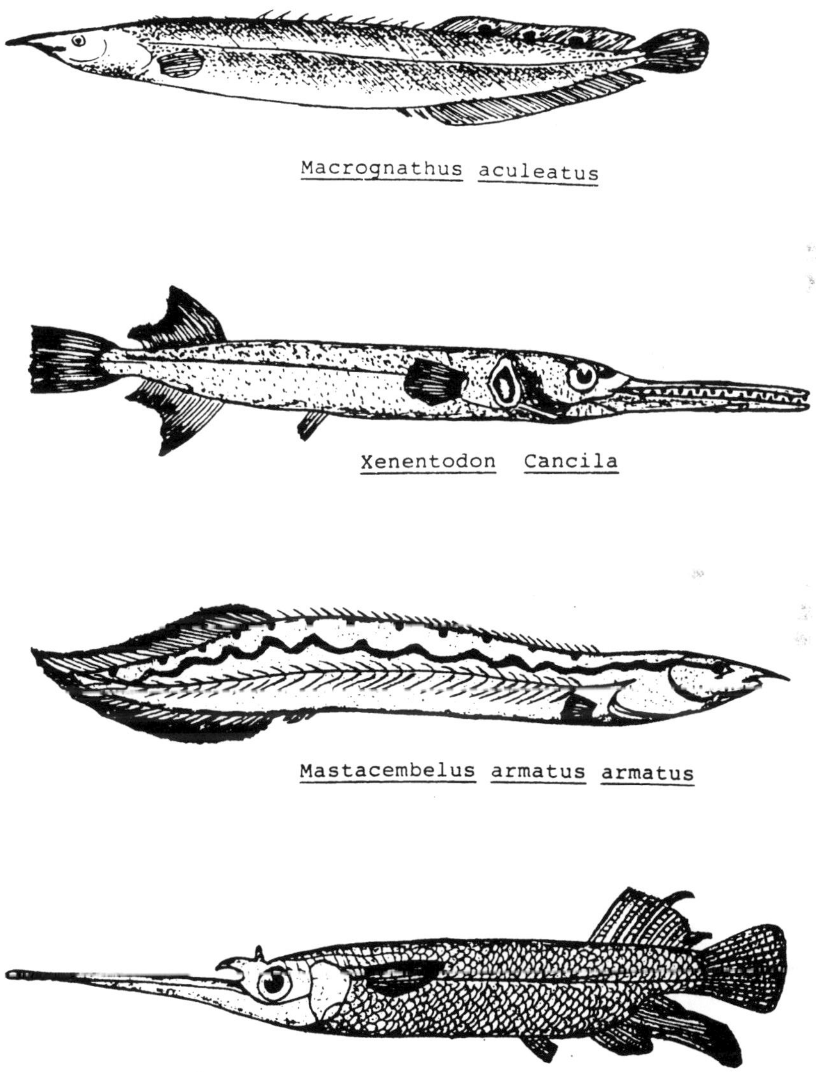

Fig. 106: Fishes of the orders: Atheriniformes and Mastacembeliformes

No. 7 *Mastacembelus armatus armatus* (Lacépéde)

Systematic Position

Phylum	—	Chordata
Sub-Phylum	—	Vertebrata
Class	—	Pisces
Sub-Class	—	Teleostomi
Super Order	—	Acanthopterygii
Order	—	Mastacembeliformes
Family	—	Mastacembelidae

Diagnosis: This fish is of rich brown colour above, and paler below. There is a black or dark brown irregular zigzag pattern between the dorsal ridge and the lateral line. The body is fairly elongated and eel-shaped. The dorsal spines commence over the middle of the pectoral fin. They increase in size from anterior to posterior. The dorsal fin is confluent with anal fin in most of the cases and, the caudal fin is rounded. The ventral fin is absent. Scales are present and the air bladder is elongated.

Jaws are unequal. Teeth are very minute and they are present on jaws and palate. Preopercle is spiny at its base. A preorbital spine may not be present. This fish is quite good for eating. In some specimens some dark spots may be present in a row in the dorsal part of the body.

Distribution: These are distributed in India,Pakistan, China, Nepal, Sri Lanka, Bangladesh, Burma, Malay Archipelago and some west African countries.

Fin formula

$D_{37-39/78-82'}$ $P_{23-25,}$ $A_{3/75-78}$

Some other species belonging to *Mastacembelidae* are:

M. alboguttatus (Boulenger), *M. caudiocellatus* (Boulenger), *M. guentheri* (Day), *M. pancalus* (Ham.), *M. unicolor* (Valenciennes) and *M. zebrinus* (Blyth).

No. 8 *Monopterus (Amphipnous) cuchia* (Hamilton)

Systematic Position

Phylum	—	Chordata
Sub-Phylum	—	Vertebrata
Class	—	Pisces
Sub-Class	—	Teleostomi
Super Order	—	Acanthopterygii
Order	—	Synbranchiformes
Family	—	Synbranchiade

Diagnosis: The body is elongated, eel-shaped and compressed posteriorly. The gill opening is present in the form of a slit. Scales are very minute and are arranged in longitudinal rows. Mouth is wide. It is a carnivorous fish of muddy water and frequently burrows in soil. Now and then, it emerges at the surface of water to gulp air (being an air-breathing form). The dorsal fin is very much reduced. The skin is glandular. The first pair of valved nostrils open just above the orbit but the second pair is located in front of the snout. Lips are quite fleshy. Teeth are present on the Premaxillae, Palatine and lower jaw. Teeth on the palatine are backwardly directed. The fish is dark brown in colour. The dorsal and anal fins are rudimentary and are just a fold of skin. The caudal tip is bluntly rounded. The gill openings are triangular without lateral folds. The lateral line is well developed.

Distribution: It has been reported from North-Eastern India, Bangaldesh, Pakistan, Burma and Nepal.

Other species are: *M. albus* (Zuiew), *M. fossorius* (Nayar) and *M. indicus* (Silas and Dawson).

No. 9 *Notoptarus Chitala* (Hamilton)
N. notopterus (Pallas)

Systematic Position

Phylum	—	Chordata
Sub-Phylum	—	Vertebrata
Class	—	Pisces
Sub-Class	—	Teleostomi
Super Order	—	Osteoglossomorpha
Order	—	Osteoglossiformes
Family	—	Notopteridae

Diagnosis: The body is oblong, laterally compressed and deep and it is covered with overlapping scales. The dorsal fin is small. Anal fin is absent. The caudal fin is not forked. The minute scales are devoid of photophores. Barbels are absent in the family notopteridae. Eyes are moderate in size. Teeth are present on Premaxillae, Maxilla, Vomer, Palatine and Pterygoid. Tongue is also provided with teeth. Pharyngeal teeth are absent. *Notopterus chitala* has strongly humped dorsal profile and it gradually declines from the front to the tail. Snout is prominent. There are two distinct spines one on either side of the throat. Gape of mouth extends beyond hind edge of orbit. The body is brown or greyish along narrow back having fifteen silvery transverse bars meeting across dorsal ridge. The body of *Notopterus notopterus* is silvery white with fine grey spots which are dark, along narrow back. The gape of mouth does not extend beyond hind edge of orbit. This fish is relished in both fresh and dried conditions.

Distribution: N. chitala is commonly found in India, Pakistan, Burma, Bangladesh and some other places. *Notopterus notopterus* is found in Nepal, Thailand, Malaya and Indonesia in addition to India, Pakistan, Burma and Bangladesh.

Fin formula

N. chitala:

$D_{9(1/8)'}\ P_{16'}\ A_{110\text{-}118'}\ C_{12'}\ LI_{160\text{-}180}$

N. notopterus:

$D_{8(1/7)'}\ P_{17'}\ V_{6'}\ A_{100'}\ C_{19'}\ LI_{225'}\ Vert_{30/60}$

No. 10 *Syngnathus argyostictus* (Kaup)

Systematic Position

Phylum	—	Chordata
Sub-Phylum	—	Vertebrata
Class	—	Pisces
Sub-Class	—	Teleostomi
Super Order	—	Acanthopterygii
Order	—	Gasterosteiformes
Family	—	Syngnathidae

Diagnosis: The body is elongated and has distinct ridges. The abdomen is rounded. There is no spiny dorsal fin. Ventral and caudal fins are either reduced or completely absent. Anal fin is minute with one or two rays. Brood pouch is present in male which has longitudinal opening. The snout is cylindrical. There is a prominent median spinous Keel on the dorsal surface of the snout. Jaws are produced in the form of a beak. Teeth are absent on the jaws and palate. There is no barbel. Lateral line is complete. Superior cristae of trunk and tail are not continuous. Snout is longer than remaining part of the head. The trunk has seven longitudinal series of pearly ocelli. These fishes secondarily enter fresh water and are of very little economic importance.

Distribution: They have been reported from Madras, Goa and some other places in India.

S. spicifer (Rüppel) is the another important species.

No. 11 *Tetraodon cutcutia* (Hamilton)
Tetraodon fluviatilis (Hamilton)

Systematic Position

Phylum	—	Chordata
Sub-Phylum	—	Vertebrata
Class	—	Pisces
Sub-Class	—	Teleostomi
Super Order	—	Acanthopterygii
Order	—	Tetraodontiformes
Family	—	Tetraodontidae

Diagnosis: The body is short and the back is broad or it is compressed into a ridge. The head is oval, snout blunt, and the abdomen is rounded. Mouth is terminal and transverse. Lips are thick and fleshy. One or two nostrils are present on each side. Both the jaws have a median suture. The dorsal fin is inserted above slightly ahead of the anal fin. The ventral fin is absent. The caudal fin is emerginate or truncate or rounded. Body is partially or completely covered with dermal spines which may be absent in certain cases. The air-bladder is horse-shoe-shaped. The oesophagus can be dilated and the fish looks like globe. In *Tetraodon cutcutia* a simple nasal cavity is present. Body is devoid of spines. The upper surface of the body is greenish black but the ventral surface is white. Nostril is a single orifice, situated in a very short simple tube. In this species the back is broad and tapers towards the tail. Interorbital space is broad. In *T.fluviatilis* two nasal tentacles are present on each side which are solid. The nasal fossa is impervious. Spines are present on the back and also on the abdominal area. The body is cylindrical and elongated. The intraorbital space is convex. Lateral line is absent. The head is dark-grey in colour. Pectoral fin has pit at the base.

Distribution: They are found in Indian rivers (Bihar, West Bengal, Assam and Orissa) Burma and Bangladesh.

Fin Formula

T. cutcutia:

$D_{10,}$ $P_{21'}$ $A_{10'}$ C_7

T.fluviatilis:

$D_{14\text{-}16'}$ $P_{22'}$ V-absent, $A_{12\text{-}13'}$ $C_{11'}$ $B_{1\ pair}$

T. lineatus (Linnaeus) is the another important species.

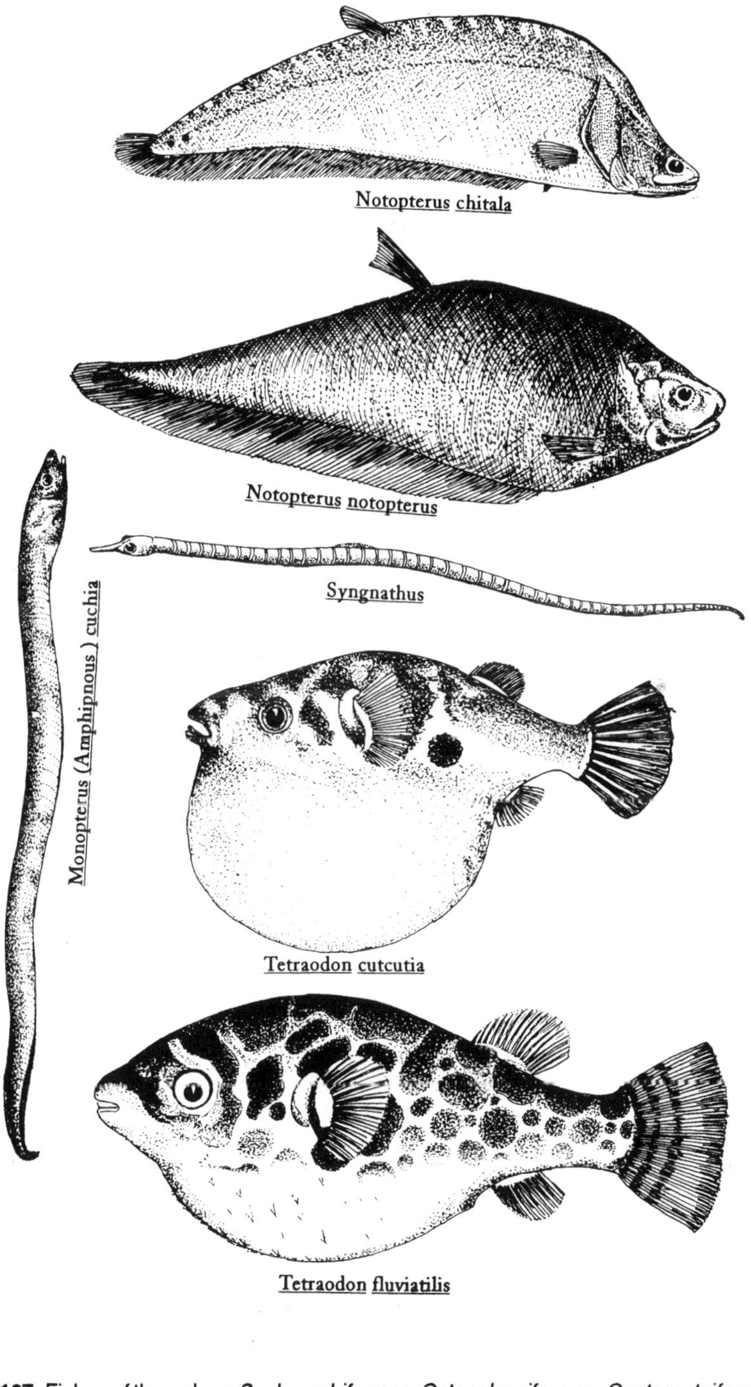

Fig. 107: Fishes of the orders: *Synbranchiformes, Osteoglossiformes, Gasterosteiformes* and *Tetraodontiformes*

No. 12 *Amblypharyngodon mola* (Hamilton)

Systematic Position

Phylum	—	Chordata
Sub-Phylum	—	Vertebrata
Class	—	Pisces
Sub-Class	—	Teleostomi
Super Order	—	Ostariophysi
Order	—	Cypriniformes
Family	—	Rasborinae

Diagnosis: The body is moderately elongated and the dorsal profile is slightly more convex than the abdominal profile. The snout is obtusely rounded. Mouth is anterior and the lower jaw is more prominent. Eyes are large and centrally placed. The upper lip is almost absent. Barbels are also absent. Silvery white lateral band is present on either side of the body which turns upwards in the tail region. The dorsal fin is inserted slightly behind the insertion of the Pelvic fin and has nine rays and no spine. Anal fin has seven rays and the caudal fin is forked. Dark markings are present on the dorsal, anal and caudal fins. Lateral line is incomplete with 65-75 scales.

Distribution: It is found in different parts of India (except Kerala), Pakistan, Bangladesh, Sri Lanka, Nepal and Burma.

Fin formula

$D_9(2/7)$, P_{15}, V_9, $A_7(2\text{-}5)$, C_{19}, $LI_{65\text{-}75}$, $Ltr_{12/12}$

The other important species belonging to the family *Rasborinae* are:

A. atkinsonii (Blyth), *A. melettina* (Val.), and *A. microlepis* (Bleeker).

No. 13 *Catla catla* (Hamilton)

Systematic Position

Phylum	—	Chordata
Sub-Phylum	—	Vertebrata
Class	—	Pisces
Sub-Class	—	Teleostomi
Supe Order	—	Ostariophysi
Order	—	Cypriniformes
Family	—	Cyprinidae
Sub-family	—	Cyprininae

Diagnosis: It is a silvery fish with a pinkish tinge. The body is short with rounded abdomen and the dorsal profile is more convex in comparison to the ventral one. It has wide mouth with prominent lower jaw. Eyes are large and situated in the anterior half of the head. Pores may be present on the snout. Barbels are absent. Upper lip is absent and the lower lip is very thick. Lower jaw has a movable articulation at the symphysis. Dorsal fin is inserted above tip of pectoral fin, and has 17-19 rays. There is no spine. Anal fin has 8 rays out of which five are branched. Caudal fin is forked. Lateral line is complete with 40-43 scales.

Distribution: It is distributed throughout India, Pakistan, Bangladesh, Nepal and Thailand. In south it is found in the Krishna river. It has also been introduced into the Cauvery river system later.

Fin Formula

$$D_{18-19}(3/15-16),\ P_{19},\ V_9,\ A_{8(3/5)},\ C_{19},\ LI_{43},\ Ltr_{7\frac{1}{2}/6\frac{1}{2}},\ B_{1\ pair}$$

No. 14 *Cirrhinus* (*cirrhina*) *mrigala* (Ham.)
C. *reba* (Ham.)

Systematic Position

Phylum	—	Chordata
Sub-Phylum	—	Vertebrata
Class	—	Pisces
Sub-Class	—	Teleostomi
Super Order	—	Ostariophysi
Order	—	Cypriniformes
Family	—	Cyprinidae
Sub-family	—	Cyprininae

Diagnosis: The body is elongated and compressed. The mouth is wide and lips are thin. The body is silvery but dark grey along back. The snout is obtusely rounded and it may have some pores. The upper lip is either fringed or entire and it is not continuous with the lower lip. The lower jaw is sharp with a small tubercle at the symphysis. Barbels are of very small size and its number may be two or four. In certain cases it may be absent.

In C. *mrigala* the upper margin of the body is concave particularly in the posterior side. The dorsal fin has 15-16 rays and lateral line scales are 40-45 in number.

In C. *reba*, the scales are more exposed and it looks larger. Both profiles are convex (dorsal being more convex). Scales have dark edges. Sometimes, bluish longitudinal bands may be present on the body. The dorsal fin is less than body height. Lateral line scales are 35-38 in number.

Distribution: They are found in Pakistan, Bangladesh, Nepal, Burma and East Indies.

Fin Formula

C. *mrigala:*

$D_{16(3/13)}$, P_{18}, V_9, $A_{8(2/6)}$, C_{15}, $LI_{42\text{-}44}$, $Ltr_{6\frac{1}{2}/6\frac{1}{2}}$, $B_{1\text{ pair}}$

C. *reba:*

$D_{11(2/9)}$, P_{16}, V_9, $A_{8(2/6)}$, C_{19}, $LI_{36\text{-}37}$, $Ltr_{7/5}$, $B_{1\text{ pair}}$.

The other members of the family *Cyprininae* are—

C.cirrhosa (Bloch), *C. fulungee* (Sykes), and *C. horai* (Lakshmanan).

No. 15 *Crossochelius latius latius* (Hamilton)

Systematic Position

Phylum	—	Chordata
Sub-Phylum	—	Vertebrata
Class	—	Pisces
Sub-Class	—	Teleostomi
Super Order	—	Ostariophysi
Order	—	Cypriniformes
Family	—	Cyprinidae
Sub-family	—	Garrinae

Diagnosis: This fish if found in hill-streams. Its body is slender and its colour is dull oilve above and dull silvery below. Dorsal and caudal fins are yellowish grey and other fins are orange-coloured.Irregular black blotches are present along the sides of the body. The ventral profile of the body is horizontal or a bit curved. The abdomen is rounded. Snout is prominent and obtusely pointed. The head is small and mouth is inferior. Postlabial groove is present. The pectoral fin is as long as the head. The caudal fin is forked and the upper lobe is slightly longer than the lower one. Lower lip has no suctorial disc. One pair of barbels are present on the rostrum. Sometimes one pair of short maxillary barbels may be present. Pectoral fins are shorter than the head. Lateral line is continuous with 37-40 scales.

Distribution: They are found in India, Bangaldesh, Nepal, and Pakistan. They are present in the Ganges and Brahmaputra river systems and also some rivers of Maharashtra.

Fin formula

$D_{11(3/8)}, P_{15}, V_{9}, A_{7(2-5)}, C_{19}, LI_{39}, Ltr_{6/6}, B_{1\text{-}2Pairs}.$

Other species are —*C. oblongus, C. punjabensis* (Mukerjii), and *C. burmanicus* (Hora).

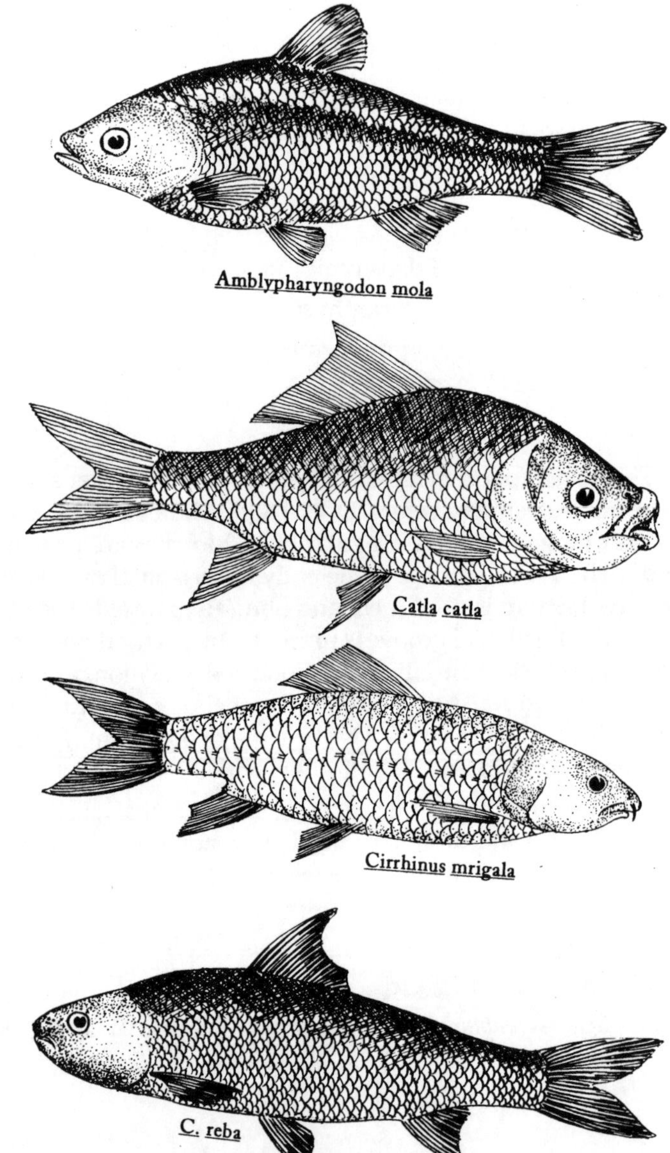

Fig. 108: Fishes of the order: *Cypriniformes*

No. 16 *Ctenopharyngodon idella* (Valenciennes)

Systematic Position

Phylum	—	Chordata
Sub-Phylum	—	Vertebrata
Class	—	Pisces
Sub-Class	—	Teleostomi
Super Order	—	Ostariophysi
Order	—	Cypriniformes
Family	—	Cyprinidae
Sub-family	—	Cyprininae

Diagnosis: This fish is also known as grass-carp or white Amur. The body is elongated (moderately) and compressed posteriorly. Head is depressed and flattened. Mouth is terminal and lips are thin. The upper jaw is slightly longer than the lower jaw. Eyes are large and lateral in position. Barbels are absent. Dorsal fin is inserted slightly ahead of pelvics. It has ten rays, out of which, seven are branched and three are simple. Anal fin is short with eight branched and two simple rays. Caudal fin is forked. Scales are cycloid. Lateral line is continuous with 40-42 scales.

Distribution : It was found in Siberia and Manchuria, China, U.S.S.R. but now it has been introduced into India also.

No. 17 *Garra gotyla gotyla* (Gray)

Systematic Position

Phylum	—	Chordata
Sub-Phylum	—	Vertebrata
Class	—	Pisces
Sub-Class	—	Teleostomi
Super Order	—	Ostariophysi
Order	—	Cypriniformes
Family	—	Cyprinidae
Sub-family	—	Garrinae

Diagnosis: The body is comparatively short with rounded abdomen. It is a well known hill-stream fish. Head is depressed and snout is blunt. Pores may be present on the snout. Mouth is inferior and semicircular in outline. Eyes are small in the posterior half of the head. Lips are thick and the upper and lower lips are continuous. On the chin a suctorial disc is present. It is a semicartilaginous pad. Interorbital space is convex. One or two pairs of barbels may be present in the various species of *Garra*. Barbels may be absent in certain species (e.g. *G. imberbis*). Jaws are not equal. Dorsal fin is inserted slightly ahead of Pelvics. Anal fin is short. Caudal fin is slightly emarginate. Lateral line is complete. Probosics is trilobed. Body depth is less than 5 times of the standard length. The colour is greenish and there is a bluish green band along the centre of body and extends along the middle of the caudal fin. The abdomen is yellowish green. A dark spot behind the gill opening may be present.

Distribution: It is found in different parts of India, Nepal, Pakistan, Bangladesh and Burma. In Assam they are distributed all along the Himalayas. In Bihar it is found in the Chota-Nagpur area and Kakolat hill stream.

Fin Formula

$$D_{11\frac{3-2}{8-9}}, P_{15}, V_{9}, A_{8(2/5)}, C_{17}, Ll_{32-36}, Ltr_{4\frac{1}{4}/5}, Vert_{18-14}, B_{2\ pairs}$$

Other species belonging to the sub-family *Garrinae* are— *G. annandalei* (Hora), *G. biocornuata* (Rao), *G. hughi* (Silas), *G.lamta* (Hamilton), *G. mullya* (Sykes), *G. nasuta*(McClelland), *G. notata* (Blyth) and *G. satyendranathi* (Ganguly and Datta).

No. 18 *Labeo calbasu* (Hamilton)

L. dero (Heckel)

L. gonius (Hamilton)

L. rohita (Hamilton)

Systematic Position

Phylum	—	Chordata
Sub-Phylum	—	Vertebrata
Class	—	Pisces
Sub-Class	—	Teleostomi
Super Order	—	Ostariophysi
Order	—	Cypriniformes
Family	—	Cyprinidae
Sub-family	—	Cyprininae

Diagnosis: All the above species possess moderately elongated body and rounded abdomen. Snout is truncated or rounded and it overhangs the mouth. Mouth is mostly inferior. Jaws are provided with transverse folds. Lips are thick and fleshy and also fringed. They cover both jaws and are continuous at angle of mouth forming a labial fold. Barbels when present may be four or two. Pharyngeal teeth are hooked and are in three rows. Dorsal fin is inserted ahead of pelvic fins. Anal fin is short. Caudal fin is forked or emarginate. Scales are moderate or small and the lateral line is complete.

In *Labeo calbasu* 5-6 scales are present between lateral line and pelvic fin. Dorsal fin has 16 to 18 rays. One pair of each rostral and maxillary barbels are present. These fishes are blackish with scarlet in the centre of the scales and fins are generally black.

In *Labeo dero,* 6 scales are occasionally present between lateral line and pelvic base. The snout has a distinct deep groove across. Dorsal fin is inserted above last quarter of pectoral fins. The pectoral fin does not reach the pelvic fin. One pair of maxillary barbels are present, the rostral pair is absent. The colour is brown in the dorsal side but the belly is silvery. Some species are olive green above and white below.

In *Labeo gonius,* 9 to 13 scales are present between lateral line and pelvic fin base. One pair of rostral and one pair of maxillary barbels are present. The dorsal side is of greenish black colour and the ventral side is silvery white (upto lateral line area). In this species black longitudinal bands extend from the anterior to the posterior end of the body.

In *Labeo rohita,* 6 to 6 $^{1}/_{2}$ scales are present between Lateral line and Pelvic fin base. One pair of maxillary brabels are present which are short and thin. The colour of the fish is bluish-black along the back, reddish black along the sides and silvery in the abdominal area.

Distribution: All these species are found throughout India, Pakistan, Bangladesh, Nepal and Burma.

Fin Formula

L.calbasu; $D_{17(3/14)}$, P_{19}, V_9, $A_{7(2/5)}$, C_{19}, LI_{41}, $Ltr_{7\frac{1}{2}/8}$, $B_{2\ pairs}$.

L.dero: $D_{12-13(3/9-10)}$, P_{16-17}, V_9, $A_{8(3/5)}$, C_{19}, LI_{38-43}, $Ltr_{8/6-7}$, $B_{1\ pair\ maxillary}$

L.boga: $D_{2/8-9}$, P_{16}, V_9, $A_{2/5}$, C_{19}, LI_{36-40}, Ltr_{15}, $B_{1\ pair}$

L.rohita: $D_{16(3/13)}$, P_{17}, V_9, $A_{7(2/5)}$, C_{19}, LI_{40-41}, $Ltr_{6\frac{1}{2}-7\frac{1}{2}/9}$, $B_{1\ pair}$.

Some other important species are : *L. bata* (Hamilton), *L.dyocheilus dyocheilus* (McClelland), *L. dyocheilus pakistanicus* (Mirza and Awan), *L. fimbriatus* (Bloch), *L. gonius* (Hamilton), *L. kontius* (Jerdon) *L. pangusia* (Hamilton) and *L. sindensis* (Day).

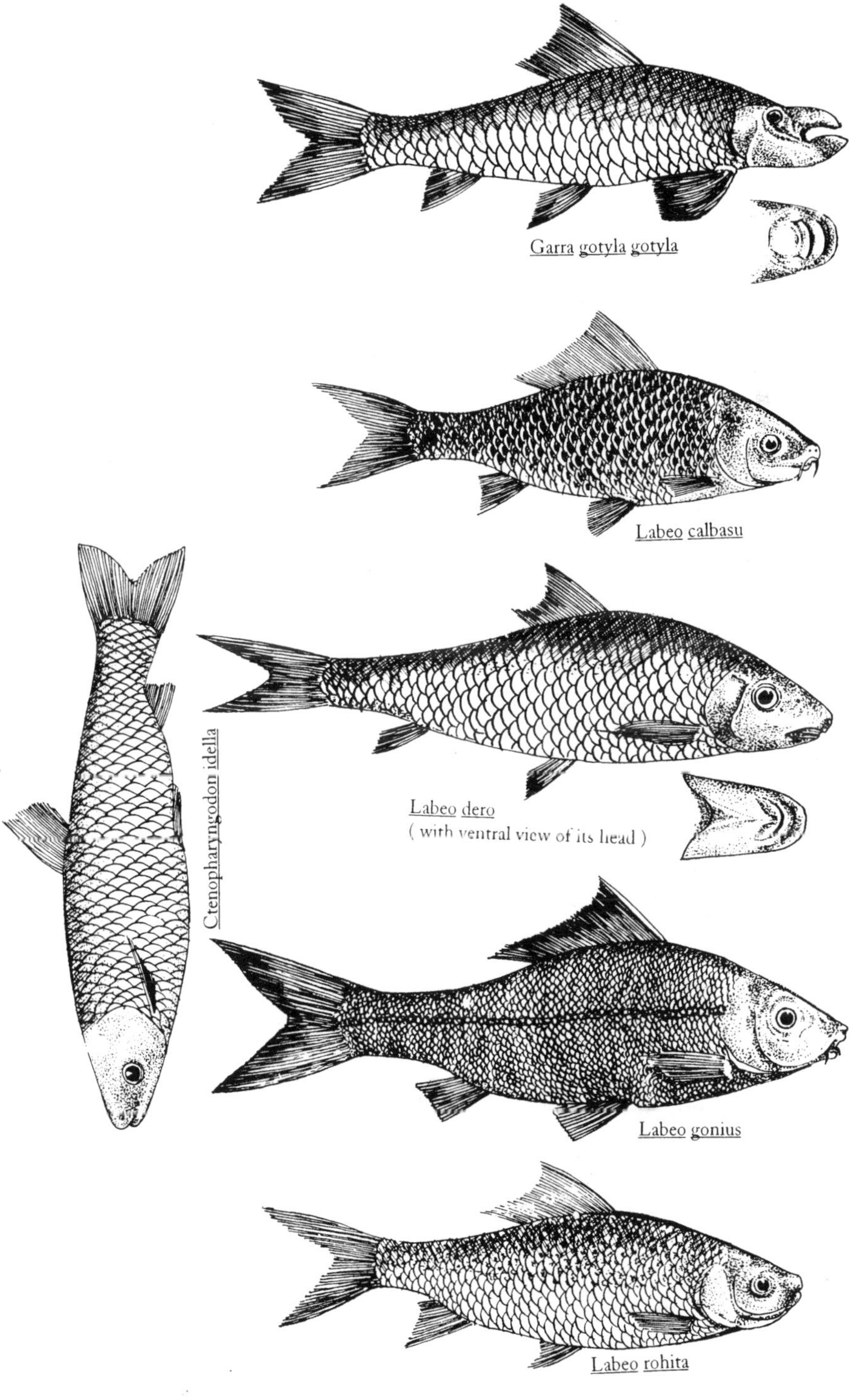

Fig. 109: Fishes of the order : *Cypriniformes*

No. 19 *Lepidocephalichthys guntea* (Ham.)

Systematic Position

Phylum	—	Chordata
Sub-Phylum	—	Vertebrata
Class	—	Pisces
Sub-Class	—	Teleostomi
Super Order	—	Ostariophysi
Order	—	Cypriniformes
Family	—	Cobitidae
Sub-family	—	Cobitinae

Diagnosis: Body is elongated and moderately compressed. Head is short and conical and the abdomen is rounded. Mouth is inferior and slightly arched. Eyes are small and superior in position. Lips are thick and fleshy, and the lower lip is interrupted in middle. Two pairs of rostral and one pair of maxillary barbels are present. The maxillary barbels reach the middle of the orbit. Two pairs of barbel like mental lobes are present and they join the maxillary barbels. A broad longitudinal black band extends dorsally from the occipital region to the base of the caudal fin. Dorsal fin is inserted slightly ahead of pelvic fins. In males, the inner ray of pectoral fin is ossified as a flat osseous plate like structure, caudal fin is truncate or rounded. Suborbital spine is without convex side elevations or it curves on the anterior side. Numerous rows of dark spots are present on the caudal and dorsal fins. These fishes are present in rivers, hill streams and other freshwater bodies. The colour of the fish is dirty yellowish brown.

Distribution: It is found in different parts of India, Bangladesh, Pakistan, Nepal and Burma.

Fin Formula

$D_{8(2/6)}$, P_{8}, V_{7}, $A_{7(2/5)}$, C_{16}, LI_{115}, $B_{4\ pairs}$.

Other important species of the family *Cobitinae* are—

L. annandalei (Chaudhuri), *L. berdmorei* (Blyth), *L. caudofurcatus* (Tilak and Hussain), *L. dibruensis* (Sen), *L. goalparensis* (Pillai and Yazdani), *L. thermalis* (Valenciennes) and *L. irrorata* (Hora).

No. 20 *Noemacheilus rupicola rupicola* (McClelland)

Systematic Position

Phylum	—	Chordata
Sub-Phylum	—	Vertebrata
Class	—	Pisces
Sub-Class	—	Teleostomi
Super Order	—	Ostariophysi
Order	—	Cypriniformes
Family	—	Cobitidae
Sub-family	—	Noemacheilinae

Diagnosis: These are hill-stream fishes. The body is elongated and somewhat compressed. The dorsal profile is almost horizontal. Head is cylindrical, anteriorly pointed and has no preorbital spine. The snout is obtusely rounded. Mouth is inferior and the eyes are small or moderate. Lips are thick and fleshy and they are continuous at the angle of mouth. Jaws and palate are without teeth. Dorsal fin is situated opposite the ventrals. Number of barbels may be 2 pairs, 3 pairs or 4 pairs in different species. Anal fin is short and caudal fin may be emarginate, truncate or lunate. Lateral line complete in some species or may be incomplete in others. In *N. rupicola rupicola* a processus dentiformes is present. The upper jaw in this species is produced into process with a broad, truncate apex while the lower jaw is deeply incised in order to receive this process. Dorsal fin has 7 to 8 branched rays. In *N. botia botia* the body has irregular blotches and the lateral line is complete. A black ocellus is present near upper margin of base of caudal fin. Caudal fin has 7 irregular bars.

Distribution: It is distributed in different parts of India and Nepal. These are present in Kashmir, Doon, Simla, Poonch Valleys, Naga hills, Eastern Himalayas and Western Himalayas.

Fin formula

N. botia

$D_{12\text{-}14(2/10\text{-}12),}\ P_{11,}\ V_{8,}\ A_{7(2/5),}\ C_{17,}\ B_{3\ pairs.}$

There are several species of *Noemacheilus*, however, a few more important species are:

N. anguilla (Annandale), *N. beavani* (Günther), *N. brevis* (Boulenger), *N. horai* (Menon), *N. kangrae* (Menon), *N. kashmirensis* (Hora), *N. manipurensis* (Chaudhuri), *N. marmoratus* (Heckel), *N. microps* (Steindachner), *N. monilis* (Hora), *N. montanus* (McClelland), *N. nasseri* (Ahmad and Mirza), *N. pakistanicus* (Mirza and Banarescu), *N. poonaensis* (Menon), *N. pulchellus* (Day), *N. punjabensis* (Hora), *N. rajasthanicus* (Mathur and Yazdani), *N. striatus* (Day), *N. triangularis* (Day), *N. vittatus* (Heckel), and *N. zonatus* (McClelland) etc.

No. 21 *Puntius chola* (Hamilton)
P. sarana sarana (Hamilton)
P. sophore (Hamilton)

Systematic Position

Phylum	—	Chordata
Sub-Phylum	—	Vertebrata
Class	—	Pisces
Sub-Class	—	Teleostomi
Super Order	—	Ostariophysi
Order	—	Cypriniformes
Family	—	Cyprinidae
Sub-family	—	Cyprininae

Diagnosis: (Characters of the genus)— The body is moderately elongated, deep and compressed. Head is short. Snout is obtuse, conical or pointed and may overhang the jaw. Mouth is arched and it may be anterior or inferior. Jaws are simple and have no horny covering. Eyes are moderate to large and dorso-lateral in position. Barbels may be four, two or none. Dorsal fin is short and is inserted opposite pelvic fins. Anal fin is short and the caudal fin is forked. Scales are small, moderate or large. Lateral line may be complete or incomplete.

In *P. chola,* a dark blotch is present from the 23 to 25th scales of the lateral line. The number of predorsal scales is 10-12. A dark spot along base of the 1st to fourth anterior dorsal ray is also present. A black spot behind the gill opening may be present. Only one pair of maxillary barbels is present. Lateral line is complete.

In *P. sarana sarana,* lateral line scale 30-34, and scales between midline and lateral line are $4\frac{1}{2}$ to $6\frac{1}{2}$ in number. There are two pairs of barbels. In *P. sophore,* body is not very deep. A round black blotch is present at the roof of the caudal fin. The barbels are absent.

Distribution: These species have been reported from different parts of India, Pakistan, Bangladesh, Nepal, Sri Lanka and Burma. *P. sarana sarana* is not present in Peninsular India. *P. sophore* has been reported from Yunnan also.

Fin formula: *P. chola:*

$D_{11(3/8\text{-}9)}$, $P_{14\text{-}15}$, V_9, $A_{8(3/5)}$, C_{19}, $Ll_{27\text{-}28}$, $Ltr_{6\frac{1}{2}/5\frac{1}{2}}$, $B_{1\ pair}$

P. sarana sarana:

$D_{11\text{-}12(3/8\text{-}9)}$, $P_{15\text{-}16}$, $V_{8\text{-}9}$, $A_{8(3/5)}$, C_{19}, $Ll_{30\text{-}34}$, $Ltr_{6\frac{1}{2}/6}$, $B_{2\ pairs}$.

P. sophore:

$D_{11(3/8)}$, $P_{15\text{-}16}$, V_9, $A_{8(3/5)}$, C_{19}, $Ll_{25\text{-}26}$, $Ltr_{5\frac{1}{2}/5-5\frac{1}{2}}$

Some other species are—*P. amphibius* (Valenciennes), *P. apogon* (Valenciennes), *P. dorsalis* (Jerdon), *P. simaculatus* (Bleeker), *P. singhala* (Duncker), *P. terio* (Hamilton), *P. tincto punctatus* (Day), *P. muzaffarpurensis* (Srivastava, Verma, Srivastava), and *P. vittatus* (Day).

No. 22 *Tor tor* (Hamilton)

Systematic Position

Phylum	—	Chordata
Sub-Phylum	—	Vertebrata
Class	—	Pisces
Sub-Class	—	Teleostomi
Super Order	—	Ostariophysi
Order	—	Cypriniformes
Family	—	Cyprinidae
Sub-family	—	Cyprininae

Diagnosis: The body is elongated and compressed. The ventral profile is more arched. The abdomen is round. The head is broad but pointed. Mouth is inferior and arched. Eyes are large but its size varies according to age. Lips are thick and fleshy, continuous at angles of mouth. Median lobe may not be present in the posterior lip. The post-labial groove is continuous. The dorsal fin is inserted above pelvic fins and a scaly sheath is present at its place. Anal fin does nor reach the base of the caudal fin. The caudal fin is deeply forked. Scales are large and the lateral line is complete. Pharyngeal teeth are present in 3 rows of 5, 3, 2 teeth. The colour is dark grey along the dorsal side. Sides are golden and the abdomen is silvery with slightly golden tinge. The fins are reddish yellow in colour.

Distribution: They are present in India, Pakistan and Bangladesh. In India they have been reported from the bases of the Himalayas, Madhya Pradesh, Bihar, Assam and North parts of Bengal.

Fin formula

$$D_{3/9},\ P_{17}, A_{7(2/5)},\ Ll_{25},\ Ltr_{4\frac{1}{2}/4\frac{1}{2}},\ B_{2\ \text{pairs}}.$$

Other important species are:

Tor putitora (Ham.), *T. khudree* (Sykes), *T. khudree malabaricus* (Jerdon), *T. mosal* (Sykes), *T. mosal mahandicus* (David), *T. mussullah* (Sykes), *T. progenius* (Mc Clelland) etc.

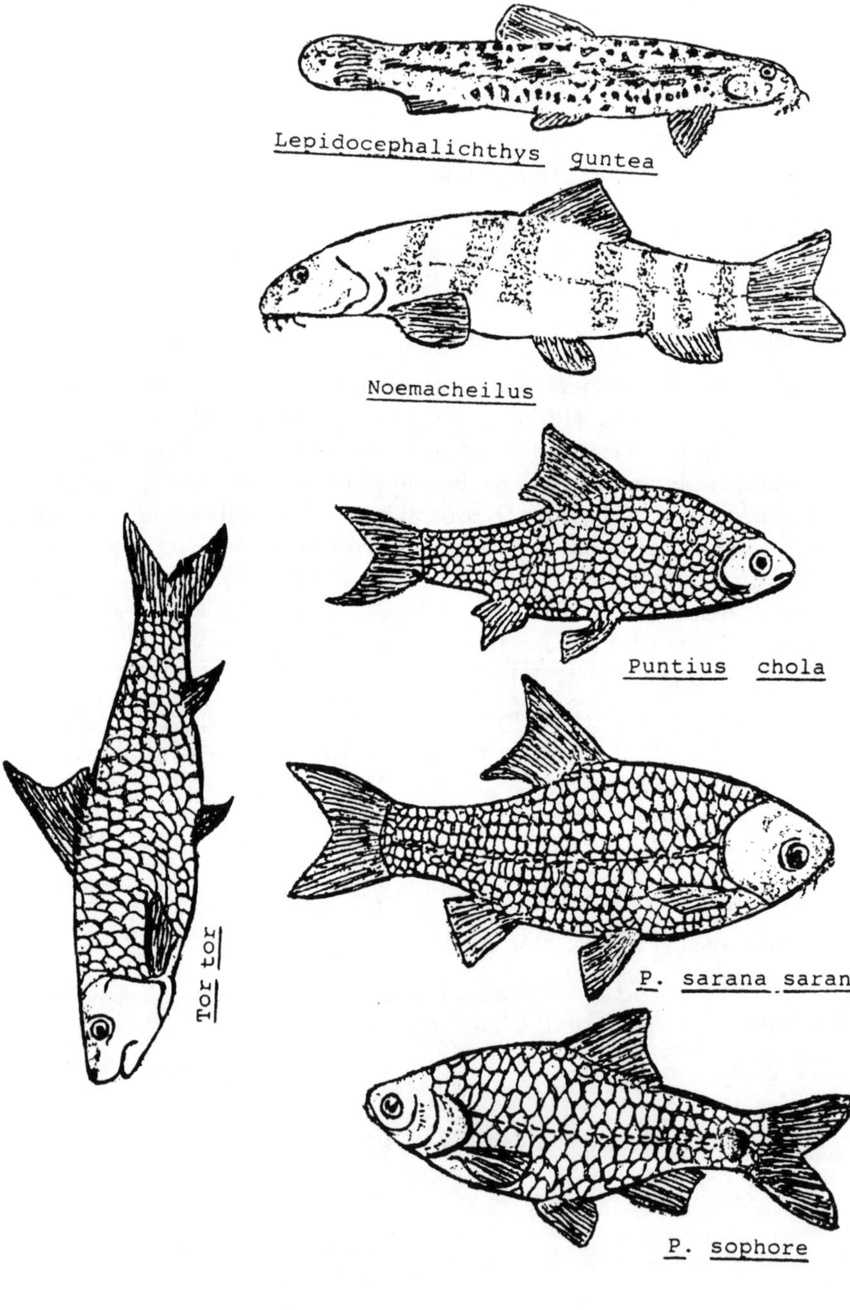

Fig. 110: Fishes of the order: *Cypriniformes*

No. 23 *Anabas testudineus* (Bloch)

Systematic Position

Phylum	—	Chordata
Sub-Phylum	—	Vertebrata
Class	—	Pisces
Sub-Class	—	Telecstomi
Super Order	—	Acanthopterygii
Order	—	Perciformes
Family	—	Anabantidae

Diagnosis: Body is stout, oblong, almost cigar shaped and compressed. The abdomen is rounded. The head is greenish brown in colour. Snout is slightly conical. The jaws are equal and lips are thin. This fish has got accessory respiratory organ and it can survive in moist air for about six days. There is a single dorsal fin covering the entire length of the trunk and is inserted above pectoral base and has variable number of spines. Caudal fin is rounded. Ctenoid scales are present. Teeth are absent on the palatines. The outer row of villi form teeth in the jaws are of largest size. Teeth present on the vomers are small. Eyes are large and lateral. Lateral line is interrupted at 18th scale and the 19th scale is perforated. This fish is very popular as food.

Distribution: Distributed at several places in the fresh and brackish waters of Asia and South Africa.

Fin formula

$D_{17/9\text{-}10}, P_{15}, V_{1/5}, A_{10\text{-}11}, C_{17}, Ll_{29}, Ltr_{4/9}$

Another important species is :

A. oligolepis (Bleeker).

No. 24 *Chanda nama* (Hamilton)
C.ranga (Hamilton)

Systematic Position

Phylum	—	Chordata
Sub-Phylum	—	Vertebrata
Class	—	Pisces
Sub-Class	—	Teleostomi
Super Order	—	Acanthopterygii
Order	—	Perciformes
Family	—	Chandidae

Diagnosis: They have short, deep and compressed body. Head is also short and compressed and the snout is sharp. Mouth is wide and turned upward in these two species particularly. The lower jaw is longer than the upper one. Lips are thin. Villiform teeth are present not only on the jaws but also on the palate and tongue in certain species. The lower limb of preopercle has a double serrated edge, and the opercle has no prominent spine. Two dorsal fins are present which are continuous. Also, dorsal fin has forwardly directed recumbent spine. Caudal fin is forked. Scales are cycloid. Eyes are large and superior.

In *Chanda nama,* Lateral line is not distinct, rather it is discontinuous or absent. A dark blotch is generally present on the upper edge of the dorsal fin. Anal fin has spots at the base of the spine. Two large and curved canines are present on either side of the lower jaw.

In *Chanda ranga,* a dark shoulder spot is present. There are no teeth on the tongue.

Distribution: They are found in India, Pakistan, Bangladesh, Nepal, Malaya, Burma and Thailand. In Sind and Punjab, they are in abundance.

Fin Formula

C. nama

$D_{1+7/1/16\text{-}17,}\ P_{12\text{-}13,}\ V_{1/5,}\ A_{3/16\text{-}18,}\ C_{17,}$
Lr scales deciduous

C. ranga:

$D_{1+7/1/13,}\ P_{11\text{-}13,}\ V_{1\text{-}5,}\ A_{3/14\text{-}16'}\ C_{17,}$
Ll scales deciduous.

Other important species are — *C. baculis* (Ham.), *C. thomassi* (Day), *C.nalua* (Ham) etc.

No. 25 *Colisa faciata* (Schneider)

Systematic Position

Phylum	—	Chordata
Sub-Phylum	—	Vertebrata
Class	—	Pisces
Sub-Class	—	Teleostomi
Super Order	—	Acanthopterygii
Order	—	Perciformes
Family	—	Belontidae
Sub-family	—	Trichogastrinae

Diagnosis: Body is elevated but laterally compressed. It has a blunt snout. Mouth is turned upward and jaws are unequal and slightly protractile. Villiform teeth are present on the jaws. Branchial arches have toothed tubercles. A single dorsal fin commences above from near pectoral base. Caudal fin is truncated. Dorsal, caudal and anal fins are spotted orange in colour. The pelvic fin is present in the form of single, elongate, filiform ray. Lateral line, if present, is interrupted. Scales are slightly ctenoid. 14 or more orange coloured oblique bands are present on the body. Eyes are large and black with a red spot in the white area.

Distribution: It is found in India, Southern Pakistan, Bangladesh, Nepal and Burma.

Fin Formula

$$D_{16\text{-}17/10\text{-}11}\ P_{10}, V_{1},\ A_{16\text{-}17/15\text{-}16},\ C_{15},\ LI_{29\text{-}30},\ Ltr_{5\frac{1}{2}/11-12}$$

Other important species are:

C. *labiosus* (Day), C. *latius* (Hamilton), C. *sota* (Hamilton) etc.

No. 26 Glossogobius giuris (Hamilton)

Systematic Position

Phylum	—	Chordata
Sub-Phylum	—	Vertebrata
Class	—	Pisces
Sub-Class	—	Teleostomi
Super Order	—	Acanthopterygii
Order	—	Perciformes
Family	—	Gobiidae
Sub-family	—	Gobiinae

Diagnosis: Body is elongated and anteriorly cylindrical. Head is depressed and generally pointed. Snout is obtusely rounded or pointed. Mouth is slightly oblique and lips are thick. Villiform teeth are present in several rows. Outer and inner rows of teeth are enlarged. Tongue is bilobate. Anterior scales are cycloid and the posterior scales are however ctenoid. Anal fin is posteriorly pointed. Caudal fin is oblong. Ventral fins are united at their bases forming a cuplike structure. The two dorsal fins are separated by a short interspace. The first dorsal fin is inserted above half or three-fourth of pectoral fin. In the transverse line 9-14 scales are present. One black spot is sometimes present on the first dorsal fin. The fish bears variable cream colour. Light black markings are present on the head. Irregular markings are generally present on the body.

Distribution: It has been reported from different parts of India, Pakistan, Bangladesh, Sri Lanka, Burma and Nepal. They are also found in some parts of Japan and Australia and along the east coast of Africa.

Fin Formula

$D_{6/1/9'}\ P_{20'}\ V_{1/5'}\ A_{1/8'}\ C_{17'}\ Ll_{35'}\ Ltr_{12}$

Another important species is—

G. biocellatus (Val.).

No. 27 Lates calcarifer (Bloch)

Systematic Position

Phylum	—	Chordata
Sub-Phylum	—	Vertebrata
Class	—	Pisces
Sub-Class	—	Teleostomi
Super Order	—	Acanthopterygii
Order	—	Perciformes
Family	—	Centropomidae

Diagnosis: It has oblong, deep and compressed body. Head is also of moderate size and is compressed. The snout is obtusely rounded. Mouth is wide and gape extends to anterior border of eyes. Eyes are moderate and supero-lateral in position. Lower jaw is always longer than the upper one. Lips are however thin. Villiform teeth are present on the palate, tongue is devoid of teeth. Preopercle has a strong spine at its angle. It is denticulated along horizontal limb with 3 or 4 spines. Two dorsal fins are continuous and they are united at the base. The first dorsal fin has 7-8 spines but the second has 11-13 rays. Anal fin has 3 spines and 8-9 rays. Caudal fin in this fish is truncate or rounded. Lateral line has 52-60 scales and it is slightly curved. Scales are ctenoid. Lateral line scales reach the margin of the caudal fin and they are in three series. *L. calcarifer* is a game fish and has better food value.

Distribution: They are found in different parts of India, Pakistan, Burma, Bangladesh, Thailand and Malaya.

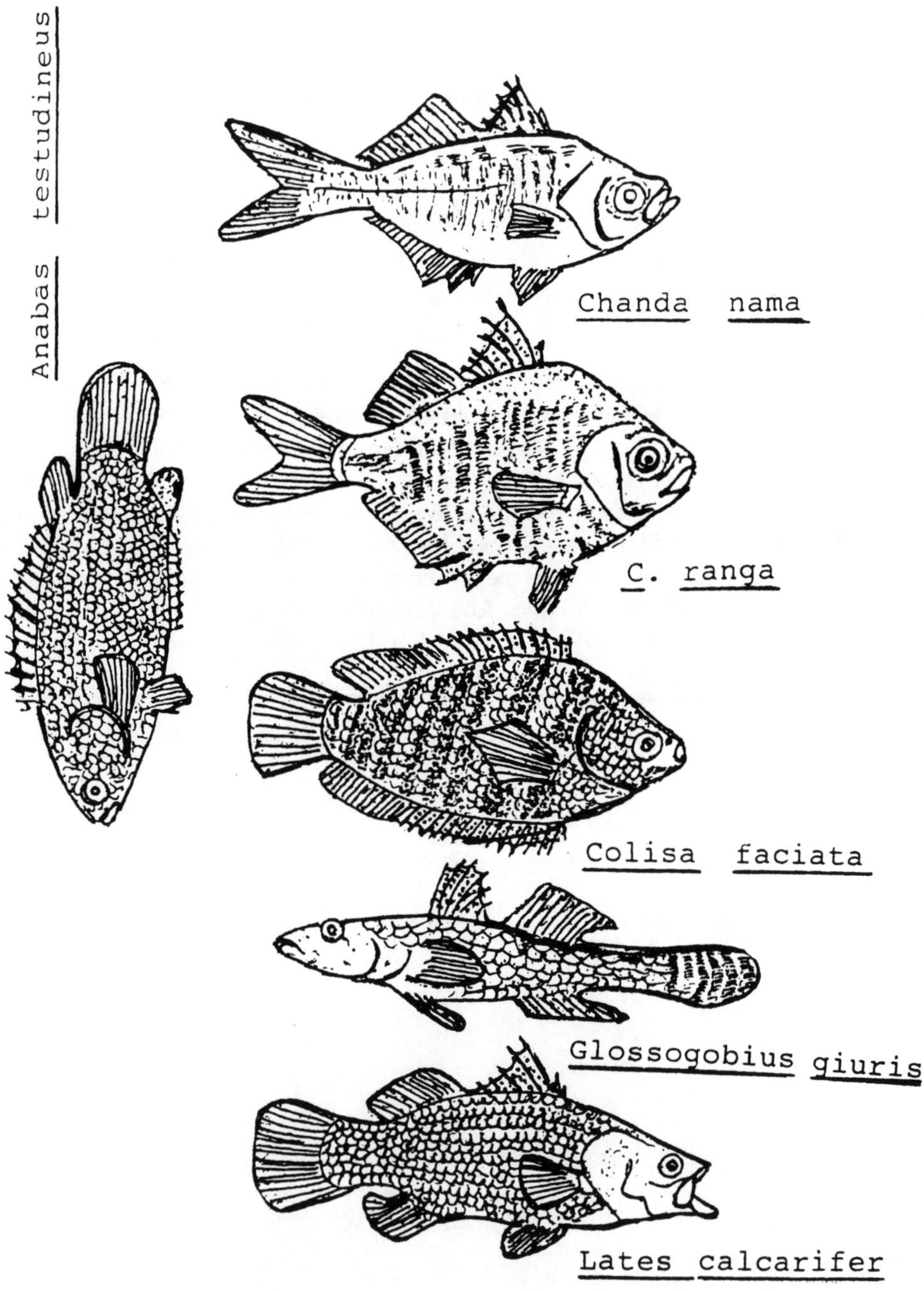

Fig. 111: Fishes of the order: *Perciformes*

No. 28 *Nandus nandus* (Ham.)

Systematic Position

Phylum	—	Chordata
Sub-Phylum	—	Vertebrata
Class	—	Pisces
Sub-Class	—	Teleostomi
Super Order	—	Acanthopterygii
Order	—	Perciformes
Family	—	Nandidae

Diagnosis: Body is oblong and compressed and has rounded abdomen. Snout is pointed and the head is large and compressed. It has terminal mouth with wide cleft which extends protractile posterior border of the eyes. Eyes are large and lateral in position. Lower jaw is longer and lips are thin. Teeth are villiform and are present on palate and tongue. Dorsal fin is inserted above pectoral base. Dorsal spines are strong and their bases being lodged in a groove. Soft portion of the dorsal fin is rounded. Anal spines are very strong and the second one is the largest. Cudal fin is rounded or square shaped. Scales are ctenoid. Lateral line is interrupted at about 36th scale. There are 46-48 scales in the lateral line. There are three vertical broad wavy bands on the side of the body . In addition to this, there is a fourth short band with a black blotch which crosses the free portion of the tail. Opercle has one spine. Preopercle, preorbit, sub-opercle and inter-opercle are serrated or entire. This fish is a piscivorous species preying upon small carps mainly.

Distribution: It is found all over India, Bangladesh, Pakistan, Thailand and Burma.

Fin formula

$D_{13/12\text{-}13,}\ P_{15\text{-}17,}\ V_{1/5,}\ A_{3/8,}\ C_{15,}\ LI_{46\text{-}48}$

No. 29 *Tilapia (Oreochromis) mossambica* (Peters)

Systematic Position

Phylum	—	Chordata
Sub-Phylum	—	Vertebrata
Class	—	Pisces
Sub-Class	—	Teleostomi
Super Order	—	Acanthopterygii
Order	—	Perciformes
Family	—	Cichlidae

Diagnosis: Tilapia mossambica is an exotic species introduced in India in as early as 1952. It has a short, compressed and elongated body. The abdomen is rounded. The upper profile of the body is concave. Mouth is terminal and very wide. The snout is rounded and jaws are equal. Teeth are present in two series, the outer teeth are bicuspid and the others are tricuspid. Dorsal fin is inserted above the base of the pectoral fin and has 15 or 16 spines and 10-11 rays. Anal fin has three or four spines. Caudal fin is rounded. Scales are cycloid in this fish. Lateral line is incomplete. Upper one has 18-21 scales and the lower one has 10-15 scales only. This fish is not suitable for culture along with the major Indian carps because of its depredation on fry. This fish starts breeding at the age of only two months and it breeds four to six times in a year. Its survival rate is very high and they rapidly increase in number.

Distribution: Originally these fishes were present in East Africa but now they have been introduced into India and Pakistan.

No. 30 *Gadusia chapra* (Hamilton)

Systematic Position

Phylum	—	Chordata
Sub-Phylum	—	Vertebrata
Class	—	Pisces
Sub-Class	—	Teleostomi
Super Order	—	Clupeomorpha
Order	—	Clupeiformes
Family	—	Clupeidae
Sub-family	—	Alosinae

Diagnosis: Body is oblong, compressed and converted with small scales. Abdomen is serrated with 18-19 pre-pelvic and 8-10 post-pelvic scutes. Maxilla extends to the middle of the orbit. Adipose lid is present in the eye. Barbels are absent. Head is short, high and compressed and mouth is terminal and slightly upturned. Eyes are large and lateral in position. Abdominal profile is more complex than dorsal profile. Lower jaw is not projecting over the upper one. Dorsal fin is inserted above pelvic origin with 14-15 rays. Caudal fin is forked and the anal fin has 21-24 rays. Lateral line is absent in this species. Teeth are absent. Margin of the caudal fin is dark and sometimes black spot may be present on the shoulder. There is no cross bars on the side of the body. *Gadusia chapra* is an edible fish.

Distribution: They have been reported from India, Pakistan, Bangladesh, Nepal, Burma and Malaya.

Fin formula

$D_{14\text{-}15(3/11\text{-}12)}$, P_{13}, V_{8}, $A_{22\text{-}24(2/20\text{-}22)}$, C_{17}, $LI_{80\text{-}120}$, $Ltr_{33\text{-}35}$

Another important species is:

G. variegata (Day).

No. 31 *Hilsa ilisha* (Hamilton)

Systematic Position

Phylum	—	Chordata
Sub-Phylum	—	Vertebrata
Class	—	Pisces
Sub-Class	—	Teleostomi
Super Order	—	Clupeomorpha
Order	—	Clupeiformes
Family	—	Clupeidae
Sub-family	—	Alosinae

Diagnosis: Body is oblong and compressed. Maxilla extends upto the middle of the orbit. Eyes are provided with adipose lids. 15-16 pre-pelvic and 11-16 post-pelvic scutes are present in the abdomen. Head is large, high and compressed and the snout is rounded. Mouth is terminal but the cleft does not extent to orbit. Eyes are large and lateral in position. Jaws are not equal and the upper jaw has a median notch at the centre. Occipital ridges converge behind. Dorsal fin originates opposite to the place of origin of the ventral fin. Anal fin is long and single. Caudal fin is deeply forked. The abdominal profile is more convex than that of the dorsal profile. The caudal lobe is as long as head. Scales are large and Lateral line is absent. There are seven faint bars beginning from the dorsal side and reaching the middle of the body on either side. There is a rounded blotch at the base of the caudal fin. *Hilsa* is an edible fish and is quite delicious.

Distribution: They are distributed in India, Pakistan, Bangladesh, Sri Lanka and Burma. There is abundance of this fish in the various river system of India i.e. Ganges, Yamuna, Narmada, Krishna, Tapti, Godavari, Cauvery systems mainly.

Fin Formula

$$D_{19(3/16)}, P_{(15-18)}, V_8, A_{21-22\left(\frac{2}{19-20}\right)}, C_{19}, LI_{50}, Ltr_{17-19}$$

Another important species is :

H. toli (Valenciennes).

No. 32 *Setipinna phasa* (Hamilton)

Systematic Position

Phylum	—	Chordata
Sub-Phylum	—	Vertebrata
Class	—	Pisces
Sub-Class	—	Teleostomi
Super Order	—	Clupeomorpha
Order	—	Clupeiformes
Family	—	Engraulidae
Sub-family	—	Engraulinae

Diagnosis: Body is elongated, compressed and it tapers behind. The abdomen is serrated with 15-23 pre-pelvic and 6-12 post-pelvic scutes. Snout is obtused. Head is short and compressed. Mouth is sub-inferior and the cleft is wide, and the latter extends beyond posterior margin of the eye. Eyes are large and lateral in position and are located in the anterior part of the head. The adipose eye lid is present. Maxilla extends behind the eye. Jaws are unequal and the lower jaw is shorter than the upper one. There are very small teeth present on the jaws and palate. Dorsal fin is inserted behind the anal fin. The dorsal spine is short but strong. A free long spine is present before dorsal fin. The anal fin is very long. Lateral line is absent. Caudal fin is forked and the lower lobe is larger than the upper one. Also, the upper lobe is truncated.

Distribution: Different parts of India, Burma and Bangladesh.

Fin formula

$D_{1/14}, P_{14\text{-}15}, V_{7}, A_{71\text{-}75}, C_{19}, LI_{52}, Ltr_{14}$

Other species are:

S. breviceps (Cantor), *S. tenuifilis* (Valenciennes), *S. taty* (Valenciennes) etc.

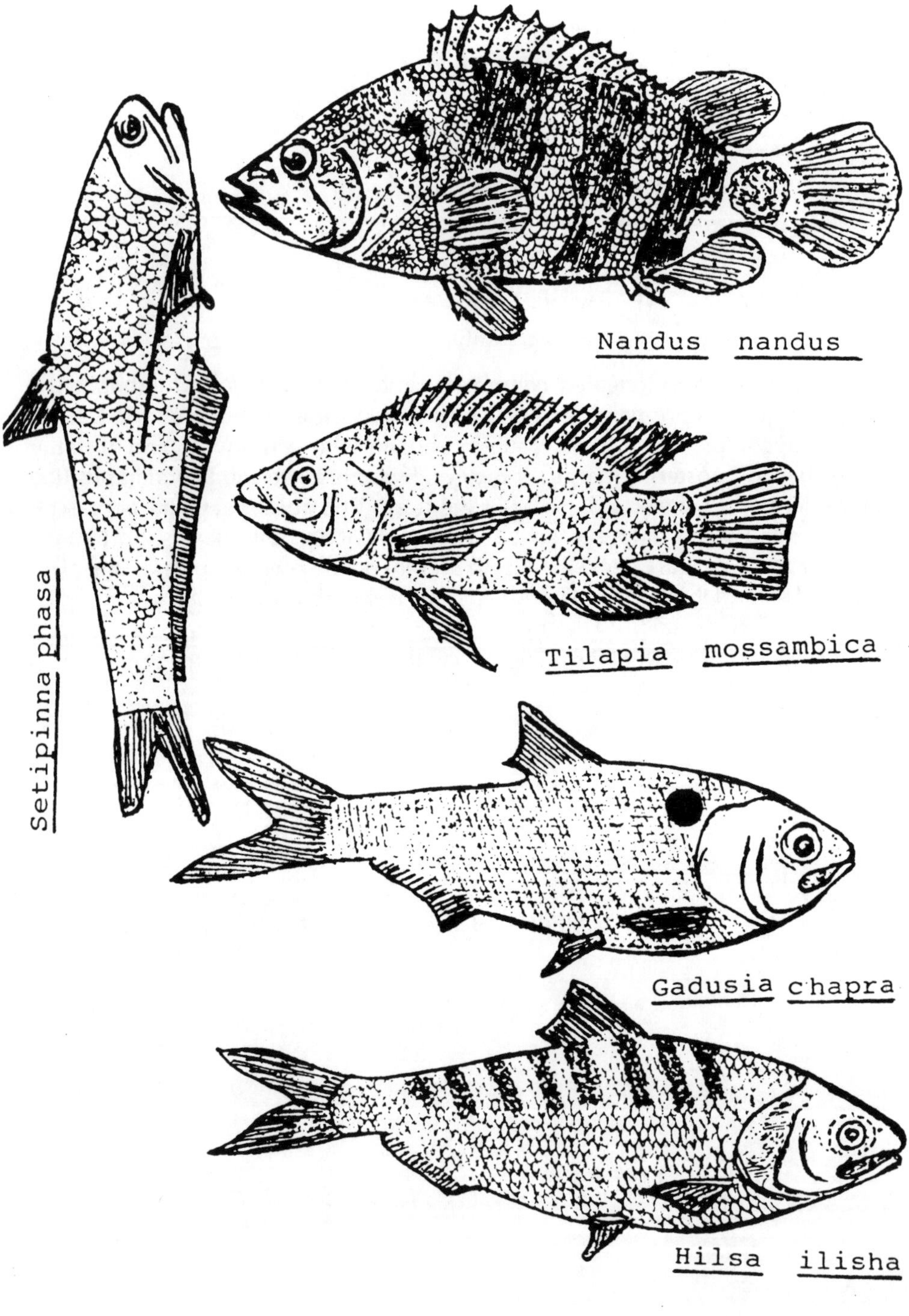

Fig. 112: Fishes of the orders: *Perciformes and Clupeiformes*

No. 33 *Bagarius bagarius* (Hamilton)

Systematic Position

Phylum	—	Chordata
Sub-Phylum	—	Vertebrata
Class	—	Pisces
Sub-Class	—	Teleostomi
Super Order	—	Ostariophysi
Order	—	Siluriformes
Family	—	Sisoridae

Diagnosis: It has elongated body and abdomen. Head is large and depressed with its upper surface osseous. The upper surface is rugose in irregular bands of lines. Snout is conical and the mouth is ventral, wide and crescentic. Eyes are small and dorsally placed at posterior half of the head. Lips are thick in this fish. Branchiostegals are twelve and the gill membranes are not confluent with the skin of the isthmus. There are four pairs of barbels. The maxillary barbels have broad base and is longer than the head, reaching anterior one third of Pectoral fin. The nasal pair is short and the outer mandibular pair is long, but the inner mandibular barbel is shorter in comparison to the outer one. Teeth are present in both the jaws and they are of unequal size. The outer row of mandibular teeth are widely separated. The dorsal fin is rayed and inserted above base of pectoral fin. Adipose dorsal fin is moderately long, and posteriorly free. Caudal fin is deeply forked. The upper lobe of the caudal fin is longer. Both lobes are produced into soft filamentous prolongations. Lateral line is complete and simple. Air bladder is small and enclosed into two bony capsules. Fins are provided with a black base and a dark band across each. Numerous black spots, round in shape are present over the entire body excepting belly only.

Distribution: This species is distributed in India, Pakistan, Bangladesh, Nepal, Burma, Malaya, Thailand, East India and Tonkin.

Fin Formula

$D_{1/6/0,}\ P_{1/12,}\ V_{6,}\ A_{13(3/10),}\ C_{17,}\ B_{4\ \text{Pairs.}}$

No. 34 *Clarias batrachus* (Linn.)

Systematic Position

Phylum	—	Chordata
Sub-Phylum	—	Vertebrata
Class	—	Pisces
Sub-Class	—	Teleostomi
Super Order	—	Ostariophysi
Order	—	Siluriformes
Family	—	Clariidae

Diagnosis: Body is elongated and compressed with rounded abdomen. Head is depressed and is covered with osseous plates dorsally and laterally which form a cask covering, a diverticulum of the gill cavity. The width of the interorbital space equals one half the length of the head. The greatest width of head is equal to its length. Upper jaw is longer than the lower one. Villiform teeth are present in broad bands or patches on jaws and palate. Four pairs of barbels are present—Two pairs of mandibular, one pair of maxillary and nasal each. Gill membranes are deeply notched and they are free from isthmus. On the head there are some fine granules. The size of the eyes is smaller which may be considered to be an adaptation to cope with the muddy habitat. Anterior depression on the head which is deep and oblong is present behind the eyes and the posterior depression is present midway between the posterior extremity of the anterior fossa and the end of the occipital process. The posterior depression is oval and shallow. The occipital process is rounded behind and the width of its base is more than double its length. Pectoral fin reaches below the commencement of the dorsal fin. The external serrations of the spine is prominent. Dorsal fin is very long, reaching the base of the caudal fin. Caudal fin is round and free. Lateral line is complete.

Distribution: This species is distributed in India, Pakistan, Sri Lanka, Nepal, Burma, Bangladesh, Malaya, Thailand, Java, Philippines, Malacca, Singapore, Borneo, and some other places.

Fin formula

$D_{65\text{-}70}$, $P_{1/8}$, V_6, A_{47}, C_{17}, B_4 pairs.

Other species are—*C. dussumieri dayi* (Hora), *C. dussumieri dussumieri* (Valenciennes) etc.

No. 35 *Eutropiichthys vacha* (Hamilton)

Systematic Position

Phylum	—	Chordata
Sub-Phylum	—	Vertebrata
Class	—	Pisces
Sub-Class	—	Teleostomi
Super Order	—	Ostariophysi
Order	—	Siluriformes
Family	—	Schilbeidae
Sub-family	—	Schilbeinae

Diagnosis: Body elongated and compressed, and the abdomen is rounded. Head is of moderate size and is conical in shape. Snout is pointed. Width of the head equals its length behind the middle of the eyes. Mouth is sub-terminal and transverse and the cleft reaches below orbit or slightly beyond. Jaws are unequal. Teeth are sharp, and, teeth on palate in a band is wider than premaxillary band. There are 4 pairs of barbels and the nasal barbels reach hind border of head or slightly beyond. One pair of maxillary, one pair of nasal and two pairs of mandibular barbels are there. Eyes are moderately large and lateral in position. Rayed dorsal fin is inserted above half of pectoral fin. Adipose dorsal fin is short and posteriorly free. Anal fin is long and caudal fin is deeply forked. Pectoral and caudal fins are edged with black. Pectoral fins reach the base of the ventral. Their spines are externally rough and internally serrated. This fish is silvery, greyish along the back. Lateral line is complete and simple.

Distribution: They are found in India, Pakistan, Nepal, Burma, Thailand and Bangladesh.

Fin formula

$D_{1/7/0}, P_{1/15}, V_{6}, A_{48(3/45)}, C_{17}, B_{4}$ pairs.

Other important species are:

E. goongwaree (Sykes), *E. murius* (Hamilton) etc.

No. 36 *Glyptosternum maculatum* (Regan)

G. reticulatum (Mc Clelland)

Systematic Position

Phylum	—	Chordata
Sub-Phylum	—	Vertebrata
Class	—	Pisces
Sub-Class	—	Teleostomi
Super Order	—	Ostariophysi
Order	—	Siluriformes
Family	—	Sisoridae

Diagnosis: Body is elongated and compressed and up to the pelvic base the abdomen is somewhat flat. Head is small and flat and snout is rounded. Mouth is inferior. Eyes are small and superior in position and is situated in the middle of the head. Jaws are unequal and upper jaw is larger, overhanging the lower one. Villiform teeth are present in bands on the jaws. Four pairs of barbels are present, i.e., one pair of nasal, one pair of maxillary and two pairs of mandibular. Gill membranes are free from each other and are not united with isthmus. Mandibular barbels have broad bases and bear striated pads of adhesive skin on outer halves. In *G.maculatum,* the adipose dorsal fin is not continuous with caudal fin. But in *G.raticulatum* the adipose dorsal fin is continuous with caudal fin. Dorsal fin is inserted above tip of pectoral fin and it has 6-7 rays and there is no spine. Pectoral fin has 11 branched rays and there is no spine. Pelvic fin has only 6 rays. The first ray of the paired fins is soft and skin on ventral surface is corrugated in pinnate folds for adhesion. Caudal fin is rounded or truncate. Anal fin is short and has 5 or 6 rays. Lateral line is complete and simple. Air bladder is enclosed in bony capsule.

Distribution: G.maculatum has been reported from different parts of India, China,Tibet and Sikkim. *G. reticulatum* is distributed in Ladakh and Kashmir area of India, Pakistan, China, Afghanistan and other places.

No. 37 *Glyptothorax saisii* (Jenkins)

Systematic Position

Phylum	—	Chordata
Sub-Phylum	—	Vertebrata
Class	—	Pisces
Sub-Class	—	Teleostomi
Super Order	—	Ostariophysi
Order	—	Siluriformes
Family	—	Sisoridae

Diagnosis: Body is elongated and moderately depressed and granulated. Abdomen is flat or slightly rounded. Head is small and depressed and snout is conical. Mouth is inferior in position and it is narrow. Eyes are small and dorsal in position. Lips are thick and fleshy and possess papillae. Upper jaw is longer than the lower jaw. Villiform teeth are present in the jaws and palate is endentate. Ventral surface of the body is between the pectoral fins (slightly anterior) is provided with adhesive apparatus which is a hill-stream adaptation. Four pairs of barbels are present, i.e. one pair of nasal, one pair of maxillary and two pairs of mandibular. The maxillary barbels are provided with broad bases. Gill membranes are United with each other and they are attached with isthmus. Adipose dorsal fin is short and posteriorly free, also, adipose dorsal base is equal to rayed dorsal fin base. 6-11 rays and one spine are present in the Pectoral fin. This fin is broad and quite strong and is serrated with teeth along the inner edge. Pelvic fin has 6 rays. Paired fins are generally plaited on the ventral surface. Anai fin is short and it has 7-14 rays. Caudal fin is deeply forked. Lateral line is simple but complete. Air bladders are enclosed in the bony capsule like some other hill stream fishes.

Distribution: It has been reported from various parts of India including Parasnath hills in Bihar.

Fin formula

G.telchita (Ham.) $D_{1/6/0,}$ $P_{1/9,}$ $V_{6,}$ $A_{12(2/10),}$ $C_{18,}$ $B_{4\ pairs.}$

Other species of the genus *Glyptothorax* are—

G. annandalei (Hora), *G. brevipinnis brevipinnis, G. brevipinnis alaknandi, G. cavia* (Hamilton), *G. gracilis* (Günther), *G.horai* (Shaw and Shebbeare), *G.Kashmirensis, G.nelsoni , G. naziri, G. pectinopterus* (Hamilton), *G. platypogonoides* (Bleeker). *G. punjabensis, G. striatus* (McClelland), *G. telchitta* etc.

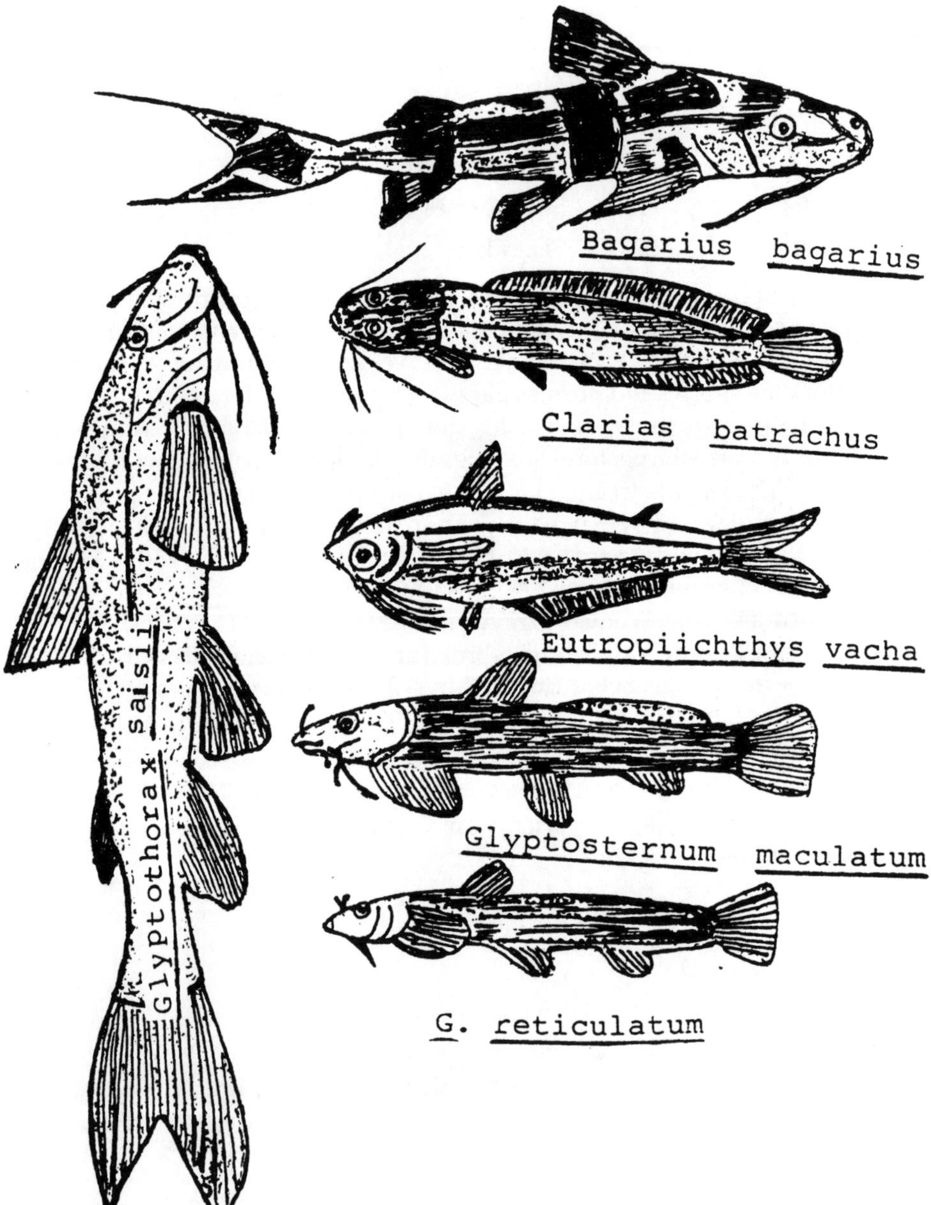

Fig. 113: Fishes of the Order: *Siluriformes*

No. 38 *Heteropneustes fossils* (Bloch)

Systematic Position

Phylum	—	Chordata
Sub-Phylum	—	Vertebrata
Class	—	Pisces
Sub-Class	—	Teleostomi
Super Order	—	Ostariophysi
Order	—	Siluriformes
Family	—	Heteropneustidae

Diagnosis: Body is elongated and compressed. Head is of moderate size and is greatly depressed. Mouth is narrow and terminal and snout is nearly flat. Lips are fleshy and are provided with papillae. Jaws are unequal. Villiform teeth in board bands are present on jaws and in the two oval patches on the palate also. There are eight barbels— To maxillary, two nasal and four mandibular. Gill membranes are not united with the isthmus. They are separated by deep notch. Accessory respiratory organ is present in the form of airsacs which extend into the caudal region. Paired fins are horizontally inserted. Dorsal fin is short and has no spine. Paired fins are inserted horizontally. Adipose dorsal fin is absent in this case and a low adipose ridge is present in the caudal region. Pectoral fin has a strong spine serrated along inner edge. Caudal fin is rounded and anal fin is separated from the caudal fin by a deep notch. Anal fin is very long. This fish is dark brown in colour but the young one is reddish. Lateral line is complete and simple. This is a nourishing food fish and is tasty.

Distribution: This species is distributed in India, Pakistan, Sri Lanka, Bangladesh, Nepal, Laos and Thailand.

Fin formula

$D_{6,}\ P_{1/7,}\ V_{6,}\ A_{62\text{-}66,}\ C_{19,}\ B_{4\ \text{Pairs.}}$

Another important species is *H. microps* (Günther).

No. 39 *Mystus cavasius* (Ham.)
M.tengra (Ham.)
M. vittatus (Bloch)
M. aor (Ham.)

Systematic Position

Phylum	—	Chordata
Sub-Phylum	—	Vertebrata
Class	—	Pisces
Sub-Class	—	Teleostomi
Super Order	—	Ostariophysi
Order	—	Siluriformes
Family	—	Bagridae

Diagnosis: Body is moderately elongated, and compressed. Head is also compressed. Snout is rounded or obtuse. Mouth is terminal and transverse. Eyes are small and superior with free circular eyelid. Villiform teeth are arranged in the form of an uninterrupted semilunar band on the palate and on upper jaw, however, on the lower jaw the band is interrupted. Gill membranes overlap one another but are free from each other. They are not attached with the isthmus. There are 4 pairs of barbels— one pair of maxillary, one pair of nasal and two pairs of mandibular. Dorsals fin is inserted above last quarter of pectoral fin. Adipose dorsal fin is low. Rays and spines are present in the pectoral fin. Anal fin is short and caudal fin is forked. Lateral line is present. In *M.cavasius* maxillary barbels reach the base of the caudal fin or beyond it. A dark spot is present at the base of the dorsal fin. Median longitudinal groove of the head reaches the base of the occipital process. In *Mystus, tengra,* maxillary barbels reach the base of the pelvic fins. The nasal barbel is as long as the head. The maxillary barbel reaches the base of the ventral fin. The external mandibular barbel reaches the middle of the pectoral fin and the internal barbel reaches only up to the base of the pectoral fin. Mandibular barbels are white with a black streak. At the base of the ventral fin there is a black round blotch but at the base of the anal fin there is an elongated faint black blotch. In *Mystus vittatus,* a dark shoulder spot is present. At the base of the caudal fin there is no spot. Median longitudinal groove on the head is shallow and does not reach the base of the occipital process. External mandibular barbels reach the middle or beyond the middle of the pectoral spine but the internal barbels reach nearly the base of the pectoral spine. Caudal fin is forked and the upper lobe is longer than the lower. In *M. aor,* the maxillary barbels are exceptionally long, reaching nearly base of the caudal fin or even beyond it. The median groove on the head reaches the base of the occipital process. Snout is broad and spatulate.

Distribution: This species is found in India, Nepal, Pakistan, Sri Lanka, Burma, Bangladesh, Thailand, Indo-China, Malaysia, East Indies, Syria and West Africa.

Fin Formula

M. tengra:

$D_{1/7/0,}\ P_{1/9,}\ V_{6,}\ A_{11\text{-}12\ (3/8\text{-}9),}\ C_{19\text{-}21,}\ B_{4\ \text{Pairs.}}$

Other species are— *M. bleekeri* (Day), *M. gulio* (Hamilton), *M. menoda menoda* (Hamilton), *M. punctatus* (Jerdon), *M. kelatius* (Valenciennes), *M. malabaricus* (Jerdon), *M. microphthalmus* (Day), *M. pulcher* (Chaudhuri) etc.

No. 40 *Rita rita* (Hamilton)

Systematic Position

Phylum	—	Chordata
Sub-Phylum	—	Vertebrata
Class	—	Pisces
Sub-Class	—	Teleostomi
Super Order	—	Ostariophysi
Order	—	Siluriformes
Family	—	Bagridae

Diagnosis: Body is short and compressed. Head is large and depressed and the snout is obtuse. Mouth is transverse and jaw are unequal— upper jaw is longer than the lower. Nostrils are separated by wide gap. Eyes are comparatively small, dorso-lateral, and without free circular margin. Villiform teeth are present on the jaws. Molariform teeth may be present on the mandibles and the palate. Teeth in *Rita rita* are present on palate in two elliptical patches.

Three pairs of barbels are present— one pair maxillary, one pair nasal and one pair mandibular. Nasal barbels are very small having a valve like base. Dorsal fin is inserted above half of pectoral fin. It has a strong spine. Dorsal adipose fin is moderate in length and it may be short. Pectoral fin has a spine serrated along both the edges. Caudal fin is forked. Ventral fin is present behind the base of the dorsal. Lateral line has well developed scutes along anterior quarters.

Distribution: This species is found in the rivers of northern India. It is also widely spread in Nepal, Pakistan, Bangladesh, Burma and Yunnan. In Southern India, this fish is found in the river Krishna.

Fin Formula

$D_{1/6/0,}\ P_{1/10,}\ V_{8,}\ A_{13(4/9),}\ C_{19,}\ B_{3\ pairs}$

Other Species are—*R. kuturnee* (Sykes), *R. chrysea* (Day), *R. gogra* (Sykes) etc.

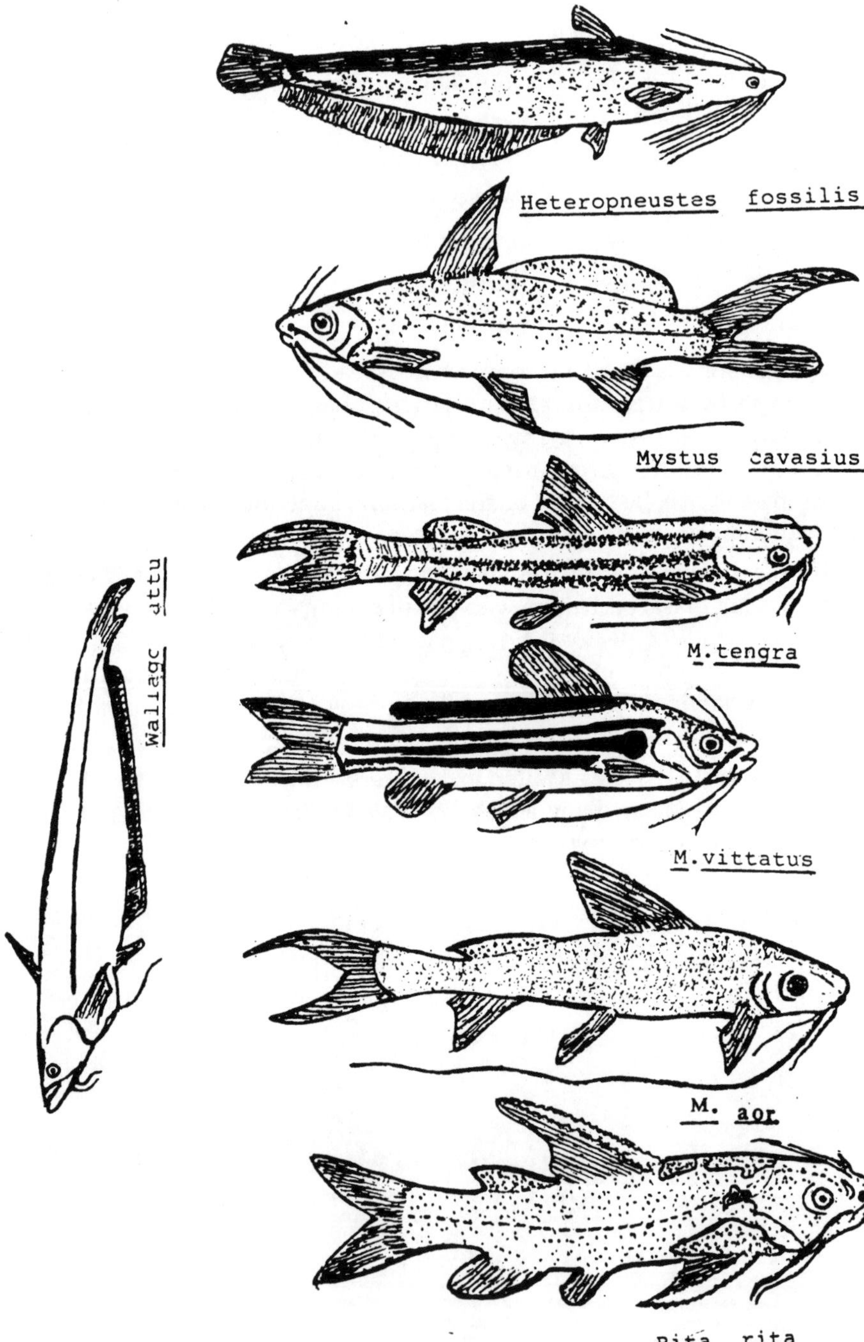

Fig. 114: Fishes of the order : *Siluriformes*

No. 41 *Wallago attu* (Schneider)

Systematic Position

Phylum	—	Chordata
Sub-Phylum	—	Vertebrata
Class	—	Pisces
Sub-Class	—	Teleostomi
Super Order	—	Ostariophysi
Order	—	Siluriformes
Family	—	Siluridae

Diagnosis: Body is elongated and compressed and the head is depressed. Mouth is sub-terminal and oblique. Gape of the mouth is wide reaching to or beyond the anterior border of the eye. Snout is spatulate and a bit protruded. Lips are thin and jaws are unequal—lower jaw being longer than the upper one. Villiform teeth are present in bands on jaws and in patches on palate. Tow pairs of barbels are present—one pair maxillary and one pair mandibular. Maxillary barbels are longer than the mandibular barbels.

Dorsal fin is inserted above half of Pectoral fin. There is no adipose dorsal fin in this case. Pectoral fin has caudal fin. Caudal fin is forked and its lobes are rounded or sometimes pointed. The upper lobe of the caudal fin is longer. Cardiform teeth are present on both the jaws. The palatines are devoid of teeth. Lateral line is complete and simple.

Distribution: It is found in several parts of India, Pakistan, Bangladesh, Sri Lanka, Thailand, Burma. They have been reported from Java, Sumatra and Borneo.

Fin Formula

$D_{5'}$ $P_{1/14'}$ $V_{10'}$ $A_{86(4/82)'}$ $C_{17'}$ $B_{2\ \text{pairs}}$

Two other important species are:

Wallago dinema (Bleeker) and *Wallago attu valeya* (Deraniyagala).

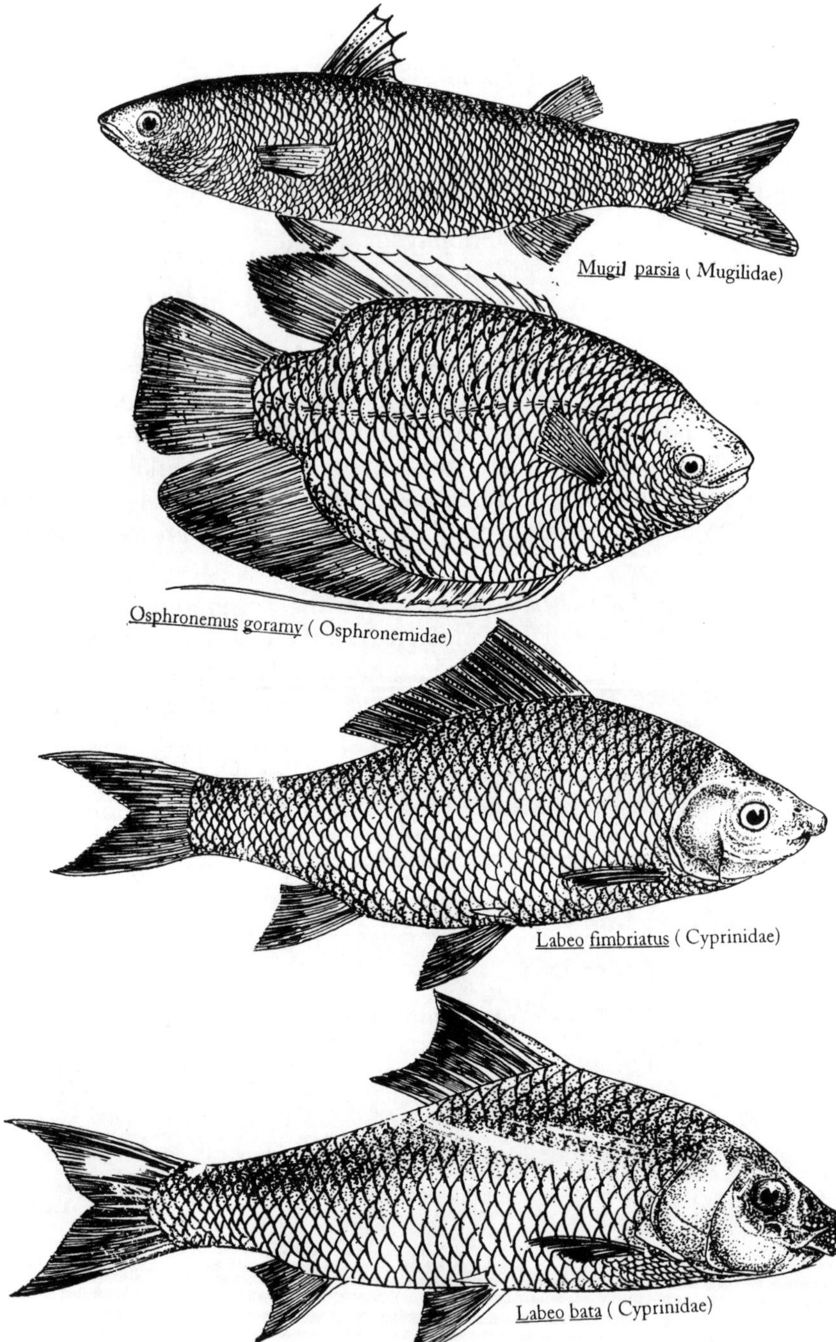

Fig. 115: Some Other Important Fishes

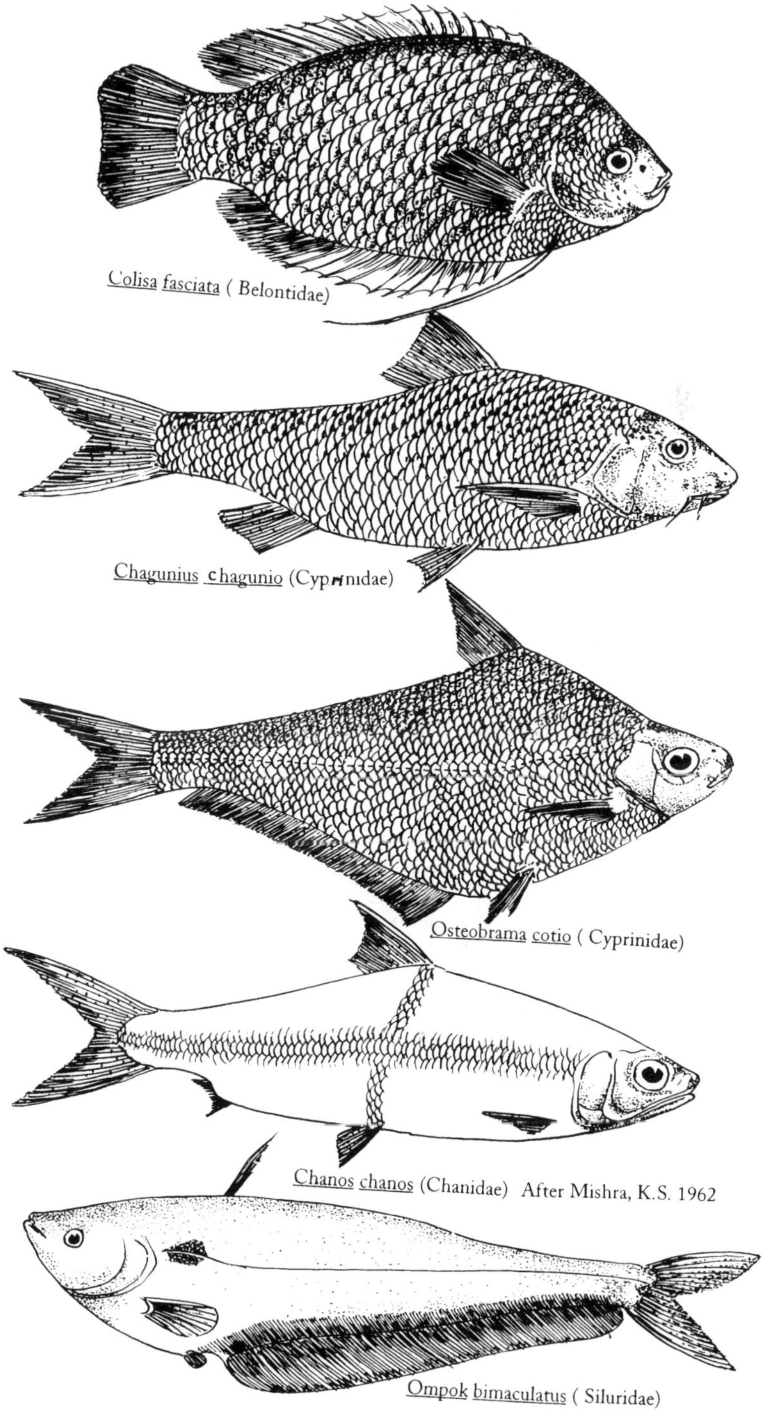

Fig. 116: Some Other Important Fishes

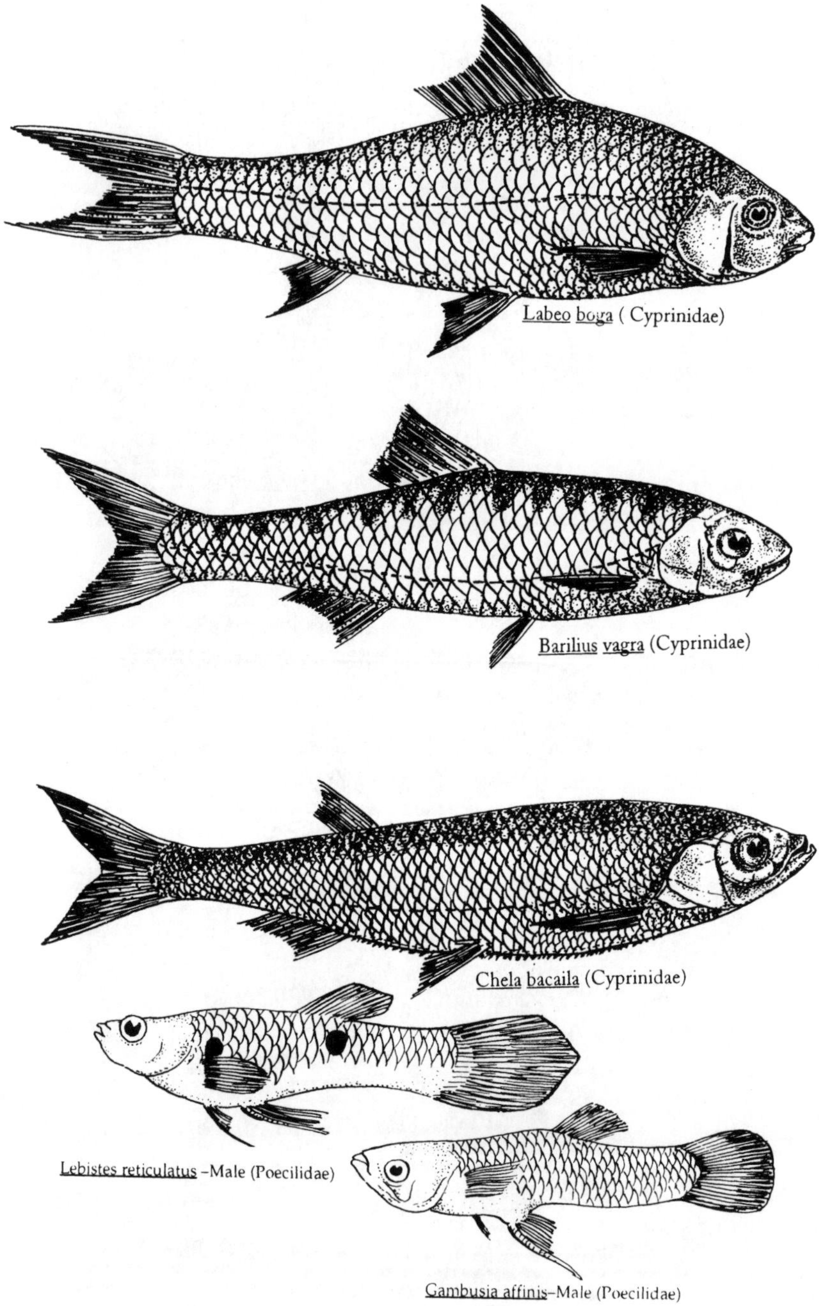

Fig. 117: Some Other Important Fishes

CHAPTER 34

FISHERIES INSTITUTES IN INDIA

Establishments and functioning of all the important fisheries institutes are directly or indirectly controlled by *Indian Council of Agricultural Research* (ICAR), with its Head Quarter at New Delhi (Krishi Bhavan, Dr. Rajendra Prasad Road, New Delhi-110001). The Fisheries Research Institutes (Freshwater and Marine) have been mentioned below alongwith some other details.

(1) *Central Institute of Freshwater Aquaculture (ICAR Fisheries Research Institute),* Kausalyaganga, Bhubaneswar-751002 (Orissa).

This institute was established in 1986. The institute is spread over an area of 147 hec. and is supposed to be the largest freshwater fishfarm in India. It conducts research particularly in *Fish Nutrition, Fish Physiology, Fish Genetics, Fish Pathology, Pond Environment Monitoring* and *Aquaculture Engineering* for developing intensive warm freshwater farming system of commercially important fin-fish and shell-fish. Researches are conducted in weed management and organic farming, Frog culture, Freshwater Pearl culture, Cat fish culture, Carp culture, Carp breeding and Hatchery management, Freshwater Prawn culture and Aquatic microbiology. The Institute also conducts specialised training and extension programmes in freshwater aquaculture. The institute makes efforts for economic utilization of the cultivated and cultivable freshwater resources of the country. It contributes much in providing scientific and technology transfer for freshwater aquaculture development. More than 350 employees are working this institute including Scientific, Technical, Administrative and Supporting staff members.

Some Operational Research Project (ORP) centres of CIFA are:

(i) Shri Ramkrishna Mission Lokasiksha Parishad, Narendrapur-743508 (West Bengal)

(ii) Society for Rural Industrialisation (SRI) Fish Farm Bareya Kanke, Ranchi - 834007 (Bihar)

(iii) Fish Seed Farm, Mujhar, Waraseoni-481331, Balaghar (M.P.)

(iv) Fisheries Department, Hanuman Chowk, Civil Lines, Gondia- 441601, Bhandara (Maharashtra)

(v) Penamaluru Fish Seed Farm, Penamaluru-521139, Vijayawada (Andhra Pradesh)

(vi) Kuttand Integral Development Society, Darshanpuram, Sanathanapuram, Alappuzha-688003 (Kerala)

(vii) Sewage-fed Fish Farm, Ganjia, Arail, Naini, Allahabad-211008, (Uttar Pradesh)

(viii) Centre for Research on Sustainable Agricultural and Rural Development, 3rd Cross Street, Taramani Institutional Area, Madras-600113 (Tamil Nadu)

(ix) Peninsular Aquacultural Division of CIFA, 170, 8th Cross, 7th Main Road, Malleswaram, Bangalore - 560003 (Karnataka)

(2) *Central Marine Fisheries Research Institute, Govt. of India (I.C.A.R.),* Cochin - 862031 (Kerala)

This institute was established in 1947 by the Ministry of Agriculture and Irrigation and later on brought under the Indian Council of Agricultural Research in 1967. The Head Quarter is located at Cochin and its regional centre at Mandapam Camp. There are as many as eleven research centres and twenty eight Field centres situated along the east and west zone sea coasts. The institute is engaged in developing in suitable mariculture technologies for fin-fish and shell-fish production in order to transfer technology, short-term and long-term trainings and Post-graduate programmes. There are eight major divisions of research programmes which include— *Physiology, Nutrition* and *Pathology* Division, *Fishery Environment Management* Division, *Fisheries Resources Assessment* Division, *Pelagic Fisheries* Division, *Demersal Fisheries* Division, *Molluscan Fisheries* Division, *Crustacean Fisheries* Division, *Fisheries Economics* and *Extension* Division. The institute is affiliated to Cochin University of Science and Technology which conducts M.Sc. and Ph.D. programmes in Mariculture.

(3) *National Bureau of Fish Genetic Resources,* 351/28, Dariyapur, Talkatora Road, P.O. Rajendranagar, Lucknow-226004 (U.P.)

The main objective of this Bureau are collection, classification and evaluation of information on fish genetic resources, cataloguing of genotypes, Maintenance and Preservation of fish genetic materials and monitoring of introduction of exotic fish species in Indian waters. Researchers are attempting genetic upgradation of some commercially important fish species for enhancing their production.

(4) *National Research Centre on Cold water Fisheries (I.C.A.R.)* P.B.No. 28, Roopnagar, Haldwani-263139, Nainital (U.P.)

The institute conducts research assessment and management of Coldwater fishery resources. Technologies are being developed for improvement. Training and extension programmes are also being conducted there. Mahseer (*Tor putitora*) hatchery management and seed production programmes have also been taken up.

(5) *Central Inland Capture Fisheries Research Institute (I.C.A.R.),* Barrackpore - 743101 (West Bengal)

It was established in as early as 1947. CICFRI developed certain technologies like riverine carp spawn prospecting carp seed production and composite fish culture. Later on in 1987 attention was paid to capture fisheries. Under the new mandate CICFRI started conducting research and developed systems for monitoring and improving production in natural and man-made water resources through stocking. The major divisions of research are riverine, reservoirs and estuarine. It investigates causes, effects and remedies of riverine, estuarine and locustrine pollution. It also conducts training, education including extension education programmes and provides institutional consultancy services.

There are as many as 20 (twenty) Research/Survey centres associated with CICFRI.

(A) Central Inland Capture Fisheries Research Institute,
Barrackore- 743101 (West Bengal)

(B) Central Inland Capture Fisheries Research Institute,
Rajajinagar, Bangalore - 560010

(C) Central Inland Capture Fisheries Research Centre,
Ujjain, Tika Nather, Zamanabad Road, Kangra - 176001 (H.Pradesh)

(D) Allahabad Inland Capture Fisheries Research Institute,
24, Pannalal Road, Allahabad - 211002 (Uttar Pradesh)

(E) Calcutta Research Centre,
Central Indian Capture Fisheries Research Institute,
M.S.O. Building (2nd Floor, 'C' Block), DF Block, Salt Lake, Calcutta - 700064.

(F) Central Inland Capture Fisheries Research Institute,
(Canning Survey Centre), M.S.O. Building (2nd Floor 'C' Block), DF Block, Salt Lake, Calcutta- 700064

(G) Digha Survey Centre,
Central Inland Capture Fisheries Research Institute,
Digha, Midnapur - Dist. (West Bengal)

(H) Kolleru Lake Research Centre
Central Inland Capture Fisheries Research Institute,
24-B/10-53 Panugantivari House and Street,
P.O. - Ramchandrarao Peta, Eluru - 534002,
West Godavari district (Andhra Pradesh)

(I) Diamond Harbour Survey Centre
Central Inland Capture Fisheries Research Institute,
House of Bidhu Bhushan Bhuiya, New Madhavpur,
P.O. - Diamond Harbour, 24, Paraganas (South) West Bengal

(J) Guahati Research Centre
Central Inland Capture Fisheries Research Institute
Nutun Sarania, Guwahati - 761003 (Assam)

(K) Vadodara Research Centre
Central Inland Capture Fisheries Research Institute,
Gaikwad Building (Opposite Bhimnath Mahadeo Temple)
Sayajiganj, Badodara - 390005

(L) Lalgola Survey Centre
Central Inland Capture Fisheries Research Institute,
Lalgola - 742148, Dist. - Murshidabad (West Bengal)

(M) Agra Research Centre
Central Inland Capture Fisheries Research Institute,
Bhagwatisadan, First Floor, 47, Heerabagh Colony,
Dayal Bagh Road, Agra-282005 (Uttar Pradesh)

(N) Raidighi Survey Centre
Central Inland Capture Fisheries Research Institute,
Raidighi, 24 Parganas (South), (West Bengal)

(O) Pune Research Centre
Central Inland Capture Fisheries Research Institute,
Flat No. 6, Indraprasta House Society,
Godital - Hadapsar - P.O.
Pune - 411028 (Maharashtra)

(P) Patna Research Centre
Central Inland Capture Fisheries Research Institute,
1st Floor, Shambey House, Kankarbagh, Patna - 800020 (Bihar)

(Q) Coimbatore Research Centre
Central Inland Capture Fisheries Research Institute,
15/3, Bharathi Park Road, 7th Cross, Saibaba Colony - P.O.
Coimbatore - 641011 (Tamil Nadu)

(R) Uluberia Survey Centre
Central Inland Capture Fisheries Research Institute
Uluberia, Dist. –Howrah (West Bengal)

(S) Raipur Research Centre
Central Inland Capture Fisheries Research Institute
326, Ashirwad, Shankar Nagar, Near Bottle House,
Raipur - 492007 (Madhya Pradesh)

(T) Krishi Vigyan Kendra
Central Inland Capture Fisheries Research Institute
Kakdwip, 24 - Parganas (South) (West Bengal)

(6) *Central Institute of Brackishwater Aquaculture (I.C.A.R.)* 141, Marshalls Road, Egmore, Madras - 600008

The institute conducts research in techno-economically viable and sustainable culture systems for finfish and shellfish in brackish-water. Researches lead to improved brackish water productivity. They undertake transfer of technology through training education and extension education programmes and institutional consultancy services. Breeding and Seed production of grey mullet (*Liza macrolepis*), mass culture of diatoms, pen and cage culture of milkfish, Diagnosis and treatment of prawn diseases, Microlevel Survey of coastal land for soil, water and other features have been taken up by this institute here.

(7) *Central Institute of Fisheries Technology (C.I.F.T.)*, Matsyapuri - P.O., Cochin - 682029 (Kerala)

The institute was established in 1957 under the Department of Agriculture, Ministry of Food and Agriculture, Govt. of India. It was brought under the administrative control of ICAR in October 1967. Though the Head Quarter was located at Cochin, its research centres are at Veraval (Gujarat), Burla (Orissa), Mumbai (Maharashtra), Kalinada (Andhra Pradesh), Panaji (Goa) and Calicut (Kerala). Attempts are being made for the development of better qualities of crafts and gears. The institute conducts training programme for the fishermen. Researches are carried on in Fish processing, Biochemistry, Microbiology, Engineering, Electronics and Statistics.

(8) *Central Institute of Fisheries Education (I.C.A.R.)* Deemed University, J.P.Road, Seven Bunglows, Versova, Mumbai - 400061

This institute was started in 1961. There is administrative control of ICAR (Govt. of India) over this institute. The institute conducts Post-graduate and doctoral degree programmes and also Post-graduate diploma and certificate courses in fisheries. Master of Science in Fisheries Management (M.Sc., F.M.), Master of Science in Inland Fisheries Administration and Management (M.Sc., IFAM), Diploma in Fisheries Science (D.F.Sc.), Certificate Course in Inland Fisheries Development and Administration and certificate course in Fisheries Extension are also imparted here. There is also one year certificate course in Inland Fisheries Operational Management. There is also Ph.D.Course which normally takes three years in completion. Several training programmes in *inland fisheries, marine fisheries, fisheries extension education, fisheries economics, fish processing, fish breeding* and *culture, hatchery technology* and *fish seed production technology* are conducted time to time for Scientists and Fishermen.

(9) *College of Fisheries* : University of Agriculture Science, Bangalore - 575002 (Karnatak)

This college of Fisheries was established in 1969. Courses for Bachelor of Fisheries Science, Master of Fisheries Science and Ph. D. are conducted there. Teaching in *Industrial Fishery Technology* and *Fish Production and Management* are also there. Ph. D. courses have been arranged in *fishery Biology, Aquaculture, Microbiology, Aquatic biology, Fishery oceanography* and *Fish Processing Technology.*

(10) *Tamil Nadu Veterinary and Animal Science University*, Fisheries College, Tuticorin - 628008

Here, the following courses are offered :

(a) Bachelor of Fisheries Science (B.F.Sc.)

(b) Master of Fisheries Science (M.F.Sc.)

(c) Ph.D.

In the Master of Fisheries Science Course, there are five disciplines e.g. *Aquaculture, Fisheries Biology, Fisheries Environment, Fish Processing Technology* and *Fishing Technology and Fisheries Engineering*. For Ph. D. course, research work is done in *Aquaculture, Fisheries Biology* and *Capture Fisheries*. Several research projects have been taken up and they are being successfully continued.

(11) *Konkan Krishi Vidyapeeth* (Agricultural University), Dapoli-415712, Ratnagiri (Maharashtra), Fisheries College, Pethkilla, Ratnagiri-415612.

This agricultural University was started in 1972. There are three different faculties e.g. *Faculty of Agriculture, Faculty of Veterinary Science* and *Faculty of Fisheries*. Courses offered are— Bachelor of Fisheries Science and Master of Science (Fish). Mainly Freshwater Fish, Marine Biology and Marine Fisheries are taught here. Bombay Veterinary College is located at Bombay-12. In the college of fisheries, there are several departments like - *Fishery Biology, Hydrology, Technology, Aquaculture, Engineering, Fishery Economics, Statistics* and *Extension Education*. Several research projects have been taken up by this institute.

(12) *College of Fisheries*, Gujarat Agricultural University, Rajendra Bhavan Road, Veraval - 362265 (Gujarat)

The courses offered here are Bachelor of Fisheries Science, Master of Fisheries Science and Ph.D. Teaching and research works are offered in Zoology, Ichthyology, Management and Computers, Crafts and Gears, Fish Farm Engineering, Marine and Freshwater Capture and Culture, Oceanography, Social Science, Language, Mathematics and Statistics and some other applied aspects.

(13) *University of Kalyani, Faculty of Science, Department of Zoology*, Kalyani - 741235 (West Bengal)

Teaching in fisheries specialization has been offered at the M.Sc. (Zoology) stage. Other specializations are Cytogenetics, Cell Biology, Parasitology, Entomology, Reproductive Zoology and Endocrinology. Some research projects related to Fisheries Science have been granted by the U.G.C. and other agencies.

(14) *Kerala Agricultural University, Kochi*, College of Fisheries, Panangad-Cochin

This college was started during the academic year 1979-80 with the approval of I.C.A.R. and the Govt. of Kerala. Courses offered are Bachelor of Fisheries Science and Master of Fisheries Science. P.G. courses in *Aquaculture, Fishery Biology. Fish Processing Technology* and *Fisheries Extension* have been started there.

(15) *College of Fisheries* (Orissa University of Agriculture and Technology), Rangailunda, Berhampur - 760007 (Orissa).

The courses offered are Bachelor of Fisheries Science (B.F.Sc.), Master of Fisheries Science (M.F.Sc.) in Aquaculture and Ph. D. (Aquaculture). Some research projects are also there. The P.G. Programme is conducted in collaboration with the Central Institute of Freshwater Aquaculture, Kausalyaganga under the Centre of Advance Studies in Aquaculture sponsored by I.C.A.R.

(16) *College of Fisheries* (Rajendra Agricultural University), Dholi, Muzaffarpur, Bihar

Course offered — Bachelor of Fisheries Science (B.F.Sc.). There are seven departments e.g. *Aquaculture, Fishery Biology, Aquatic Biology, Fishery Economics and Statistics, Fishery Microbiology, Fishery Extension* and *Fishery Engineering.*

(17) *Andhra Pradesh Agricultural University College of Fishery Science,* Muttukur Road, Nellore- 524004

This college was started in September 1992. In this college, there are seven departments: *Fishery Biology, Aquaculture, Limnology and Oceanography, Fish Processing Technology, Fishery Engineering, Fishery Economics and Statistics* and *Fishery Extension and English.* Bachelor of Fisheries Science (B.F.Sc.) is the only course offered here. Also, some research projects on Hydrobiological studies and Faunestic Survey with special reference to crustacean larvae are being conducted there.

(18) *Indian Institute of Technology,* Aquaculture Engineering Section, Department of Agricultural Engineering, Kharagpur - 721302 (West Bengal)

The Post-Graduate Course (M.Tech.) in Agricultural Engineering was started at this institute (I.I.T.) during the year 1984. Here survey work is done concerning location of suitable sites for aquaculture and associated activities like hatchery, feed mill, pre-processing zones etc. Design of Aquaculture farm, water intake systems, Development and construction of other aquaculture facilities, updating the modern techniques, formation of aquaculture complexes, satellite farming etc. are being taken up. Workers contribute in the preparation of major equipments for aquaculture such as discharge pumps, aerators, feeders, feed plants, effluent treatment plants and several mechanical and electrical equipments. Attention is being paid to develop some other aquacultural facilities like species-specific or multi-species hatchery, case culture, pen culture etc.

(19) *The Central Food Technological Research Institute (CFTRI),* Mysore.

It is an International Centre for Training in Food Technology. Researches are conducted in food processing technology and related matters with sea food processing and packing.

In addition to above institutes there are some more Institutions imparting teaching and research in fisheries science which have been given below:

1. Centre of Advanced Study in Marine Biology, Annamalai University, Parangipettai-608502, (T.N.)
2. Fishery Survey of India, Botawala Chambers, Sir P.M. Road, Mumbai-400001, (M.S.)

3. Central Institute of Fisheries Nautical & Engineering Training (CIFNET), Dewan's Raod, Ernakulam - 682016, (Kerala)
4. School of Marine Science, Cochin University of Science and Technology, Fine Art Avenue, Cochin-682016, (Kerala)
5. Bay of Bengal Programme for Fisheries Development, 91, St. Mary's Road, Abhiramapuram, Madras-600018, (T.N.)
6. West Bengal University of Animal and Fishery Science, Calcutta-700037
7. College of Fisheries (G.B. Pant University of Agriculture and Technology), Pantanagar-263145, (U.P.)
8. College of Fisheries (Assam Agriculture University), Raha-782103, (Assam)
9. National Institute of Oceanography, Dona Paula, Goa-403004

Index

H

R

T